Wm Vaughan Moody.

Letters *to* Harriet

BY

WILLIAM VAUGHN MOODY

EDITED, WITH INTRODUC-
TION AND CONCLUSION, BY
PERCY MACKAYE

Boston and New York

HOUGHTON MIFFLIN COMPANY

The Riverside Press Cambridge

1935

The Riverside Press
CAMBRIDGE · MASSACHUSETTS
PRINTED IN THE U.S.A.

CONTENTS

Contents

Illustrations

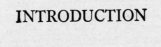

INTRODUCTION

I wish I might let you know how the beauty of your life has been revealed to me, and how the revelation has brought me near to the centre of all life, to the eternal secret — the Open Secret which from the beginning every created thing has been breathless to declare, has been breathlessly declaring.

W. V. M. to HARRIET

There is a shine in all directions that indicates the return of W. V. M.... The permanence of his place is one of the self-evident things.... Nearly all of his poems are stamped with genius as with a signature.... Thank God he lived to do his work — enough of it to place him among the immortals.

EDWIN ARLINGTON ROBINSON to HARRIET MOODY

INTRODUCTION

I. THE LETTERS: THREE ELEMENTS: THEIR MAJOR EMPHASIS — THE THEATRE

THE seventeenth of October, 1935, marks the twenty-fifth anniversary of the death of William Vaughn Moody, at the age of forty-one (July 8, 1869 — October 17, 1910).

During that quarter century since his passing, a world both substantial and unsubstantial has passed away, rolled up like an Apocalyptic scroll from the eyes and almost from the conception of a new generation nurtured upon the ravages of the Great War — a world here partly glimpsed again in the large serenities of these 'Letters to Harriet,' written by an excelling poet to the excellent friend of his life and art.

Expressed to only one other soul, they lay bare the quick of sensibility, the wellsprings of courage and the mystic sources of creative growth in a mind astonishingly poised, unsullied and self-mastered, at a period of psychology when *Psyche* was still a Spirit inviolate, before strange mob-termites had invaded her temple to permeate its lintels and pillars and crumble her pristine image.

In English speech, volumes of letters by outstanding poets wherein each communes with one dearest friend are as exceedingly rare in genus as they are almost obsolete. Because of ever-accelerating life, this book is perhaps the last of its kind. Of such by poets in the past, one thinks of the letters of Keats to Fanny Brawne or of Browning to Elizabeth Barrett but, even counting them on one hand, each poet by his nature uniquely creates his own

[3]

species. In our time, contrasted with its whirling *ephemera* forever tinselly pursuing their mass novelties, this shy 'deep-damasked' being, William Vaughn Moody, may well be hailed supreme in novelty for the sustained balance and psychic serenity of his homage to Harriet.

Written with no slightest thought of their publication or even of their survival, that very obliviousness to our aftertime makes these letters the more appealing to us and all the more sure of survival. Their appeal, however, is not as 'love letters' in the usual connotation of that term, but as many-sided revelations of the poet's mind — the mind of a poet permanent in literature, whose intrinsic style renders them valid literature in themselves, and whose sincerity of acute observation makes them signally important as original source material of an historic period. Commencing in 1901, with almost unbroken continuity during eight years, they comprise in large measure a behind-the-scenes commentary, at once factual and formative, upon the first decade of our century with respect to American poetry in relation to the theatre, which has been largely ignored or misconceived by historical scholarship, owing to inadequate published records of its source material.

According to its main inhering elements, this volume of letters might be entitled (spiritually) *The Story of Will and Harriet*, or (stylistically) *New Poems in Prose*, by W. V. M., or (factually) *Historical Sketch of Broadway, by a Poet-dramatist: 1904–1909*. Though these elements, of course, are interwoven throughout, the dominant motif is the last.

'The theatre is my grand resource' wrote Moody to Harriet, in 1904, and from then onward at least two thirds of his letters express that major emphasis in his life and art. For that reason the major emphasis of this Introduction is devoted to the sources and the associations of his work for the theatre in its vital relationship to poetry. So, likewise, having been asked to make these commentaries as his fellow-worker and friend, I do so in a capacity as editor which necessarily involves my personal relationship with Moody as participator in those dominant events and issues of his life during its culminating period.

Dealing with the three inhering elements above mentioned, it is my aim to integrate their spiritual story with its background and its after-horizons as suggested in this Introduction and its sequent Conclusion; to appreciate their poetry through brief citation and comment; to annotate their factual history by supplementing it with new source material in correlated records. In this undertaking, my incentives spring from my own friendship with Will Moody, and from my many years' equal friendship with Harriet herself — the great personality whose name entitles these letters, now through them first revealed to the general public as the deepest personal influence upon Moody's career.

II. A STEP IN THE DARK: DRAMATIC UNION OF DESTINIES

Sprung from deep soils of Indiana and Ohio, in both Will and Harriet, at their full soul-stature, our native America rose to its cosmic plane. In the dramatic juncture with which these letters begin, when at Lakeside near Chicago, during an outdoor May party at night, Harriet suddenly mistrod in the dark and direly broke her ankle, thwarting by that fall the supple ease of her glorious car-

[5]

riage for the rest of her life — so it befell that bodily defeat became spiritual destiny to them both, 'the immense thing of all the years ahead, for it carried her and Will together with such a rush that they were never again divided. Their union, the marriage of their souls, was sealed from that moment.'

These last quoted words were written recently to me by one of their dearest mutual friends, Prof. Ferdinand Schevill of the University of Chicago, the 'Ferd' of these letters. Since there is none living who can speak with more authority of this crucial incident, I quote further from his own words in regard to it.

Will and Harriet met occasionally before the year 1900 but developed no particular intimacy. I came back from England in the spring of 1901 and was told by Will that he had a surprise in store for me. I was to meet a Mrs. B——— * and I was to meet her under happy circumstances. In her very grandiose way she had taken a house on the North Shore for the spring, where she planned to meet her friends during the week-ends.

It happened that the first week-end I was invited fell on May 16. The date is unforgettable, for not only did I meet Harriet for the first time on this occasion, but just past midnight, while the remnant of the large party was still crouching around the fire, Harriet had the disastrous mischance of breaking her ankle.*

Often in your friendship with Harriet you must have divined what this accident meant to her, and what it brought of both good and ill. — For months she lay on her back on that swinging couch you remember in the front room at 2970 Groveland Avenue.

There wasn't a day that Will didn't turn up there for talk and reading aloud. When the hot summer was over, Harriet

---

* Cf. *Notes*, at back of this volume, to which all asterisks throughout refer.

could think of recovery in the country and took a house up on the charming island of Mackinac. They spent several months in that little northern paradise, lulled by the peace of an Indian summer of unforgettable magnificence. I am not moonshining about this chapter of their experience, for I was with them there for at least part of the time.

Harriet recovered very slowly, and only gradually awakened to the fact that her foot was gone and that she would be lame for the rest of her life. I spoke above of good and ill resulting from her harrowing fall. The good, of course, was her spiritual union with Will. The ill was chiefly her mental suffering, for she had lost the perfection of her Junoesque carriage, her unrivaled dignity. As you recall Harriet after her fall, she will appear to your mind's eye sufficiently proud of bearing for any human purpose. That was the pose she forced herself to take to cover the confusion which threatened almost from moment to moment to overwhelm her in the face of her disability.

But she never did let it overwhelm her. About four years after this time Schevill records, I first met Harriet through Will, at her home. So intrinsic were her courage and imagining tenderness toward the needs of others, that none who knew her friendship, as I did for twenty-five years, ever was made to feel for an instant any sense of pity toward one maimed or in pain, but rather a charmed admiration for one so surprisingly self-commanding and irradiant of cheerful wisdom. These qualities indeed set her superbly apart among those who were merely good-natured and amiable.

III. HARRIET: 'DISENGAGED FROM ILLUSIONS'

In her brief diaries, kept chiefly for Will's sake during his last year of life, I find no introspective reference by Harriet to herself except in this one passage,* revealing a

[7]

profound inward conflict of which she gave no outward intimations.

> I started off this morning in that mood of pagan forgetfulness of the sightless powers of the air which sometimes seizes me. It must be a mood in which I have passed another life and is probably temperamental, for it is the state of being that most comports with joy and love for me. But the astral influences under which I move, and have always moved in this life, will not permit it to me, and crash their terrible thunder about me whenever I forget them. So a day into which I passed with childish and oblivious gayety changed into one of blind and uncomprehended darkness.

In his earliest letter to her,* Will Moody himself wrote concerning that subtle apartness from things transitory which outwardly seemed often to immerse her: 'I only know your mind and character stand out before me as if disengaged from the illusions and interruptions of this world.' And again *: 'I always follow the movement of your nature with the conviction that whatever else in the world be illusory or negligible, this at least is very truth and not to be passed by.'

That 'disengagement from illusions,' that 'very truth' of her pervades all these letters increasingly throughout the years as an unworded but sensed reality between their lines. Although between letter and letter the actual text of her responses is here lacking, their instigating charm is none the less felt by the reader, who has intuitively grown into agreement with Moody's own tributes before reading them in these two passages *:

> Several more letters came today, each one a poem of life. You quarrel with me for not answering your letters, but to answer these would be like 'talking back' to sunlight and brook water.

Your letters about A—— constitute a little masterpiece. They convince me anew that unless you turn your gifts of expression to some overt use, the world will be the poorer by one great and delightful talent.

'Delicately walking in most pellucid air,' a phrase of hers re-echoed by Will through these letters, is a lovely instance of her blending 'sunlight and brook water' in effortless expression.

Harriet's own style, indeed, in its swift capture of word and image to release and interpret her poetic feeling for life, though less structural than Will's, was as well mated with his as her mind and heart were. But it was native to air, not to ink. Sprung from the French Huguenot heritage of her mother, Harriet Converse, her style took wing in her conversation with a Gallic ease that — artless but sure, and 'like a slanted gull for motion' — dipped, careened, floated or gracilely poised, but never floundered above those 'gulfs of meaning' which Will himself has imaged atavistically from his own Dutch-English pauses of reticence on frail footpath-spannings of the infinite — in this note to her *:

> If you and I could ever say *Good morning* in such a manner as to really express our meaning, we should go straight on to glory, towing the astonished universe after us. — 'Is it not so?' 'Good morning,' — 'Goodnight,' — 'I am happy,' — 'Did you rest well?' — 'Is it becoming?' — over what gulfs of meaning we walk on these little bridges, what loads of cosmic matters we lift and swing into place with these frail levers! I wish you would make a poem about it

He himself made a poem of it in those words, as doubtless she answered it by another fresh idyll. Back and forth from roiling metropolis to metropolis their untainted spirits flew to each other, east and west. A few days later,[1] anticipating her coming, he wrote again:

> The shop-girls who pass me in the street have heard of it and offer me their mute congratulations. The newsboys refrain good-humoredly from offering me their wares, knowing that I have the only news in the world worth attention. The waiters as by conspiracy serve me with exquisiteness and unction, perceiving that I am one of the favored of the earth. For in a week, or maybe less, you will be here. It would be too good to be true, if it were not, according to the happier formula, quite too good *not* to be true.

But for lack of her personal presence there was compensation at least in the arrival of her 'counterpart presentment' as this passage * from one of his letters the following spring illumines:

> The little portrait * came yesterday and has made a radiance in my room ever since. The likeness is not perfect but there is enough of you in it to make it infinitely precious. I wish you had sent the old Florentine frame; it will be difficult to find anything quaint or naïve enough to go with it. The hair is a thing to dream of, and the eyes and all the upper part of the face — a luscious heritage.

Amid the changing horizons of America, Europe and Atlantic Ocean, where the starry 'creatures' of constellations were to be his 'tremendous comfort in the summer nights' these further passages express his profound comradeship with Harriet in varied phases.

> Boston; Nov. 25, 1901. Out of this, as out of everything great and generous, my heart turned to you, saying 'See!' or rather, saying nothing, but looking for the soul's intelligencer, the speaking light of your eye understanding in secret.

> Boston; Dec. 27, 1901. Your pictures are a great support to

[1] Sept. 30, 1904. Cf. Note under 'Acknowledgments' at back.

me. They remind me that, as Keats said, 'Life is the Valley of Soul-making.'

En voyage; April 28, 1902. Do you remember? — The Northern Crown; Arcturus, largest star in Boötes; Castor and Pollux; and Berenice's Hair — the lovely cluster, or rather tangle, or rather mist of tiny stars at the right and even with the Great Bear, distant about thirty degrees. These creatures are going to be a tremendous comfort and delight to me in the summer nights, and if you pick them out and look at them nightly, that will be a kind of language between us — a kind of cosmic telegraphy.

Athens; May 16, 1902. I plucked a handful of poppies for you yesterday on the slope of Hymettus. Did you get them? ... The many great things I have learned and have to learn from you, dear.... In four or five hours this mighty moon will be hanging over your dear head — alas, I fear with unhandsome thrift of silver.... Let us look about us again and yet again for a way. Meanwhile, of course, you contrive to live both lives and to send me pussy-willows. The little woolly rascals kept quite fresh — I mean, quite woolly — and made me homesick for the American spring, with its myriad life and stir, in this untenanted majesty of bare mountain and reverberating light on forsaken fanes.

Athens; May 20, 1902. Your words, whatever they are, never fail to quicken and strengthen me toward the life which is for both of us the only reality in a world of phantoms coming and going — beautiful and terrible and in their order dear, but still phantoms.

Athens; May 29, 1902. I perceive that it is impossible for one spirit to glorify another unduly, in descrying and asseverating its nobility, which now we see as in a glass darkly, but then face to face. *'Who that has ever heard a strain of music,'* said Thoreau, *'will speak of exaggeration any more ever after?'* If you have caught through me a strain of the eternal music, it is well. I had meant to scold you for idealizing me, and this is what it has come to.

[11]

New York; Nov. 17, 1903. I enjoyed a meditative and delighted grin over your absurd effectiveness, thus again signalized.

New York; Sept. 8, 1904. I am glad, for a time, not to be a disturbing influence, so precious to me is the clear stream of your individuality, with its eddies of bright whim and its wave-crests of flashing contradiction... a life-friend, a spirit so large, and radiant and fruitful, so tender and swift to respond along all the far-flung lines of our communicating natures.

New York; Jan. 21, 1905. I am dreadfully alone without my gay and disquieting and ever incalculable companion upon whose shifting moods I have learned to build from hour to hour my house of life.

Florence; May 1, 1907. The total inability to 'see out' of a mood of discouragement, to remember, to discount, to strike a rational balance, is one of the most amazing and awful things in life. It is the suggestress of suicide and the mother of dead dogs. It lies at the root of all our pitiful bungling and waste with regard to the issues of our lives. You will know what I mean by this... you will understand, and understand, and understand, above pity or forgiveness or regret. You will do this and you are the only woman on earth who could.

Things merely factual seem hardly of substance to cling to Harriet's remembrance, yet for their bearing upon facts of Will Moody's life and his after-memory, I have recorded some such data concerning her in the Conclusion and in the Notes at the back.

In his words before quoted, Schevill says: 'Will and Harriet met occasionally before the year 1900, but developed no particular intimacy.' Will, however, writes in his poem concerning their 'sacred day' of her accident:

'We had been sweet friends long before.'

Elsewhere he has painted with 'rich and liberal' strokes

such a motion-color portraiture of her, companioning him
on horse-back,* in his poem, *A Prairie Ride* —

> 'When league on league between ripe fields of corn,
> Galloping neck and neck, or loitering hand in hand,
> We rode across the prairie land
> Where I was born —'

that, though anonymous, the on-rushing rhythmic lines
declare aloud for all that have known her undaunted self
the withholden name of Harriet, where he portrays her

> 'Like a slanted gull for motion
> And the blown corn like an ocean
> For its billows and their rumor and the
> tassels snapping free
> As whittled foam and brine-scud of the sea —'

or, at pause, where

> 'On the proud fields and on her proud bent head
> The sunlight like a covenant did fall;
> Then with a gesture rich and liberal
> She raised her hands with laughter to the sun, —
> And it was done,
> Never in life or death to be gainsaid!'

IV. WILL: REVELATIONS OF THE POET'S MIND

Of Will Moody himself these letters disclose on every
page their own varied revelations of the poet's mind, in
his innate mysticism, moral passion, sensitivity to moods
of wild nature and to human friendship; his heights of
droll humor and Dantesque gulfs of depression; his adoration for 'winged words' and his meticulous choice of them;
his keen five senses aura'd by a sixth of divination; his
Old Testament seerdom; his fresh skill in painting and
worship of noble music; his studious addiction to religious
experience, Christian and pagan, especially the ancient

[13]

Greek, with excursions into the primitive, Indian and
negro; his inward revolts against the academic, while still
clutching Laokoön coils, combined strangely with outward
stolidity; his faun-like love of beauty in women and in
art; his sturdy athletism and fecund scholarship; his
whimsical courtesy to children and playful badinage; his
slothful shyness; his yearning life-search for a home-farm,
brotherly companionship with dogs and horses and tramps;
his selfless consecration to poetry — wondering devotion
to the theatre — unselfish passion for his country, America; his loving honesty toward all his fellow beings. These
brief excerpts express a few instances of such qualities:

Colorado; Aug. 27, 1901. I wish I could give you a conception of these mountain meadows ten or eleven thousand feet
high, set in a cirque of desolate grandeur, flower-starred floors
of richest, softest green, rivulet-enlaced and aspen-fringed,
swept by silver skirts of rain which the sun chases and glorifies.
They are the poetry of these mountains, not to be known save
of him whose strenuous right elbow can buckle a mule-pack in
place.

One tremendous afternoon we had two on the summit of
the divide, with a world of peaks in circle, far as the eye
could reach — an awful Senate. We crawled down the side
of the thing before sunset, with the frost beginning to settle
lightly on the rocks, and camped by a little cold green lake
which was held like a cup on a shelf of granite a thousand
feet high, that again rested on another and another, a stairway to make the brain faint as it felt down it for a resting place.

Andritzena; June 12, 1902. When man is at rest over the
face of the earth, it is then that the earth spirit seems most
passionately awake and intent upon its own business.

New York; Feb. 4, 1904. The excellent balanced play of the
heart, mind and imagination together, without which there
is no sufficing art.

New York; Nov. 8, 1904. This is election day. Portentous issues for each of us, for the country and the world, are being decided by that silent snow of white ballots, falling by millions and millions all over the land. My imagination is strangely possessed.... Our different destiny may be greater, but the America that we have known and passionately believed in, will be no more.

Florence; May 1, 1907. Yesterday, burst upon us a day of glorious brightness, of lustre altogether unworldly.... As I was walking along the street thinking of nothing but the good feel of the sun and the good taste of the air, suddenly something clicked inside my head, a kaleidoscopic down-rush and up-thrust and over-tumble of broken pictures and half-thoughts passed before my mind, whirled a minute, settled into place, and behold! there was the third part of my trilogy. For an hour, or a quarter of a second, or however long it lasted, it was as plain as print and as perfect as the atomic structure of a jewel. This morning it is dim and disjointed again, but that does not much discourage me, for I have seen it once, and I shall see it again.

Concerning now certain stages and personal associations of Moody's career it is needful to supply some factual records as background.

V. PUBLISHED WORKS AND BIOGRAPHERS

A detailed chronological list of seven volumes by Moody and one play-anthology including his *The Great Divide*, issued by the present publishers (1901–1935), is printed at the front of this book. Only one earlier volume, his earliest, *The Masque of Judgment*, was issued by another publisher (Small Maynard: Boston; 1900), later included in his collected *Poems and Poetic Dramas* (Houghton Mifflin; 1912).

Of his scholarly prose works, his *Life of Milton* is pub-

lished as an Introduction to 'The Complete Poetical
Works of John Milton' (Houghton Mifflin; 1899, 1924).
Signed only with the initials, W. V. M., and practically
lost there, it eminently deserves to be reissued as a book
by itself, for its nobly eloquent discernment of one Mil-
tonic mind by another.

The editorships of the volumes published since his death
have sprung from a few profound friendships of his life-
time, expressed — through their Introductions — in the
sensitive scholarship of John M. Manly, the artist insight
of Daniel Gregory Mason, the finely perceptive correla-
tion-power of Robert Morss Lovett,* and the present commentaries by myself. Those Introductions by Manly,
Mason and Lovett contain facts and viewpoints invaluable
to an all-round estimate of Moody and his works, and to
those I refer the reader, as their substance is not duplicated
here.

One recent important volume, concerned with his life
and total creative output, is *William Vaughn Moody; A
Study*, by David D. Henry (Boston, Bruce Humphries,
1934) — a book which dispenses with any need of pre-
senting here a digest of its large scope. Thoroughly in-
dexed, its 274 pages assemble exhaustively the many
sources of its theme with extraordinary diligence and
sympathy, and lay the foundations for a definitive biography of Moody.

Such final biography must await further publications.
Hopefully it may be based also upon the yet unwritten
reminiscences of Ridgely Torrence and Ferdinand Schevill,
whose intimate companionship with the poet in high adventures abroad and at home are hinted, but not enlarged
on, in his letters to Harriet, and also upon such still un-

published letters (to Josephine Preston Peabody, E. A.
Robinson, Torrence, MacKaye, Schevill, Lovett and other
friends) as were not included in Professor Mason's slender
collection * as well as upon the letters and memorabilia of
Moody's family, especially the yet unpublished volumes *
compiled during many years with affectionate zeal by his
sister, Julia Moody Schmalz, comprising data about the
poet's ancestry and early life, together with critical essays
on his works, nowhere else collected.

VI. THREE PERIODS OF LIFE AND WORK

Exclusive of his five sojourns abroad in Europe and
England (1892–1893, 1894, 1902, 1907, 1909), Moody's life
in America falls naturally into three periods: his childhood
and youth, largely in the Middle West (1869–1889); his
academic years, at Cambridge and Chicago (1889–1902);
and his unshackled, ripening years (1902–1910), in the
main devoted creatively to the drama, in New York and
Cornish, N.H. (interrupted by four trips — 1901, 1904,
1906, 1909 — into the Far West).

Concerning the earliest of these western American trips,
Hamlin Garland has written me:

> I put into my *Companions on the Trail* (Chapter Six) a short
> account of my trip with Moody in 1901, but I can add some
> details. The whole expedition began with a dinner table
> meeting, a year or two before, when he said to me: 'I want you
> to introduce me to the Rockies. Any time you wire me, I will
> come.'
>
> He came, and his delight amounted to ecstasy as we topped
> the divide more than 13000 feet above the sea, and saw before
> us range after range of other peaks nearly as high. He rode
> most of the way with his soft hat rolled and tied to his saddle,
> his face uplifted to the sun. I knew that his brain was boiling

with new imagery. How much this ride had to do with *The Great Divide* I do not presume to say.

He was in Colorado Springs, a guest of the Ehrichs (Walter and Alma), when some news came from Harriet and he left so precipitantly for Chicago that he forgot to take his favorite pipe and a number of other belongings.

Moody's letters, of August 19 and 29, 1901, to Harriet enlarge and clarify these allusions of Garland to 'topping the divide' and to Colorado Springs.*

Concerning the second western trip, Ferdinand Schevill records for this Introduction:

> Early in April of 1904, Will and I went to Arizona together. We made the trip across the desert on horseback and stayed for several weeks among the Hopis, chiefly at Oraibi and Walpi. Will often declared that this desert trip was the perfect complement to his journey with boy and mule through the mountains of Peloponnesus. He was deeply struck, too, by the inner relationship between the dances and religious ceremonies we shared together and the spirit which gave birth to the Greek tragedy. However, the literary outcome of this invasion of our west was not another poem like *The Fire-Bringer* but the prose drama which he called *A Sabine Woman*, later renamed *The Great Divide*.

Moody's letters from Greece,* June 9, 1902 ('I and the mule-boy left Sparta in bright starlight') to June 18, 1902, and from Arizona, March 31, 1902, to May 11, 1902 (especially April 4th) round out eloquently these references of Prof. Schevill.*

The first period of Moody's life awaits its full documentation from the memorabilia of his ancestry,* childhood and early youth, before mentioned.

The second period, as we have seen, has been almost fully recorded by the memorials of his university friends,

Manly, Mason and Lovett, whose writings have naturally given special emphasis to those young-manhood, 'Harvardian' and Chicago University years, which have thus far tended to impress the public with an academic connotation of Moody, the poet, which Moody, the man, in his later years, was almost exasperatedly eager to throw off.

The third period receives now, for the first time, its long-overdue emphasis in these letters, which commence when the poet was just beginning to throw off his scholastic 'shackles' in real earnest.

With this third period my own intimacy with Moody is associated both in gala companionship and in fellow-workmanship for the theatre. In the second period, during two college years (1893-1895), though we were not yet personally acquainted, he and I may often have brushed elbows along Harvard paths,* for I was then in my Freshman and Sophomore years when he was a graduate student and then a graduate-instructor at Cambridge. Anonymously then he may have corrected some of my themes written for an English course, attended by me, in which he was assisting his friend, Prof. Lewis Gates, with whom he travelled in Europe, during summer vacation. At Harvard also we had mutual associations with Sanders Theatre and *The Harvard Monthly*.

In June of 1893, at Sanders Theatre, on graduation, Moody delivered his *Ode*, as Class Poet. In June of 1897, at Sanders Theatre, on graduation, I delivered my Commencement Part address,* *On the Need of Imagination in the Drama of Today.*

In view of our then-future hopes and works in common for a 'Poets' Theatre' in New York's metropolis, those Sanders Theatre dates have their pertinence, for when we

were at Harvard, college courses in the modern drama or
theatre were still undreamed of, and Prof. George Pierce
Baker was then teaching 'Argumentation,' as the only prophetic forerunner of his '47 Workshop,' nearly a decade
afterward.

Of *The Harvard Monthly* as an undergraduate, Moody
was an editor. Concerning that period Norman Hapgood
has written me recently this valuable comment of his own:

> The mail for *The Harvard Monthly* used to come to the
> Editor-in-Chief, and in the first half of 1889–90 I was editor-
> in-chief. One day I opened a contribution. It was six lines in
> verse, summarizing a poem by Uhland. In my memory they
> ran thus:
>
>> One touched the hair where yet the soft light played,
>> And said, 'I should have loved her, had she stayed.'
>>
>> One turned with passionate sobbing to the wall,
>> 'So long to love, and this the end of all.'
>>
>> One stooped, and kissed the pale lips with a smile,
>> 'Patience, dear love, 'tis only for a while.'

Greatly excited, I felt a poet had come to Harvard, although up to then I had not seen the name of William V.
Moody. There were these two rules on the *Monthly* — (1)
No Freshman was to be elected to the board. — (2) Nobody
was to be elected until three contributions had been accepted
for publication.

When I read the little poem at the next meeting the editors
agreed that, in spite of rules, Moody we must have. We abro-
gated the rule about Freshmen, and I was authorized to call on
Moody and take any other two poems I pleased. They did not
use the words, 'take them out of the waste-basket,' but that
came near to being the meaning. One at least of the editors
had heard of him, through seeing a contribution in the *Advocate*, and this increased our determination, for we felt that for

anybody worthy of the *Monthly* to be on the *Advocate* would
be a sin against literature. — Moody was shy, almost silent,
when I visited his room (rather far down Cambridge street, as
I recall), but he gave me two poems that also were above our
average standard.

The friendship that developed between him and me was
essentially literary and intellectual, rather than temperamental. We took numberless long walks together in the outskirts of Cambridge, spent one summer abroad together, and
for years did not meet, then picked up the friendship again in
New York, and had our last meeting in a walk in Central
Park, where I felt I was breaking further through his shyness
than ever before. — On the trip abroad he was the most earnest of our party of four, wishing to see every beauty, every
spot of historic suggestion, every masterpiece in every gallery.

Of the *Harvard Monthly*, as a ten-year graduate, I was
elected an honorary member, in 1907. At the time, in the
Harvard Graduates' Magazine (April, 1907), an article entitled *Recent Harvard Graduates as Men of Letters*, by
J. M. Groton, was illustrated by Portraits of Wm. Vaughn
Moody, '93, and Percy MacKaye, '97. Other Harvard
publications indicative of our association as poets and
dramatists are the following: December, 1908 — *Harvard
Poets*, by William Roscoe Thayer (with portraits of Wood-
berry, Santayana, Moody, MacKaye), in *Harvard Gradu-
ates' Magazine*. June, 1909 — *A Group of Harvard Drama-
tists*, by G. P. Baker (with portraits of Moody, '93, Mac-
Kaye, '97, Allan Davis, '03, and Edward Sheldon, '08), in
Harvard Graduates' Magazine. April, 1911 — a special
'Harvard Dramatists Number' of the *Harvard Monthly*.
In 1907–1908, at the Sorbonne, Paris, G. P. Baker, as ex-
change professor, lectured on the American theatre poets,
Moody, J. Peabody, and P. M-K.

VII. THIRD PERIOD: AMERICA'S FIRST GROUP OF THEATRE POETS

Our Harvard days, however, lay seemingly ages behind us when, in 1904, Moody and I first met face to face in New York City. There, almost literally hand in hand with two other poets of that turbulent 'town down the river' — Edwin Arlington Robinson and Ridgely Torrence — we plunged into a poets' onset upon the theatre which, both in its successes and failures, was to influence the after-development of poetry and drama in America. Another poet-friend of us all, Josephine Preston Peabody, joining us at times from Cambridge, made us a phalanx of five.

The annals of that onset have never been written, and only two of us are now living who could write them from the knowledge of creative participation — Torrence and myself. Fully to do so would fill a volume in itself. But here at least some epitome is needful for the right comprehension of that large portion of these letters concerned with Moody's championship of the common aims of 'our little group'[1] (as he himself called it), three of whose names were first publicly conjoined in these initials of my Dedication to my first book of collected *Poems* (Macmillan, 1909), as follows:

To W. V. M. — E. A. R. and R. T. — *In Fellowship.*

An earlier but unpublic conjoining of our names is still engraved in silver on a loving-cup — presented by us four to the fifth, Josephine Peabody, on her wedding in Cambridge (June 21, 1906) to Prof. Lionel Marks — inscribed with a Greek verse of Theocritus, reading in translation:

May there always be concord in the house of the Muses.

[1] Cf. his letter of Oct. 16, 1907.

Dissimilar though we were in our ways and work, we all shared in that American heritage of 'pioneers' which Walt Whitman was first to hymn in poetry — the unstinted zest of 'comrades.' These brief excerpts of letters, written to me by the other four, may serve to give hint of that instigating group-comradeship.

From Robinson, in 1907 (April): Thank you very much for your letter to Frohman. I left the *Van Zorn* Ms. at the theatre with your note. *Nous verrons*, I wish you were here to digest the scenario of *The Porcupine*. It ends 'in two keys' like R. Strauss's *Zarathustra*. (July): I have just finished the first draft of *The Porcupine*.... Have you heard anything from Moody?... Torrence is in Xenia, fat and hearty since his trip abroad (with Moody).... What you say about *Van Zorn* is so sensible that I shall think no more about it until Mr. Fiske puts in an appearance. Meantime is there any reason why I should not send the same product to His Majesty's Theatre, London?... Don't think from this that I take myself too seriously — or that my handwriting is worse than your own.

From Josephine Peabody (April, 1905): Tell me of things dramatic and poetic, and what you are doing, and what I *ought* to be doing, and what hope — or fear — there is for all of us who are growing pale and thin watching for signs of American drama.... (Feb., 1914): You can't think how sweet to my ears are your enthusiastic words of my *Gubbio*!... Glorious to think of your play playing on to delighted thousands!

From Torrence (Oct., 1908): Hurray for the continuation of *Mater*! E. A. and I rejoice with you. It is our success as well as yours, for it doesn't matter who writes what we all want written. Have you heard from Will (Moody)? Is he coming east?... What delightful news about your other play on the road — after such mountainous bumps.

From Moody (Jan. 11, 1906): I have not had a chance to talk with Robinson and Torrence yet, but I fancy that they have no conflicting arrangements. For myself, I am eager to glimpse the Cornish landscape fascinations your letter suggests, and still more eager for some walks and talks with you, in which we may get a better mutual understanding of where we find ourselves.... (Sept. 13, 1907): I am crawling along with the *Eve* play; but finished? Brass-bowelled man, have pity! It is just barely so to say begun and before it is finished I shall be leaner.... Delighted that the rehearsals of *Sappho* are going well.... (Sept. 29, 1908): In New York, 9th of Nov. rehearsals of *The Faith Healer* begin. I have rewritten it... substantially improved.

In 1904, Moody and I had begun to correspond by letter when on August 5 (from 2970 Groveland Avenue, Chicago), he wrote to me:

Let me thank you very heartily for your generous words concerning *The Fire-Bringer*. Such words would be very pleasant to hear from anyone, and they are trebly so when that one is a fellow-workman in the poetic drama. It is true that I am heart and soul dedicated to the conviction that modern life can be presented on the stage in the poetic mediums, and adequately presented only in that way.[1] If I am anywhere near Cornish this summer, as is not improbable, it will give me genuine pleasure to look you up. In any case you will find me, from the first of November on, at 51 West 10th Street, New York; and I hope you will come to see me there.

VIII. FIVE POETS' COMRADESHIP IN LYRIC ARMS

So it was at his Tenth Street Studio, the following autumn, that I first met Moody. I went there with Torrence

[1] In such 'poetic mediums' for the stage-expression of modern life I had also been making experiments (afterwards published) and had written to Moody concerning our mutual interest in them. Cf. his letter to Harriet, Feb. 6, 1904: — 'I have jumped into a big piece of work.... I seem to myself to be on the point of solving the great problem of the application of blank verse to the realistic treatment of a modern theme in drama.' Cf. also letters Feb. 10, 15, 24, 1904. This 'big piece of work,' which he never completed, is apparently lost.

whom, shortly before then, I had met through Edmund Clarence Stedman at another studio, that of Augustus Franzén, who was exhibiting there his portrait of my little son. In the Tenth Street building I remember how Torrence and I sprang eagerly up the long, broad stairway of the dusky hall, mounting to Moody's eyrie on the last floor where, just before we knocked, the ever-twinkling Torrence waved a mystic air-charm with one lithe arm, and murmured: 'Lo, now, the Cloud-Compeller on his topless tower!'

With that, he struck a loud, hollow *clap* on the door-panel, and the wide, dark door swung inward, revealing against sun-shafted light the firm, stocky figure of the Cloud-Compeller himself, in ochre jacket and close-clipt, tawny beard, peering at us — through curved, all quizzical lashes — eyes of pure-blue quietude. From an amber-stemmed pipe in one hand the lately 'compelled' clouds were still curling upward above a smile of dawning welcome. Near by, on a large, bare table, lay some paper sheets of manuscript. After a warm handshake, he brushed the papers back and said, in his musical, low voice, with a shy sort of shrug, half apology: 'Just some work I'm at — prose, not our kind of stuff. Sit down. It's mighty good to meet you — at last.'

He did not speak further of the manuscript, that may perhaps have been some literary editing for school-texts in which he was then 'working in slate like a hard-luck miner,' * but we launched immediately upon a happy voyage of friendship toward horizons which I find myself still seeking here; for, from that first moment, Moody and I were drawn together by a telepathy of understanding independent of time and place which even now, after many years, makes me eager to construe for a new generation some of the significances of his life and personality.

The key to his personality was kindness — his innate capacity for deep friendship. Both as artist and man, his loving attributes were as imaginatively keen as they were deeply endearing to his fellows. The same meticulous conscience which made him give to his work: 'that kind of slow intense scrutiny and testing which constitutes the *really* immeasurable difference between a thing done as well as one can do it, and a thing done *almost* as well' * made him as instinctively prodigal of his own best towards those who shared his companionship. Ridgely Torrence writes me in a recent letter:

> When I think of Moody's personal characteristics, his patience and long-suffering kindness occur first to me. As an instance of these qualities, I recall a night we spent in a bleak and primitive Italian hotel. It was in a fourteenth century castle, its mediaeval discomfort in no wise relieved. About two o'clock in the morning, as we lay sleepless from the damp, icy agony of our thin pallets and insufficient covering, Will suddenly rose and left the room. After a time he returned and cast some cover on my bed. Too thankful to ask I blessed him and soon fell asleep. When day came I discovered that he had groped barefoot down the long flights of stone stairs to the hall and found in the darkness one small rug which he gave me and then lay shivering and awake till day.

The story of another midnight occurrence — his assisting a down-and-outer whose lost clothing he sedulously rescued from various dingy pawnshops — is recorded in one of these letters to Harriet, whose large nature * was commensurate with his own.

In 1904, E. A. Robinson, friend and poet-interpreter of 'poets, rogues and sick physicians,' was himself almost down and out in material substance. In that year I first met him in New York through Moody, to whom I am happily able to accredit here (for the first time publicly) three acts of imagining friendship towards 'E. A.,' two of which were of vital import to Robinson's after-career. All three present Moody as Robinson's unselfish advance-agent behind the scenes. The earliest is revealed by this excerpt of a letter from Moody to Harriet, April 14, 1902: 'Robinson's book *Captain Craig*, has been accepted by Houghton Mifflin, partly at my solicitation, I am proud to say.'

At this time, Robinson was known only to a tiny public through two slim books of poems, both published at his own expense, while Moody had already sprung into nation-wide acclaim through his *Ode in Time of Hesitation* first printed by Bliss Perry in the *Atlantic Monthly*, May, 1900, and included in his first collected *Poems*, published by Houghton Mifflin (1901). Thus Moody's personal initiative in securing his own publishers for *Captain Craig*, was critically helpful in launching the very volume which first made E. A. known to a national audience through the personal endorsement of the President of the United States.* Exactly how that happened is now first revealed through the following letter from Moody to E. A. himself, in Boston (incidentally mentioning an 'eloping' interloper who, just thirty years later, borrowed * twenty-five dollars from E. A. on his death-bed). It is dated from 51 West 10th St., New York, March 31, 1905.

Dear Robinson — I ought to have answered your letter long ago, and meant to, and live in the world of reality, so here goes for good measure. I wanted ——'s address because he had eloped with my overcoat — my only one. For three days I planned bloody plans for getting it back; at the end of that time I reflected that he needed it more than I did. The belated telegram doubtless thus contributed to my adoption of a reasonable line of conduct, so it is all to the good.

It may interest you to know that you have been discovered by the national administration. Roosevelt is said to stop cabinet discussion to ask Hay, 'Do you know Robinson?' and upon receiving a negative reply, to spend the rest of the session reading *Captain Craig* aloud. R. W. Gilder, who told me this, stands in with Teddy, and has promised at my suggestion to tell him you ought to have a nice lazy berth in the consular service in England. If this seems to you officious on my part, write a bad name on a postcard and mail it to me, whereupon I will call off the genial Gilder.

Do you see anything of Josephine? Write me something about her, and about yourself. I may be drifting through Boston before long, if you can make it sound worth while. Yours, W. V. M.

P.S. — O, he (Gilder) won't say 'lazy' to Teddy!

Moody's 'suggestion' to Gilder led almost immediately to Robinson's appointment by Roosevelt to a 'berth' in the office of the special Agent of the Customs Department in the port of New York.

A third instance of Moody's advocacy of Robinson, equal in warmth though not in efficacy of results, is recorded in his letter [1] to Harriet wherein he relates how he bearded the redoubtable Charles Frohman in his den on behalf of Robinson's play, *The Porcupine*.

Before I knew it, I was pouring out my heart to him on what our little group dreamed of trying to do by way of crusade.... Before I left, he promised to read E. A.'s play at once, and bade me tell the other crusaders (I mentioned Percy and Ridgely, too) that whenever they wanted tickets to any of

[1] Oct. 16, 1907.

his theatres they were to be had for the asking.... I swore the daylight black and blue cracking up *The Porcupine*.

These anecdotes suggest the endearing personality of Moody in relation to our little group of poets then beleaguering the theatre under the aegis of Parnassus.

IX. THE ONSET: POETRY BESIEGES BROADWAY

'Parnassus is no place for a poet to slip!' Moody once said to me laughingly. Though he told me then of his accident in Greece,* not till thirty years afterward was I to read the following words of his to Harriet, written from Greece, May 28, 1902:

> Here I am in Athens again, laid up a few days for repairs. Coming down Parnassus I slipped and strained my hip-joint, and two days hard walking and riding have irritated it so that it seems wise to give it a complete rest for a little while.... (June 1) — My lame leg is so far restored that I expect to leave tomorrow for the Peloponnesus.

The import of the above few lines was more ominous than Moody could then have imagined, for they were latent with his own death eight years later. Strangely intuitive, however, far away in Chicago, Harriet was then writing him words of foreboding whose echo we catch in these words of his from Paris, July 23, gently remonstrating her 'troubled and troubling pages,' forwarded from Athens:

> I know of nothing in my history which could have affected your mood disastrously.... You know from my letters that these were among the greatest days which have ever been handed down out of Heaven to me.... My accident worried me a little... a day or two of illness — too light to mention. I should have known, and helped somehow... your loneliness,

which touches me more being wholly past than if I had known of it without delay. I suppose it is because the past is so majestically isolated and fixed apart from any help... it wears something of the lonely pride which is the feature of all others that breaks our spirit as we look on the face of the dead.

That slip on Parnassus in 1902 led to a New York Hospital operation in 1905, which then promised complete recovery, but — aggravated by typhoid and intensified by his battling endeavors against cruelly adverse conditions of the theatre to save the integrity of his second play's production — eventuated in his mortal illness, as recounted further in these commentaries. Thus strangely two physical missteps affected the destiny of both Will and Harriet. Will's led to his death; Harriet's to her marriage with Will. 'Cloud-treaders, both, on the rim of the world' — Ridgely Torrence has called them.

In her Arts and Letters, America has had her own Trojan Wars, and in the battles of Broadway many an 'unknown soldier' has fallen unrecorded; but of one illustrious casualty — Moody, the Parnassan — the reasons for his untimely fall are shadowed forth through the aims and personnel of that small phalanx of his fellow poets with whom he was fighting creatively in a common cause. Adequately to portray that historic clash, with its *élan* of ardors, hopes, works and endurances, would require a larger canvas than this Introduction; but here sketchily I must try my hand, because it still feels the good pressure of Will Moody's.

In 1904 we were all emerging from our apprenticeships. Our literary catapults in our siege of the theatre were our plays, both verse and prose. Though our college days * had influenced our early work, we had put them behind us, out of mind. At the time of my first meeting with Moody (Harvard, '93) he was thirty-five, six months older than Robinson (at Harvard, 1891–93), while Josephine Peabody (at Radcliffe, 1894–96) was thirty, Torrence (Princeton, '97) thirty, and I (Harvard, '97) twenty-nine.

Josephine, about 1902, I had met at Boston through E. H. Sothern, who was then interested in her first two verse-plays, *Fortune and Men's Eyes* (1900), and *Marlowe* (1901), though he did not produce them. Her charming play, *The Piper* (1909), was first refused as 'too beautiful' for the famed New Theatre by its director, Winthrop Ames, who as soon as *The Piper* had been acted at Shakespeare's birthplace and received there the Stratford-on-Avon prize (1910), promptly cabled to England for the American rights and produced it with great success at the New Theatre and on the road (1911).

Beginning with our group-onset, Robinson put aside all his poetry for several years * working incessantly at two plays, *Van Zorn* (first entitled *Ferguson's Ivory Tower*) and *The Porcupine* (both afterwards published), only one of which, *Van Zorn*, was produced years later by Henry Stillman, with Wright Kramer as Van Zorn, for a week's run at the Brooklyn Y.M.C.A., Feb. 26, 1917.

Torrence won his early literary recognition by his two verse-plays, *Eldorado* (1903), and *Abelarde and Heloise* (1907). His admirable prose play, *The Madstone* — sprung imaginatively from his native soil, Ohio — was then announced for production by the famous Russian actress, Nazimova, but not till after Moody's death were to appear his still-unequalled negro plays, *Granny Maumee* and *The Rider of Dreams*, notably produced in New York, with settings by Robert Edmond Jones (1917).

When I first met Moody, I had published only one play, *The Canterbury Pilgrims* (Macmillan, 1903), a commission from Sothern, who had been interested in my earlier play, *A Garland to Sylvia* (begun at Harvard, 1897, but not published until 1910), which had enlisted an enthusiastic two-column review in the New York Commercial Advertiser (Nov. 30, 1901), from Norman Hapgood, then dramatic critic of that journal. Having received a second play-commission from Sothern (*Fenris, the Wolf*), I fled in 1904 from New York City to Cornish, in the New Hampshire hills, my home ever since then. Other early plays of mine and theatre books are listed in the footnote.[1]

To these group activities in the drama (all, of course, individually conceived and executed), Moody contributed his early masques in verse, *The Masque of Judgment* (1900) and *The Fire-Bringer* (1904), and his two plays in prose, *The Great Divide* (1906) and *The Faith-Healer* (1908).

Here, then, was a nucleus of dramatic literature, ready for and in part availed by the stage, toward which further works for a valid Poets' Theatre in America might then very possibly have been contributed by other American poets, except in large measure for the critical occurrence of two commercial failures on the part of plays by Moody and myself, which turned the managerial interest in our movement into different channels.

[1] By P. M-K. — published plays: *The Canterbury Pilgrims*, 1903; *Fenris, the Wolf*, 1905; *Jeanne d'Arc* (1906); *Sappho and Phaon*, 1907; *Mater*, 1908; *The Scarecrow* (written 1903), 1908; *Anti-Matrimony*, 1910; *A Garland to Sylvia* (written 1897), 1910; *Tomorrow*, 1912; *Yankee Fantasies* (5 one-act plays, written 1901–06), 1912; *The Playhouse and the Play*, Essays and Public Addresses, 1909; *The Civic Theatre, in Relation to the Redemption of Leisure*, 1912.

X. POTENTIAL SCOPE OF NATIONAL REINFORCEMENTS

Among poets outlying our group, at varying spacial distances, were notably four — Olive Tilford Dargan; Vachel Lindsay and Robert Frost (then both unknown); and Edgar Lee Masters.

Living then in New York, Olive Dargan* published through Scribner's *Semiramis, and Other Plays* (1904), *Lords and Lovers, and Other Dramas*[1] (1906), and *The Mortal Gods, and Other Dramas* (1912), a dozen of her collected plays in verse and prose which won for her richly imaginative gifts the highest literary acclaim from Stedman,* Brownell and other critics of America and England. For one of her plays, *The Poet*, dealing with Edgar Allen Poe, I had myself secured an imminent production by Sothern, when my professional difficulties with Julia Marlowe, alluded to by Moody in his letters, in part resulted at the time in deflecting her brilliant talents for our stage to other channels of lyric and novel.

Living also in New York, unacquainted as yet with any of our group, Vachel Lindsay was even then discouragedly peddling his artist wares to magazines until Torrence, as managing editor of *The Critic*, first detected his qualities as poet in some verses, appended to some drawings of his, which Torrence published in *The Critic* * — nine years before the appearance of Lindsay's *General William Booth Enters Heaven* in Harriet Monroe's magazine, *Poetry*,

---

[1] First published in *Lords and Lovers*, Olive Dargan's play of the Russian Revolution of 1905, *The Shepherd*, was the first play produced by Alice and Irene Lewisohn at the Neighborhood Playhouse, New York City, where (directed by Mrs. Sarah Cowell Le Moine) its extraordinary success launched, in 1911, the long career of that significant theatre organization.

which began its career two years after the death of Moody.*
But for the Great War,* which soon after shattered that
earlier cycle, Lindsay's unique genius would have helped
to carry our theatre onset beyond Moody's casualty, as I
know personally, for I interested him in certain dance-
forms of chanted poetry for a new kind of theatre-ballet
and drama, related to Gordon Craig's art,* for which I had
made experiments with Isadora Duncan, and we were
planning to stage together a dance-poem developed from
the strange caesuras of his own chant: 'Down *céllar*...
said the cricket.'

Robert Frost was six years younger than Moody, his
first book appearing twelve years after Moody's first book
and three years after Moody's death. During the first
decade, Frost was farming and teaching school in the New
Hampshire hills, remote from all theatres and unknown to
our group. Still unrecognized in his own land, his deeply
indigenous gifts were to be first acclaimed abroad, in England. He is labeled always *poet*, never *dramatist;* but
long ago I read plays of his in manuscript (still unpublished) which showed his rich potentiality as a native
dramatist.

Not till seven years after Moody's death was Amy Lowell to launch in 1917 her 'new' school of imagists through
her critical volume, *Tendencies in Modern American
Poetry*, which holds no reference whatever to the theatre
work of her poet contemporaries, or to their potential
tendencies as dramatists.

To help clarify this background of poetry and drama in
respect to the chronology and correlation of its creative
factors, the poets themselves, I have tabulated the following chart, in which the five italized names indicate the

New York dramatic group, among whom Moody was the eldest.

TEN AMERICAN POETS BORN IN ONE DECADE

Year of Birth	Name	Birthday	Birthplace	at date of first	
				Age	Book *
1869	*W. V. Moody*	July 8	Indiana	31	1900
1869	E. L. Masters	Aug. 23	Kansas	33	1902
1869	*E. A. Robinson*	Dec. 22	Maine	33	1902
1874	Amy Lowell	Feb. 9	Mass.	38	1912
1874	*J. P. Peabody*	May 30	N. Y. City	26	1900
1874	*Ridgely Torrence*	Nov. 22	Ohio	29	1903
1875	*Percy MacKaye*	March 16	N. Y. City	28	1903
1875	Robert Frost	March 26	San Francisco	38	1913
1879	Olive Dargan	Jan. 10	Kentucky	25	1904
1879	Vachel Lindsay	Nov. 10	Illinois	34	1913

These horizon vistas * are needful in glimpsing also the first decade works of Edgar Lee Masters,* who was then brunting courageously the sparse conditions of his life in Chicago. Referring to that time Masters himself has written me for this Introduction:

I was living in Chicago during the years that Moody was a teacher and lecturer at the University of Chicago. But he was away a good deal. In 1902 he went to Greece and by 1903 he was lecturing in Chicago only one quarter of the year. At the same time I was deeply immersed in the practice of law and had scarcely any literary associations, though I was reading in poetry and philosophy, and cherishing the ambition of writing poetry when I had accumulated a competence at the law. With all things put together I did not meet Moody. I read his verse as it appeared; I saw his play *A Sabine Woman* when it was produced at Powers theatre in 1906. We were similarly influenced by the times and the events of those days. He wrote his *Ode in Time of Hesitation* at about the time that I wrote my Tyrtaean verses against our conquest of the Philippines,* gathered up at last and published in 1905 in a book entitled *The Blood of the Prophets*, under the pseudonym of Dexter Wallace. I was then leading an anonymous life as a writer in order not to harm my business as a lawyer.

In 1900, I wrote a play in verse entitled *Maximilian*, by way of scoring our imperial adventure, then being carried on by Theodore Roosevelt, Albert J. Beveridge, John C. Spooner, and the trusts. *Maximilian* was published in Boston in 1902 with myself boldly announced as the author. I had hopes of that drama, but though it was well spoken of in reviews it had no stage bidders. One day in Chicago, Donald Robertson told me that Moody had spoken enthusiastically of my *Maximilian*. I was greatly delighted to win praise from a source as high as his.

After 1915, I met Mrs. Moody and was frequently at her charming house in Groveland Avenue, where I saw Moody's paintings, and heard much from her about him. In many ways he was the most imaginative and creative talent of those born in America in the last third of the nineteenth century. If he had lived and retained his strength he would have deepened and enriched the art which he was developing to handle the Promethean myth. As the record stands, his best work will always attract discerning lovers of the art of poetry.

Could Masters' fecund genius have joined forces then with our eastern group, it would have advantaged greatly the nationally representative scope of our movement.

Out of the west had come indeed one richly endowed spirit nurtured upon her 'Amerind' landscape and lore — Mary Austin, whose all-Indian play, *The Arrow Maker*, was the only native work by an American (except *The Piper*) produced by the New Theatre,* of New York, for the dedicatory opening of which I wrote a Choral Ode, little imagining then that the United States Federal patronage and metropolitan high finance represented there by Elihu Root, Secretary of State, and by J. Pierpont Morgan, presiding there on the stage platform, would soon afterwards so lightly desert the permanent cause of an endowed American institution of theatre art by handing it back to the speculative interests of Broadway. But Moody was more perceptive of its inhering weakness when he wrote, three years earlier, concerning its loudly heralded pretensions to national dignity and permanency this passage to Harriet (Nov. 12, 1905):

> By telepathic process, New York has got wind of our Chicago theatre project and this morning puts out a gigantic counterpart to save its own metropolitan reputation. It appears that the ground has been secured on Central Park West, a whole block front costing a million, and plans for the National Theatre have been drawn. Building and decorations to cost two millions are to be raised by the sale of thirty box-stalls, at a hundred thousand dollars each, the owners to possess them in perpetuity — two nights a week to be devoted to 'Opera Comique' (not Comic Opera, thank heaven!) and the remainder to standard drama, native and foreign — I rather guess especially *foreign*! Conried,* the man who so successfully built up the German theatre here and who for two years has run the Grand Opera is to be Manager. The thing has a rank money smell and seems built on the presumption that anything earthly or heavenly can be quickly bought for money down, but it may get into better hands and develop into the consummation we have been sighing for so long. But I think our modest plan more hopeful for sound results.[1]

[1] On Nov. 20, 1905, Moody wrote to Harriet: 'There is no time to be lost, for our fame is spreading. The Editor of the New York *Cosmopolitan* told me that some time ago he received an official communication from the Manager of the theatre in Prague, stating that he had learned there was quite a revival of literary drama in America and asking for some specimens to be sent him. The editor sent Miss Peabody's *Marlowe*, Torrence's *Eldorado* and my *Fire-Bringer* and Hovey's *Taliessen*. The manager said that he expected to have at least one of those translated into Bohemian and given this winter on the stage. *Ecco!*

With Moody himself, the valid poets of America were then, as now, vitally potential factors for creating a Poets' Theatre. But creative *potentiality* in art is nearly always the last factor to be understood or recognized by art patronage, as Moody implies in his comment on the 'New' Theatre of our century's first decade.

XI. NESTOR'S 'LONG–AGO PREDICTION OF DRAMATIC RENAISSANCE'

Very different in spirit from that 'money down'-presumption was the creatively critical spirit of Edmund Clarence Stedman, who was then the acknowledged Nestor of our native poetry in the New York metropolis. To his home in Bronxville, N.Y., poets and authors from England and America made pilgrimage. There, in 1900, Moody had despatched the first advance copy of his first published book, *The Masque of Judgment*, writing him (Oct. 30), 'Doubtless you are overwhelmed with tributes of this questionable kind, yet I am bold enough to hope you will read the book, even if it remains in your mind as a symbol of grotesquely ambitious "first volumes."' In the spring of 1907, Stedman wrote to me concerning the achievements of our group.

I am glad to have lived far enough into the twentieth century to see the rise of a young, inspired phalanx of American poets, impelled by instinct and no less by conditions to composition in the highest of poetic forms. Our country has had a period when poetry went more directly than now to the hearts of the people at large, but we never have had writers who were more absolutely poets than Moody, Mrs. Dargan and yourself, and I think that Torrence is just on the edge of something very fine.... (Then after favorable comment on my *Sappho and Phaon*:)

[38]

All the same, and much as I love the glory that was Greece and the grandeur that was Rome, I look upon this classical play as I looked upon *Fenris the Wolf* as upon some superb gallery piece of a rising painter, after the composition of which he has attained such mastery of his form that his proper and predestined work becomes easy for him. To more clearly explain my meaning, let me say that while I do not consider Moody's *The Great Divide* as his proper and predestined work, it does show an adaptability to the handling of any kind of work pertaining to his own line which he would not have possessed if he had not first composed *The Masque of Judgment* and *The Fire-Bringer*.

In short, I have been recently impressed by two things: first, the fulfilment of my long-ago prediction of the dramatic quality which must attach to any renaissance of poetry. 'Wisdom is justified of her children,' and you, Moody, Torrence, Mrs. Dargan, of yourselves, form a school which I have looked for. But second.... You will not have done your work at all until you show some evidence in it of the spirit of a New World.... You only show your own limitations when you profess to show yourselves unable to find American atmosphere and themes for American dramas.... You fellows are all in your prime and possess a dramatic market unknown in my nineteenth century, and I don't want you to disappoint me. Give me a chance to say *nunc dimittis*!

On January 15, 1908, I spent a long evening with Stedman at his New York apartment where we talked of Moody, and our dramatic group, and of our future plans, and he recounted to me his own projected plan for a critical volume interpreting the first decade of the twentieth century in its tendencies of the new American poetry. The next day he died suddenly. Had he lived six months longer, Amy Lowell's volume above mentioned would have been nine years preceded by an authoritative critical survey from Stedman's pen, which would now have rendered needless these commentaries in respect to a period of our literature still to be recorded correctly, in which William Vaughn Moody holds his permanent creative place in our dramatic renaissance of poetry.

Throughout most of that period there existed as yet in America no organized dramatic movement, no little theatre, no drama league, no university theatre, no university course in modern drama (except one, at Harvard, just beginning), no civic or municipal theatre, no poetry society, no anthology or critical summation of American poetry since Stedman's, no poetry journal, or college course in contemporary poetry and drama. Our group began its work without any such things existent. Our incentive was to create them, and some of us helped to attain them.

XII. *A SABINE WOMAN*: SHOCK OF THE FIRST ENCOUNTER

'*The theatre is my grand resource*,' Will wrote to Harriet (Oct. 29, 1904), as stated at the outset of this Introduction and here repeated; for such is the separative pigeon-hole influence of card-catalogues in our time that poets and dramatists are classified, studied and collected in anthologies as if they were wholly distinct species of literary fauna — an inept trick of mechanics which, for his public fame, has already severed the unity of Moody's creative work into two worlds, mutually unknown to each other: the lyric world of poetry and the dramatic world of Broadway. The poet *in se* can never be mechanically classified, for his spirit focuses the diverse unity of nature. Moody was no less the lyric author of *Gloucester Moors* because he dramatically revealed the meanings of *The Great Divide* to Broadway.

With that play indeed he began a new apprenticeship which his untimely death cut off from full mastership. With his growth that led up to it I was intimately in touch. One of its earliest versions * he had read to me and my wife, during his first visit to us at Cornish with Torrence in February, 1906. It was on a long snowy evening by lamplight, beside a roaring wood-stove in my little studio at that time, formerly used by George de Forest Brush. That night, we had a round-robin of each other's plays, Moody reading aloud his play, then called *A Sabine Woman*, Torrence reading his *Abelarde* and I my *Scarecrow*, all from our own manuscripts. On the way home after midnight in our small overloaded family-sleigh, our old roan nag stumbled in a drift, almost overturning us, as Moody pulled a taut rein, exclaiming: 'Whoa, Bucephalus! Bury us not in the snows of Ida, or what will become of the nurslings of American Drama?'

During that stay of his in my Cornish home, while Moody and I were discussing his play, I suggested Margaret Anglin for the part of the heroine. Returning with him and Torrence soon afterward to New York, I went to see Sothern (then on tour) concerning my play, *Fenris the Wolf*, completed as a commission for him just before his co-starship * with Julia Marlowe. On that trip I told him of my enthusiasm for Moody's play, and he asked to read it on behalf of his wife, Virginia Harned. On Feb. 13, 1906, Moody wrote to Harriet:

> I am just back from Cornish, which turned out to be a most enchanting spot in its winter dress.... Two days ago came word from Sothern (whom MacKaye had meanwhile seen and

spoken to him about my play) that he wanted to see it at once, with a view to production by his wife (Virginia Harned) who needs a new play immediately, so have been working day and night to get it into presentable shape and typewritten. I shall send it to him tomorrow.

Virginia Harned, however, sent it back as too much of 'a problem play' for her use, so releasing it to be shown to Margaret Anglin. Meanwhile Moody had sent a carbon copy to Harriet, who read it to Donald Robertson in Chicago.

About six weeks later, I was visiting Harriet in Chicago, where I was delivering some lectures on the theatre of the future, during a brief theatrical engagement there of Margaret Anglin. Moody was then in New York, just on the point of starting with Torrence for Europe. Knowing Margaret Anglin, I joined with Donald Robertson in urging the play upon the attention of Miss Anglin, who on reading it was filled with instant enthusiasm which she communicated by long-distance telephone to her associate, Henry Miller, in New York, and arranged for an immediate try-out in Powers theatre, Chicago, before her engagement ended there, the next week. Then followed hectic preparations in Harriet's home — telegrams to Moody, midnight clickings of typewriters copying out the parts of actors, and equally hectic preparations at the theatre, where, knowing the play well, I directed the rehearsals and attended to the printing of programmes and playbills until Moody, having given up his trip to Europe, arrived on the eve of the opening.

That première night (April 12, 1906) is unforgettable. Hastening out from the stage door at about 7.45, with a large last-minute playbill for the outside theatre entrance,

I superintended its plastering-up there, watched by a garish young chap, with his derby tilted over one eye and his best girl's arm tucked under one elbow. Cocking his other eye at the playbill, he grunted to her:

'Say, what t'hell of a woman is a "*Sabbeen* Woman"?'

I still have a duplicate of that playbill in memento of that hallucinatic night, when I sat on a left-hand orchestra seat between Harriet and Will Moody, in a house packed by all the notables of Chicago. After the first-act curtain's tumultuous applause, word came by an usher that Moody was wanted in the box-office inner-sanctum and I went with him there, to learn from the lips of the local Shubert representative that a telegram had just come from 'higher up' in New York, demanding that a contract be signed and sealed with the author before the end of that performance. Together with this contract of some two dozen legal Articles already miraculously typewritten and thrust under the author's startled gaze, was presented also a 'verbal' message purporting to be from Miss Anglin herself then in her back-stage dressing-room, 'requesting the same'—so the lips of the local representative icily averred. From the audience a lawyer was called into consultation.

Then followed a fifty-five minute intermission — as awful and world-cleaving as the gap of the Grand Canyon itself, wherein far roaring waters rise up in evanishing mists. The distinguished audience and the critics, catching wind of a mystery, discussed it amid groups in the foyer, sauntered back and gossiped in the aisles, sank into seats and ever-tensening silence.

Meanwhile I played errand-boy for the desperate poet. Further performance had been refused until he should sign the document. From box-office sanctum to back-stage dressing-room, I conveyed his bewildered enquiries through confused shiftings of far-western sets, amid which the hero 'lead' took self-consolingly to drink and the heroine star — transfixed in her orbit by the adroit local representative's astrology — peered at me through a slit of her dressing-room door and gasped 'Yes, yes, *I must have it!*'

Receding to the front-house inner sanctum, I reported that final dictum and listened to dulcet dronings from lips of the local representative, whose icy bands had now thawed in a springtide purling of 'party of the first part, party of the second part,' while — glancing an instant at the red sticking-seals — the poet held his closed eyes with pressing fingertips and murmured from out his own elegy of ancient Thammuz:

> ' " Crimson stains where the rushes grow...
> *What is this that I must know?* "

It looks like a hold-up. Hand me the pen! — Where do I sign?'

I watched him sign.

'Curtain up!' sounded the buzzer, and Moody and I groped back down the darkling aisle to our seats, where whispered asides to Harriet imparted the cryptic outcome, while the première of the 'Ode in Time of Hesitation' poet's first-enacted play unrolled its greatly dividing vistas to another curtain-fall — this time, of trickling applause.

The last act, interpreted by harrowed nerves and distraught undiscipline of its lesser roles, dragged to a ghastly *finale.* That after première midnight, as Will and Harriet and I ducked our heads to enter a hackney coach at the empty theatre's portico, I heard him murmur again: 'O, for a draught of Lethe!'

The next morning, a messenger boy rang at the door of Harriet's home and handed in a note from Miss Anglin, disclosing the happier sequel: It was not at all the crimson-sealed-and-signed, many-articled 'party of parts' contract of the averring local representative which she had said she 'must have': it was simply — an option! In the confusion of the night before, on both sides of the footlights it had looked like 'a hold-up.' Behind the scenes, owing to cross-purposes, coolly fomented by the local representative who had probably hoped thus to advance himself with those 'higher-up' in New York, Miss Anglin had been as bewildered as the author. She was naturally as hurt and chagrined while supposing that he refused merely to give her a signed *option* on the play (to which she had devoted her fine gifts so whole-heartedly in producing it) as Moody, who had just arrived and had scarcely met her, was hurt and chagrined while supposing that she was holding the last-act's curtain of his play's première until he was forced to sign a contract whose details would require some weeks of conference to consummate. I myself, as errand-bearer, had had opportunity only to ask through a door-slit — 'Do you really want it?' ('it' meaning 'complex contract') and I had carried back the exasperate answer: 'Yes, yes, I must have it' ('it' meaning 'simple option'). On that monosyllable, 'it,' had hung all the misunderstanding, which has passed into published chronicles.*

XIII. RE-ARMING IN THE HILLS: *THE GREAT DIVIDE*, ROAD 'FAILURE'

In early May of 1906, at New York, Moody first met Henry Miller, who was then just joining forces as co-star with Miss Anglin. No sooner did Miller set eyes on the contract which Moody had signed in Chicago, than he tore it up in wrath. 'Get your own lawyer and dictate your own terms,' he said to Moody, and soon preparations were harmoniously under way for an autumn production in the east. But the playbill incident of the '*Sabbeen Woman*' title had its weight, and early that summer, at Cornish, N.H., in the tiny sitting-room of our home, 'The Snuff-box,' Moody, my wife and I sat at a small table where — like the game of alphabet in Jane Austen's *Emma* — lay an assortment of paper slips, on which had been written various suggested titles. These we proceeded to pick out and discuss. On one of them, picked out by my wife, was written *The Great Divide*. After that, by acclamation the others were relegated to the waste basket. 'MacKaye is enthusiastic about the new title,' wrote Moody to Harriet soon after that auspicious shuffle-game.

Far from auspicious, however, the next autumn, were the first three weeks of *The Great Divide* on the road, from Albany to Pittsburgh. So devastating were the reviews and the consequent disastrous fall in box-office receipts, that Lee Shubert himself hastened to Pittsburgh to persuade Miller and Anglin to shelve the play entirely. But despite their own personal losses, the co-stars stood firm. 'No,' they answered, 'not till we know how New York takes it. We believe in this play.' Had they weakened then and shelved it, Moody's fate as a playwright would have been sealed, and his plays would not now be studied in our universities.

The following Tuesday night occurred the New York dress-rehearsal, commencing quietly at sunset and ceasing cataclysmically at dawn. From far New Mexico Moody had fetched, a few weeks earlier in his own hands, a soul-prized vase of antique Indian craft, to splotch with authentic color and contour the far-west stage-setting of his play. Moment by moment into the midnight hours the surcharged rehearsal had been swelling with its omened thunderbolt, when — flashing one circumferencing eye-glance — Henry Miller lifted the priceless vase aloft in both hands and crashed it into atoms at the feet of the petrified poet, as the actor-star reverberated (in a line from his own part) '*Smashed to hell is smashed to hell!*—There will *be* no "Great Divide"!' and rushed out of the stage door.

That Wednesday evening (October 3, 1906) at about eight o'clock, cautious and crestfallen, Moody approached the Princess Theatre, half incredulous of the electric beacon blazoning there *The Great Divide*. Skulking through the stage-entrance, he tapped shyly at Miller's dressing-room door, which flew open with a burst of genial hilarity:

'Hello, Moody! Top of the evening to you! House sold out. Success — success my dear boy! Smell it in the air! Everything smooth as silk — company in high spirits — public pouring in — So glad to see you. Got it all primed — eh? your curtain speech? A perfect night — *par excellence!* Here's to the famous author!'

XIV. BROADWAY 'SUCCESS': 'AN IMPOSTUME TO BE LANCED'

The next morning is written large in theatre history. Miller's tenacious faith and exuberant prophecy were colossally fulfilled. 'Success' pervaded the air from New York to San Francisco. Four months later (Feb. 28, 1905), Moody wrote to Harriet:

> The town is plastered with gigantic signs, announcing that owing to the pressing demands from diplomats, statesmen, etc.,... to witness the long-awaited GREAT AMERICAN DRAMA, etc., etc.,... The gorge rises at it! — Miller has sunk a pile of money in new scenery to fit the larger stage; this will avail, however, for next year on the road.*

'The gorge rises at it!' Such was the poet's comment on what he termed his own 'blatancy' of notoriety, from which — refusing from Charles Frohman fifteen hundred dollars down on a 'fat' contract for his next play — he fled to the serene sincerities of his friend Dan Mason's home, in the hills of Connecticut.

The play which New York extolled was exactly the same play which Washington and Pittsburgh had vilified — the deeply brooded work of an uncompromising artist. The next season, Pittsburgh and Washington out-clamored New York in extollings.

To Moody's charming honor and the illumination of the gross anilities that encoil every sibilant of the word 'success' in American public acclaim, it is fortunate for his country that the brave beauty of these letters of his to Harriet have survived to gladden the *credo* of his valid successors. Concerning a dinner of the American Dramatists Club, on Jan. 20th, 1907, through which Moody and I sat together, he wrote to Harriet:

> The speeches, taken together, constituted a more naïvely blatant mumbo-jumbo ritual before the shrine of 'Success' than I would have thought possible in a civilized gathering. The idea that any other standard of judgment existed than that furnished by the box-office tally-sheet never for one instant, even by innuendo, lifted its head. All plays and all playwrights were ranged in a hierarchy of merit according to cash receipts... an august line, in which even I, God help me, had for the nonce my quasi-conspicuous place!
>
> 'O, fie on't!' why not write a play to show up in its true colors this success madness? It is certainly a dreadful organic disease in our society, an impostume that cries to heaven to be lanced, and lanced deep. I hear you saying that no work of art with so moralistic an origin ever got anywhere. But I am not so sure that moral passion (if it be really that) is not as good a motive-spring of art as any other passion; it may include most others, if it reach the creative tension and the apocalyptic elevation, as it certainly sometimes does — as in the Bible.

'Moral passion' assuredly imbued Moody's championship of the aims of our group. On October 16, 1907, he wrote to Harriet:

> Your letter came just in time to inspirit me before I entered the den of Apollyon, i.e. the private office of 'the Syndicate,' with Robinson's play in my hand, and terror battling with disgust in my pericardiacs.... But — shall we ever learn that... the Devil is not so black as he is painted ... and his sins are due to ignorance and necessity rather than inherent baseness or even essential vulgarity?

In that one text of Moody's are blended both ardent contempt and tolerance — youth's keen edge and maturity's ripening insight. He and our group were young. Our aim was to cleanse our temple of Apollo, the stage, from the sins of Apollyon, the commercial speculation of Broadway — 'sins due to ignorance and necessity.' To that cause, however, we dedicated ourselves not as religious, economic, or social reformers, but as poets. It is no wonder that our aim met its defeat then. The wonder is that it met at least two outstanding victories, for we were aiming to 'lance deep' the impostume of success with which Apollyon infects every age of society. But even as poets we shared at least one of his sins of ignorance — blindness to the truth that no one unit of society, such as the stage, can be healed without cleansing the whole organism. It was not 'the Syndicate' but Society itself that required our sharpened 'lances' — not of enmity but of insight — to be healed. Youth seeks for understanding friends in every generation, and it is eminently youth who shall rediscover in Moody a friend of both ardor and insight in the ever-oncoming 'new age.'

XV. SHARING AND ASSAYING A DOUBLE VICTORY

In 1906, within a single fortnight of October, Moody and I won our first stage victories. On October 11, 1906, he wrote to me at Philadelphia, where I was then plunged in last rehearsals of *Jeanne d'Arc*, produced there by Sothern and Marlowe, October 15, 1906:

Dear Percy: Thanks for your cordial note about the play. (*The Great Divide.*) Broadway the formidable has indeed roared us as any sucking dove for this once. It's like taking candy from a child. I am making my plans to get down to Philadelphia for your opening. Save me a ticket!... *Will.*

I saved him a ticket and a room in the St. James hotel, where he joined our party of friends who had come from Cornish for the opening night of *Jeanne* at the Lyric theatre, as this excerpt from my wife's diary records:

> Will Moody came and Hal (MacKaye)... At the theatre we forgathered with Stephen and Anne Parrish, Homer (Saint-Gaudens), Barry (Faulkner) and the Converses.... Fred Converse's music began and we sat tense. Everything went off without a hitch... enthusiastic applause... flowers... but too long, lasting till 11.30.... Went back stage where Percy introduced Will Moody to Miss Marlowe.... At the hotel, he had a bite of supper with us, talking it all over.

That night and the next morning, Moody shared our feelings toward the warm public acclaim of my play's success (continuing prosperously onward for two seasons, in America and London) — 'success' tinctured with hemlock of professional differences and of problems for poetry's rendition in the theatre. Moody wrote to Harriet that morning:

> Last night the audience was cordial and today's newspapers are very complimentary, though the performance dragged and the many lovely passages of poetry went for next to nothing, being badly rendered and lost in the vast spaces of the theatre.... This has given me to think — I mean about the problem of the verse-play on our stage.

Such experiences in common served to deepen our natural fellowship as poets. Again he attended my play, with Harriet and friends of 'the Grove,' at Chicago, where he wrote me at Cornish (Dec. 21):

> We went *en masse* to see Jeanne, the second week. The house was packed and followed the play with absorption. The shortening process has made the movement brisker, without materially harming the literary effect. They murder your

verse pretty badly, some of them, but enough emerges to amply make good. The stage is badly lighted... too dark throughout. How about the *Sappho*? I see they are advertising it still in their prospective repertory.... Glad you liked the *Eve*. You must be having great times up there in the snow. Nothing here but slush and coal-dirt. Affectionate regards to Marion.

We had both just experienced the *Sturm und Drang* of our first public recognition in loud-resounding 'successes,' of the theatre — Moody's in prose, mine in verse. The theatre is especially susceptible to the swift onslaughts and adulations of white-heat journalism — its creatures as seasonal as August flies or humming-birds, equally in the fierce moment's glare oblivious of the all-including Zodiac. So inevitably there soon rose from the presses a buzzing of partisan cults, sportily wagering on Moody and me as 'rivals,' as if we were contending for some illusive prize of mastership. Such comments continued till Moody's death, and were reechoed even by staider voices over-seas.* For us, of course, such thoughts of rivalry were non-existent. We were having our joint repute; we were soon to have our joint disparagement. Mine came first, with my play, *Sappho and Phaon*; his followed shortly after, with his play, *The Faith Healer*. Unfortunately, the mutual ties of our loyal small group were entangled in the thwartive results.

XVI. ALLIED CHAMPIONS OF THE COMMON AIM

Our common hopes for a poets' theatre on Broadway were centred in two then commanding stage-figures, both actor-producers, E. H. Sothern and Henry Miller. Since the days of my father's first Lyceum Theatre in

the 1880's, I had from my childhood known Sothern, who
had acted there with my elder brother, Will, a gifted
young artist and poet who died soon afterwards. In New
York, while teaching in a private school for boys (1900–
1904), I stayed with Sothern often in his home, where we
planned glowingly a whole decade's repertory of productions by American poets, even before I knew Moody and
our group.* One day, there, the doorbell rang and a new-
comer stepped diffidently into Sothern's study — a slight,
dark, youngish man, with whom Sothern was closeted
for several hours. When he had as demurely departed, I
said to Sothern, casually, 'Who was that, Eddy?' 'Oh,'
he answered musingly, 'That's the future, Percy. Our
morning-glories are seeding mandrakes. From now on,
our cloud-capped towers are for rent. In brief, dear boy,
we must join "the Independents" and buck "the Syndicate." Little Charlie Frohman is "the Syndicate."
That was Lee Shubert — of "the Independents."'... That
moment's shadow was forecast far across our country's
landscape.

Intrepid of spirit, Moody's staunch actor-friend, Henry
Miller, was generously lavish of his own talents and shifting fortunes on behalf of the best in the theatre. He first
came to the states from Canada to study with Charles W.
Couldock, then starring in my father's *Hazel Kirke*, in
which Miller afterwards acted. Though British-born like
Sothern, he was like him whole-hearted in his high aims
for the theatre's art in America. In two commissions for
him I experienced his rare qualities of 'intellect, imagination and kindness,' so gratefully given tribute by Moody.
In 1908 under his management, Edith Wynne Matthison
and Walter Hampden, in acting, and Charles Rann Ken-

nedy, in authorship, near the start of their careers in America, were engaged by him for the notably skillful production of Kennedy's play, *The Servant in the House*, in which Hampden acted *Manson*, 'the Servant,' and Tyrone Power the *Drain-Man*. During the San Francisco engagement of that company, on August 9, 1908, Miller produced there my American comedy, *Mater*, acting in it admirably the part of Cullen, a subtly genial politician. All these theatre threads are interwoven with Moody's comments to Harriet in these letters. Miller was as eager as Sothern to head the repertory of a Poets' Theatre, but for all 'on the road' to Stratford and Weimar it was bumpy hard-sledding by route of Medicine Hat and Kalamazoo. So Miller's many years' investment in Moody's *The Great Divide* was for him a salvaging bonanza.*

XVII. 'ALARUMS AND EXCURSIONS' OF SUDDEN REVERSAL

Such in barest hint of background were some of the contemporary theatrical factors involved for Moody and us all in our stage 'successes' and 'failures.'

'How about the *Sappho*?' he had written me (Dec. 21, 1906). 'I see they (Sothern & Marlowe) are still advertising it in their prospective repertory.'

In the previous summer, while I was completing at Cornish my *Sappho and Phaon* as a commission for Sothern and Marlowe, they had bought from Mrs. Patrick Campbell her contract with me for *Jeanne d'Arc*, which I wrote for her: a contract which permitted no textual changes in the play without the author's approval. Differences * on that point between Miss Marlowe and me were the reason for the transfer of rights in *Sappho and Phaon* from the Sothern-Marlowe repertory to the management of Harrison Grey Fiske who produced it with Madame Bertha Kalich as Sappho, in Providence, R.I., Oct. 14, 1907, and in New York, a week later. Published by Macmillan the previous May, the full-versioned play, with its new structure of intermetric verse-forms and rhythms of interflowing contrasted scenes, had been welcomed enthusiastically by literary reviewers, and (in its curtailed stage-version) by its first 'road' theatrical critics and its 'standing room only' during its first week's run at Providence. Thus the spice had been perfectly prepared for the New York theatre critics, who as gleefully thumbed their noses at their Providence colleagues in reversing the road 'success' of *Sappho* as they had thumbed them at those of Pittsburgh in reversing the road 'failure' of *The Great Divide*. So Moody and I were to share our rue, 'with a difference' — exactly transposed.

Accidentally missent by train to New London instead of to New York, the stage-sets of *Sappho and Phaon* barely arrived at the New York Lyric Theatre on Monday evening at 8.15, at the moment when the long-heralded American première of *The Merry Widow* was opening just across the street on 44th St., where the critics of both productions co-fraternized between the acts.

In the Lyric Theatre, splendid special curtains of Greek design concealed the stage. Seated again with Moody in the orchestra parquet, as once before at his Sabine Woman 'tragedy' in Chicago, there now began my Aegean Woman tragedy, but now our roles were reversed and *he* was to administer for me the chloral anodyne. Of our party were

[55]

also my wife, Robinson, Torrence, George Grey Barnard,
W. D. Howells and Stedman. The last brilliant old veteran, in full dress,* nudged his young poet friends and
spoke glowingly again of his 'long-ago prediction of the
dramatic renaissance of poetry.' — Not till nearly 9.30
did the double Greek curtains part, disclosing a pillared
temple on a cliff of the isle of Lesbos overlooking the
Aegean sea. From then until after midnight, 'unmerciful
disaster followed fast and followed faster,' in an epical
series of accidents which I reserve for my own memoirs.
One only is chronicled by Moody in his letter to Harriet
the next morning.

Old Greek myth tells us that Sappho invented the lyre
by bridging a hollow tortoise-shell with cross-strings — so
providing an incidental theme for my play, in which Phaon
is a dreamy sea-slave. Helping him to mend his fish-net,
Sappho encoils him in subtler meshes. On that New York
opening night at the imminent climax of that love scene,
there entered a *dramatis persona* not set down in the play's
published text. Moody described to Harriet the fateful
entrance:

> A cat strayed on from the right wing, sat down in the middle
> of the stage near the footlights, looked meditatively around on
> the Leucadean landscape, wiped his nose with reflective paw,
> and padded solemnly out on the left.

At that moment, from the seat next to mine, this anodyne was poured in my ear from the lips of Moody: —
'Never mind, Percy — it's a *tortoise-shell* cat!'

The Greek tragedy's première ended long past midnight.
Across the street the cabmen were all humming the rival
première strains of 'The Merry Widow's' *Blue Danube*.
Such, however, is the glamor of *any* first night to the author

[56]

and his friends, oblivious of critics even then dangling their Damoclesian swords, that when our little group adjourned to the Arena restaurant nearby to celebrate the Glory that was Greece by festively toasting * the 'dead-alive' author, only Norman Hapgood, who joined us there, uttered ominous morning-edition forebodings from his all-critic-fathoming mind. And Norman's prophetic acumen was amply confirmed.

The next morning *The Merry Widow* waltzed her triumphant way through showering petals from the theatrical columns, snowing-under five fathom deep old Stedman-Nestor's 'long-ago prediction of America's dramatic renaissance of poetry.' After reading the morning editions, Moody epitomized for Harriet 'the strange eventful history' of that opening night and closing day of our mutual hopes:

> We are all in the dumps. Last night... we good men in buckram, together with a large Cornish contingent, kept up alarums and excursions of applause all through, to the good end that we dragged Percy before the curtain, more dead than alive. Today the cynical crowd of newspaper critics are slaughtering him in good style, with all the cosmopolitan refinements of torture.

XVIII. 'THE FAITH HEALER': COURAGEOUS TENACITY AND STALEMATE

The play was withdrawn at that week's end and has not since been acted professionally.* The repercussions of its sounding demise shook the nerves and the creative outlook of our group for a long while. This may be sensed within these lines, five weeks later (Nov. 29), from Moody, to Harriet:

> After a week of discouragement, I am again feeling hopeful about it. I feel now that it will surely be interesting to read,

whether any mortal manager will ever have the spunk to produce it, or any actor to play it.

This passage ushers in a year of doubts, hesitancies, feverish overwork, sudden serious illness, recuperation too quickly forced, new high expectations and abrupt stalemate for his play, *The Faith Healer*, which he had been meditating off and on during many years.

In the autumn of 1907, within a space of four days (Oct. 18–22), his faith in our common cause had been sorely battered by disillusionizing facts.* So it was in present need of healing, that now, more sadly wise, he continued patiently to 'file' the too 'crumbling' substance of his *Faith Healer* — as these passages to Harriet in the winter of 1908 suggest.

New York; Jan 15. I am still hard at work on the play. I thought it was as good as done, but it isn't. The first and second acts have at last stopped crumbling under the file, but the third act is still full of soft places. In fact I have been on the point of despair concerning it.

Jan. 22. As for the play I have written *finis*. I have done for it all I can do. The verdict is either negative or hostile, with one exception. If it were not for your conviction about it I should be greatly cast down.

Jan. 25. I am making very slow progress with *The Faith Healer*. It is a vastly more laborious job than writing a wholly new play would be. It is like building a new house out of the materials of an old one, plus a lot of quite disparate material, while a family for whom you care is occupying the premises. Your scattered comments are of help to me whenever you are moved to make them.

Towards spring of 1908, hopes for his play's early production were mounting high, when he was stricken with typhoid fever.

Boston, Feb. 6. To the main news: I had an all-night session with Miller, reading the new play. We started in at midnight and finished at five-thirty in the morning.

New York, Feb. 19. I shall retreat to The Players Club or the Harvard Club for a brief season. Thence I shall issue, under Miller's guidance, with a mask and a dark lantern, to watch a few actors and actorines at their unconscious gambols, with a view to sizing them up for the new play.

March 3. I spent the evening with Tyrone Power — the *Ulysses* in Stephen Phillips play. There is a taint of melodrama about him... of the magniloquent and seedy tragedian turned tramp — but Miller thinks that all this could be made valuable if chastened.

Telegram. March 22. Doctor forbids writing for day or two. Making good progress.

In the little old apartment, artistic but ramshackle, up four steep flights, on the top floor of 107 Waverly Place, he lay severely ill for nearly three months, nursed by his devoted sister, Charlotte, visited at times by his neighboring friend, Mrs. C. P. Davidge, * and always under the constant ministrations of Harriet, who came on from Chicago to look after him. By late May he was well enough to go, under doctor's care, to the shore of Long Island Sound, where he wrote again to Harriet on her return to 'the Grove' in Chicago.

Port Chester, N.Y., May 25. It seems a long, long time since I lost your dear presence, symbol and pledge of the life which I feel slowly — O so slowly — returning. I spend vast stretches of time — whole existences — sitting in a porch chair in the tender spring sunshine, looking at the sky and water, playing with the pup, and thinking about eternal mysteries.... On your lips seems hovering the answer to the everlasting riddle, of the world out there and the world within.

Cos Cob., June 15. I think it will be necessary now to let

Miller go on. Before the rehearsals are over, I can get the third act rewritten to my satisfaction, and can insist on his making the necessary changes.

During that summer of 1908, after receiving at Yale the honorary degree of Litt. D., he made a brief visit with Torrence to Monhegan Island, Maine, and soon afterward took a cottage in Michigan on the island of Mackinac * where with Harriet and Charlotte he spent three months of recuperation, painting and companioning his dogs on long walks. In early November he wrote again from Waverly Place to Harriet in Chicago:

New York (after three months in the west) Nov. 4. Since I got here I have been distractingly busy, to little purpose, Miller has done nothing toward assembling a cast.... Since plunging into this maelstrom, it is 'me for the country!'

Nov. 12. Miller accepts the new version unreservedly. Great difficulties have beset us in preparing the production. Things seem to me to be going badly enough. Meanwhile I am getting *The Faith Healer* and *The Great Divide* ready for press.... This means work, as the Ms. has got badly mixed up.

Nov. 22. These have been and are tremendously busy days. ... To stop the clamor of the printers, I hit on a first rate name for my man — *Michaelis*. I found it in the New York City Directory. For first name I will call him Ulrich — *Ulrich Michaelis*.... A love and a dream... a ten-year-old girl — is to play *Annie*... a gem of child acting. Tyrone Power... in the title role... does better than as the *Drain-Man*... I feel quite illogically buoyant about the outcome.

Nov. 28. I am in a bushel of trouble about the question of copyright protection. Our enlightened Congress has refused to join the Berne Convention, which makes copyright easy and automatic throughout European countries, and has ranged itself with Patagonia. The result is a mountain of red tape to untie... a law compelling plays (for English Copyright) to be submitted to the Lord Chamberlain of England *in printed form.* This functionary takes his own time... to grant permission for the play to be performed in England, which then only acquires copyright standing.

But while all this is being done, here must sit our good friend, Henry, with an expensive company on his hands, doing nothing except wait upon my lord's pleasure.... God bless our Congressmen and those in whose favor these barbaric laws exist... to provide them ampler forage upon the brains of men who are misguided enough to write plays. I am writing this in a restaurant after a day of hurry, perplexity and unconscious starvation.

Telegram, Dec. 7. Production of play postponed. Am going west.

The letters in full relate the arduous details of preparing a production of his play in Boston which our uncivilized copyright laws brought to naught: an admirably cast production, which might well have achieved success for his play and new life and works for himself. Instead, he went west to California with his painter friend, William Wendt, only to be plunged again into hectic labors at St. Louis, recounted in this letter to me (1935) from Ferdinand Schevill.

In March, 1909, I went from Chicago to St. Louis to attend the try-out of *The Faith Healer* and was shocked at the condition in which I found our dear friend. We had to drive to the rehearsals and a few hours of remonstrance with the actors left him a complete wreck. Henry Miller was very gentle with him.

At St. Louis, Harriet was with him for at least a week. Will was so nervously exhausted with recurring, perhaps perpetual headache that without her constant care he could not have gone through the rehearsals. However, he sat in the dark auditorium day after day and stayed for the Opening Night, which was not an unequivocal success. I went down from Chicago a day or two before the play opened. The black cloud had settled so close above Will's head that the whole episode remains with me as one of the most tragic I have ever experienced.

Will Moody's own account of this St. Louis experience is given in the following letter to Charlotte, written just before his last ocean trip to England. There with Harriet he sought recovery but too late, for the latency of his fatal illness had been grimly roused by his final battle with the forces of Broadway. How in the winter of 1910, at Santa Barbara, California, under on-coming blindness, he received the news of his play's New York première is recorded in the Conclusion of this book. His letter to Charlotte is dated from The Harvard Club, April 30, 1909.

My dear sister: I am afraid I have neglected you pretty badly of late, but if you knew how busy I have been you would forgive me.... In the first place, I was called back from California, where I was again on the up-hill road to getting my health and strength back, to St. Louis by news that Miller had decided to produce the play there. Back I scooted — then followed two of the most strenuous weeks I have ever lived through; first a week of rehearsals, and then a week of try-out performances with the papers shrieking — one half of them praise and the other half furious condemnation — the latter chiefly on the score (bless your heart) of sacrilege! *Michaelis* if you please, was declared by these latter far-seeing gentlemen to be intended as a 'Christ figure' (whatever that is), and one paper ran a standing description of the play throughout the week thus: 'Weird and absorbing drama but appalling in its sacrilegious handling of sacred things.' So much for the critics.

The audiences, so far as I could make out, were simply flabbergasted and didn't know whether to be pleased, shocked or merely eternally puzzled. In other words, they didn't understand the play at all, the real difficulty being — as I very soon saw clearly — that in my desire for condensation I had condensed too much and had failed to make the motive and upshot of the play clear to the average mind. An amusing confirmation of this hypothesis has just reached me from a lady in Boston who has been giving expository readings of *The Faith Healer* at which she says you, Henri * and Julia * were present, and in the printed outline of which she makes it abundantly clear that she has totally misconceived the whole matter.

Well, to return: That much being established, I vetoed all further performances until the play was rewritten. This I have now done after six or seven weeks of very strenuous labor. The play — Miller thinks, and I also — has been very much improved dramatically and at any rate there is now no slightest excuse for misunderstanding.

I have been spending much time with Miller at his Connecticut farm and the relaxation and country air with riding and driving have kept me from going to pieces again, though I am on the ragged edge and am about to take an ocean trip to tone up. With much love — Will.

XIX. METROPOLITAN FELLOWSHIP WITH PLAYERS AND ARTISTS

But I must not convey an overemphasis of tragedy in Moody's life. During the years of my own companionship with him, we shared many happy and zestful experiences. In New York I was present with him at nearly all the social functions * described by him in these letters. On the night of Isadora Duncan's first appearance at the Metropolitan Opera House, Moody, George Grey Barnard and I sat together there, spellbound as by some vision out of Beethoven's mind become then unbelievably corporeal, and afterward in Isadora's blue-curtained studio at the Windsor Arcade (East 45th St., and Fifth Ave.), I introduced to her our group of poets whom her autobiography refers to as 'young revolutionists': a time that is glimpsed in this passage of Moody's to Harriet: New York, Nov. 18, 1908:

> There is a wondrous dancing creature here called Isadora Duncan, fresh from European triumphs, who dances to a full symphony orchestra the seventh Symphony of Beethoven and others. I saw her fill the huge Metropolitan Opera House stage in a fashion quite incredible. Also I saw her do impromptu things in her own studio no less than marvellous. I can imagine nothing which would give you more pleasure.

In these letters there are more gaps than inclusions of events in our companionship, of which there were more than a chapterful at his studio; at our clubs and favorite cafés, (especially at Guffanti's * on Eighth Avenue); at theatres and theatre-rehearsals; at the Judson, on Washington Square, where Robinson and Torrence and Olivia Dunbar (afterwards Mrs. Torrence) were then living; and at the Windsor Arcade studio of George Grey Barnard, whose early great sculptures towered about us there, some still in clay. These experiences were shared in the city where, despite all urban charms, our mutual longing was embodied in Moody's 'plunged in this maelstrom, "it's me for the country!"'

XX. FRIENDSHIP IN THE HILLS: 'SIMPLE, FREE, OPEN-HEARTED'

So it was in the Cornish hills [1] of New Hampshire (as his first letter to me had desired) that we 'found ourselves' in many an exchange of ideas or on rambles together: in first readings aloud to each other of our lyrics and evolving

[1] Also in the lower hills of Massachusetts, near Mt. Wachusett, W. V. M. visited with me my boyhood home at Shirley Center, Mass.,* in the summer of 1906.

plays; in congenial meetings with neighbors, and — companionly with my wife and me — by the fireside of our home, where still his is a mythic presence endeared to their childhood memories by his philosophic matchings of wit with our son, Robin, and by his Provençal deference toward Arvia, our little girl, to whom on her birthday (St. Valentine's Day, 1906) he dispatched from New York a volume of Stevenson's *Child's Garden of Verses*, with this inscription on the fly-leaf:

> To Mistress Arvia MacKaye, on her fourth birthday, from her servant and well-wisher, desiring he might subscribe himself her Valentine.

A few days afterwards (Feb. 27) he wrote to my wife:

> If Cornish is always as delightful as it was during those days we spent there, it is an awful waste of time to live anywhere else.... As for the poem to the little lady, Arvia, on the 14th I was horribly busy getting my play in shape for Mr. Sothern to look at. When the feast day of her Saint was past both Saint and Muse refused to look at me. But this only means postponement — not defection.

Of that first trip to Cornish my wife's diary records:

> That morning (Feb. 8), we started from New York for Cornish with Will Moody and Ridgely Torrence. Otis Skinner accompanied us as far as New Haven where he was opening in a new play. We had a delightful journey up, going through the snow-storm, the poets darting about from side to side of the nearly empty car for views of the country winter — especially for a first view of Ascutney as we neared our destination. We were greatly distressed to find that Arvia had cut her eyebrow, coasting.
>
> We enjoyed their visit very much and they seemed delighted with everything. One evening we took them to dine

with the Saint-Gaudens — going over by the snow-path through the woods to the studio. Saint-Gaudens had his latest things all ready to show us in the clay — the $20 coin with its beautiful figure, the Phillips Brooks and the head of Christ. He was interested in this first meeting with Moody and spoke to him pleasantly about his ode.

With his gentle concern for Arvia's hurt brow began Moody's courtly endearments toward the child, to whose wide-eyed wonder I recall his reciting in soft, strange cadences his poem of *The Counting Man:*

> *Eeny, meeny, miney mo,* —
> All the children in a row,
> *Cracka feeny,* who is he,
> Counting out so solemnly?
>
> *Eeny meeny,* look how tall,
> Like a shadow on the wall!
> When did he come down the street,
> Muffled up from head to feet?
>
> Listen! Don't you hear the shiney
> Shadow-man count *meeny-miney?*
> Hush! when all the counting's done
> May be — *I* might be The One!

In tingling weather we all took to snowshoes, trailing the woods and pastures home again to our hedged garden where Moody assisted the children in packing the walls of a snow labyrinth of hide-away paths. Of another winter visit, on a piercing zero twilight of January, 1908, I recall Moody and Torrence — in meagre city-gear, bare-headed, biting their thumbs, having rejected our country furs — dashing off down a drifted back-road on a two-mile run to the village. Concerning this later visit, Henry Hering, the sculptor (then Saint-Gaudens' assistant) has recalled

to me his encountering the two poets by black night
on a lower road, doubled over beside a one-horse sleigh
with an oil-lantern, desperately trying to dislodge with
their fingers the icy balls of snow packed in the horse's
hooves.

At Cornish, in those days, Saint-Gaudens' charming,
dynamic personality was the magnet which had drawn
around him there, during many years, a circle of all-the-
year-round neighbors diversely gifted in arts and letters.
Having been deeply stirred by his bronze memorial in
Boston, Moody — whose moving ode begins:

> Before the solemn bronze Saint-Gaudens made
> To thrill the heedless passer's heart with awe —
> And set here in the city's talk and trade
> To the good memory of Robert Shaw —

had long desired to meet the sculptor of that young Civil
War commander of negro troops, whom — also in tribute
to Saint-Gaudens — I had described

> Sitting his horse in proud simplicity,
> His lifted brow clouded with battle dreams
> Where the imagined drum-beats roll in bronze,

in my Prologue to the Saint-Gaudens Masque, about
eight months before Moody's first visit to Cornish. In that
Masque * written and performed to celebrate the twentieth
Anniversary of the founding of the Cornish Colony by
Augustus and Augusta Saint-Gaudens, some sixty artists
and writers of repute took part, to music of Boston Symphony Orchestra Players. On that very spot today —
mecca of thousands of art pilgrims, yearly — the sculptor's
ashes rest in the altar of a small pillared temple — a re-
plica in marble of the stucco temple, in front of which

[67]

Saint-Gaudens himself — toward twilight of June 23, 1905 — watched his Cornish neighbors enact

> Their frolic Masque of satyr, muse and faun
> In honor of their only pagan saint.

The history of the Cornish Colony, significant for its workers in the arts for half a century, has never been written in its varied ramifications, artistic, literary, social and governmental. If it ever shall be, the sojournings there of William Vaughn Moody will contribute to a charming chapter of its middle period, for which portions of these letters are important source material. Writing from Cornish (July 2, 1906) to Charlotte Moody, he touches further on certain allusions of his letters to Harriet in these passages to his sister.

> The social life here is charmingly simple and free from stiffness, the people both open hearted and clever, (not a frequent coincidence of qualities) and I am enjoying this kind of summer colony existence for the first time in my life.
> I see Miss Barrymore * every day and like her immensely. She is simple, hearty and boyish as can be imagined. She has a tennis court and a great cement-lined bathing pool, both of which we indulge in nearly every day, and the combination, with a high-ball and a cigarette afterwards on the big stone-flagged porch, is difficult to beat.
> She is preparing to stage — in the studio of her house here — a one-act play * of my friend and chum, Percy MacKaye, and I have been asked to undertake one of the parts — that of a Maine sea-captain. I don't quite see myself as a Maine sea-captain, and besides I am far too busy to spend the time required for rehearsals, but I am tempted nevertheless to go in for it, for the *fun* of the thing.

This apparently first and only temptation of Moody's to turn histrion and appear as Ethel Barrymore's 'leading man,' turned out after all a non-appearance, for both he and I were 'far too busy' that summer, wrestling with the writing of plays for early production, to take share in that projected studio performance, so it never came off. But that self-glance of Moody anticipating it 'for the *fun* of the thing' glimpses a unique moment in his life, 'enjoying this kind of existence for the first time.'

XXI. WILL AND HARRIET: THEIR 'SACRED DAY'

In this Introduction I have tried to recall and correlate phases actual and spiritual of my friendship with Will Moody which — looking back through long years — I realize are perhaps expressible, if at all, only through the unpremeditated urge of poetry; so that I think I have far better than here intimated them in the poem *Uriel*, which I wrote to his memory, a year after his death; for today, even more than then, I feel

> his kindling currents run
> Quickening within me gladness and new ken
> Of life, that I have shared his prime with one
> Who wrought large-minded for the love of men.
>
> But not alone to share that large estate
> Of work and interchange of communings —
> The little human-paths to heavenly things
> Were also ours...

and feeling this, I know how sparsely here I have disclosed those paths, or intimated the heavenly things.

So, too, of Harriet. Now that both are gone, only to return together on compulsive tides of memory, I see how inexpressibly intertwined her great spirit is with my thankful share in their mutual largesse of life; and I realize anew how impossible it has been for me to assume a dispassionate editorial aloofness in commenting here on our mingled friendship.

Throughout these letters, though from their varied sequence of place and time, Harriet herself is bodily remote — absent always in her far off 'Grove,' impalpable under a Chicago 'moon with unhandsome thrift of silver' — yet we have that bodily absence to thank for her spiritual embodiment in the letters, which else would not have been written.

From one of them now, in closing this prologue (which opens again in the letters' epilogue), I return to the theme of that 'sacred day' which occasioned their commencement, in quoting this passage written by Will to Harriet, from Cornish, May 17, 1906, six years after his first letter which begins their sequence.

> By some unaccountable lapse of memory I forgot yesterday that it was the anniversary of our sacred day, forever to be remembered with hymns and trances of the spirit. As some slight atonement (to myself) I am going to copy out and send you the little poem which you know. I have given it, provisionally, the title of *The Three Angels*.* The only other I can think of is *Dies Angelica*.

Enclosed in the letter was the poem, in which these stanzas reveal her — as throughout all his communings with her — 'disengaged from the illusions and interruptions of this world.'

> Last night I sat at her right hand:
> Though Death upon the left hand stood,
> Our hearts were ne'er so light and bland;
> As in a moonlit summer wood
> Friend unto happy friend we spake,
> As swan by swan on a windless lake
> We drifted down God's glassy flood.

WILL AND HARRIET

We had been sweet friends long before,
But till this evening's dark mischance,
Aye, never till this deep death-hour
Had such a heart been ours to dance
Childlike upon the hills of glee;
So on those hills she played with me,
Through swooning pain and ether trance.

And yet had not been breathed a sound
Of love, nor a thought of love been thought.
With light of light her brow was wound
When mutely she made question, 'What
Means this strange light about your brow?'
And I made answer mute, 'You know
It is the love that we have found.'

Like flame afar her life did rise
And from the ends of being came,
Bare as at birth, without disguise,
To meet my spirt's naked flame
Which towered from out the primal mist
To her. — Her lips lay all unkissed;
We made no sign, we named no name.

LETTERS TO HARRIET

Letters to Harriet

29 NORTH HALL
CHICAGO, *May* 20, 1901

I do not know whether letters are allowed, but in the confidence that this will be intercepted if they are not, I am going to yield to an impulse which I can no longer resist to speak a word to you. I have thought of you so much these last days and nights that my desire to write a line at least has by accumulation outgrown my sense that you ought not to be disturbed. What is it that I want to say, you will wonder. I hardly know myself. I only know that your pain and danger have made your mind and character stand out before me as if disengaged from the illusions and interruptions of this world, and filled me with a sense of deep — bear with me if I say religious — gratitude for the gift of your friendship. I feel that in knowing you I have had a rich blessing — one which will enter for good into all that I do or become. When you are well and strong again, I shall probably not have the courage to say this; so let me say it now, and afterwards remember it silently.

If it is any comfort to you in these painful and tedious days of your convalescence, you should know, as I think perhaps you do, that any one of us, from Hannah up (or down), would joyfully have taken your place, if by so

doing we could have saved from suffering you, our brightest and noblest one.[1]

En route via Union Pacific Railroad
Outside Denver, Friday Morning
(Postmarked August 16, 1901)

The good word reached me before I had got far beyond
the Mississippi. Until it came, rolling the weight off with
that great sentence, I did not realize how heavy my anxiety had been. Now there are only a few weeks more of
patience and then the climb to health and the joy of life
renewed. We shall all go up the slope with you step by
step, sharing in the gain.

These incredible plains! It's hard to believe them as
level as they look, with the car surging like a ship on a lee
shore.

An hour ago I saw a man on foot, crawling God knows
whither antlike over this enormous monotony.

These words have remained with me from my morning
reading, from hour to hour revealing all kinds of good
meanings. Take them.

'*Chiedete, e vi sarà dato; cercate, e troverete; picchiate e
vi sarà aperto.*'

W. V. M.

COLORADO SPRINGS, *Saturday*
(Postmarked August 18, 1901)

Garland [2] is at Wagon Wheel Gap, somewhere in the
southwestern corner of the state, and I leave for there, by
train and stage, tonight. I have spent the day getting my
outfit ready. Naturally nothing that I brought would do,

[1] Cf. first two notes at back, under Introduction Notes, II.
[2] Hamlin Garland.

and a mad career of acquisition has been mine — water-proof boots, blankets, corduroy trousers ('pants,' I mean), 'slickers' (which being interpreted is oilskin wrappings) and leather leggings. I look like a Cripple Creek desperado, and feel like Buffalo Bill on a spree. The latter simile is for rhetorical purposes only — in point of fact I feel like a fellow who has left his best friend behind in sore plight and who has a mind to go back and try to comfort him. An hour of golden silence or quiet converse beside a certain sick bed seems more to be desired than the mighty secret of the mountains for which they are calling me to wrestle.

Mr. Ehrich, who turns out to be a capital fellow (an intelligent and cultivated Jew, generously helpful and nobly hospitable), has been immensely kind. He will take care of my mail and forward it to me as long as I am in reach of a post-office.

The mountains here are disappointing in a garish light, but at morning and evening they take on an indescribable majesty. There will be more to tell when I know their minds better and am admitted to their privacies. Just here they seem a little worldly and shabby, from being photographed and be-circulared and be-tripped. The camera and the watering-place hotel are among the prime inventions of the devil to circumvent the glory of God. The yawning mouth of a packing-case, hungering to be filled; excuse me while I fill it.

It is filled, but there is only time to say goodbye. Be of good courage. Throw up the water into the sun.

W. V. M.

WAGON WHEEL GAP, COLO. *Aug.* 19 (1901)

Here I am on the roof of things. Met Garland yesterday, and today we are getting ready to start on trail. Shall take mountain ponies to ride and a pack mule for the camping stuff. We are going up the Rio Grande to its source, over Marshall Pass into the Ouray region, then over Trident Mesa and Uncompahgre Peak, returning by way of Slumgullion Gulch. (God bless the man who imagined these names!) This is the highest part of the Continental Divide, and the crazy little torrents are all destined to great fates. They will not stop short of the Pacific or the Gulf of Mexico. Even here in the Gap we are several thousand feet higher than the top of Mt. Washington. The mountain air has already made me feel equal to — to — well, to Slumgullion Gulch, begad. Can expression farther go?

This morning it has rained, and now that the sun is breaking through above the savage peaks of sheer stone and rolling a luminous chaos of cloud through the valleys and cañons, I can only — as a better man than me once did — 'stand in my shoes and wonder.' They are calling me to pick out a pony. Goodbye and good cheer.

W. V. M.

ANTELOPE SPRINGS
RIO GRANDE DEL NORTE
COLORADO

Our trailing expedition has been brought to a premature end by an accident to Garland. In crossing a high meadow, covered with an almost impenetrable tangle of scrub-willows and made soft by the snow from surrounding peaks, his horse got into a bog, and in scrambling out fell on the slope of the bank, crushing his (Garland's) foot painfully, though, as it turns out, not dangerously. We were thirty-three miles from the nearest settlement when it happened, and the way thither lay through what G. declares to be the wildest piece of country he has seen in the States. There was nothing for it but to put him on his horse and push for cover. Fortunately the accident occurred early in the morning, and by riding hard all day through fallen timber, bog, 'slide-rock,' and creek-beds, we managed to get in *before* it was too dark to see our horses' ears, the last three hours through drenching and freezing rain.

G.'s foot was badly swollen, but the injury proves to be not great, and he will be about again in a week. Meanwhile, however, camping on the trail, which has made the last week an experience long to be remembered, is over. We tackled the stiffest proposition in reach — a country of great cañons narrowing up to strange green mountain meadows, overlooked by savage peaks of sheer rock. We started with a trail, which tradition declared to continue across the Continental Divide and down again into the habitable valleys; but before we had gone one day's journey the said trail became dim and interrupted, and by the middle of the second day disappeared altogether, except for a dubious and ghostly reappearance at long intervals and in surprising places. Probably it has not been travelled since the Indians, who made it, left the country. There was of course much exhausting labor involved, especially as our pack horse and his burden required constant care. Then pitching the tent, unharnessing and hobbling the horses, getting wood for fire, cooking, fixing bedding to keep us warm when the sun dropped and the thermometer with it far below freezing point — all this

meant work, I tell you; so that as yet the physical difficulties of the trip almost obscure the aesthetic impressions
(how I hate that phrase!). But this will not be for long;
already the essentials are fast emerging from the accidents.

I wish I could give you a conception of these mountain
meadows, ten or eleven thousand feet high, set in a cirque
of desolate grandeur, flower-starred floors of richest,
softest green, rivulet-enlaced and aspen-fringed, swept
by silver skirts of rain which the sun chases and glorifies.
They are the poetry of these mountains, not to be known
save of him whose strenuous right elbow can buckle a
mule-pack in place. One tremendous afternoon we had
two on the summit of the divide, with a world of peaks in
circle, far as the eye could reach — an awful Senate. We
crawled down the side of the thing before sunset, with the
frost beginning to settle lightly on the rocks, and camped
by a little cold green lake which was held like a cup on a
shelf of granite a thousand feet high, that again resting
on another and another, a stairway to make the brain
faint as it felt down it for a resting place.

Well, trailing — with its thrilling joys and exhausting
labors — is over for me for this time. I am doing the next
best thing — in some ways even a better thing, since it
leaves me with more energy to enjoy what I see. I have
put Garland in good hands and started out with a single
horse to explore the country around Ouray, a compara-
tively settled region, so that by figuring ahead pretty
sharply I can be sure of a roof to sleep under at night and
a shed for my horse. Tonight I am staying with a ranch-
man in the upper Rio Grande, who by grand good luck
owns pen, ink, and paper. Tomorrow I go over the Divide

to Lake City; the trail goes very high and I expect to have a gorgeous day.

You will pardon all this chatter; I don't forget that you are cooped up in bed, and for all I know suffering weary pain — certainly suffering the weariest pain of all — that of confinement and ennui.

This I will not talk about, since it avails not. And after all you are with me here, and your heart is made strong with the mountains.

W. V. M.

Please read something of this to Ferd.[1] It is too late to write him tonight and I don't know when I shall have another chance.

I don't understand why I hear nothing from you or from him. I have had no word at all. — Every now and then I am seized with anxiety as to the result of the operation, and half suspect you are keeping back something from me. *Please* do not.

Tuesday, Aug. 27.

Thursday, Aug. 29 (1901)

The dirty and crumpled condition of these sheets is due to the fact that I took the wrong trail to Lake City and found myself at nightfall with eighteen miles and a mountain between me and a bed; the condition of these sheets isn't due to that, but to what follows, to wit: friendly curl of smoke through trees on mountain side; approach by benighted tenderfoot; greeting by band of tramp miners; deserted cowpuncher's hut (notice that hut not c.p. was deserted) made festal by a log-fire kindled reck-

[1] Ferdinand Schevill.

lessly in the midst thereof; baking of 'dough-gobs' and boiling of inexpressible coffee; ravenous eating of same; stories; bed *au naturel* on dirt floor, with benighted tenderfoot wrapped in his raincoat. The dirt and crumpling of these sheets is due to their position in an exposed pocket in too intimate contact with dirt floor, charred logs, and dough-gobs.

I return to Wagon Wheel Gap tomorrow, and start at once for Colorado Springs where I shall spend a day or two. Shall probably be in Chicago by Tuesday or Wednesday of next week. I am going to fill up the rest of this sheet with writing, in hopes that the grime may be in part concealed. If you knew what good fellows some of these tramp miners were you would regard more reverently the dirt which is their secular element.

(Postmarked Boston, Mass., Nov. 25, 1901)

Sunday night, and you are gathered about the fire, warmed also and illuminated by another light, that never was on land or sea, shed from some deathless lyric which someone has just said. The blessed expansion of these firelit hours, and how we found each other in the wind of the poetry, and went down it together to the unguessed-at goal! Here is a night of rain and wild Atlantic wind; inside, sleepy domestic happiness, and for me *tedium vitae*. I think I am still of the unregenerate in whom sleepy domestic happiness induces *tedium vitae*. Other people's at any rate; perhaps my own wouldn't, but I doubt it would. Or perhaps (a happy thought) my own wouldn't be sleepy. Basta.

I am trying to obey your injunction and think of you as happy and possessed in soul, but for some reason, some underworld reason, it is not easy. Both last night and the night before I wakened several times with the feeling that you were in distress and that I must go to you at once. This, in a more shadowy sense, has persisted through the daylight, filling me with vague uneasiness. Let me know that you are well, that you rest confidently and joyously on the larger facts of our mutual life, and that the days bring you each after its kind their mystic increase. Write me quite concretely and matter-of-factly about your daily life — as I mean to do. As an evidence of good faith I will state that I have a bad cold, caught at the football game, and a small price to pay for it too, for it was a glorious spectacle and a great generous excitement. Out of this, as out of everything great and generous, my heart turned to you, saying 'See!' or rather, saying nothing, but looking for the soul's intelligencer, the speaking light of your eye understanding in secret. You do not know how I turn to you for that sweet secret understanding.

Good night and good cheer for the morrow.

I think of getting a room in Cambridge, to be near the library.

W. V. M.

1 WILLOW STREET, BOSTON
Wednesday
(Postmarked Dec. 5, 1901)

DEAR HARRIET:

Your first good letter came some days ago, and relieved my mind much. Here is another, telling of your social dissipations. Don't do it. Peace is not to be found that way.

'Shine inward rather thou, and all the dark
Illumine.'

[83]

Mason [1] has just been playing me Beethoven's second symphony, which we are to hear at this week's concert. His music is a tremendous resource to me. How I wish you might share it. Some day you will know him and add one more noble soul to the number of those whom to have known in this life is life and to have missed is the great misfortune.

I am working night and day, trying to push the book [2] through by the first of the year. It looks now like a forlorn hope. Lovett is very good-natured about working his stuff over, and I am recasting much of mine to approximate it as nearly as possible to some common standard of form and tone. This soul-destroying work makes me feel like a turnip in the head and a rotten walnut in the — well, not in the heart, I guess, let me say the sensorium. I keep boring away in the dark, like a captive tunnelling his way under the prison flags to daylight and fresh air. Barring suffocation or a cave-in I shall get away with my life, I think. Once out and in the woods I shall lie for a week forgetting, and then — *basta*, as Signor G. Mantellini now has the privilege of saying in his debased American accent to one accustomed to the right Tuscan tang. Which reminds me that I heard yesterday of a place called Cornish, on the Connecticut River, on the New Hampshire-Vermont border, said to be a great region, where there is a small house for sale. It is on a high hill outside the village, the last house, with a big view of the river, etc. Does it sound? Has it a flavor?

What you say about *Hedda Gabler* is very exciting; I shall read it as soon as I can find an hour not roosted on

[1] Daniel Gregory Mason.
[2] The Moody-Lovett *History of English Literature.*

by the Incubus. The Incubus is discouragingly catholic and exhaustive as to his roosts. Your account of Herrick's book is disappointing, but I hardly hoped he could handle the theme metaphysically. He seems to have pictured vividly the world of unreality, in which he believes, and been unable to picture the world of reality because he doesn't believe in it, at least not with the vital belief which is the substance of things hoped for, the evidence of things not seen.

For fear you have lost count let me remind you that today (Wednesday) you should be reading the 13th chapter of John. Aren't you a little disappointed in John? He is so anxious to establish the god-head of Christ that he robs him of a great deal of the humanity which the simpler Evangelists let us see in him. Already his features have begun to stiffen into those of an idol, under the freezing touch of theology. Yet it was John that He loved best — dear me!

Was on the point of sending for the *Faith-Healer* last week, when I discovered that Willard was here, but there was hardly time. When you send it let me know your last impression, however unfavorable. Also any suggestions that have occurred to you, for rewriting.

It is late, late, and here is a great lot of nothing, meaning merely that I wish to talk to you, and fear if I stop you will go away.

Yours,   WILL

(Postmarked Boston, Mass., Dec. 16, 1901)
Sunday night

It is eleven o'clock, and I have been writing since nine this morning, almost uninterruptedly, so that my head is putty; but I must send you a line. You write of many interesting things, but fail to answer my questions about your operation and resultant state of health. I begin to be worried by your reticence, and shall appeal to little Alice for the truth. Send the programs by all means. This accursed book has got on my nerve so that I can think of nothing else awake or asleep except pushing it through. However, perhaps the knowledge that I am listening to your music will relax the tension and permit me to hear.

The pictures (of which Dyer sent me rough proofs) were uniformly base. I sent one or two back to be finished up, for luck, but if they are as bad as they promise to be you shall never see them. A kind of rudimentary self-respect survives, amid the ruin of my faculties, and it takes the form of wishing to preserve my image in your breast undisfigured by photographic caricature. If you notice any incoherences in this letter, forgive them. They are due only to the fact that I keep thinking of you and forgetting my pen.

W—

Friday night
(Postmarked Boston, Mass., Dec. 17, 1901)

DEAR HARRIET:

I am sorry that you worried about my cold. It has been bothersome, but at no time serious. I was unable to achieve a temperature of more than a hundred, tho' I used the thermometer as per directions. What is much more to the purpose is that they have been butchering you again and that you are once more in the grip of the Cocaine devil. Poor dear! I wish I could be there to help you bear what at last grows, does it not? unbearable.

It's really too much, too much! But keep a heart in your breast, and don't let go the 'forward-looking thoughts.'

I wish I could send you one thing which is a constant source of vague happiness to me. For days I couldn't fix on what it was; but each time I stepped out doors my heart gave a lift — vague, delicious. Last night I went out for a walk in the frosty starlight before going to bed. Again the sudden impalpable sweet pang, like a harp-string softly struck in the core of my being. I stopped and tried to analyze the sensation, and succeeded in tracing it to the nostrils. All at once it came over me — the Sea! I had been smelling it for days, and thrilling to it, without knowing it.

The streets are full of Christmas. I wonder by what chemistry the very quality of the air changes in festival time? If the snow holds I shall go up into the mountains during Christmas week. Be of good cheer; this *must* be the last of a bad business.

W.

(Postmarked Boston, Mass., Dec. 27, 1901)

Dear Harriet,

This morning your note of Christmas greeting came, and started the day for me bravely. Except that you are ill again, alas! And except that you speak of me in terms which make the drudging, un-uplifted reality of me wish to be blotted out and there an end. Think of me as one who has been human and may in the fullness of time be so again, but who is at present a maker of textbooks and an offence to the sunlight. Lovett is not sailing on the 28th and the book is still far from done. The unholy thing has had to be practically rewritten from start to finish, compressed and recast, to make the parts fit together. It has been a business! I am working ten hours a day, and have been doing so since I came East. By good luck I shall be done in another three weeks. Then? I think I will tumble into the first train or steamer headed south, travel until I find a big field with a tree in the middle of it, and lie under said tree for forty days without moving a finger. Will you come along? There will be room for two under the tree, if you promise not to stir or speak for forty days. If you said *Boo!* I'm that nervous I should fly to pieces like a Prince Rupert's drop.

Your pictures are a great support to me. They remind me, in these days when I need to be reminded, that there is such a thing as human great-heartedness, and that, as Keats said, Life is the Valley of Soul-making. Which reminds me that the volume of Keats you speak of has not reached me. Seymour's book[1] is very interesting. I am surprised by the faithfulness of several of his drawings to the seventeenth century spirit — I mean the spirit of seventeenth century graphic art. Is this an accident of temperament, or has he studied the contemporary engravings? At any rate the book is a pious and admirable piece of work. I read the poem over in a crowded street car Christmas Eve, going out to Newton, and its majestic melody, its imagery, for all it is so quaintly elaborate, always eager and awe-struck, made that bouncing, screaming electric car a fore-court of adoration, and the bundle-laden people nothing less than 'star-led wizards' and shepherds tendings their flocks by night — under the helmèd Cherubim and swordèd Seraphim. I here check my pen with the uncomfortable suspicion that this verges

[1] Ralph Fletcher Seymour's edition of *The Eve of Saint Agnes.*

on Scenery, and that some lines ago you gave this letter up and laid it beside the last rhapsody from —— ——. Pick it up again, do. I promise plain russet, and no sarcenet surety for my oaths. And in plain russet, I wish you a happy New Year, and in plain love I pray God to send you speedily health and all joy.

W.

1 WILLOW STREET, BOSTON
Jan. 13, 1902

DEAR HARRIET,

I have neglected you sadly of late, I fear, so far as writing goes. The fact is I have been straining every nerve to get this infernal book done, and after each day's stint was over, have been too fagged and dead to have anything to say, even to you. It was good of you to send the little books. The Milton especially is a wonder of bookmaking and almost solves the problem of a library for people who live in their trunks.

I shall be through with my job in another week or ten days, and shall then go down to New York with the manuscript, and arrange about having the proof forwarded to me somewhere. After a day or two in N.Y. recovering the rudimentary use of my suspended faculties, I shall be off — somewhere. I want a month or two of absolute rest and solitude, in a soft country — a soft country. The buds are pushing out on the laurels below Amalfi, and the blue, blue water is lapping in the Capri caves. What shall I do?

W.

(Postmarked Jan. 23, 1902)
1 WILLOW ST., BOSTON
Saturday

DEAR HARRIET:

Your letter has just come, and I send a hasty line of information about my necessary movements without waiting to answer your large-hearted message. I leave for New York on Monday the 25th. I shall probably have to be there for a week, in consultation with Scribner about the book, and in getting the printing under way. I do not think it would pay you to come to New York. The Virginia Coast is far better, and after a week I can come there perfectly well. The news of your health alarms and pains me — but I will not talk about that. When you start send word to me care ——, where you have decided to go, and I will join you and little Alice as soon as I can.

W—

SALMAGUNDI CLUB
(Postmarked New York, Feb. 11, 1902)

This unimaginable textbook hangs on. I thought I had it done two weeks ago, but on looking at the bibliography I found it had to be done over again, and the result has been a fortnight of about as strenuous drudgery as the devil ever meted to a just man. I am still working eight hours a day, but the end is at last in sight. Gloria in excelsis and hoop-la! I expect to take the three o'clock boat on Friday afternoon, and reach Norfolk the next day, about noon.

Stephen Phillips's *Ulysses* is out. I bought it this morning but haven't had time to read it. I saw Mrs. P. Campbell in *Beyond Human Power* last week, and share your lack of enthusiasm, both for player and play.

Have you got books enough? If not telegraph me what to bring, or write if you think there is time. Also hunt up that tree — the Nirvana tree.

W. V. M.

(Harriet, accompanied by Alice Corbin and Elizabeth O'Neill, went to Cape Henry, where the only place she could find to live in was an old inn. Here they were joined by W. V. M.)

NORFOLK, VA.
(Postmarked April 10, 1902)

I am unable to get out of town tonight after all, and am wandering like a lost soul in this Gehenna of a hotel. A certain fireside in a seaside shanty, with the elements outside, and a loved life inside; Shakespeare, and big important conversation, and the Little Talk within — why didn't we know a good thing when we had it? There is nothing for it but bed, where at least these strident noises and uninhabited faces will give way to oblivion; not that oblivion isn't something in my line tonight, with only an hour's sleep out of last night's allowance in my shy-a-bed pate. In spite of weariness your spirit is vividly with me, and thank God it is a glad spirit tonight, and not sorrowful. Dear spirit, may He keep me true to you, and through you to the best I have to hope for, and learn, and attain unto.

WILL.

(Postmarked April 12, 1902, New York)
Friday night, 11:30

I have had a long day on the train, and am correspondingly used up — so much so, that I feel anxious to hear how you stood your long ride. There is small likelihood of my getting off tomorrow, as the boat sails at 10 A.M., instead of two in the afternoon as at first advertised; but I have heard of another sailing Tuesday, which I shall probably take. I shall get some word from you before that. May it be one of good cheer, which I can lay to heart for comfort on the voyage.

On the train I read the *Winter's Tale*, rereading the first act in order to hear your voice on the lines. I did observance at all our shrines coming along past Cape Henry this morning. To tell the truth, however, I was surprised and shocked to find everything there just as if nothing had happened. The stolid existence of things in space and time, when all reason for their existence has disappeared, is among the hardships. The fruit trees in Maryland were a joy to the heart; I hope you found them singing all along your route.

W.

(Postmarked April 13, 1902, New York)

I have taken passage on the Città di Milano, sailing Tuesday morning for Naples. She is small and slowish (fourteen days) but I expect to get a good deal of fun out of the crew and passengers, who will doubtless all be Italians. I had a regular love feast with the '*Genovese, si, Signore, sono da Genova, bella città*,' who sold me my ticket. I save twenty-five dollars over the German line, and gain, I think, more than that in *imponderabilia*.

W.

(Postmarked New York, April 14, 1902)

I have been dining with Robinson [1] tonight, and we have sat late over the coffee and cigars; so I shall take time only

[1] Edwin Arlington Robinson.

[92]

for a word. Robinson's book *Captain Craig* has been accepted by Houghton and Mifflin, partly at my solicitation, I am proud to say. Get it when it comes out, and let me know what you think of it. Your judgment of his work has, I know, hitherto been adverse; I shall be curious to know whether this volume changes it at all. The mortal day I have been reading proof, finishing the last pages; I tremble to think how ill they will bear your scrutinizing eye. Reading them alone was dreary work; thoughts of my dear comrade came between me and the page more than once; I longed for the Cape Henry fireplace, the half-heard boom of the sea, and the sense of glad intimate understanding.

Tomorrow will be an exceedingly busy day, but I shall snatch time for a word spoken in secret to the noblest and tenderest of earthly hearts. Spoken in secret — such these hasty scrawlings are, as you know, though matters of fact and things of no moment, except for the unspoken things beneath.

WILL

NEW YORK, *April* 14 (1902)

My trunk is packed, and the wind sits in the shoulder of the sail. Freedom is somewhere near. I feel her as a presence veiled with light, and her blessed eyes are on me; but when I turn about to catch her at it she is gone and I am left still mewed up in my heaviness. Her coyness and my lack of spirit may be due to the fact that I have not heard from you after your home-coming, and I have a vague fear about you. This I know is not according to our contract, and a night's sleep will give me once more my happy confidence in the strength and joyousness which I know uphold you. Goodbye, and may all the great powers shield you. If possible I will send a line from Gibraltar. In case we do not touch there, it will be between three and four weeks before you hear from me. Meanwhile, the water into the sun!

WILL —

(Postmarked New York, April 15, 1902)

We are going down the harbor, and my mood, which has been rather low, has been so raised by your letter, handed me as I left the hotel, that I begin to feel the glory of the world, and know that it is well for us both that I go. No man since the first who went down to the sea in ships ever left behind him a braver or sweeter heart; and I shall rest confident in your power to take your life and mine in the largest way, to feed yourself and me from the eternal cisterns. It is great news about your walking; but I told you so. Indeed, let it be an omen.

I shall try and send you a line from Gibraltar. Goodbye once more, and may the Lord make his light to shine upon you.

WILL

April 16 (1902)

We are on a halcyon sea, smooth as silk, rippling into long lazy lines of light. The boat proves, so far, unexpectedly comfortable. When I saw her lying at the pier I was half-inclined to give her the go-by and forfeit my passage money. But though small she is clean, and bids fair not to roll too outrageously. We are about thirty souls in the first cabin, and some hundred in the steerage. Most of the cabin passengers are Italians of the middle

[94]

class — a retired sea-captain, a doctor, a lieutenant in the navy, a musician (member of the Thomas orchestra), merchants, etc. I sit at table with the sea-captain and his wife and baby; we are already good friends, thanks to the baby. The most picturesque members of our company are a nun of the Order of St. Francis of Assisi, and the mother superior of the order, who have in charge six or eight Irish-American girls on their way to Rome to take the veil. Seen against this gigantic laughing pagan sea, the black hoods and unbetraying faces of the nuns give one strange thoughts. I have had a little talk with the 'Madre'— a remarkably intelligent woman, so far as her absolute devotion to her church allows her to be. There bids fair to be plenty of diverting humanity here, but for now I lie curled in my steamer chair, with my warm rug about me, contemplating all things and luxuriating in laziness. I am more tired than I supposed. I can think of nothing so blessed as to lie in a steamer chair in the sun, and to be borne softly along over sleepy seas, to the day before Judgment.

It is still too cold to sleep on deck at night, but I hope that as we make south I shall be able to. I shall jot down a word or two now and then, to chronicle my course across the sea. I take it for granted that all the petty facts as well as the few large ones, that go to make up the days for me, interest you — a hugeous assumption, I know.

April 17 (1902)

It is a cold and rainy day off the Banks of Newfoundland. It seems we are taking the northern passage, which means several days of bad weather. All the passengers have been driven indoors, and all their facile Italian tongues are going at once, to say nothing of the fog-horn, the piano, the pounding engines, the shuddering wrench of the screw as it comes out of the water, and — triumphantly audible above everything — the ship baby. I remember several rings of Dante's hell which seem by contrast Elysian. My distresses are added to by the fact that the old gentleman who shares my stateroom is very ill; and between pity for his groans and the vain attempt to relieve them, I don't get much sleep. And you know what I am without an ox's share of sleep.

All this sounds doleful, no doubt; but I am, as a matter of fact, enjoying most of it. I forgot to tell you (or did I tell you after all?) that I finished the last bit of proof on board, and sent it back by the pilot boat. A pretty neat fit, it strikes me.

I have read two books of the *Odyssey* since the ship started. I intend to read at least a book a day during the voyage, not attempting the drama until a more strenuous time. Here is a sentence which I found in Hesiod, about the rich: 'They know not how the half is more than the whole, nor the great joy there is in mallow and asphodel.'

Sunday, April 21

For two days we have been in the grip of a tremendous sea, which has tossed and shaken and pounded our poor little ship as a cat treats a mouse. Rain and cold, together with the sky-larking of the boat, have made it impossible to do anything but hug one's berth, so that my 'correspondence' has languished along with other things. Today it is bright again, and the sea after its anger is glorious — the color of bright iron, roaring and shouting past in mountainous play. The boat is in for the fun too — standing now on its head and now pirouetting on its beam-end, ducking its taffrail and covering itself amidships with crisp green avalanches of brine. Poseidon is a great god and a merry. I am setting down these remarks on the weather as I skate past my paper — a word on the starboard roll and a word on the port. How you would glory in the gigantic mirth of this sea!

April 22 (1902)

This has been a great Homeric day, and the gods have been seated again upon the clouds. It has been a great experience to read Homer against this background of unreclaimed primeval sea. The rhythms especially take on a new meaning when timed with the swing and swell of the water, here in mid-Atlantic. The hexameter would never have arisen except among a race of sailors or coast-dwellers. This strikes me as an ornamental variety of Lautverschieb; I shall embody it in my forthcoming textbook on the subject.

There is an extraordinary complex of human life on board, even more than is usually to be found on these small steamers, where the passengers, since they travel the seas not for pleasure but for serious business, are almost always at some crisis of life. I wish hourly that you might be here, to share my absorption in the curious human stories that are poured into my ear whenever I stop to listen. The smallness of the boat, the three days of dreadful weather, the pressing in upon us of the immensities of sky and sea, make everybody eager to share his heart's inmost secret, an eagerness which these dear Italians are apt to experience at all times.

We have among our types a buffoon and a madman. The latter is a Piedmontese peasant who was refused admission to the United States by the immigration authorities, and who has gone out of his head with the disappointment. For a day or two he roamed the ship, but is now confined. The buffoon is still at large.

There is a young Englishman on board, an engineer, whom I knew in Cambridge, and who may go to Greece with me. He is a capital fellow, and will make a first-rate companion for rough travel, I think.

W—

April 23 (1902)

Last night and today has been rather a solemn time. The old gentleman whom I spoke of as being ill in my cabin, proved to be far more seriously afflicted than anybody dreamed. He got rapidly worse during the three days of storm. I did what I could for him, which was very little. For several nights I slept in the smoking room, (or made a bluff at sleeping) as his condition made it impossible to sleep in the cabin, and the stewards needed the room in order to take care of him. Day before yesterday he was removed to the hospital and last night at sunset died. As I stood on deck after everybody was in bed, and thought of the old man lying there in the majesty of death, it seemed as if he were piloting the ship toward the unearthly shore where his business now is. An inventory of his papers and effects revealed the fact that he was a Catholic priest, with a natural son — a nice boy who came on board with him and saw him safely fixed. He will be buried tonight at nine, somewhere off the Azores. There is another priest on board to read the funeral service. This tragedy, and some others, not so catastrophic but even more affecting, which have come to light from day to day among the steerage passengers (they are easy to come at and talk with, in so small a ship) have cast a pall over the sun, and I shall be relieved when land is sighted. We shall pass Gibraltar the day after tomorrow, and be in Naples three days later.

W—

April 25, 3 P.M. (1902)

This is dated from mÿ bunk, which is the only place I can find steady enough to write in, and it is to be accomplished here only with the aid of an elaborate apparatus of bracing gear, contrived of suit-cases and shawl-strap bundles.

Yesterday I was too depressed by the happenings of the night before to write. At nine o'clock a little knot of passengers — as many as had the courage to cross the open space of howling wind and rain intervening — gathered in the hospital, and clung to the tiers of iron bunks while the French priest read his Latin over the dead; the two nuns and the girls who are going to Rome to enter a convent, muttering the responses. When we came on deck the storm which had been brewing all day had broken, and the burial was a thing to remember for gruesomeness. It was made tolerable only by the sense of majesty which death seems always to bring, which no claptrap or hugger-mugger can injure, or even human callousness much. These good Italians came back to the saloon afterwards, and gave the whole thing a grand talking-over, spiced with wit and with nice points of difference, uproariously debated.

The weather continues vexatiously bad. All day yesterday, last night and today, a gale of wind has been blowing, and the sea has been getting more and more angry. The boat plunges and rolls like a crazy thing. One can cross the deck only by clinging to a safety-rope, and then at some peril, as we keep shipping seas. At four o'clock this morning an unusually simple and earnest business wave struck us, smashing two life boats, flooding the engine room, and putting out some of the fires. We have been compelled temporarily to leave our course and run before the wind, as the ship is hardly powerful enough to cope with the cross-seas. If the gale holds for twenty-four hours, we shall probably have to put in at Lisbon, which will mean two days delay at least. The sea is a glorious sight now, especially from the bow of the boat, where one moment you see the hills of water slanting fifteen or twenty feet above you, and the next you hang poised on the crest, with sliding green abysses round you. All the same I wish the wind would behave itself and let us go decently on our course. There isn't the slightest danger, not even enough to give continued interest to the situation, and this vague dubbing-about begins to grow wearisome.

W—

April 28 (1902)

Since day before yesterday, when the storm ceased and we got back into our course, life has been growing worth while again at a rapid rate. We came through the Strait of Gibraltar just before sunset yesterday — a wonderful hour, with curtains of mist and rain sweeping and lifting about us, giving glimpses of ethereal mountain slopes, nestling white villages, etc. Supply scenic details. The coast of Africa, which we ran unusually near, was about the most unearthly thing, the most impalpable and dream-like in its loveliness, that I ever saw; yet marvelously distinct in its pencillings. Once in the Mediterranean, the Italian passengers (who have been dispirited during the bad weather) new-tricked their brains, and all day the gay language has gone up and down the boat like a song. The steerage children are playing London Bridge (or its old-world equivalent) on the lower deck while their mothers are hanging out the clothes to dry on improvised clothes-lines, and screaming good-naturedly at the sailors when they come too near with the buckets of paint which are to make us fine for our grand entry into Naples Bay. A waiter just passing announces confidentially in my ear that there is champagne for dinner, and 'gelato all' Americano.' It seems years since that ghostly business of the burial. Perhaps I dreamed it. Yes, now I remember, I did; but all the same I can't find the old man anywhere. Doubtless the whole thing was a dream from the beginning.

Ever since we came near these beautiful and tragic lands, I have wished with an especial longing that you were here. This is the home of your heart. How much longer will you bear to live in exile? Chicago? Did I dream that too? I hope and pray that you may find it possible very soon to ship the burden of that life, which you have borne with such quiet heroism, and get away into a better country. Try, try.

                                                              W.

EUROPE

NAPLES, *May* 2 (1902)

I have just finished dinner, and over the coffee and cigar
(ah, for a real one, instead of a straw and peach-leaf imitation!) I must follow the example set me by the *jeunesse
dorée* at neighboring tables, and write a letter.

The past two days have been a bewildering whirl of
sensations. First there was a bridal procession of islands,
miraculous shapes and colors, and veiled Vesuvius as
chief paranymph. Then a pandemonium of custom-
house, hackmen, crazy-eyed gesticulating screaming *fac-
chini*, then the thousand-voiced, myriad-vested streets
of this incredible town — soldiers, priests, pastry-venders,
fruit-venders, water-sellers, goats, pigeons, bare-legged
contadini, and the rest of the indescribable jumble. The
first impression is that they are all drunk — including the
goats, donkeys, and pigeons; the next and lasting one is
that they are all stark crazy, as well as the God who made
them. In sober earnest I would inquire if, in view of the
things he creates, the Creator is really at all times strictly
temperate in his habits? Looking out upon the Via Roma,
from the vantage ground of my restaurant table and a
good dinner done, I am forced to answer in the negative.

By great good luck I find a steamer here about to sail
direct to Athens. This saves two weary railway journeys
and much trouble in transferring baggage, etc., which I
had been dreading. The chap I spoke of who thought
something of going on with me doesn't feel up to the trick

of horseback travel and bad inns. He looked staunch enough but, like everybody else in the civilized world, has just had nervous prostration, and has gone to sleep at Capri for a month. He may follow me later. I have been making feints at beginning to learn enough modern Greek to get along with when alone in the interior, but it seems dreadfully hard. I feel discouraged by the language difficulty. The whole success of my enterprise will, I fear, depend altogether on my finding a good guide and interpreter within my means. There is also the possibility of falling in with some American or English student in Athens who knows the language and who is bent on the same kind of jaunting that I want to do.

I sail tomorrow morning, and there will be three days at sea.

W—

ATHENS *May 6 (April 24)*

In disembarking on these shores I have tumbled into a little gold-mine of gratuitous days. Yesterday it was the fifth of May; today it is the twenty-fourth of April. Hamlet's quip to Polonius seems to have come true. The prosaic explanation is that the Greek calendar is unreformed, and is thirteen days behind that of the rest of the world.

The sail from Naples to the Piraeus (the port for Athens) was very repaying. Early yesterday morning, when I looked out of my porthole we were passing close to 'Sandy Pylos,' where Nestor entertained Telemachus and Athene, when Telemachus came thither in search of his father. A few hours later we rounded Cape Matapan into the Gulf of Sparta, and for a long time had the grand snowcapped peak of Taÿgetos (which marks the site of old Sparta) as the dominating presence in a world more magically colored than it is possible for anyone who has not seen it to conceive. I had retained a vivid recollection of this Greek coloring, so much higher in the scale, so much more spiritual and intellectual than that in which Italy is steeped, but I found that my recollection of it was a very sorry thing compared with the reality. So long as this atmosphere endures the old gods cannot die, but will go on 'delicately marching through most pellucid air.' By great good luck we succeeded in colliding with a Greek steamer during the afternoon, which detained us two hours for the ascertaining of damages, and made our approach to Athens fall at the sunset hour, when a supernatural splendor and hush lay upon Aegina and Salamis, the mountain ranges above Eleusis, and the dimly discerned Acropolis. (I am afraid all this is scenery, or manners and customs, or phrases, or something else that you justly dislike and have charged me deeply not to perpetrate; but these are the things which have been in my mind, and how can I avoid setting them down, wishing to speak to you as to my other self. I know you are scolding me for this parenthesis, and I deserve it. A momentary panic seized me. Please tell me that I may be as scenic and guidebookish as I like.)

As I take my coffee this morning the streets outside are full of music, soldiers and holiday-makers. It is the feast of St. George, the king's patron saint. I shall go up to the American School this afternoon. The school is still open, I hear, and the Shoreys are doubtless here. I feel that my fortunes hang pretty much on what they can do for me. The prices of the professional dragomen and camping outfitters are hopelessly out of my reach, and the impossibility of mastering modern Greek sufficiently to travel alone seems to be absolute. I will let you know tomorrow what they tell me.

W—

May 9 (1902)

Yesterday was a day of small disappointments, which were lost in the light shed by your letter, the first word I have had from you for nearly a month. I found it waiting for me at the American School, and read it as I came down through the cypresses and pepper-trees of the garden. It cheered and gladdened me much, and I was in need of such cheer, for I had found the school deserted, all the students scattered, the annual excursions over, and the library (which I had hoped to use) in the hands of workmen, who had nailed the books up. Later in the day I found the Shoreys at their hotel, on the wing for Italy. So I beheld myself left high and dry, and the problem of inland travelling unsolved and apparently insoluble. In this crisis, I rushed off to the Piraeus, and took a berth in a tiny steamer which by good luck I found just started for a tour of the islands. All day we have been threading the marvellous lace-work pattern which the Cyclades make on the blue surface of the Aegean. It is now half-past nine at night; we have just left the mountain-locked harbor of Seriphos and are standing off for Melos. I remember that She of Melos is your patron goddess, that she is you in some other incarnation, so I shall stay on deck, wrapped in my rug and bag, and defy the drenching dew until we pass the sacred earth whence her statue was taken.

I hope you can read this. It is written by a dingy

decklamp, and the coil of rope on which I sit is wobbling badly. I haven't the face to get out my palatial sleeping-togs until the Greek and Armenian peasants round me on the deck have gone to sleep. I should be shunned for the rest of the journey as an aristocrat, and should forfeit the golden opinions I have won by my simplehearted struggle to pick up from them a few phrases of their out-rageous tongue.

W—

May 10 (1902)

This is Cänea, in Crete, on the threshold of the Orient — white domes and minarets of mosques and latticed se-raglio windows against a sky of passionate blue. It is the last stronghold of Greece toward the East, too, and the mountains and the sea are all Greek. This meeting of the east and west may have given color to a scene which I be-held this morning and which will haunt me for many days. On the beach at the outskirts of the town a num-ber of fishing boats were drawn up, and the nets drying. The sailors were lying about asleep in the fierce sun — except one, who had heaved his boat on her side and was caulking her. By him stood a man dressed in a long dark robe of coarse stuff, bareheaded, talking earnestly to the stooping sailor. I took him for a Greek priest, by reason of his long hair and spiritual profile. There was something in the spare frame of the man, the slight stoop of the shoulders, and the calm intensity of the attitude, which made my heart stop beating. Presently he turned to look at me, and it was indeed He. This has happened to me twice now — once before at Sorrento seven years ago.

W—

May 11 (1902)

We are standing off Melos. As I told you we passed here before at night, and although I did my devotions in both our names I had to come and see the home of that figure of light at a fitter season. The island is bare of trees (as are most of the Cyclades), but this seems almost to be an added and last sumptuousness, for the light plays over the noble forms of shore-rock and upland and peak more richly thus, as over the naked form of the goddess herself. Ah, Harriet, Harriet! Share it with me; my heart aches with its lonesome joy.

W—

ATHENS, *May* 14 (1902)

Here I am back in Athens, settled down for a week or two of reading, before trying any of the up-country trips I have planned. I am pleasantly fixed here. My room has a balcony which commands a stunning view of the Acropolis and the Gulf of Aegina, the house is clean (for a wonder) and the food good. There is a flat roof with a parapet, to which I can retreat when it gets too hot to sleep in bed. The early morning hours on the roof or the balcony are delicious. It gets very hot in the middle of the day, and I fear it is only a question of weeks until I shall be driven to Switzerland for a breath of cool air. It is also very dry and dusty here about Athens, but I hope to find the country less parched.

Dullness and the blues are on me tonight — one of those times that are so hard to bear because of their meaninglessness, when one simply feels emptied of power and purpose, and there is nothing to say about it. A part of it I suppose is due to the heat and disappointment at finding the season so far past the prime, and a part to the fact that I went to see Colonus this afternoon (where Sophocles's lovely play *Oedipus at Colonus* is laid) and found it a dust-heap, inhabited by goats and dogs. The attempt to see old Greece through the Greece of today is not always easy. Really, however, this is silly whining, and induced by an overmastering desire to be petted and condoled with as a victim of ill-fortune, when I know perfectly well my luck is shamefully and indecently good. I know also that a man who can't find here the things which the antique spirits found, or something as excellent, merely because there are smokestacks in the Piraeus, and a steam-tram to Eleusis, is a fellow of no metal. *Basta.*

W—

ATHENS, *May* 15 (1902)

This has been a festival day. They handed me out at the bank — where I had previously inquired in vain — twelve letters, ten from you. Two of them I read coming home through the blinding white streets, and the rest on my pretty balcony, with Hymettos and the Aegean isles singing chorals of congratulation. Since then I have walked in the radiance shed from their pages, not of this earth, but homely and comfort-bringing with the earth-warmth and earth-fragrance.

In the realm of tangibles the most important news they bring is your reconquest of the art and mystery of locomotion. The second claim on my heart's attention was made by the news about Little Alice.[1] Happy news it is, and may it prove still happier in the sequel. Dear little girl-

[1] Alice Corbin.

woman! Give her my love and blessing; I think of her often, and am the better for it. May all the healing powers of earth and air, and of the unseen gods that dwell there, be quick to help her. The good hope of her recovery carries with it the assurance that you will not have that great weight of care to keep you from winning back to the glorious health Heaven meant you to walk arrayed in. Remember your sister of Melos, and see that you keep up the family tradition. Your cry for the country fills me with rebellion against the conditions which keep you cabined there. Is there no way out into the simple life for which you were made, and which God knows you have by this time earned five-fold the right to?

May 16 (1902)

I have just had a glorious afternoon walk around the bay of Phaleron, and back by moonlight. The colors of this land are unbelievable in their purity and intensity. I am itching to get my fingers on a palette. My box of oils I sent with you back to Chicago, as it was too heavy and bulky to carry, and I can't think of any way to carry oil sketches without great risk and inconvenience. I think I shall try what I can do with water colors; perhaps I can give you a faint suggestion that way of the cosmic soap-bubble in which I sail through space these days.

ATHENS, *May* 17

The weather has been much cooler today and yesterday — perfect May weather in fact. I begin to hope that the extreme heat of the week past was only a flurry such as we often have at home in May.

I have got hold of a bicycle, and have been exploring
Attica by means of it. It (not Attica) is rather less picturesque than a donkey, but more effective. Today I went
to Eleusis, the principal seat of the Demeter worship —
a very strange cult, as far as I can make out, involving
many mystical conceptions such as we usually think of
as foreign to the Greek mind. I came home by the old
'Sacred Way' over the Pass of Daphne. It was late when
I reached the top of the pass, and the sun was setting behind me. The Attic plain was a great pool of purple
shadow, out of which Hymettos and Parnes rose up intense with the very spirit of light — living flame, and the
ghost of flame. In the midst of the glory lay Athens, as
white and proud as she must have looked to the ancient
pilgrims to Eleusis who first caught sight of her from this
point, as they came from the south. The City of the Vio-
let Crown, they used to call her; and her brows were
wreathed today as of old.

This bicycle idea is a great one. It has disadvantages
of course, but it gives one vastly more liberty than any
other means of travel which I have been able to hit upon.
For short distances, it solves the problem perfectly; but
one can't travel very far in Greece without colliding with
a mountain over which a wheel can't be dragged. Never-
the-less I expect in a few days to put a dictionary in my
pocket, and a few cakes of Baker's sweet in my *rucksack*,
and start out to seek my fortune that way. One slight
drawback to bicycling here is that every donkey you pass
goes into hysterics, deposits his rider in a ditch and his
load of water-jars in a neighboring field, and disappears
forever, leaving the solicitous and apologetic bicyclist
to be knifed by the owner of the animal. Another is that

the dogs, which are larger and fiercer than any dog has a
right to be, are visited by only one deep perplexity in
life, namely, whether to make the necessary daily meal
off the rider of a passing wheel, or off the wheel itself.
Either decision interferes with one's pleasure as a traveller.
Moreover, any injury to the dog (digestive or other) results in an immediate uprising of the community; if it
is the wheel which has gone first, the traveller is fed to the
dog as a requital for his injuries — I mean the former's injuries at the hands of the latter — no, I think I mean the
other thing. Former and Latter, since they were laid up
in Michmash between the covers of a certain epoch-making historical work, both look alike to me.

I return the page which you sent me from Ferd's letter. It was very heartening. You are all far too good to
me, both for what I do and what I am. Perhaps after a
few lives of failure and success and failure again I shall
begin to be worthy of such friends. Something too much
of this, are you thinking?

I was glad to hear that the sketches came through all
right. Today I hope to get a water color outfit, and attempt the impossible task of fixing on paper for you at
least a far-off hint of the miraculous light which lies over
these mountains and seas.

W—

ATHENS, *May* 20 (1902)

You must not think that I am indifferent to what you
tell me about people liking my poems and finding themselves touched by them to a keener sense of life. Indeed,
I am not so. Nor is there any danger of my finding what
you say 'fulsome.' Your words, whatever they are, never

fail to quicken and strengthen me toward the life which is
for both of us the only reality in a world of phantoms coming and going — beautiful and terrible and in their order
dear, but still phantoms.

As for me, I am simply prostrated by the Greek drama,
now that I am beginning to see it as it was and is, in all
its simplicity and grandeur. I have just finished the
Oedipus at Colonus, and am perfectly bowled over by it.
It is, for one thing, so *un*classical. A more romantic conception than the coming of Oedipus to Colonus, and his
passing into death in the grove of the Eumenides, does
not exist in poetry. The choruses are inconceivably good.
I haven't yet mastered the intricate metres, and I see the
lyrics therefore through a veil, but even so they are mad-
dening. I sometimes take my book down to the old Dionysiac theatre on the south slope of the Acropolis, and read
there, evoking the chorus and watching them dance while
they chant the tremendous lines. Ah, me!

Tomorrow I go to Delphi on a coasting steamer which
touches at Itea, a little port on the Gulf of Corinth from
which Delphi can be reached easily on foot or by horse.
If it is possible to live there I shall stay for some days,
and take some walks or rides in the mountains — perhaps climb Parnassus, for a sign. Would that you might
be with me there, at that centre of old-world religion.
I only hope they haven't made a dust-heap of it with their
d——d excavations. Archeology here attacks all human
organisms, as the dry-rot; they would shovel Olympus
into the sea in order to unearth a seventh century stew-
pan, at least if there was a chance to quarrel over its
date. The people at the American School — the few lin-
gerers I have seen — are as hopelessly pedantic in this

respect as the rest. I dare say they do some good, though, and have a place in the cycle.

Some day, and not too distant, you must come here. There is much in the revelation of life which was made here, and which is still made in a sense, to thrill you with a native joy, to make you realize your own nature, as perhaps even you have never yet realized it. I am constantly reminded of you, and turn to point out to you your affinities.

WILL

DELPHI, *May* 23 (1902)

I landed at Itea about four this afternoon, and since then have been climbing through olive orchards, and over bare rocky ridges, up to the old shrine of Apollo and the centre of the antique world. It is now eight o'clock, and the splendor is fast fading from the tremendous valley below, though the cliffs which cluster above are still dyed with rose and gold. There is to be a moon, and by her light I shall go up to the ruins above the town and consult the god. Meanwhile I have been using the last rays of light to make a sketch of the valley for you. It turns out a poor thing, for I haven't yet got any skill with water colors; but it will give you a faint hint at least, so I will send it.

There is no inn here, but one of the villagers, who rejoices in the name of Alexandros Pappalexandron, has taken me in and seems disposed to minister to such physical needs as one can be gross enough to retain in such a place. There is nobody in the town who speaks anything but Greek, and my having in that is still a younger brother's portion. Fortunately I have brought a dictionary, and have picked up a few of the essential phrases, so that I shall get on.

Dear Harriet, noblest of woman souls! would that you were here, so that we might do together the acts of piety which are here to be done. You are constantly in my thoughts, and no day passes but I thank God for the inspiration, the strength, and the pure desires that flow from you to me.

W—

May 25 (1902)

The donkeys are browsing on the scant grass among the rocks and snow patches, and my guide is asleep in the sun, though I can't see how he manages it in this icy wind which sweeps down from the peak. We are on Parnassus, just at the snow line, and all Greece is spread out below, mountains and islands and bays and tiny white towns. I had hoped to get to the summit, but that means spending the night here and freezing to death. I am going to hunt a sheltered place in the rocks, wrap myself in my rug, and follow my guide's example, in the hope that the Muses will appear in a vision and suggest a way.

ARACHOVA, *May 26*

The Muses failed to appear, the jades, and there was nothing for it but to leave the mountain to the stars and the late moon, and seek shelter in this mountain village. It is a marvellous little place, hung like a swallow's nest among the clouds, at the head of the valley above Delphi. It is noted for its hand-woven carpets and its handsome women. I haven't seen the carpets, but I'll take oath as to the women. A group of them drawing water at the

fountain in the square yonder would serve as caryatids
for a temple of Artemis. Unfortunately the men are hand-
somer still; the standard is so high that, after a struggle,
I have abandoned the idea of marrying and settling down
here, though I am sure I should have a career in carpets.

DESPHINA, *May* 27

This afternoon I crossed the valley from Arachova, and
climbed up to a village which seemed to invite me to adventure. Nor was adventure lacking. I was met outside
the town by three old men, who shook hands with me
solemnly and gave me a grave welcome. They abandoned
their errand, whatever it was, and turned back to do the
honors of the village for me. The place was in festival,
owing to the marriage of the demarch's daughter; the
boys, dressed in their Sunday best, were dancing under a
great plane-tree in the public square, at the side of an
old church, while the women and girls looked on in dazzling groups. As soon as they heard that a stranger had
come, dropped from Mars or the moon, all other business
was suspended, and I found myself the centre of attraction for the rest of the afternoon. I was never so fêted
and toasted and done grace to since I came home from
Crusade with Barbarossa. The demarch (mayor), the
bridegroom, the bride, the priest, the town-clerk, the inn-
keeper, and other persons whose callings and dignities I
could but dimly guess, plied me with wine, sweetmeats,
and questions, took me from house to house for varying
hospitalities, and finally insisted on my staying all night,
with a promise that I should be conducted back to Delphi
the next day by a delegation of chosen youths. This
sounds like exaggeration, no doubt, but I assure you it is

all true. It has been really a touching experience, and has taught me something about the *gentilézza* of the human heart when it is still innocent and primitive. Tonight there is to be more dancing, by torchlight, and some mysterious solemnities which my very meagre stock of Greek doesn't enable me to understand, in spite of elaborate explanations. I wish you were here to kiss the bride, and to lead the woman's dance — the Χόρος γυναἰχων — which is to be danced, while I foot it with the lads.

W—

ATHENS, *May* 28 (1902)

Here I am in Athens again, laid up a few days for repairs. Coming down Parnassus I slipped and strained my hip-joint, and two days of hard walking and riding have irritated it so that it seems wise to give it a complete rest for a little while. It is nothing to worry about, and will be all right in a week. My trip to Delphi was a great experience — quite enough in itself to repay a journey across wider seas than I have crossed. I have drunk of Castaly and slept on Parnassus, so that henceforth inspiration is mine by right.

Better than Castaly were the four beautiful letters which I found awaiting me here. The glimpses you give of the American spring have made me homesick. If there were a chance to recapture it I should be sorely tempted to leave these alien splendors and fly to see those mysteriously budding trees which are making love to you over there six thousand miles away. The aspect of sap-filled branches which you describe I have never noticed; but the budding has all been done by my orders, just as I thought you would like it.

[116]

This morning I read the story of the Shunem woman
and the man of God. I had forgotten how touching it
was. *Brand* I can remember only very vaguely. It
seemed to me doctrinaire — as you say — and at the same
time misty and undigested — a poor combination of qualities. Fiske is altogether wrong in saying that the Greeks
had no conception of the after life save as a shadowy and
joyless existence. This is indeed true of Homer and the
early poets; but the Orphic poets, the teachers of the
Dionysiac cult and the hierophants of Demeter at Eleusis
seem to have taught something far different — a doctrine
of mystic regeneration, to be achieved however not
through denial of this life but by a complete entering
into it.

ATHENS, *May* 29 (1902)

The letters which fell to me this morning were a god-
send, for confinement to the house and the prince of the
powers of the air had made me very blue. They came
bringing warm life and hope, breathing such tenderness
and courage as I think few men have ever had to fall
back upon at need. Sometimes I cannot bear to have
you make so much of me, knowing how ordinary are the
levels on which most of my life is led, how utterly un-
heroic I am in all the relations of life. But this morning a
better thought came to me. I perceived that it is impossible for one spirit to glorify another unduly, in descrying
and asservating its nobility, which now we see as in a
glass darkly, but then face to face. 'Who that has ever
heard a strain of music,' said Thoreau, 'will speak of
exaggeration any more ever after?' If you have caught
through me a strain of the eternal music, it is well. I

had meant to scold you for idealizing me, and this is what it has come to.

My sore hip is better today, and will be all right in a little while. It is deuced irksome to be cooped up, though, while it is mending. When I think of your year of it, I stand in my shoes and wonder.

You must not think, by the way, that the anniversary of that most sacred night and day at Lakeside went by me unremembered. I could not write about it, that was all. Instead, I watched the hours of it away, with many thoughts.

ATHENS, *May* 30 (1902)

I sent you today three little water-color sketches, confiding them to the mail with much trepidation, for although they are very crude and botchy I want you to see them, and the Greek mails are a by-word for unreliability. If they go through all right I shall be emboldened to send more. The colors here are a passion and a despair—to try to catch even a suggestion of them with a ten-franc box of paints is a height of naïveté to which even I rise with difficulty. Shall a cake of ultramarine ensnare the myriad-minded sea, or a tube of chrome-yellow mock the insufferable sun? I guess nit.

Today I have been reading, or rather digging out with pick and hammer, the *Prometheus Bound*. Doubtless it is unwise to judge it until I have mastered the text sufficiently to read it currently; but my first impression is one of disappointment. There is a certain dryness — *sécheresse* — about it, in conception. The language (as I dimly perceive it through a maze of difficulties) is grand beyond conception, however, and the choruses will keep me awake

nights when I have got once fully into their musical se-
crets. They picked out with unerring judgment the least
interesting of Ben Jonson's plays [1] for the University
jamboree. Still, I should like to see it.

ATHENS, *June* 1 (1902)

Is Robinson's book out yet? I am anxious to see it,
and still more anxious to know what you think of it. I
gather from your late silence about the textbook that
Cooley has not been ravished by its charms out of his
official self-possession.

My lame leg is so far restored that I expect to leave
tomorrow or next day for the Peloponnesus. I have been
waiting for Gates, who wrote that he was coming; but
he has failed to appear, and I shall trudge off *mutterseelenallein*. I should have preferred to have a companion,
to help make light of the discomforts, which sometimes
require a very sturdy sense of humor to reduce to their
proper level of unimportance. But there is a gain, too,
in being alone. It is so hot in the middle of the day that I
shall have to travel in the early morning and late afternoon and night. The mornings and nights are delicious
— still, still as the inmost heart of love, colored (the mornings) like the centre of an opal, and fragrant with all
mysterious sweetness. When I came down from Delphi, I
started at half-past three, with the moon still two hours
high, and dropped down the ridges into the happy valley
of Itea (of which I sent you a feeble sketch in water-
color), as the light was making up over the sacred mountains behind me. It was a morning to remember for a
hundred lives. You were with me, as always when the

[1] *The Case is Altered.*

wonders of life most declare themselves. I seemed often to be walking, not through those mountain paths, but through the heights and morning splendors of your divine heart.

W—

June 2 (1902)

I have been wrestling all day again with the mighty lines of the *Agamemnon*. It is exceedingly difficult reading for me, with my very imperfect linguistic equipment, but I can't rest until I have mastered it. However I managed to live these thirty-odd years upon the same planet with it and remain a stranger to its terrible grandeurs, is more than I can understand. I told you I was much struck with the 'unclassical' quality of the *Oedipus at Colonus*. The *Agamemnon*, both in conception and execution, is romantic *à outrance*. I wonder how Messrs. Pope, Boileau and Co. ever succeeded in foisting into the canons of art that absurd category of classicism, anyhow? But *basta!* This is a letter to you, and not a history of literature. I wish each day that you were going along with me in this madly exciting exploration of the Greek drama. But I know well that as you are situated at present it is out of the question. Some day, however, you must do it, by which happy time I shall, I hope, be able to act as mystagogue.

Your perturbation over the misspelled word I was not able to enter into with intelligent sympathy, because of the inability to decide which one you referred to. One and all they give piquancy to your pages, me dear, so let not your heart be troubled. If I ever objected to them it was in some unreclaimed pedagogical mood. Now that I am a free soul, I cherish even the least of them; and some of them have an ineffable unworldly grace.

I can't get a boat to Gytheion (the port of Sparta) until Saturday, so that my dash into the Peloponnesus is delayed until then. Tomorrow I am going to Laurion, and thence on foot along the coast to Cape Sunion, where there is a fine ruin of a temple to Poseidon, set high on the promontory for the Athenian sailors to see on their homeward way. Byron wrote things about it, but that's not the temple's fault.

W—

June 3 (1902)

Several more letters came today, each one a poem of life. You quarrel with me for not answering your letters, but to answer these would be like 'talking back' to sunlight and brook water.

I have wreaked myself on the choruses of *Agamemnon* today until I haven't a mouthful of music left anywhere in body or soul, except enough to say good night with. I have an invitation by today's mail from a college friend to spend the summer with him in Paris. He has been there seven years, studying Greek, and has a nice apartment in the Latin Quarter. Perhaps I may go there later, when I have seen what I want to see, and am looking for a quiet place to work. The heat, however, gives me pause. The Lovetts are summering on the Seine, below Paris, and Ferd and his sister will probably drift along that way in July. There is something in it.

W—

Dionyso, *June* 4 (1902)

I have made a pious pilgrimage to the earliest home of the Greek drama, the old Attic deme of Icaria. It was in this valley on the north slope of Mount Pentelicon, that the rustic worship of Dionysus first flowered out into the drama, under the hand of Thespis. They have preserved the name of the god in the village, before the inn-door of which I am sitting to write to the only person I know who understands what a gift it was that Dionysus and Thespis, the god and the god's minstrel together, gave to mankind. It is a deserted country now, for the blessed water, after which all this land pants and prays, has failed it. All day I have not seen a brook of living water, not even a spring or a well. Still it manages somehow to keep green and joyous; the trees must manage to find out water somewhere in the depths of the hills. I have a long road before me, with small prospect of a bed even then, so goodbye till tomorrow.

W—

ICARIA, *June* 5 (1902)

I feel like taking back what I said in dispraise of this wonderful valley on the score of its water-supply, for coming back this way today I have found a fountain, with world-old mammoth plane-trees keeping guard about it, and with a gushing stream of water clear and cold. Until you have ridden for a day in a southern sun, without a hint of water on a hundred marble hills, you don't know what that elemental liquid stands for in human and sub-human life. Some pious ancient who knew it well has carved a word of praise to the god (I daresay) on the fountain stone, since nearly obliterated by generations of hands rested here while the owners stooped to drink. I have been lying all afternoon in the grass, listening to the gush of the water, the rising and falling of the wind's voice in the trees, and watching the shadows creep around the mountains. The old sanctuary of Dionysus, near by, was excavated a few years ago by the American School; but in the little time which has elapsed since they left it to the silence of its primeval valley, nature has taken it once more into her busy mysterious hands, and almost covered it again with trees and flowering shrubs, so that I came upon it quite suddenly, and thought for a moment that I had made a great discovery. You mustn't mind the dirt on this paper; the most of it is good honest goat's cheese and black bread, and the rest is Attic dust.

W—

SPARTA, *June* 8 (1902)

I have had a long and hard ride today from the coast, very hot during the high hours of the sun, but I will write a word to let you know where I am at least. Sparta proves to be rather a dull little town, and I doubt if it was ever much more, even in 'classic' days; but the valley is exceedingly beautiful, rich with orange, olive, and fig, and mad just now along the streams with oleanders and a kind of blue daisy-like flower which I never saw before, while the maize fields are washed with great sweeping tracts of poppy. You can actually hear the colors clashing and melting together, in the prodigious brilliance. They reminded me of what you said of the Valkyrie ride — only in terms of utter sunlight instead of moonlight. Apollo is by good right the first of the Hellene gods; all this land is a temple of light builded to him.

I passed an awful night at Gytheion, the port where I disembarked; and I fear it is a sad presage for the future. This is to be taken in a purely physical sense; I mean the bed was awful, the floor worse, and sleeping out impossible because of the mosquitoes. The glories of the day had erased these memories, but as it draws on to twelve they recur with force, as the conditions appear to be repeated. Tomorrow I go through the great Langhada Pass, across Mount Taÿgetos, which dominates the whole Peloponnesus with its snowy dome. An hour or two of sleep would be a good thing to have with me.

THE LANGHADA, *June* 9 (1902)

This morning we (I and the mule-boy, to wit) left Sparta at four, in the bright starlight; the day broke as we rode through the orange groves and vineyards, where for an hour before the tinkle of my mule-bells had been the only sound. It is now afternoon, and we have reached the top of the pass. The plain of Messenia lies several thousand feet below, a tapestry of dyes such as Fez nor Samarcand ever knew. It might be a robe that Aphrodite had dropped from her as she flew to her chosen island of Cythera out yonder in the inexpressible sea. The trail up here has been exceedingly beautiful, walls of fern and ivy hundreds of feet high washed with rich green glooms and played through by showering light, century-old plane-trees and pines, innumerable icy springs and waterfalls chiming together. One of these springs I shall never forget. We had been crossing some barren ridges and rocky fields which even the goats had given up for lost, and where the sun smote down intolerably. Suddenly we dipped into a hollow filled with patriarchal trees and carpeted with flowers and grass. I left my mule and climbed up the hollow to find the spring which I knew must be the nourishing spirit of all this blessed green life. I found it soon, but so small and so miraculously clear that I stepped into the water before I saw that there was water there. It lay at the foot of a vine covered rock, in a little amphitheatre open to the sky, so withdrawn and virginal, so happy in its thoughts and so unconscious, yet the creator and supporter and comforter of its green world, causing trees to grow wherein all the fowls of the air might be gathered together. Thus it is. Out of sweetness doth He bring forth strength. Out of the girl the heroic manchild, savior of the host and breaker of cities.

W—

ITHOME, MESSENIA
June 10 (1902)

These words come to you from the top of a bare mountain where they used to make human sacrifice to Zeus Ithomas, in the days before the father of gods and men had taken to a tamer and more refined diet. These earlier habits of his were never referred to in the polite circles of Olympus, but were well known, as were other particulars of the Thunderer's shady past. Now there is not even a fragment of the savage altar left, but where it stood there is a ruined chapel of the prince of peace. I pushed open the crumbling door of the courtyard, and found an old man living there as a hermit, the oldest man he seemed who ever wore grey hairs. He was glad to see me, offered me water and bread (the only hospitalities he had to offer) and talked eagerly as he showed me over the ruinous place and pointed out the towns and mountains of the tremendous landscape below. He said he had been there thirty-three years, absolutely alone except for a stray traveller at rare intervals. He had so much dignity that I did not dare offer

him money, though he must have to buy his food, since
the rocky summit of his mountain affords no chance for
things to grow. I am afraid that, in my shamefacedness, I
hid the money I left so effectually that he will never find it.
He spoke a far better Greek than the peasants, and looked
as if he had had a past. As he shook hands in farewell at
the gate, he touched me to the heart by saying simply,
in words which I shall cherish to the end, 'εἰσι καλὸς
ἄνθρωπος' — 'Thou art a good man.' Alas, alas, how far
from that; yet if to feel brotherhood with such as he be
a part of goodness, that I can claim without flinching.
Dear woman-heart, I yearn over you today, and over myself, and over all these souls who suffer with us this destiny
of life. What are we? What do we here? Alas, alas!

W—

ANDRITZENA, *June* 12 (1902)

This is a little mountain town on the borders of Arcadia,
hung like a bird's nest here whither I have been climbing
for two days, up and on the road by starlight, with a good
piece of the day's journey done before the sun comes
scattering abroad his terrible glories. I am glad, all things
considered, that the season is as far gone into the mid-
passion of the summer as it is, for it seems to me that these
suns are needed to reveal the central secret of that art and
religion which once was here, and which by virtue of its
truth and beauty is forever here.

This morning I crossed some wild pastures and barren
gorges, then climbed for a long time through oak-woods,
to a temple of Apollo, set on the forehead of a vast slope,
looking over a mighty concourse of mountains, so far from
everywhere that for many centuries (until the end of the

18th, I believe) it remained unknown except to the shepherds who drove their flocks into these upper reaches for summer pasture. It is a beautiful piece of building, and almost perfect so far as the columns are concerned. I tried to get a sketch of it for you, but made nothing of it.

I have seen nothing except Delphi so eloquent as this temple and the wilderness where it is set. Tomorrow I go on toward Olympia, by a road which I hear is more than ordinarily difficult — a fact which worries me a little, as my beast shows signs of lameness. I shall humor him by walking most of the way. I have given up sleeping now altogether, but the mountain air is so bracing that I do not feel the need of it. Knowing my hypnogluttonous disposition you will find it hard to believe that I am quite contented with an hour in the middle of the day, and devote the night to wandering and contemplation. I made two trials of the beds, and found them first-class horrors. If I could get accustomed to the excitement of night out of doors I could sleep very nicely here in the higher country in my sleeping-bag, but at present there is far too much doing between midnight and dawn. When man is at rest over the face of the earth, it is then that the earth-spirit seems most passionately awake and intent upon its own business.

OLYMPIA, *June* 14 (1902)

The past two days I have spent riding through lonely valleys of Arcadia and Elis, hardly seeing a human being. Here and there a shepherd, or a silent wonder-stricken child watching his goats and amazed at the portent of a stranger in outlandish clothes. It was in these lonesome valleys that the god Pan first appeared to men, and after seeing them one understands better the listening, the brooding, the lonesome music, the sudden terror ('Panic terror'), the animal yet mystic mirth, and all the other attributes of that wonderful god that the Arcadian peasants dreamed out for themselves.

My beast did not give out, as I feared, but my boy did, so he has ridden while I walked. I had to leave him here at Olympia — not because of his fatigue, which he got over soon, but because he didn't know the road any further. He has gone back to his mountain hut in Messenia, and I am left quite desolate, for I had got fond of the silent little beggar. I am drooping tired and ripe for sleep.

W.

MEGASPAELION, *June* 16 (1902)

I wrote last from Olympia, one of the three or four great strongholds of Greek paganism, and with its ruined temples, altars, palaestras, stadiums, and votive statues still very eloquent of the older Greece. Two days of travel through the mountains and valleys of Arcadia have brought me to a very different place indeed, to the greatest stronghold of mediaeval and Christian Greece, if you can imagine such an anomaly. This is one of the most curious and astounding places it has ever been my lot to behold. It is a monastery, once vast and still very large (supporting over a hundred monks), built in a cave at the top of a tremendous cliff of sheer stone. As I approached it last evening from below it seemed incredible that it should cling any longer to the face of the precipice. At the gate of the courtyard I was received by a monk whose business it is to bestow the hospitality of the monastery on wayfaring strangers, and was ushered by him into a large guest-room where ten or fifteen other persons had already found asylum — Greek farmers, shepherds, and village folk who had got benighted between Kalavryta and Aigion, and had turned in here for the night. We were served a primitive supper — a single great dish of boiled meat and cucumbers, with cheese, bread, and resined wine, young acolytes with beautiful masses of uncut hair and dressed in flowing black robes, serving us. When it was discovered that I was an American, the pent-up curiosity of the table could no longer be restrained, even by the stringent rules of politeness which obtain; a flood of questions was poured in upon me about friends and relatives who had gone to America to seek their fortunes — to be 'fruit-merchants' and 'musicians,' it was proudly explained. I had to confess to a lack of personal acquaintance with one and all of the persons named, a fact which puzzled and disconcerted some of them visibly. The gift of a cigar (a fabulous luxury here) to the chief spokesman of the party, reinstated me socially. Two girls thereupon left the room, and returned soon with some leaves of lettuce and some green peas which they had evidently got leave to pluck in the monastery garden. These they gave to me, smiling and blushing. After a moment of embarrassed ignorance as to the purport of the gift, I made out that the vegetables were to be eaten, in a state of nature, and that they were regarded as a toothsome dainty. Accordingly I divided and ate. I assure you that lettuce leaves and raw green peas, without any other salt than that of human kindness, are a dish for a king. We spent the evening roaming about the gardens, courtyards, and chapels of the place, looking out through century-old ilex-trees to the darkening country spread out a thousand feet below. We slept all in one big room, the men on one side and the women on the other — on the floor of course; and at dawn we all went together to the gloomy little Byzantine chapel and heard mass. No breakfast was offered us except a tiny cup of black coffee, on the strength of which I should have had as much as I wanted to do to make my way to the next town where food is procurable, were it not that like the provident soul I am, I have a cake of chocolate in my *rucksack* and can laugh at fate.

W.

CORINTH, *June* 18 (1902)

It is an intensely hot day, all things on land and sea being merely varieties and shapes of flame, wonderful to look upon but not wholly good to be amongst. I shall be back in Athens in another couple of days.

I think I shall leave Greece shortly for Italy, and thence north into the Tyrol or the French Alps. It is getting too hot here for comfort, and I have seen much of what I came to see, besides much else that I did not dream of, and these things are always the best. I think my sojourn here has not been in vain; but that is for the gods to determine.

W.

78 RUE D'ASSAS, PARIS, *July* 13 (1902)

I have not written since I left Greece, three weeks ago, and if it were not that you will be anxious, I should not write now, for I have a tale to tell only of wasted — worse than wasted days, of that failure of will and courage which is the ultimate affliction, of defeat after defeat by the dark powers of unrighteousness and division of soul.

Often I have been tempted to keep all this from you, seeing that from others you have much of this to bear, and from me have a right to look for something better. But though I can wrong you, it seems, I cannot deceive you by passing over, even in anguished and expiating silence, a vital passage of my life.

When I left Greece, whether it was by reaction from the vivid excitement and physical strain I had been under in the Peloponnesus journey, or whether from some more mysterious cause, I do not know, but I went down at once into such a valley and shadow of despair as I have never, I think, had to pass through before. Feeling round through my darkened kingdoms I could find no hopeful thing, no joy, no sovereignty. This is a rather large way of saying that I was profoundly discouraged at not having recovered my tone of body and mind, that I felt spiritually deserted, God-forgotten, without power or hope or purpose, as if some Finger had been laid upon me saying 'Thus far and no farther'; and again 'Why, is it not simple? We have finished with thee!' and 'Behold, these many things were ill done, and these few well enough. This is the Book. Why dost thou tarry?'

I think I went through Italy, and stood in many a holy and well-beloved place. I know that at Rome I laid two roses on Keats's grave — and an ivy-leaf on the slab that covers Shelley's ashes. But none of these things availed. After a time came rebellion, and reckless grasping after life or what bore the semblance and wore the red flower of life, careless whether — nay, even glad if its heart were poisoned. I took — O sweet and noble soul, this will pain you cruelly, but I must tell it — I took the ring from my finger, for it burnt my flesh with its impossible summons and its intolerable reproach. The worst of it is that I did this at the moment rather callously, with a kind of dull satisfaction at the ease with which a man might slip his soul off his finger and put it in his pocket, when it got to be a bit too much of a bother.

After that I tried to find the mountains, but there was nothing there but some piles of rock and dirt on which hotels were built and over which people were senselessly swarming, like ants without the ant's dignity of an end in view.

Then I came to Paris, simply because it was a place to come to. Since I have been here I have been sunk in unfathomable sloth, a torpor more than narcotic. I sit in the green Luxembourg Gardens or in front of the pleasant cafés, listening to the music and watching the queer delightful people as from an interstellar distance; and I would as soon lift the earth over the moon as lift my hand from the chair to the table. The struggle of the past three weeks seems faint and far away, like everything else. All is silvery-soft and muffled — a haze of colors that would be bright and sounds that would be gay if they were not so filmy fine, so filmy fine, a breath would scatter them.

In the sifting sunlight under the grand old trees I ponder your comment on the parable. You speak for the one who welcomes back, and how well! But what of him who is welcomed? What of the robe and ring? How think you he wears them, and how do the festal wines and the meats set out in gladness taste to him? Doubtless he neither truly sees nor feels nor tastes; all is silvery-soft and muffled, a maze of filmy color and sound, through which beat the wings of healing. But there will come a time when in clear day he will stand up healed, and with the strength thus given must somehow or other work out his expiation and establish his soul out of these perils. Then the implacable coils and swift-playing inescapable fang of the Serpent — for whom I wait, but childishly, quiet, soothed, almost amused, by the flutter and flash and rumor of the world about me. There is my hand widowed of its circle of light wherein the sworded angel stood and sang, touching the East and the West with burning plumage of his wing, but just now it does not seem so very grievous. What can be very grievous in a world so impalpable, so silvery-soft, so ghostly glad, so dreamily grief-smitten! I think after a while I will raise my hand and break and brush it all away.

I have had no letters from you since I left Greece. Today or tomorrow they will come, perhaps. How strange!

78 RUE D'ASSAS, PARIS, *July* 16 (1902)

I am afraid that my last letter may have given you, by its vagueness, unnecessary anxiety about my physical welfare. I have not been and am not ill, in any ordinary sense of the word. Nor am I any longer a prey to the harpies of the spirit which pursued me for so long. Indeed, a wonderful peace has settled round me; and though it is still grey, I know that the light is journeying toward me, and I know that soon I shall be able to take up my life again.

Your letters which reached me from London three days ago, have been an unspeakable help to me, and solace, though every word has pierced me through with grief, especially the light and merry words. They broke up the strange torpor into which I had fallen, and are gradually

preparing me to go down into the terrible waters of puri-
fication. Something tells me that on the other side of the
stream a new life awaits me, a life of stronger faith, of
larger acquiescence in the laws of life and death. I begin
to see that the trouble with me always has been that I
was one of little faith. All along my life I see how a too
quick despair has hurled me out of the path to which I
had to struggle back with punishment and loss. It is this
too which has made my human history incoherent, has
made me take and cast away, claim hearts and deny them,
handle the most precious gifts of time like a fool and a
spendthrift. By God's help, it shall be so no more.

I realize now that, though I did not know it at the time,
I lived at a fierce pace while in Greece. Besides the
excitement and fatigue of travel, I read ten plays (the
equivalent of two college courses), got up enough modern
Greek to travel with, gutted the libraries of the American
and the British school for what they had consonant to
my purpose, and behaved generally like a man who was
to be hanged o' Friday. When I came to Italy, eager to
begin the work for which this had been a preparation,
and called on my soul to arise and spread its wings, it
withered and sank in sick refusal. I was at first astonished,
then terror-stricken, and from that went astray down all
the winds that blow for the confusion of impatient, faithless men. Even you I lost in the tempest of darkness and
then I was lost indeed.

> *Mi ritrovai per una selva oscura,*
> *Che la diritta via era smarrita.*

The right way — how easy to lose, how hard to find, how
hard to keep when found! But I will say no more of all

this. As between me and you there is no need to say so much. I may not write very often for a while; in this healing silence where I sit, words are not best. But know that now it is well with me. The news of your steady recovery, and the signal stages thereof, comes to me just now with a special sweetness.

W—

I am staying with a college friend, Joe Stickney,[1] who has been here at the Sorbonne seven years, studying Greek. We are going to read Euripides together, and then he promises to show me Pindar. He has a very nice apartment back of the Luxembourg Gardens, with all the comforts of life as it is lived in Paris. It is a good place to rest.

78 RUE D'ASSAS, PARIS
(Postmarked July 23, 1902)

A batch of letters reached me from Athens today; evidently they arrived very shortly after I sailed, and as I had notified my London banker a week before sailing, of my change of address, it was only by the merest chance that I sent word to Athens to have mail forwarded. A happy chance, for I could not have afforded the loss of these troubled and troubling pages. They were written in early June. I know of nothing in my own history which could have affected your mood disastrously. During those days I was at Delphi, and you know from my letters written there that these were among the greatest days which have ever been handed down out of Heaven to me. To be sure, my accident worried me a little, and I had after

[1] Joseph Trumbull Stickney.

coming back a day or two of illness — too light to mention — due doubtless merely to bad food or water, or an overdose of sun. But however that may be, the fact remains that you were sad and deeply troubled, and felt no support from me. I should have known, and helped somehow or other. For some reason the knowledge of this difficult time through which you passed in loneliness touches me more as being wholly past than if I had known of it without delay. I suppose it is because the past is so majestically isolated and fixed apart from any help, and even from any of the busy pretenses of help with which we dissemble our helplessness. It wears something of the lonely pride which is the feature of all others that breaks our spirit as we look on the face of the dead. Of course you must write me out of the heart of the hour, whether it be dark or bright. That I thought we had agreed upon. You must not be afraid of depressing me, and above all you must not think of my 'disapproval.' I never disapprove of you, as you well know; I always follow the movements of your nature with the conviction that whatever else in the world be illusory or negligible, this at least is very truth and not to be passed by.

I was glad to get the clippings about Cuba, and Senator Hoar's speech. Poor blundering, grudging, generous land! To free Cuba with one hand, and with the other quietly remove all possible chance for her to live decently — or indeed to live at all. Of course I know that the one hand is that of the whole people, and the other that of a commercial interest, and I don't mean to belittle the magnanimous deed; but why, O why, did it have to be smutched and spoiled? As for the recent disclosures in the Philippines (which were doubtless the real occasion of Hoar's speech) they are too sickening to talk or think about. Shall we ever be able to hold up our heads again? The little flag you sent me on the Fourth of July seemed striped and stained with that innocent blood. I wonder how we shall wash it out, and let our flag take the air again like a thing of joy; till then it cannot gladden me nor any other eyes over the whole earth.

Remember that I am being well taken care of as to the eating and sleeping man, and that as soon as I recover, and feel able to take up my work, I shall be saved; I shan't then have time to bother about myself. But it is weary waiting!

WILL

78 RUE D'ASSAS
July 24 (1902)

When I woke this morning, the sky had cleared, both without and within. I felt the breath of health and joy in my lungs; life seemed once more the possible and excellent thing it is when unfevered either by over-striving or by the sickness of weariness which follows over-strife. (I am not preaching the 'golden mean'; I am not preaching anything; we must be as we are.) The heavens of poetry, which have been draped so long, were thrown open, and there were presences plain in the place. The Prometheus,[1] which has heretofore refused to take shape, had started up overnight into all sorts of surprising growths, and though it hangs vague in a vague sky, is surely there. To celebrate the day I went to a fascinating little paint-shop in the Rue du Dragon (Street of the Dragon! — The names of the streets here are a never-ending delight: 'Street of the Old Dove-House,' 'Street of the Dry Tree,'

[1] *The Fire-Bringer.*

'Rue Madame,' 'Rue des Quatre Vents') and bought an oil sketching kit, one which enables me to carry wet sketches without bother. Then I took one of the funny little Seine steamers, and went down to Saint Cloud through the green summer country, along with a boat-load of these friendliest, merriest and most human French people. I made a sketch for you, of Saint Cloud seen from the bank, below Sèvres. It is really very pretty. I wish I had some way to send it to you. How I wish you were here, to enjoy with me this happy country, which has taken hold of me in quite a new way this time. Life is, and is made, supremely possible here. When one is open to it — as I have been today — the *pleasantness* of it is intoxicating. We can afford to spend one life here, in spite of the fact that, as you say, Parisian French is a tongue which 'does not carry far.'

W.

78 RUE D'ASSAS, PARIS
July 30 (1902)

Here are several letters of yours which, in their revelation of the life of practical heroism you are leading, make me again ashamed of making a fuss about ghosts and shadows. Besides, I feel my health coming back, the fever going out of my veins, and with it the phantoms of perplexity and despair out of my brain. In a few days I shall be myself again, and no longer feel it necessary to make a great whining about the very simple, universal, and inescapable fact that the problem of living well is not an easy one, and that the mysteries and dangers of the spiritual existence are many, as are its blessed asylums and sweet assurances.

The weather here is delightful, very bright, and cool as autumn almost. In a week or two more I shall make for the mountains, or perhaps join Ferd in Siena. I should unhesitatingly do the latter, but fear that the heat which he reports there will keep me from working. If I don't go, I shall ask him to stop in the Tyrol for a while with me as he goes through to Vienna to join his sister.

Can't you possibly contrive to get hold of a good translation of the *Bacchantes* of Euripides? It is my latest discovery and rapturously good. I myself know of no translation which is not worse than a caricature, but there must be such. Otherwise I shall have to make you one myself, for you must read it.

You must not interpret the words about 'returning health,' 'fever,' etc., in any physical or otherwise alarming sense. I have been rather fagged out, but otherwise master of the machine, and I am getting rested fast, so that in a week or two I shall be preening and prating with the best duck in the pond.

W.

78 RUE D'ASSAS, PARIS
Aug. 1 (1902)

I was wakened this morning by the maid putting a bundle of letters on my pillow. These letters were written during the days of my silence and defection, and it put a veil over the sunny morning for me to see the vague suffering emerge from the lines not meant to betray it. Well, enough of that. Just now I cannot bear to go back over that path, nor count the stations of it. I want only to remember that the sky is a keen blue, that the babies and the gorgeous-capped beribboned *bonnes* in the Garden are having the time of their lives, while the birds discuss last night's rain pro and con — the pro's having by long odds the best of it. This old garden and the human beings who haunt it are a never-ending delight. In my present mood it is a piece of pure good fortune to find not one person or a group of persons, but a whole city, a whole nation, which does not have to be taken seriously; and for the whole nation to concentrate and poetize itself into a queer old garden at your door, full of happy, careless human life, is more than I had a right to ask. I sit for hours under the blossomy bushes and beside the dreamy old fountains adorned with shabby moss-covered eighteenth century gods, and watch these gay groups of people who are so miraculously untroubled by any suspicion of a doctrine that life was not meant to be enjoyed, who wear the awful gift of being like a ribbon or a flower, and if they like your *beaux yeux*, will toss you their youth like a bon-bon. It's a strange world, Harriet, a strange world.

W—

Aug. 3 (1902)

The heavens have spoken tonight, after long silence, as I walked by the Seine in a sunset splendid after rain. I feel that I can soon put on the ring again, with your word as my warrant, though it will have to be with a more human and less ethical conception of its meaning than before. I am not going to deny my nature, nor cramp it, for it and the natures of the sisters and brothers whose lives I see and share, is all that I know of God. I have a whim about putting it on, which is to go to the mountains and ask a mountain child to do this service for me, some brown-legged, merry-eyed, unspoiled little thing, worthy to be your vicar herein. It sounds sentimental, and I wouldn't tell another human being under the sun but you whom it befits to know and who would not blame or question a far more extravagant whim than this, if, as this, it were born of an instinct such as drives beasts in sickness to eat of certain herbs of grace.

W—

PARIS, *Aug.* 4 (1902)

I am still loafing here with Stickney, reading Plato and Euripides with him, and chasing down an occasional Promethean hint in the *Bibliothèque Nationale*. My impatience is at times great, but I am not going to let impatience defeat me this time, especially as I feel that the light half-conscious touching and touching of the subject which this leisure permits me, is moulding it into a good shape. It is so manifold in its implications, embraces so much unorganized and perhaps unorganizable matter of thought and feeling, that it keeps holding me off and luring me on in a most tantalizing manner. Sometimes it dissolves and disappears altogether, and then again, as yesterday in a windy rainy sunset over the Seine, looms up all but perfect in the clouds, mysteriously turning upon itself and unfolding new patterns — bothersomely many.

W—

PARIS, *Aug.* 8 (1902)

I am going to the Dolomites in the South Austrian Tyrol. I feel well and strong again, renewed in body and mind. The great lassitude which weighed me down for a while, and under which the mere thought of exertion,

especially mental exertion, was sickening to me, has
entirely passed away. Without having been really ill, I
am blessed with an exquisite lightness and clarity of
bodily sensation which I remember from periods of convalescence long ago in childhood. It is such an impalpable
joy that I am half-afraid to mention it for fear of scaring
it away, but the mountains will establish it. I shall not
be in any great hurry to get to work; it is this wretched
haste which spoils all. I have written to Ferd to meet me
in the Dolomites for a week's or a fortnight's tramp, and
I earnestly hope he can. I will show him among other
notable things the Valley of Judgment; it lies in the heart
of the business, up by San Martino di Castrozza, and a
terrific old gully it is.

PARIS, *Aug.* 10 (1902)

I leave tonight for Innsbruck, and from there shall
prospect on foot until I find a promising place. I have in
my mind's eye an eagle's nest called St. Vigil, seen once
and remembered forever. Perhaps that is the place.
You may not hear from me for some time.

ST. VIGIL, TYROL
Aug. 16 (1902)

This place is all that I hoped to find it — a primitive
but well-to-do Tyrolese village, with a respectable hos-
telry, near the head of a grand valley, with incredible
peaks climbing heaven on three sides. It is at present
very cold, too cold to sit in one's room with comfort, but
that is said to be a passing phase, as it was at Cape Henry,
absit omen. The inn, a great rambling affair which has
grown by fits and starts to accommodate foot-travellers
between Cortina and San Lorenzo, is conducted in a very

mysterious fashion. The proprietor is invisible and apparently non-existent. The only person in authority is an old waitress, who seems to be in league with the guests to 'do' the said nonexistent proprietor. Whatever you order comes, and no account taken. People come and go, eat and drink as only Germans can, yet nobody pays nor does the idea of cash anywhere taint the mountain air. We toil not neither do we spin. The first day of my stay, before I had realized into what a four-dimensional economy I had stepped, after giving an order I mentioned the number of my room. The old waitress looked at me in vague astonishment, and then said, as with a dawning perception of my friendly attempt to make conversation, '*Ya, ya, ein schönes Zimmer; siecht nach Süden. I' wünsch die Herrschaft glückliche Stunden darin!*'

Yesterday a crowd of soldiers bivouacked in the village, and gutted the inn of all its meat and beer, but I never saw a coin passed. These hyperborean manners are highly to my taste, and they moreover fit the present state of my purse as by a foreordained harmony. I think I will live and die here. I made a sketch today of some peaks at the head of the valley; I take it to be my best effort, but perhaps that is because it is my last. I will send it for you to judge, thou rhadamanthine mind. W—

ST. VIGIL, *Aug.* 17 (1902)

It has been raining all day, but tonight cleared a bit, so that I got a royal walk up the valley, with a plunging moon and a few careering stars, the mountains twice their size in the misty light and cloud-drift. If the Lord had only seen fit not to have created the German race and language when he created St. Vigil he would have done well; or even if he could have spared us the language. There are some forty (Germans) here, and I'm afraid they'll drive me to Italy merely by force of excoriating my eardrum. O for the ripple and gush and musical fall of that delicious language! Ferd writes from Siena that he probably can't come to the mountains, because of *Lautverschieb* and lack of cash. His unpardonable hand-writing led me to read Vienna for Venice, and I made sure he would stop here on his way to Vienna, otherwise I should perhaps have braved the heat and gone to Siena, for I am really very lonesome to see the boy. The conditions are good here, however, and I suppose it will be the wise thing to put my lonesomeness in my pocket. I need the air and the exercise that this place affords, for I haven't managed yet to pull my nerves very firmly together. When I paint or write I get more excited than there is any possible occasion for, and then follow periods of lassitude when I feel like an old lady I once knew in Maine, who took boarders in summer and sewed quilts in winter until she had saved enough to buy an annuity and pay for her funeral, whereupon she went to bed and has been there ever since, her fifteen year siesta only interrupted by one summer spell of work to which she was goaded by the thought that she had failed to provide silver handles for her casket. The parallel is perfect except that I have no hankering for silver handles and am shy the annuity in every sense financial and spiritual.

ST. VIGIL, TYROL
Aug. 18, 1902

I have spent the afternoon down the valley at an old sawmill, which is run by one of the mad little rivers that tumble down from the glaciers hid somewhere back there in the clouds. If there is any more absorbing and profitable human occupation than to sit and see a five-foot saw eat through a cedar log as if it were cheese, then I have failed to find it. The weather is perfect here now, just warm enough in the daytime to say it is warm, and a delicious crisp chill at night. I have taken a room outside the hotel, in one of the houses of the village, so that I am free from the German terror, except at dinner and supper. Breakfast I take in the open, wherever I can coax or bribe the Anna to bring it to me. *Die Anna* is the marvellous old housemaid I told you of, who runs the hotel establishment and incidentally the rest of the village and township. She has only one eye, and a face that seems to have been carved on a mallet handle by a satiric savage of the stone age, but she is the salt of the earth. My heart tells me that she begins to reciprocate my affection. Indeed tonight, when I got in long after dark to supper, she met me with ill-concealed emotion, and said she had been worried for fear I had *verunglückt* myself. O love's young dream, how fond and fair!

ST. VIGIL, *Aug.* 20, 1902

This morning I awoke with this thought, that I had nothing to do with the motto of the ring, that that was wholly yours, your wish and prayer for me thus hinted at and bodied forth, that it laid me under no constraint, involved no vow of life other than the knowledge of love and high thoughts in another heart must involve, that therefore I could wear it freely, however unable I know myself, here and now, to lead the life of martial saintliness, however often I may be forced to find myself neither by God's side nor of his following.

[145]

This seems so clear to me now that I wonder why it has never struck me just this way before. I turned it over and over all the morning, and could see no flaw or subterfuge in it. This afternoon I went up to the head of the valley and climbed the highest sun-steeped peak I could reach, and there put on the ring, the sun just sinking with me and standing at noon with you. These harebells I found under a friendly rock sheltered from the wind, where I stood. There were awful witnesses around, if one had been taking a vow; but I declared and protested to them, as now to you, that I took no vow. Only thus can I wear the ring. I cannot afford to fall from the height to which such a vow must lift a man; I cannot live continually in such an air; it is as much as I can do if here and there in a good hour, with all the powers consenting, I can rise into it for a heart-beat or two. Thus it stands with me, and thus I trust and long that it may seem good to you to have it.

W—

St. Vigil, *Aug.* 21 (1902)

Another day of grand rolling storm, speaking a mighty language in the mountains, and lifting for a great golden sunset. During the height of the storm all the church bells in the valley rang like mad. This is believed to be efficacious in averting thunder and whirlwind, and so in fact it proved to be.

W—

Cortina d'Ampezzo
Aug. 31 (1902)

I have been on tramp through some out-of-the-way valleys and over some stunning passes of these mountains.

The rain has interfered with me somewhat, but the mountains were never so grand as in this crazy summer of storm and cold, and it is worth an occasional ducking to get the effects of mist and rainy light on these (old Gray's word) 'monstrous creatures of God.'

Ferd has made the great refusal. Like all the wicked he gets the righteous man's just reward along with his own individual punishment appertaining; as for the latter he loses the mountains, as for the former he will see you almost as soon as this paper does, and will smooth his feathers in the comforting shadow of the Grove.[1]

ST. VIGIL, *Sept.* 7, 1902

Back again in St. Vigil. This remote little village in its dreamy valley has got to seem much like home, and I am glad to get back, although I had some great times afoot. I have got so used to being in the wilderness that after a few days I feel cramped if there is any other human being on the horizon. I shall probably end my days as a professional tramp, preferably in Central Africa. I found one valley with a heroic poem all its own, written in the local dialect, 'Ladinisch,' a variant of Low Latin. From the verses that I made out with the help of a cultured barmaid, the poem is really good, and must be several centuries old. It has never been printed, but some wandering painter had copied a part of it on the walls of the inn dining-room, and illustrated them with enthusiasm and talent. The same village had a romantic double murder to its credit, the recital of which by mine host of the inn made an exciting evening. Another high point,

[1] Harriet's home at 2970 Groveland (renamed Ellis) Avenue, Chicago, was called the Grove by W. V. M. and some of Harriet's friends.

humanly, in my journey, was an afternoon spent drawing 'portraits' of the fifteen children of a mountain guide and inn-keeper. Their joy and wonder over the crude scrawls was a thing to see. The eldest daughter, a beauty of sixteen, had spent one miraculous week in Innsbruck, and immediately recognized me as an inhabitant of that place of dream. Fortunately I knew the names of a few streets and buildings in the tame little town, and was able to keep my reputation unsullied, being assisted by the fact that the family was 'Ladinisch,' and spoke even a worse German than mine. When my Zaubergesang was gesungen, she brought me her one great earthly treasure, a pair of earrings, parcel-gilt, bought in that same incredible Innsbruck, and to be donned at her next birthday. How absurdly, deliciously, and tearfully human human beings are!

W—

ST. VIGIL, *Sept.* 10 (1902)

Several letters came today, containing the important news of your journey to your native village and to Niagara. I have been wishing I might send you the fragrance of these mountain meadows now in the last hay-harvest, early in the morning when the sun begins to dry the hoar-frost or late in the afternoon, when the heat has penetrated to the middle of the shock. But you have something better. Are there any smells like those of the earth where one grew up? I remember certain such — even pantry and kitchen smells — that I would travel round the world to get again; yet I shall never have the courage to go back for them, as you have had.

I leave here tomorrow or next day for Riva, a town on

Lake Garda, where I shall stay a week or two before settling down in Florence for the rest of my vacation. It dwindles frightfully. St. Vigil has been a good home to me and a kind nurse; I am sorry to leave it. To be sure I haven't done much, but I never can in summer. The Muse now and then grants me a fleeting favor, just enough to make me want to call out all the mustachioed blades living and dead whom the harlotry cares more about. I sha'n't know for at least a couple of months yet whether anything is coming of the Prometheus. Nine-tenths of the time I am in despair about it, and the other few minutes think it's the greatest show on wheels. It will either be good or nothing, of that I am sure, so that there won't be that harrowing indecision between the printing-shop and the waste-basket.

Yesterday was the festival of the Birth of Mary. A procession carried the crucifix from the little church through the fields to a shrine of the Virgin. First came some small bareheaded boys; one of them carried the cross; then the men, bareheaded, with a red banner; then the women with a white banner. You cannot imagine the awfulness of that white figure of pain thus escorted through sunny fields of hay and barley, and under the shadow of pine woods, with the shrill voices of the women and the deep bass of the men answering each other in some kind of monotonous pleading chant. There is more deep, old-world piety here than I have ever seen anywhere; religion, in all its forms and practices, is as much the living centre of life as it was five centuries ago. To put comedy cheek by jowl with tragedy, in his favorite fashion, the Lord sent us today the Archduke of Austria. This exalted personage is evidently bent on a foot-tour in the

Dolomites, and to add to the joy thereof has brought with him, by count, nineteen fat functionaries in full uniform. Our inn was honored with the archducal presence. N.B. it was raining and there was no other place for him to go to except a hay shed. We have been crawling round on our hands and knees all day, except when ordered up by mine host to drink a health or hurrah. We have a triumphal arch, and shoot off a cannon whenever it can be persuaded to shoot. The buttery is open to who will come, and the village fountain gushes perennial beer.

RIVA, LAGO DI GARDA
AUSTRIA, *Sept.* 28 (1902)

Did I tell you that I had tried reading *Hamlet* on the top of the Nuvolau, to see how he stood it? He stood it to admiration. It seems that when a thing is really big, anything you bring against it for comparison only makes it look bigger, but its greatness then becomes somewhat haughty and distant, instead of being as before unassuming and confiding. We have not yet plucked out the heart of Hamlet's mystery. Doubtless we never shall, and doubtless W. S. never did; but I know a certain paragraph of brilliantly borrowed ideas in a certain textbook of English literature, that must be rewritten in a tone of less confidence.

The beauty of this place is so rich and soft after the sternness of the mountains that there is nothing to do with it except to weep or make love. Weep I will not, so make love I must; I have my eye upon a most appealingly feminine camp-stool; grace and allurement lurk in every line of it. Would I were a young and dashing garden-chair, and had not to o'erleap this interval of being!

W—

[150]

En Voyage — 1902

RIVA, LAGO DI GARDA
Sept. 30 (1902)

I have your 'venturesome' letter, urging me to return to America. It is tenderly and possibly wisely thought, for there is some truth in what you say about over-stimulation on the one side and malnutrition on the other. But the case is not nearly so bad as you picture it. We are both cursed with the gift of exaggeration, and with me it has taken the form of omitting to speak of the bread and roast-beef and throwing a lurid light upon the cates and wine, or at least of making them look balefully bright by isolation from the solid substance of life's meal. I have described the mountain climb and omitted to mention the consumption of beer and sausage in the comfortable refuge-hut at the top — as well as the ordinary human chances and adventures of travel, which, though the touch be not very deep, keep one from feeling 'disembodied' and have often a wonderful relish. In other words, there have been many days — the far greater number — of healthy stolidity and satisfaction in the things known as good by the *homme moyen sensuel.* True, I have been very, very restless, but I should have been so anywhere.

W—

HOLLAND-AMERICA LINE
T.S.S. RYNDAM
Nov. 21st, 1902

I got your letter three days ago in Vienna, and immediately started for Rotterdam, where I was fortunate enough to catch this boat. It was a case of coming home now or not at all, and I know that to remain abroad would have been a fatal mistake.

I caught a severe cold on the train, and several others in

process of embarkation in a cold rain. The result is *grippe*, with complications like those which I suffered in Genoa five years ago. I hardly realize yet that I am homeward bound, and soon to see you; but the happy knowledge will grow as the good ship makes westward.

WILL

HOLLAND-AMERICA LINE
T.S.S. RYNDAM
Nov. 30, 1902

We have had a very cold and stormy passage, and my illness, of which I wrote at starting, has taken a somewhat ugly turn. There is nothing dangerous in it and nothing to worry about, but it makes my days and nights a monotony of pain, like to that which you have been suffering so long, and perhaps are still enduring. Tomorrow or next day we shall be in, and my good sister Charlotte will have me sound again in a few days of her skillful care-taking. I shall stay in New York for a week at any rate, perhaps longer; if I get on my feet again I want to try and work a bit, for I have done almost nothing with my time abroad, as far as tangible results, and I am ashamed to come to you absolutely empty-handed. (You will gather the crumb of truth from this falsehood. Of course, it matters nothing what I bring — to us.)

A thousand greetings, W—

AMERICA

DECEMBER 11, 1902 — MARCH 18, 1907

NEW YORK, *Dec.* 11 (1902)

This is a hurried word of assurance that I am out of the clutches of the rheumatic fever, thanks to my sister's care and skill. I wish I might be sure that you are also restored; your letter contained no hint as to your health. I am beginning to enjoy New York, after a week of abysmal depression. My sister insists that I shall stay until Christmas is past, and the theatres are offering so much of interest that it seems the thing to do.

Scribner declares that the textbook will have to be simplified if it is to succeed in the high schools. *Ach! weh!* He wants me to leave this book to meet the college market and recast the text on simpler lines for the high schools. I am in communication with a reliable anarchist whom I think competent to blow Scribner and his whole shooting-match at the moon, in case nothing else avails to save me.

NEW YORK, *Dec.* 25 (1902)

Your Christmas greeting met me on waking this morning. I had read the Ode before going to bed last night, but without being able to hear it or feel it very well. After your note came I looked for it again and found it lifted up into its old place.

I take the Friday morning train and shall see you Sunday morning at latest. May you have a Merry Christmas and may we have together a Happy New Year.

[153]

MACKINAC ISLAND, *May* 17, 1903

The arbutus came unwithered, and is still as bright and spirit-feeding as she who plucked it and the wish with which it was plucked and sent. I have it before me as I work, and it tells of many woodland things, beside itself, of things in the woodlands of the Lord.

The work [1] is going well, though slowly. I am not forcing it, for I feel that upon the success of this portion of the poem (the return of Prometheus) the success of the whole will largely depend. I have just received a letter from one Frederick Palmer, of Andover, Mass., in which, among other discriminating things which he says of the *Masque*,[2] he speaks of the 'Prometheus' theme which it embodies. This pleased me much, for as you know I conceive the piece I am now working at as integral in thought with the *Masque*, and have in mind some day to round out the whole as a trilogy. This afternoon I made a little study in oils of the meadow. It did not turn out very well, but I shall try again. I think I can box the pastels so that they will travel safely; as soon as I can get hold of the proper sort of tacks I will box them and express them to you, with a prayer for their safe carriage.

Pup is very lame, and seems dejected over depleted household.

MACKINAC ISLAND
Date unknown
(Postmarked May 25, 1903)

I today packed and shall tomorrow express the three pastel studies which happened while you were with us,

[1] At this time and for some months following, W. V. M. was at work on *The Fire-Bringer*.

[2] *The Masque of Judgment.*

and one new one which was very fetching before it encountered this inexplicable world in the form of a fixatif
bottle. I 'fixed' them all, and they are fixed. Oddly
enough the dark and heavy tones suffered most. However,
the things are still fairly presentable, and they would not
have travelled safely in their first state of innocence.

The meadow sketch in oils, of which I wrote before,
turned out a very tight, stocky little picture. I tried it
first with oils in the usual manner, but it would not go; it
insisted on being and remaining pallid and meaningless.
Then one afternoon I arose in my majesty and my shirt-
sleeves, squeezed a gallon of paint onto my big palette,
grasped a palette-knife and began to trowel the paint on in
everlasting chunks and shovelled until all of a sudden —
ecco! the thing began to talk. I learned more about painting in that half-hour than in all my previous dabbling. It
is on the little canvas duplicating that of the Cape Henry
waves.

Brother has recovered his spirits. He spends his days
eating my wearing apparel and his nights in chasing
imaginary burglars back and forth over my form. He has
taken to guarding the house furiously, by day and by
night, doubtless in order that his own destruction of it and
its contents may not be interrupted from without, the interruption from within having become intermittent and
despairing. He returns thanks for the dog-cakes, as well as
for the ideal dog-food. Touching the latter, however, he
declares himself no idealist; Plato can have himself; as for
him, Brother Mike Siegfried Limerick Navagesha, he
prefers a plain business diet that can be smelled and
munched. Rather than subsist on an Idea, however beautiful, he will try to put up with his present hard-time diet

of books, clothing, pictures, sketch boxes, and furniture.

The weather has been very bad here for a week, rainy, windy, and very cold — though it hasn't yet had the face to snow. T—— beseeches me to assure you that she would write if she had anything to say and knew how to spell.

(Postmarked — Mackinac Island, July 2, 1903)

I enjoyed the Howells ghost stories immensely. I can't quite agree with you in your tender but deprecating judgment. I do not see in them any sign of age; on the contrary they seem to me wonderfully supple and sure — a triumphant evidence that the artistic mind need know no age. It is very striking to see, at any rate, how Howells seems to be drifting back toward the poetic envisagement of life with which he began years ago. Of course he approaches his subject nominally under the aegis of Science, but in the last two stories in the book, 'The Angel of the Lord' and 'Though One Rose from the Dead,' there is a genuine mystic efflatus. How impressive it is to see how almost all earnest minds, and exactly by reason of their earnestness, have sooner or later to abandon the realistic formula, or at least to so modify it that it ceases to have any meaning *qua* realism. I have read *Anna Karenina* in spite of your warning, and was far less depressed by its human story than I was inspirited by its artistic grandeur. Besides, the story itself is twofold, and far more happy than sad when viewed in the entirety of its thought — at least just as happy as sad, which is all we can ask of art as of life. We must read *Crime and Punishment* and *Dead Souls*.

I am getting a whole lot out of the flower-book, and begin to think it isn't as bad as we thought it. I have identified many flowers new to me, among others the

Round-leaved Pyrola (a lovely thing), Herb Robert, Cinquefoil, Golden Ragwort, Philadelphia Fleabane (O that I might be the bane of the human flea who named it that!), Blue Vetch, Brook Veronica, and Bush Honeysuckle. The island is covered with red lilies — wood-lilies the worthy Mrs. Dana calls them, but they all grow in the open.

During a spell of cold and rainy weather which we had I got wet and neglected to change my clothes, the result being a keen pinch of the malady with which I suffered so many torments last winter. After two disagreeable days and two sleepless nights I said 'Go to,' ran nine times round the island, drank nine barrels of Lithia water, pronounced nine times the word 'Bogan' and was healed.

Brother still scratches dejectedly at your door now and then, and whenever we meet a carriage in our walks he prances up to it in the hope of regaining his lost friends. His nature impresses me anew each day; he is a wonderfully charming little soul.

W—

(Postmarked July 24, 1903) MACKINAC ISLAND

Today, after a week of denials, the postmistress gave up your letter, together with various delectable-looking packages.

Yeats's *Shadowy Waters* I have read before, but shall read it again with interest; it is very watery and shadowy. Both of these epithets are intended to be complimentary. The prose play I consumed at once, without getting much nourishment out of it. 'Where There is Nothing in Particular' — would be a juster title. It is remarkable that as sensitive an artist as Yeats (for he is that, as you say)

[157]

should care to put out anything at once so flat and so hysterical. However, I am glad you did not read it before sending, and condemn it, for I am always glad to know what a man like Yeats is doing, even when he is foozling the ball. There was a disappointing dearth of personal news in your letter. It seems to me that compared with you I am a regular *gazette scandaleuse* of gossipy information.

The island has been at her loveliest, and Brother and I have made many delightful discoveries (chiefly geographical). For instance, there is a road thro' the Cathedral Woods which no white man has ever trod before we found it, by means of which a whole new region of the woods, surpassingly fine, is accessible.

Up to today I have not done much with the poem.[1] I have seen and felt much of it with great vividness, but somehow it would not flow. Perhaps I did not really feel it as vividly as I saw it; at any rate it hadn't (perhaps hasn't yet) reached the melting point. I made two or three false starts and was a good deal discouraged. But today I had a glorious morning — I mean it felt glorious, though the concrete results were no such great potatoes.

(Postmarked Mackinac Island, Aug. 4, 1903)

J—— has gone for the mail, and I am hoping for a word from you; but meanwhile I will scribble one 'for hand in hand' as Whitman says, for without doors and within I feel your presence — gentle, gay, and eager for the day's adventure. So it has been ever since you left, and so it shall always be.

The little meadow sketch I finished; it is quite fetching,

[1] *The Fire-Bringer.*

I think. Also made a dash at St. Ignace by sunset, but to no purpose.

I have thought much about the relationship of the new poem with the *Masque* since your wonderfully revealing voice recited them to me side by side. The idea of a trilogy, it seems to me now I shall have to give up. The two pieces are conceived and executed in too different a spirit, and to add a third would only make the difficulty greater. Your suggestion, of changing the *Masque* to fit, I am afraid will not do. The divergence is too great. They had better stand as companion poems, breathing different aspects of the same theme in different moods and with each its separate 'aura,' and I can add a scene to the *Masque* which will at once complete its own inherent idea and serve as a sufficient link of suggestion between the two. Tell me what you think of this.

W—

(Postmarked Mackinac Island, Aug. 31, 1903)

The weather has certainly been execrable, and shows no sign of mending. The roads and woodpaths are so soft with the everlasting downpour that walking is difficult even if one has heart to brave the dogged leaden drench.

Under the bann of the rain even painting has ceased — nearly. I have worked over the St. Ignace sketch, to its advantage I think. The portrait has thrown off all disguise and become a pretty lady in a loggia.

(Postmarked Mackinac Island, Sept. 23, 1903)

For the past three days the old island has been doing herself proud in the way of weather, having made a complete volte-face into halcyon warmth and sunshine. This is the more to rejoice in because one of the passing phases of the domestic comedy has been that upon the whole island not a stick of firewood exists and T—— and I have been burning the furniture in order to keep warm. You would be surprised to find how little real satisfactory heat there is in a piano; but the sideboard yielded unexpected results.

The Pit is really a good deal of a book; it carries big sail, but hardly too big for the breeze it invokes and gets, yes, for the most part gets, though its unequivocal celebration of the Brute and his worshippers, simply *qua* Brute, is the Lord knows young enough, and annoying enough to such as would fain have comprehended and dismissed him forsooth.

(Postmarked Mackinac Island, Sept. 25, 1903)

I send you Stickney's book,[1] which will give you some good hours, I think. It is uneven, but it has much beauty, much visionary grace, and not seldom he has found the ultimate, the desirable word. Tell me what you think of the book, *in extenso*; I should like, when I get a chance, to tell him.

(Postmarked Mackinac Island, Oct. 4, 1903)

Don't worry about the wood. We are all right again, in fact have never been wrong. I only mentioned it as an amusing piece of island shiftlessness. Mike has roused himself and filled our bin with logs — a bit green to be sure, but when coaxed emitting a very comfortable blaze.

Great news about Ferd. Bring him up *vi et armis.*

I enclose the last of the chorals, with which the poem is to close. There are yet three songs to write.

W—

[1] *Dramatic Verses* by Joseph Trumbull Stickney.

AMERICA — 1903

The night-song, going down, is to Dionysus; the dawn song is to Apollo. Here it is, in the rough.

CHORUS OF YOUNG MEN (*ascending*)

One large last star, not yet persuaded well,
Expected till the mountains should declare;
But from his hesitant attitude,
From his wild and waiting mood,
Wildly, waitingly there came
Over sea and earth and air
And on our bended hearts there fell
Trembling and expectation of thy name.
Now the East to the West has flung
Sudden hands aloft, and sung
Thy titles and thy certain coming-on;
Wheeling ever to the right hand, wheeling ever to the dawn,
The South has danced before the North,
And the text of her talking feet is the news of thy going-forth,
Apollo! Apollo!
When radiance hid the Titan's face
And all was blind in the altar-place
Then we saw thee, we cried upon thee then,
Apollo! Apollo!
Past thee Dionysus swept,
The wings of Eros stirred and slept,
And we knew not the mist of thy song from the mist of the fire,
As out of the core of the light thy lyre laughed and thundered again!

Eros, how sweet
Is the cup of thy drunkenness.
Dionysus, how our feet
Hasten to the burning cup
Thou liftest up;
But O how sweetest and how most burning it is
To drink of thy lightsome and radiant chalices,
Apollo! Apollo! Today
We say we will follow thee and put all others away.
For we know, we have seen it of thee
That with more frenzy yet thou makest the frenzied free,

And singing leadest the rapt Spirit on
Where never mortal thought has gone,
Till, by the ultimate stream
Of vision and of dream
She stands
With startled eyes and outstretched hands,
Looking where other suns rise over other lands,
And rends the lonely skies with her prophetic scream.[1]

MACKINAC ISLAND
Sunday, Oct. 4 (1903)

I am inexpressibly sorry that I seemed to treat your letter with coldness. I sent the 'choral' in answer to it — an answer too vague and indirect, I confess; but I could think of no better way to express my sympathy for your great mood, my joy in your radiant nature, and my sense of our kinship in the blood of beauty.

It is disappointing news that you will not be here for another week yet. I had more than half expected you today, and T——, infected by my confidence, got up early to sweep the porches, and put the new cover on the swing-bed, intended to give a festival touch to the scene of your arrival. Even Brother was practically convinced, and gave the velvet cloak an extra nozzling. I haven't made a new cover for the swing-bed, but I have been doing some very pretty work tinting trees and bushes, covering the wood paths with gold and russet, arranging effects of mellow mist, and even stretching a few preliminary spider webs. Perhaps though on the whole I am proudest of my

---

[1] In this letter was enclosed the above version, 'in the rough,' 'The Chorus of Young Men' with which *The Fire-Bringer* closes. See pages 269–70–71, *Poems and Poetic Dramas*, by William Vaughn Moody, Houghton Mifflin Company, 1912. By comparing the two versions, the reader may note the significant improvement made by the poet in changing four words and substituting three new lines for three rejected ones.

little effect in odors. The whole island smells like a god's cider press; it is rare.

I think I understand what you mean about Stickney's poem, and I think I agree. 'Progress is progress' is what he has meant to say, achievement is achievement, and the achievement of each is inscrutably conserved for all, in spite of the ingratitude and indifference of those who immediately inherit. Then he has softened the crudity of the immediate rejection (very beautifully I think) by Pyrrha's confidence and hope in the outcome:

> 'Tomorrow brings again
> The sun he gave us, and the hope — the life.'

I am sorry you are not more impressed with the volume as a whole, but as you say, your situation is perhaps not favorable for tasting toward an ultimate decision. I like the *Oneiropolos* extremely, though Browning's mood and accent is too evident. The volume is certainly uneven — exasperatingly, maddeningly so, and this unevenness exists not as between poem and poem alone, where it could be neglected, but within the body of each piece, or nearly every one. Still the real stuff is there, and concerning how many books that come to hand these days can one say that?

Monna Vanna I have read and saw acted in Munich. It is rather a good little play, curiously un-Maeterlinckian, dealing with supposedly real people in a historical setting, and with only a sentence or two (put in the mouth of a Greek-chorus old man) in the mystic-melancholy vein. It represents at any rate an odd *volte-face* from his previous attempts to express the inexpressible by means of the inexpressive, and if your analysis of his case is correct, it seems rather a regrettable departure. But I read it hurriedly and saw it acted in a barbarous tongue, so there may be more of the man's philosophy in it than I gathered.

The weather continues notional; for the last three days we have had tremendous storm and rain; the thunder night before last rolled and burst and rolled and burst over our heads until not the house only but the very island seemed to rock under it.

I send you a letter just received from one of the tiny band of the faithful. I don't know why I send it, except that it came at a moment of depression and cheered me, so frail is the flesh! I thought everybody but you and Ferd had forgotten the *Masque* or never heard or would hear of it, and here bless my soul is a fellow reading it in Spain where the castles are, and thinking it's like Wagner! Well, I don't know who he is, but he's a good man. I only wish the devil hadn't prompted him to ask for the picture; it seems foolish to send it and caddish not to. What would you do?

Too bad Ferd can't come. I'm wearying for a sight of the lad.

WILL

NEW YORK, *Nov.* 12, 1903

I woke up this morning in the Blue Ridge mountains of Pennsylvania. Then, as I lay and watched the light grow over the russet and amber and olive-purple hills, the memories of the past few days came back with wonderful vividness upon me — from the Sunday morning in the meadow, when I felt the hardness melt within me, to the never-to-be-forgotten hour by the fire when I seemed to awaken from a sleep and to find you at last after many days and know the strong joy of your spirit. All through the day you have seemed to be at my side, behind me, across the street, beyond some door just opening, and always with that inexpressible light of joy upon you, summoning me to the joy for which all my life long I have hungered and thirsted.

The day's search for rooms has been discouraging. Tomorrow I shall do better — find some place to live that isn't either vulgarly pretentious and expensive or sordidly shabby and dark, as everything I have thus far seen seems to be.

Will

The Benedick, New York
Nov. 13 (1903)

Today began with another series of disappointments and disillusionments in my search for rooms, but when flesh and spirit were about exhausted good luck — disguised as a Forlorn Hope — led me into the Studio Building on West 10th Street. I had been told repeatedly that there wasn't a studio left in New York, and I entered the manager's office with expectation of the usual reply. The ravens that fed the prophet in the wilderness dropped into my arms a man who was going away and wanted to sublet his studio until the first of May. I hugged him to my breast and entreated to be led to view the same. It proved to be a big ramshackle place, looking very dingy in its denuded state, but in spite of all drawbacks the room was *gemütlich* and oddly delightful in an oldfashioned Bohemian way. I closed with him at once, as my telegram about the furniture has ere this apprised you. The place is a great ant-hill of artists, and in its arrangements reminds me much of the old dormitory I lived in on the 'Yard' at college. Your coal and water is fetched up from unknown regions by a grumbling humorous old dog of a porter, every occupant buys his own coal and runs his own little coal-bin. The walls are stained with the leavings of many palettes, and by other accidents. There is a skylight and two windows — one of them looking out on the church-yard of the 11th St. church, with a chance at the sunrise beyond (I am on the top floor and the building is pretty high.) All these precious advantages are offset by only two serious defects — there is no bathroom, and the only arrangement for heating seems to be by stove. Still, with an open-grate stove and a hat-tub I shall get on famously. The main thing is there — the feeling of *bien-être* and homeliness, the sense of seclusion from the insistent New York rush-and-grab, and the atmosphere, subtly diffused from half-open doors and passing figures in the corridors, of the artistic life. I count myself immensely fortunate to have found it, and call upon you to rejoice with me.

I telegraphed without taking very serious thought for you to ship me my table, chairs, rug and easel. Perhaps it will cost more money and trouble to send the things on than to buy them new, but perhaps not. Do as you think best. I also telegraphed you (perhaps you didn't under-stand) to let me know by wire if you had anything else about the house which you wanted to send. I have already bought a couch-bed, and a stove.

NEW YORK, *Nov.* 15, 1903

Dan Mason has turned over to me a lot of pretty hang-ings which he is not using, and we have spent the day putting these up. I am more and more delighted with my

[166]

find; the arrangements are just crude enough to give one a wholesome feeling and the atmosphere of the place is friendly and subtly inspiring. John La Farge, Dewing, Alden Weir, J. G. Brown and several other painters of name are in the building, and I look forward to some pleasant acquaintances among them, if the chances fall that way.

Your spirit is always with me; and I am learning to share with it every thought and experience that the passing hours bring — not merely the chosen ones, the high points, but all the futile, unilluminated, even I think the evil, if evil ever came near me here where I walk in the glad delicious light which from some unhoped-for mercy of revealment has fallen upon me.   W—

NEW YORK, *Nov.* 17, 1903

Your telegram announcing the despatch of the furniture came bright and early this morning; I enjoyed a meditative and delighted grin over your absurd effectiveness, thus again signalized. It would have taken any other woman in the world a week to make up her mind what she would send, and another to make up her mind to send it.

Dan Mason just here came in with two men whom he had asked to dine with me, and dragged me off....

After dinner I was taken round to the studio of Arthur Whiting, a composer, who played me a thing which evoked your presence uncannily — a dance-suite in free fantasia form, to be accompanied by dancing and plastic interpretations on the part of some woman — not yet discovered by the composer — divinely appointed to dance, to glorify again that discredited heaven of art.

The news about Brother is immensely comforting.

There was a sore place inside of me which your picture of him as in good spirits and allowed to run after the carriage, has put balm upon.

Do write 'the little word' — it will be of immense comfort to me, for New York, with all its brilliance and variety, is (let me whisper it) rather a howling wilderness.

W—

51 WEST 10TH ST.
NEW YORK, *Nov.* 19, 1903

It is comfortable to think that the things will be here in a few days, for the romance of living in a bare loft is beginning to wear off, and something to sit on will add to the meaning of life.

I saw Phillips's *Ulysses* the other night. It is perhaps a trifle less weak on the stage, but quite weak enough even there. As we surmised at the time of reading it the last act is dramatically far ahead of the rest of the play. It will doubtless come to Chicago, as it has petered out here by this time. There was only a handful of spectators.

Tonight I am going to Barrie's new comedy *The Admirable Crichton*, which is said to be capital. The opera season begins next week.

NEW YORK, *Nov.* 21 (1903)

The runaway, by some curious psychologic freak, has just fairly impinged upon my consciousness, in both its serious and its humorous aspects. Since no accident resulted the former can happily be dismissed, but it affords me an incommunicably humorous pleasure to note how all dogs and horses (at any rate) understand you and respond instantly to your temperamental demands. So it has been, apparently, from the beginning — as soon as you are

[168]

seated behind a horse, every drop of chivalrous blood whispers 'Escapade' to the equine heart. And the way in which from the very first instant Brother divined the rollicking boon-fellow in you is enough to put forever to shame the mole-like lugubrious view of a certain friend of yours I know, who prides himself upon insight forsooth.

Your note enclosing the pictures did me a world of good. I had come home tired from a symphony concert, and a little blue with the exhaustion of feeling which Tschaikowsky's Fifth always induces. Your bright brave words, and the delightful picture of yourself were like wine to my spirit. This picture gives as no other I have seen the essential nobility of outline of your head — a thing which you despise because of a supposed meretricious relationship which it bears to your back hair, but a thing which I prize as an adumbration of your inmost self and an accent of the Holy Ghost.

Herrick's novelette is about as heartless a piece of writing as ever blotted paper, though he tries hard to pump enough humanity into it at the end to raise it above the temperature of liquid air. I purchased today the Daskam's effusions, which I shall report on soon and send you the book; it is got up regardless with red and gold on the outside, and I dare say the inside has been prepared with as lavish a disregard of expense. *The Admirable Crichton*, when and if it comes to Chi, you must by all means see. It is a capital skit.

51 West 10th St.
New York, *Nov.* 24 (1903)

There is a most interesting loan-exhibition of portraits on here, ranging from sixteenth century Flemish masters through Van Dyck and Rembrandt, the English 18th Century School, Gainsborough, Reynolds, Raeburn, etc., down to Sargent, Whistler, and even the youngsters of the passing hour. It is a most wonderful parade of human masks, and besides the pure artistic pleasure, puts one in the way of strange thoughts to see the centuries marshalled this way, in their most human and private aspect. It's odd to see how nine times out of ten the sitter has fooled the painter or the painter has fooled himself or perhaps been frankly indifferent and not tried to go deeper than the mask, but here and there a soul has been caught and held up naked, proud, ashamed, trembling, defiant — pilloried pitilessly (but sometimes so tenderly!) for unborn generations to gape at — on the whole even at the best rather a shocking business. Some of these poor foolish eighteenth-century worldlings and court-beauties especially, look as if they were at last tired of the glare and the crowds, and would like to taste the privacy and undress of death, but the colors are as bright as they were two hundred years ago; those old fellows ground their own colors and knew what they were using.

I cannot tell you how keenly I longed for your company, as I went from canvas to canvas fascinated and baffled. How you would revel in this exhibition, or rather with what divine insight and sympathy and drollery of view, with what sweet all-comprehending, all-accepting sisterhood you would walk among these dead who are so strangely living. Dear friend, dear friend! I wish I might let you know how the beauty of your life has been revealed to me, and how the revelation has brought me near to the centre of all life, to the eternal secret — the Open Secret which from the beginning every created thing has been breathless to declare, has been breathlessly declaring. W—

51 West 10th St.
New York, *Nov.* 28, 1903

I have been a little under the weather for three or four days. My complaint is trifling. I caught a severe cold (excuse me, I know one can't do that!) with grippe symptoms, and had a sharp touch of that accursed pain in the hip which I suppose is rheumatism, but whatever else it is, is deucedly unpleasant. I took prompt measures, and am now virtually as good as new.

I saw (or rather heard, for I was a mile from the stage) the Valkyrie last night. Your dear presence, and the memories of that evening last spring when we beheld together those shining rivers and cascades, those swinging seas and cloud-shepherding trade-winds of melody, were with me all the evening. It is through music that I seem to come nearest to you, and nearest of all through this elemental welter of Wagner's, this chaos of chords continually shaping themselves into divine form only to gaze about for an instant and melt back once more into its primordial element.

There is nothing of first-rate importance at the theatres just now, but Mrs. Burnett's *Little Sister of José* (with Maude Adams). Ethel Barrymore in a play called *Cousin Kate*, and Marie Tempest in *The Marriage of Kitty* I shall look upon and judge. There is a very interesting Yiddish play on the East Side, of which I enclose a newspaper account. The students of the School of Dramatic Expression also give a play of Björnson's next week. These with a good comedy at the German theatre, three symphony concerts to choose from, and the opera, will show I am not starved for entertainment.

Yeats is here, and is coming West to lecture: you had better hear him. I have not seen him, but am invited to meet him at breakfast when he comes back East again.

51 WEST 10TH ST.
NEW YORK, *Dec.* 1, 1903

I met yesterday a young chap called Ridgely Torrence, a very charming and amusing fellow, who has just written a five-act verse-play entitled *Eldorado*, dealing with the Spanish search for the Seven Cities of Gold and other wonders. He says he is writing one on Abélard and Héloise for Mrs. Fiske. Robinson is not much use for purposes of comradeship these days. He is working, at a very dreary job, poor chap, and is too tired after he gets through to do much but roll into bed. Mason is also very busy, but we manage to sandwich in some good hours of music. I feel like the one loafer in a universe of strenuosity, for I have not been able to settle down to any work worth the name.

NEW YORK, *Dec.* 8, 1903

I saw Bernard Shaw's *Candida* this afternoon, given by a special company, and very impressive. The thing stages in a way to surprise you. I am hard at work on a new piece — a queer thing which I think I shall call *The Death of Eve*. It is about Eve in old age — blank verse narrative. The idea of it came on me out of a clear sky the other day, and almost lifted me out of my skin. I believe you'll like it, but I'm not sure. Perhaps you'll think it's too queer. I'm meeting a lot of interesting people; it's a strange place, is Babylon.

New York, *Dec.* 28, 1903

I have been writing like a madman — four lyrics (of the necessary five) in as many days. I send you one, of which I feel already pretty sure. If the others stand the cooling-off test successfully I shall forward them also. This one is sung at the climax of Act II, after Pyrrha says 'The stars, it is the ancient stars, etc.' Will it do? It seems good to me, but is still white hot to my fond eyes, and denies to be seen clearly.

Dec. 29, 1903

Here is a thing that I was visited with when (perhaps) you will think I ought to have been better employed. It means nothing, and many things, all of which you will know better than I. If you hate it, chuck it in the waste-basket, and it will be forever chucked; if you like it, lay it on your heart and think how passion slain renews itself, and evermore is young.

THAMMUZ

Daughters, daughters, do ye grieve?
Crimson dark the freshes flow.
Were ye violent at eve?
What hath stained the rushes so?
What is this that I must know?

Mourners by the dark red waters,
Met you Thammuz at his play?
Was your mood upon you, daughters?
Had ye drunken? Oh how grey
Looks your hair in the growing day!

Daughters, mourn not over much
That ye slew your lovely one.
Such ye are; and be ye such.
Lift your heads; the waters run
Ruby bright in the climbing sun.

[173]

Raven hair and hair of gold,
Look who bendeth over you!
I am not your father old,
I am Thammuz that ye slew,
Radiant Thammuz risen anew.

NEW YORK, *Dec. 30,* 1903

I am afraid the songs I have been sending you have not been such as to give you any delight, but I am going to risk another anyhow. The one I enclose is intended for the end of the second act, but I don't know yet whether it will stand — perhaps in the region it attempts to enter words are an impertinence, or even an impiety. You will know, unless (as I half suspect) I have failed altogether to say anything.

NEW YEAR'S DAY, 1904

This is for a Happy New Year. The greeting probably sounds vague to you, overshadowed as you must be by the awful cloud of bereavement which rests over the city. When I went out last night at dark, I learned for the first time of the dreadful theatre catastrophe.[1] I had a bad three minutes while I was buying a paper and devouring the headlines; even when I found that the tragedy had occurred twenty-eight hours ago, and knew that if it had touched anyone I loved I should have heard the news long before, it was a good while before the watery feeling went out of my knees. The momentary fear was shrewd enough to leave me wistful about you, and to keep me from being little short of a kill-joy I suspect, at the small gathering of choice spirits who watched the old year out at Whiting's studio, and drank the New Year in in bumpers of October ale, not without song.

[1] The Iroquois Theatre fire in Chicago.

Today I wrote the last of the Pandora songs. I have made some changes in those I sent you, and strengthened their effect also by some slight changes in their time and mode of entrance. I think they will stand now, but I am anxious for your opinion whether they do or not. I am going to spend a day or two more on strengthening and smoothing out the last act, which doesn't yet seem to me organically quite sound — I mean quite crystallinely organized — especially in the latter half. When that has been gone over, and the whole thing given a final 'ironing-out,' I shall have done my darnedest, and the thing will have to take care of itself, sink or swim. It has been a long and happy labor, and in every line and accent of it thoughts of you have been woven.

I send a draft of the aforesaid lyric passage.

Tomorrow morning there will perhaps be a letter from you, and until then I shall believe that you are dwelling, as you should be, in the Great Good Place.

W—

A Voice
Who are these coming down, etc....

Another Voice
It is Pandora and the unborn men,
Deukalion's seed, etc...

Pandora (sings, *invisible in the light*)
Ye who from the stone and clay
Unto godhead grope your way,
Hastening hither do ye see
Yonder passionate trinity?

The Stone Men and Earth Women
Save us, flaming Three!

[175]

PANDORA

Dionysus hath the wine,
Eros hath the rose divine,
Lord Apollo hath the lyre:
Three and one is the soul's desire.

THE STONE MEN AND EARTH WOMEN

Save us, sons of fire!

A WOMAN'S VOICE

Listen, they have passed.
They go with singing forward down the light

NEW YORK, *Jan.* 6 (1904)

After I wrote you last, my exuberant uplift departed as suddenly as it came, and I was left to crawl between heaven and earth as a biped of most questionable usefulness and dubious meaning. But your letter has made me a man again, and opened again the eastern windows which, when they close, leave me so drearily housed.

That you should like *all* the lyrics seems too good to be true; I had braced myself to rejecting one or two of them. I am not yet satisfied with the one beginning 'Because one creature'; I think it is good in itself, but not broad and floating and midnightish enough for the place it occupies; I think of bringing it in later—shortly before the antiphonal beginning 'Ye who from the stone and clay,' and writing another for the vacant place. What do you think? That in general they seem to you to 'swing into their places' is the best praise. I am finishing the Eve, but it seems to be getting rather crazy and raucous? I can't vouch for its turning out well. Also I have an idea for a 'dream-play'—very hazy, but *es liebäugelt mich an aus dem Schatten.*

Monday night I saw Barrie's *Little Mary* — a really delicious trifle. It has an Irish girl in it — Moira Louie — whose brogue would put thoughts of poison in your envious heart; it is very slight, just a little blur as of peat-smoke on a fair sky. The piece is a comic skit with a dash of farce, very pungent, and with a good deal of human depth too. I hope it will soon be coming your way. 'Little Mary,' whose identity remains a mystery until the last five minutes of the play, is a euphemism for the stomach, and the play whimsically purports to be a plea for the more humane treatment of that organ; not a promising dramatic theme, one would think, but it suffices. There is also a rich farce at the German theatre, called *Los vom Manne*, the heroine of which, a lady of certain age heading a movement for the independence of her sex, is hypnotically diverted from her life work whenever a possible or impossible lover appears on the horizon. These, with Shaw's *Candida* going, and another great picture show, convince me that you'll have to dash on to New York.

W—

NEW YORK, *Jan.* 10, 1904

I am not yet ready to let the poem go. I have spent a good many weeks in that kind of slow intense scrutiny and testing which shows such microscopic results to the casual eye, but which constitutes the really immeasurable difference between a thing done as well as one can do it, and a thing done almost as well. And there is much — I don't know how much — of this still to do. I chafe at times to see the weeks filing by and finding me still at this employment, but I know that in the long run I should be bitterly sorry not to have done it. Pandora's song at the end of Act II I have entirely rewritten; it is, I am sure, much better in its new form. I'm bound to give the tooth of time as hard a search as possible for soft places where it can begin its gnawing.

New York, *Jan.* 14, 1904

I have been reading a book on Brook Farm by Lindsay Swift which is wholly fascinating. The history of the place is rich in humor of the subtlest and sweetest kind, and cries out for somebody to put the quintessential mingling of whimsicality and elevation which is distilled from it into a play. Several of the characters who were at the Farm during the years of first enthusiasm and of hard-pan living — especially some of the obscurer characters only revealed in silhouette or 'back-to' are deliciously funny and touching and grand. The atmosphere that seems to have rested over the place is just the one in which to steep a work of art which should reveal the humorous in the unworldly, without any touch of satire or *parti pris*, and which should humanize to the materialistic and worldly average eye the mystic and otherworldly personality. This all expresses what I see in the subject most blindly, and will give you a notion that I am contemplating a *Tom Pinch* or a *Professor's Love Story*. I wonder if Hawthorne's *Blithedale Romance* comes anywhere near doing what I am trying clumsily to define? I must read it at once.

Have you noticed how long the days are growing? And how, on certain late afternoons, the air is recovering faintly, O so very faintly that it doesn't stand really looking for, the flame-tint of Spring—I mean that powdery diffused supersubtle essence of rosy flame that one sees on late Spring afternoons, nowhere to be fixed but everywhere apparent? Of course She is worlds away yet, but I verily believe — well, it is best not to be arrogant.

WILL

NEW YORK, *Jan.* 15, 1904

The day before I got your letter advising me to read the *Fire-Bringer* to Stickney in person, I had sent it to him, with a mention in the introductory note of what I conceived to be my indebtedness to his poem, and a letter in which I set this forth more in full, and asked him to tell me frankly whether the reference to his Prometheus pleased him, whether he would rather have it made more specific or more casual. Today I received a letter from him, written after a first reading of the play. It is a very friendly and manly letter, imperatively urging me to omit all reference to my predecessors in the handling of the myth, including himself, and to print instead a translation of the brief passages in Hesiod and Apollodorus which represent the raw material I have drawn upon. He thinks the connection between his poem and mine of only 'philological interest,' and finds the divergence in our handling of the characters and the action so great that — on a first reading at least — the attempt to adjust his preconceptions to my view makes my work puzzling and baffling to him. He finds the play extremely difficult, partly doubtless because of this difficulty in readjusting the lines of a settled mental picture. He calls it a 'superb performance,' but finds it less dramatic in the human than in the symbolic order; the characters do not as yet seem very real or 'convincing' to him — a most grievous opinion. He is coming down

[179]

in a week or two, and we shall have a chance to talk it out.

I am sending you tomorrow a queer play by the new Russian, Maxim Gorky. It has elements of great beauty and strength, but doesn't seem drawn together or quite 'floated' — at least on a hasty reading. I have also a new play by Sudermann, *Der Sturmgeselle Sokrates*, which I shall send you when I have finished it.

W—

NEW YORK, *Jan.* 19, 1904

I didn't meet Yeats after all. He must be a good man, to have made so strong an impression upon you, and I am sorry now I didn't take more trouble to get at him. But as for his thesis about folk-poetry and the folk-spirit, it is just as strong and just as weak as the weakest of the links which go to make it up, and that — as you point out yourself — is very weak indeed. It is this taking up of an artificial attitude toward folk-poetry that is the undoing of Yeats and all his 'school.' A self-conscious attempt to assimilate and reproduce what is itself of the very essence of naïveté, is bound to be a cancelling business; good old Bishop Percy over his port and his last find in broad-sheets, was nearer the heart of the matter. However, let me not be stentorian in the demonstration of the obvious, and of what, more-over, you have already granted me explicitly. In the matter of the 'tunes,' too, I am inclined not to set much store by the theory which you report Yeats as holding. That every good poet has his special *music* is of course true; but that is of course a thing made up of elements far too complex to be denoted by musical signs, and in many of its elements not denotable at all. Considering, too, the

single element of rhythm, I should say that all its grander
and more vital beauties, in the case of any poet of power,
were irreducible to notation; and that the recurrence of a
rhythmic theme so frequently as to enable one to pick it
out as a characteristic tune, would by just so much in-
validate a poet's claim to greatness in that kind. I feel
like Brother Tolman or the worthy Skeat, and know you
are hating me; so I will stop boring you with these dogma-
tisms right here. The main thing and the only thing to
care about is that, standing face to face with this young
Irishman, you, miraculous reader of hearts and knower of
souls, accept him as our brother. My brother he shall be,
so long as I have strength to claim him. In essence he cannot be wrong.

I sent you last night the first draft of *Eve*, and rather re-
pented me of it afterwards, for it is still rough and thin in
places, and is perhaps as a whole rejectable. It pretty much
went its own way; I am not primarily responsible for it if
you find it raucous and grotesque. I can say of it too that
in essence it is right, but it's got rather a queer envelope, I
guess. You may find the rhythmic movement of Eve's
song difficult; the secret of its music lies in its being read
with strong pauses; I have made them strong by every art I
know, but something is still left to the mercy of the ear that
hears it. After reading it please send it back, as I have
only the one copy.

————

New York, *Jan.* 24 (1904)

I saw *Parsifal* last night — a great show, but less rich
and high-floating in the score than I had hoped. Magical
moments — the Grail music, especially the boys' choir, and
the Good Friday Spell; — but on the whole not in it with

the *Valkyrie* or *Tristan*. Wagner was not religious, at
least not when he thought he was. The 'teaching' of this
opera, so far as it is doctrine and not beauty, is pitiably
false.

Since I wrote you last I have made a most interesting
acquaintanceship, which may prove to be a precious friendship, with one Gutzon Borglum — a Dane of American
birth and tastes — a sculptor and painter of superb
powers. I spent yesterday afternoon and most of the evening in his studio, where he has a half-dozen pictures and
three or four statues underway. One of the latter is a
group of madly plunging horses going over a hill, with
a naked figure clinging to the back of the foremost, and
throwing back his arm to compel the rest to follow. He
calls it 'Hercules Stealing the Horses of Admetus,' but it
might just as well be a stampede of Arizona ponies under
the hypnotic control of an Indian boy. This is still in the
wet clay, and while I smoked and talked, he modelled one
of the horses' heads in a way to make you weep. Another
group only sketched out is a woman turning away from a
prostrate man, and dropping a pair of pipes from her limp
hand as she goes. The rubric is 'I have piped to ye and ye
have not danced!' The expression of the woman is wonderfully imagined. Borglum talks almost as well as he works
— a big sane mind. Altogether he is the most powerful
figure of an artist I have ever encountered. As he seems to
like me and has urged upon me the freedom of his studio,
I expect to get much out of his companionship. He is, I
judge, about forty, perhaps less; and has had a career in
Europe before settling here for his life work.

I suppose you've thrown the *Eve* down hard, and no
blame to you. I was two or three times on the point of

telegraphing you to send it back unopened; but I decided at last not to permit that childishness.

W—

New York, *Jan.* 28, 1904

I have been very low in my mind for some days, perhaps owing to the failure of *Eve* (for as it stands it is unquestionably a failure), though I don't like to think so small an inducing cause could bring me down. Whatever the cause, I 'struck slate,' not for the first time in my life as you know, but each time it seems as if the heavens had fallen and buried me, or rather as if the principle of life had been mysteriously withdrawn from the world ('sucked up the fire of passion and of will') leaving it inhabited by joyless automatons, vacantly pursuing their functions under an automatic sun. Well, it is ungenerous for me even to mention these megrims. I know that I have only to wait, and the living waters will seep back somehow into the cistern, as indeed they are even now doing in a very commendable way.

How is Brother?[1] You have not mentioned him for weeks, and a panic fear seized me today that something had happened to him and that you were sparing me the knowledge of it. I had a queer dream about him last night, which may have aroused my uneasiness. Tell me about him, and do not let him wholly forget that I am in the world.

New York, *Feb.* 2, 1904

I am well and happy, and my little fit of the doldrums has given place to a mood of exciting or rather excited

[1] W. V. M.'s pet name for his dog, Sieg.

[183]

absorption in a new stunt — of which, if it comes to anything, you shall hear; but I am going to stop sending you
half-cooked dishes to taste.

I have been put up at the Arts Club, and have met there
many interesting and a few engaging people. It is a men's
and women's club, with a charming dining-room, a number
of good pictures, and a membership where Bohemianism is
of the chastened sort. Borglum is a member. I have been
seeing a good deal of him, to my continued satisfaction.
He is a most curious nature, irascible and egotistic, with
a basis of strange childlike solemnity, and a gloomy intensity that is the reverse of childish.

This is only a note to let you know I am riding the
waves again.

W—

New York, *Feb.* 4 (1904)

Your moving vindication of the *Eve* is so much better
than the exciting cause that I am ashamed to pursue the
subject. Really, though, you mustn't; for if you praise me
thus when I partly fail, what will you have left to do when
I succeed? The fact is that I wrote the part of the poem in
question under too great a strain of excitement. It often
happens that the excitement of 'vision' reaches a point
where it obscures some of the other faculties necessary for
the excellent balanced play of the heart, mind and imagination together, without which there is no sufficing art.
Usually, I am advised of this, and go out and cool my head
in the rain-barrel before proceeding, but this time I didn't,
and the result — though I think with you that it is in
substance good — is perturbed and inultimate. It will
have to settle a good while before I can draw off the pure

liquor which I feel is there. This you have already done, by the double alchemy of love and inspired insight; some day, the Muses willing, I shall be able to do in cold script what you have done in feeling.

I am hard at a new piece of poetry, and just now the thing is sliding like sand under my shovel. I can't tell what dimensions it will take; but as far as I can judge, I shall need three or four weeks, with luck.

Feb. 6 (1904)

My brief despair was entirely artistic and metaphysical, and in the happy reaction from it I have jumped into a big piece of work which makes my waking hours one debauch of stolid and silent excitement. Perhaps there is nothing in it, but I seem to myself to be on the point of solving the great problem of the application of blank verse to the realistic treatment of a modern theme in drama. This sounds at once appallingly presumptuous and also quite academic and theoretical. I mean that in handling the subject I have now in hand — one of the modern subjects we have talked over and for which I am indebted to you, I seem to myself to have hit upon or to be about to hit upon a type of blank verse essentially new, which has much of the unconventionality and unguided movement of prose, in the passages where the emotional level is low, and which yet is capable of gathering itself up, when needed, into the passion and splendor which prose is incapable of. Co-operate with me in warding off from my head the punishment sent upon presumption, by letting this be as if it had not been said, until such time as I shall have pushed the experiment to consummation, and either proved or disproved its value.

Feb. 10 (1904)

I have been sitting at my desk since morning, and it is now seven o'clock. I don't know where the day has gone to, but I know that I am dropping with hunger and brain-fag, and that the very sight of pen and paper makes me ill, so I shall not do more than send you a word of good cheer and thankfulness.

The new play is going at a good clip, and I am almost too much in love with it to eat or sleep.

ST. VALENTINE'S DAY (1904)

I had just awakened this morning, and in my still drowsy head the thought was running: This is St. Valentine's; I wonder what Harriet is doing? when a small much-uniformed boy knocked at the door and handed to my pajamed person a box of wonderful lilies, chanting of far-off spring from two dozen dewy throats. Then I knew at least what Harriet *had* been doing, and was warmed as to the cockles of the heart. They have been at my elbow all day as I worked, and have whispered of the divine freshness and fragrance of the heart that sent them.

I am working hard at the new play, of which I will say nothing except that I have finished the first act (in nine days — a genuine feat for a slow-moving mass like me — though it will, I fear, not impress the imagination of a lady who lately suggested that I should put posturing by and sit down with the sworn design of writing a whole play, presumably of five acts and seventeen scenes in three days). I am also well started on the second, after interruption by a stubborn attack of headache, due, I dare say, to a dearth of exercise and a plethora of coffee. Whether the result is going to amount to anything or not it is too early to say, but I am working with an ease and swiftness which I have never known before. If only the swiftness does not prove to be of the kind that hinders the feet, and the ease of the kind that makes hard reading. There will be, as far as I can now see, three acts; so that, even at the present rate of speed (which of course I cannot count on) it will take me into the second week of March to finish it in first draft.

(Postmarked February 15, 1904)
Thursday

Your last letter took away my lingering uneasiness about you, for it showed plain enough that you are again on the large plateaus of life — or I ought not to say again, because I think this is a new one and swept by a bigger wind of joy and trust in existence than you have known before. Of course I know that you aren't built for the level career, in however high and windy a country, and I dare say that by the time you get this you'll be upbraiding me *sotto voce* for taking you at your word. If so, pray understand that I don't. But all the same I do.

My little job is still keeping me too busy to eat, though just now the outward and visible signs of my activity are meagre. I have struck a place which puzzles and disconcerts and allures me, by turns and all at once, and there is nothing to do but sit down before it with siege guns and provisions, and wait until it capitulates, a process I am now employed in, though to the outward and carnal eye no such matter.

The theatres are looking up more and more here, after a thin winter. The unexpected, the impossible, the inevitable has happened. For five years Frohman and his gang have been ramming fustian down the good people's throats, until all at once this fall they rebelled, and the theatres, with their dramatized historical novels, their patched-up French farces, their pick-me-up Clydefitcheries simply stood empty. Frohman scratched his head, and told his leading ladies to provide gowns of more striking patterns. Still empty. F. puts his cigar in the other side of his mouth, and orders seventeen new carloads of scenery and souvenirs at each performance. Empty as a sucked egg. F. gives it up and says, Hard times; nothing to do about it. Then little Arnold Daly and a lank inspired Irish girl from a cheap subterranean stock-company, took heart of grace, and advertised a matinee performance of *Candida*. The house was packed, and now after seven weeks it is running yet to admiration. Ada Rehan and Otis Skinner saw the lay, emerged from retirement, and began giving Shakespeare and Sheridan; Mrs. Fiske put on *Hedda*; and some quixotic revolutionist staged three of Yeats's small plays; people had to be turned away from the doors. Mr. Sidney Rosenfeld sees the point, and organizes the 'Century Players' with *Art for Art* emblazoned on the banner. The *Everyman* Company, which has been picking up a living in country towns, hears the glad news and makes for a regenerated metropolis, offering *Twelfth Night* in the original text and with the original meagre stage-setting, and perhaps other good things to follow. Meanwhile Frohman has chewed that cigar till it's a sight, and his remarks upon men and things are said to have the gloom and force of great tragic literature.

I mark what you say about Yeats. If he comes this way again, I shall try to see him.

(Postmarked Feb. 24, 1904)

It is late, and I am dog-tired, having been at the desk all day, but I must send you a word.

Something tells me that I must push this task [1] through to completion now while it is fresh and plastic in my mind, on pain of losing altogether the especial quality that I am seeking for it. After a day or two of partial discouragement I am in love with it again. How long it will take to finish, I cannot say; but however long it is, strengthen me to stay by it. It may or may not turn out to be good, but at any rate it is something totally new (for me), and I'm not sure enough of it to drop the threads for a moment.

Ferd has just written me a letter of most generous and inspiriting praise of the *F-B*. It was like meat and drink to hear from him again.

NEW YORK, *Feb.* 29 (1904)

I send you by this mail proofs of the new book,[2] in galley, though the differences which this final version exhibits from your copy — labor-costing as they are — are so small as to be nearly negligible.

CAMBRIDGE, *March* 6 (1904)

I am on my way to Chicago, and have come on here to make the final arrangements about the book. I found myself at the end of last week completely tired out, and have to loaf and lark a little before going on with my present job. I am staying with Stickney here and having a mellow time.

[1] This modern play in verse seems never to have been finished.
[2] *The Fire-Bringer.*

KANSAS CITY, Mo., *March* 29, 1904

I snatch a moment between trains to send back a word of gratitude and admiration for the brave farewell you gave me, which put me at once into a fit mind to welcome the adventure and big breath of the West. I breakfasted with Norton and his wife, very pleasantly; she is rather pretty and quite honest and unaffected. Norton I like better than ever on more acquaintance; I think he is the sterling sort; has a touch of rudeness, *gaucherie*, which is stimulating, and impresses me as a creature of much elemental unformed power.

(Postmarked Williams, Ariz., Mar. 31, 1904)
HOLBROOK, *March* 31

Yesterday was a day of mild adventure. Our train was hours behind time, and was kept waiting on side-tracks for eastbound trains to pass. We utilized the intervals for hasty climbs to the top of neighboring rocks and mesas, and once had a wild scramble back as our train pulled unexpectedly out. The air and sunlight here on the Arizona plateau is the most wonderful I have ever seen except in Greece, in fact the color and form of the country, as well as the atmosphere, remind me constantly of Greece. The russet, umber, and cinnabar plains, the turquoise mountains on the horizon, and patches of sage-brush, yucca, and juniper dotting the masses of volcanic rock, make a miracle of color; and I find my fingers itching for a brush. There is still snow in the shaded places, and this morning we passed through quite a heavy snow storm, but the middle of the day is as warm as summer.

Have Ferd bring clothing for both extremes. Also hustle him off as quickly as possible, as Norton is impatient to get into the desert, and I fear I can't hold him from the trail later than Wednesday of next week. I am telegraphing Ferd to start at once, and he will have no time to lose en route if he is to reach Holbrook by Wednesday. Tell him to inquire at the telegraph station for word as soon as he arrives at Holbrook, so that if necessary he can take the same train on to Winslow or Cañon Diablo in case we find that one of these is a better starting-point. He had also better telegraph me at Bright Angel Hotel, Grand Cañon, what train he leaves Chicago by, so that I can catch him by wire on the way if necessary. We are just pulling into Williams, where we take the branch line up to the Cañon.

(Postmarked Grand Cañon, Ariz., April 4, 1904)
Easter Sunday

We reached the Cañon Thursday evening, in time for a walk along the rim of the ungodly thing, sunset and moonrise. The next morning we went down the trail to a vast plateau about four miles down, and found lodging in a camp there — a lovely spot, with white tents bosomed in clumps of willows and red-brush in glorious flower. The full moon made such a scandal that it was impossible to sleep; I spent most of the night outside, listening to what the little brook in the willows had to tell of you, though it wasn't much compared with what the mountains and the moon spoke on the same subject.

The next day was misty and showery; but the Cañon was even more beautiful than by sunlight weather. We took the three mile climb down to the river, and toiled back up the monstrous precipices to camp again, too sore and stiff by this time to care for anything but food and sleep. Today (Easter morning) horses were brought down to the camp, and we rode up to the summit in blue flashing weather; we got our money's worth out of the horses by holding them for a grand gallop through the woods. Incidentally Mrs. Norton was thrown, and after making sure she was not injured, there was a mad rush up hill and down dale for the peccant beast.

Your letter came yesterday. Yes, to feel the nature of a beloved friend so deeply that even in the midst of the most intimate sharing of life there is imminent knowledge of his strangeness, of the far unadventured places of his being, this is the secret and the great reward. Out of this way of love comes the soul's punctual spring and Easter, and there is no other way which holds the promise of life. I have often told you how keen this feeling of discovery and adventure always is with me in your company.

As for the Cañon I won't waste any words on it, except to say that when I saw it I saw the picture I was trying to realize three years ago, when I was writing the last act of the *Masque*. This is the Valley of Judgment. I send you a sketch, dreadfully inadequate, of a glimpse of the north wall of the Cañon, from the Bright Angel Trail.

Ferd has telegraphed that he leaves Chicago Tuesday night. We leave here tomorrow for Cañon Diablo, where Norton knows a man who has some good horses, and who is willing to let us ride them while we are waiting for the laggard. We shall probably outfit and start into the Indian country at a place called Winslow, instead of Holbrook; I shall have to catch Ferd with a telegram to notify him of the change.

Remember me to the pink pup, and try to believe with him that I am not as mean as I seem.

My Easter greetings to you.

W—

The Oraibe Trading Post
F. W. Vol. 2
at Oraibe Village, Moque Indian Reservation
Postoffice, Cañon Diablo, Ariz. April 7, 1904

We arrived at this trading post Monday night, being greeted at the station by the German proprietor and a magnificent Navajo, the latter in full regalia. It was a shock to find that the splendid creature was there merely for the purpose of carrying our luggage; but he did it (under a full moon) with a grandeur which made all good.

It is a queer household into which we have been admitted. The post is owned by two brothers, both married to Indian wives, and one of them, who spent many years in Moki-land, himself a thorough Indian in gait, gesture, manner of speech and even countenance. He sits on the floor or ground crosslegged, never wears a hat, and gallops bareback over the stony desert with a sinuous and savage grace. Besides a solitary station agent and a few Mexican section hands, there are no white men here, but hour by hour there straggles in some picturesque devil of a Navajo on a lean pony and dressed in wonderful colors, to trade off a blanket or a piece of pottery. I could not resist buying a couple of old jars and waterbottles, which I shall forward. I dare say I was cheated, though the prices seemed ridiculously small.

We decided to await Ferd here rather than at Holbrook for several reasons. By going in this way we cross a portion of the Painted Desert; it is indeed visible from here, a sleeping sea of incredible color, over which the super-heated air throbs and quivers at midday. The water is more plentiful by this route, and the horses cheaper. We expect Ferd to arrive by the morning train tomorrow, and shall have all things ready for an immediate start. It will be a transformation scene such as he has seldom experienced — from a Pullman sleeper to a desert trail. My only anxiety is concerning his horsemanship.

The ponies here are at best only half-broken, and up to all sorts of tricks on no notice at all. Yesterday we took a ten mile ride across the desert to an extinct crater. Owing to Mrs. Norton's experience at the Cañon a pony was provided for her which was loudly acclaimed to be a 'kitten.' Somebody tightened the back cinch on the kitten too hard, and in the twinkling of an eye the little beast had jumped out of a circle of four men (over our heads, it seemed to me), had bucked the saddle off by a couple of stiff-legged jumps with bowed back, and was off for the horizon. If — as I seem to remember — Ferd has never ridden, he may have a hard time of it at first. However, it will be educative, and incidentally amusing to anyone except the victim. Probably I myself, in punishment for the boastful comparison here implied, shall be selected by Providence to provide the entertainment.

It seems impracticable to take horses for the whole trip, and we have about decided to hire them from the Indians for short stages, turning them and their owners back when we reach places where we want to stay a few days. Our general plan is to go from here to the first Moki village, Oraibi, where we shall stay perhaps a week. Then on to Walpi, the second most interesting Moki town. From there we shall go east to Keam's Cañon, where there is a trading post. Then northeast to the Cañon de Chelley, the site of some interesting and seldom-visited cliff dwellings. The last stage of the trip will be to Guado and Gallup, where we strike the railroad again. I shall get a letter off to you wherever there is a post-office, but I doubt much whether any exist on the route marked out; if not, it will be a fortnight or more before you can hear from me again.

I am hoping to hear from you by tomorrow's mail, or at any rate to find a note in Ferd's pocket. My love and knowledge of you seems to grow vaster here in the face of these silences and immensities, and the great drama of our lives to gain both solemnity and mirthfulness from each day that it is projected against this landscape of amazing light, primeval contour, and whimsical barbaric detail. I am living in the assured trust that you are taking care of yourself as well in the body as I am taking care of you in the spirit. Remember your promises to me in this particular, and *take time* to fulfill them. I shall accept no excuses. I know that it is impossible for you to find time, but now and always it is the impossible which I expect and demand of you; in all but a few particulars you unfailingly rise to the impossible, then why not in this one, where my desires are so strong, and our mutual life so much at stake.

W—

ORAIBI, APRIL —?
(*Tuesday*)
(Postmarked *April* 13, 1904)

The man at the trading post has just told me that a Hopi runner is to start for Keam's Cañon, thirty-five miles away, and that there is a post-office there. I send a word in the hope that the messenger may succeed in getting it into official hands.

Ferd turned up all right at Cañon Diablo on Friday. He was nearly five hours late, and the ponies had been saddled since morning when he at last, about two in the afternoon, hove in sight. I hustled him into a Wild-West rig in a jiffy, and had him on a horse and streaking it across the desert before he had time to catch his breath. The trip up was great. On account of our heavy baggage we took two days and a half to make the sixty-three miles, camping twice — the last time by a well called Big Burro Springs, to which all evening and next morning Navajos kept converging to camp or water — and wonderful creatures many of them are.

Here at Oraibi — officially known as the 'third mesa' we rented a little adobe house, and have installed our camp kit most completely. The Hopi village on the cliffs is the centre of a strangely picturesque life, which keeps us at the highest pitch of excitement; and the settlement at the foot of the mesa, where the school and government buildings are situated, is as full of humors, factions, and 'characters' as it can stick.

Fortunately for us, there are two men here who each in his own way know all there is to know about Hopiland. One is Aiken, a New York painter, who has been living for six months on the mesa in the native village, and dresses and looks more like an Indian than if he were the real thing. He has an entrancing little adobe house, from the roof of which one can see all over creation... even as far as Chicago, and into the heart of the dearest and greatest of women; her 'nobility' as viewed from this place of vantage appears to such credit that even she would be satisfied.

Our other helpful friend is one Voth, a German who has spent twelve years studying the Hopi language and folk-lore, and is a mine of surprising things. Our company has today been enlarged by the arrival of a chap named Sawyer, also ostensibly a painter but really an irreclaimable tramp to whom adventure is as the breath of the nostrils. He will probably go on with us from here, and will certainly provide entertainment if he does, for he is 'the West' in little. All this is to give you a few dry bones of fact into which you can breathe life sufficient.

Write me at Cañon Diablo. Ferd and I shall stop there on the way back to the Grand Cañon; and we may fit out there for a pony-trip south through the Tonto Basin.

W—

The newspaper clipping about *The Fire-Bringer* was enough to make one forswear the pen forever, wasn't it? Send me any others that turn up, in order that I may test my allegiance to my craft.

CAÑON DIABLO, *April* 23 (1904)

We are back at Volz's trading post again, having left the Nortons at Walpi. The two weeks spent in Hopiland have been among the most absorbing I have ever had. Ferd tells me he has written you about our great luck in seeing a two-days-long 'katchina dance' at Walpi — a kind of primitive Feast-of-all-Saints dating from no telling what antiquity, but as human and amusing as possible.

The other high points of light — from the point of view of curiosity — were a night spent in an underground 'khiva' (a kind of temple and lodgeroom combined) at Oraibi, and a race which I alone of our party was lucky enough to witness while fooling with my sketch pad on the slope of the Oraibi mesa. We got admission to the khiva through Aiken, a painter (of whom I told you) who has lived for six months at Oraibi, wearing the native clothes and speaking the language. We climbed down the ladder about nine o'clock, and stayed there, smoking with the old chiefs and watching the ceremonies carried on by the young men until early morning. The room was faintly illuminated by a little fire of brushwood, fed on tiny stick after stick by a priest who looked — and probably was — a couple of centuries old. He was withered and shrunk into a mere handful of brown parchment, but the old eyes under the secular hair gleamed out in the excited moments of the ceremony with an almost shocking vitality. Another priest crouched before the semicircle of dancers, beating upon a kind of drum to mark the rhythm, and inciting the young men with cries, at times warning and admonitory, and again exultant and encomiastic. There were about twenty dancers, naked except for moccasins, loincloths, necklace, bracelets and headdress of feathers and bright cloth. All sang as they danced — a legend, Aiken said — a song of interminable verses, so old that the meaning of much of it has been forgotten, and the words are now repeated merely for their hieratic significance. The dancers remained in position, marking the portentous rhythm by stamping with the right foot (to which a tortoise-shell rattle was tied) and by flexions of their shining bronze bodies.

The race was even more exotic and exciting. One evening after I had been trying to put down an impression of the pale gold desert with Indian red mesas in the distance, and had finally thrown away my paper in despair, I heard strange cries and panting breath below me; then suddenly there appeared a couple of dozen naked runners, with brilliant loin cloths and headdresses, rushing up the steep slope of the mesa in two bodies, each set of men working together to kick forward a little cubic ball of pitch and horse-hair. They went up the dizzy trail like a shot, and disappeared over the cliffs on which the town is built. I was told afterward that they were picked racers from rival khivas, that the race had started from the plaza of the village hours before and had led down the cliffs, out through the heavy sand of the desert in a five-mile circuit, and back again to the plaza; and that the game combined the religious with the athletic intention in the same way as the old Greek games. I see I am being betrayed into description which does not describe.

I wish you could see with your own eyes some of the patriarchal and primeval pictures which Ferd and I have seen these two weeks — groups of old women weaving baskets on the borders of the 'Flute Well,' while waiting for their water-jars to fill under the slow trickle, files of girls carrying jugs of water up the rocks, a distant line of dancers returning from Walpi to their home on the 'second mesa,' in ceremonial garb, four aged priests sprinkling sacred corn-meal to mark and hallow the path across the desert. The photographs which I send (films) will give you something, and one of these days — before the thing is spoiled by the missionaries and school teachers (and they are hard at it), you must go with me and see it for yourself.

The two good letters which I found awaiting me here were an undreamed-of luxury. They came at the end of a two-days battle with sand-storms and all the other devices which the desert knows for putting the human invader at a disadvantage, and they made the arrival here at this God-forsaken trading post seem like a real home-coming. Ferd and I are now weather-bound — in the grip of the worst sand-storm of the season. All the wind in the world has gathered up all the loose matter in creation, and is hurling it pulverized in our faces. If it clears tomorrow we are going with Volz into the mountains south of Flagstaff for perhaps three days, then to the Grand Cañon for perhaps three or four more.

W—

Telegram:

ALBUQUERQUE, N.M.
May 11, 1904

LEAVE HERE TODAY   ARRIVE CHICAGO
FRIDAY MORNING TRAIN NO. 2

W V M

(Postmarked Lake Zurich, Ill., May 27, 1904)

I shall stay here until we get the text[1] hammered into shape, which may take until Sunday or Monday. I found Lovett recalcitrant on several points of the revision which I consider essential, and have had to labor with him mightily; he is by this time silenced, though I fear not convinced. Still, the work is going forward bravely under the circumstances.

Sieg is in great feather. He is reasonably contented with our slow program of life during the morning, but immediately after luncheon begins his demand for fun, and keeps it up until it is met. We had a scamper today in the rain and mud, in the course of which he covered himself with a large portion of the superficial area of Lake County.

[1] The revision of the Moody-Lovett *History of Literature* — called *A First View of English Literature.*

(Postmarked Kramer, Ind.)
Sunday, July 3 (1904)

This reaches you from a wood on a breezy hilltop some miles from salubrious Mudlavia and from the midst of one of the most glorious summer Sunday afternoons you ever saw. I find the country surprisingly beautiful — surprising, because, although you praised it, I knew your tolerant affection for anything that haphazard Nature sees fit to do, and perhaps (unconsciously) minimized your report. It is a broad, homely, fruitful beauty which speaks home to me through old and all-but-forgotten associations.

I came in the nick of time (says the doctor, who may be working me) to save myself an acute attack which would have laid me up for months. The mark and index of his truth-speaking is that that wretched sore place on my hip had begun to be swollen and very painful. The swelling has almost subsided, and I move with an ease and luxury which I have not known for more than a year.

My daily regimen is — I am in the bath by six o'clock — *vero!* — by eight I am ready for breakfast, and by nine I am at my little table fiddling with my little job. I have had as yet but two baths, but feel already immensely benefited. I am sure they are a good thing.

RIVERHEAD, L.I., *Aug.* 13, 1904

My things I found all intact, nothing of any importance either broken or lost. Another day's work after I get back will make all good. The place (51 West 10th St.) is as charming as ever. I look forward to the winter there with settled pleasure.

51 West 10th St.
New York, *Aug.* 17 (1904)

A couple of days' exploration of Long Island resulted in a complete desire to get back to my good quarters here. The country is pretty and the ocean-beaches grand, but the hotels are an abomination of desolation, and there seems to be no place else to stay. So back I packed, and here I shall stick — at least until the book is well under way. Nobody is here except my sister and Robinson. Unless I strike a good vein of invention, and get absorbed in work, I shall be miserably lonesome. Our months of dear companionship have spoiled my palate for the solitary life. Nevertheless I must lead it, and must relearn the lesson of leading it with contentment and inner exultation.

51 West 10th St.
New York, *Aug.* 22 (1904)

A hot day in the Mercantile Library digging up pictures for the M & L nuisance, has left me rather dull, and what I want to do is to sit down beside you on the big sofa, and let you talk and joke me slowly into possession of the realities once more. This is the next best thing — with what a world between! a world of emptiness that multiplies itself by all the miles that separate me from the light of your gaiety and fancy and wisdom, and the beloved brightness of your bodily presence.

The book of R. M. L.'s which you spoke of has not turned up yet. No more has his manuscript, for which I am waiting with daily lessening patience. I don't feel like going away before the book is in press, and New York is a brazier.

Yesterday, to get away from the prostrating heat, I

took a boat for Coney Island, and had an afternoon and
evening of solid fun wandering about that miracle of vulgarity. Or really it is not vulgar; it is too perfect of its
kind. I have seen the Parthenon, I have read the Tempest,
I have beheld Coquelin play comedy, I have experienced
not a few of the human grand examples, but anything
more consummate than Coney Island I have never
gazed upon. It is a Wonder. You would like it to the
ground.

NEW YORK, *August* 28 (1904)

I send you a copy of the new song I have written for the
Eve. It is still a bit rough, and I am not sure that when it
ʿgets cold I shall like it; but I remember your protest when
I said I had better not send you unfinished work, and so I
let you have it with all its imperfections on its head. Just
now, in the heat of composition, it seems to me good. At
least it embodies our great Idea — the Great Idea — that
much you will be willing to grant, whether it seems to you
to have the one thing needful, the 'float' and ecstacy of a
real song, or not. It just spouted out that way, and it will
have to lie a long time *perdu* before I can make it substantially different.

The city is giving signs of awakening from its dog-day
torpor. Several theatres open this week, and there will be
something doing to shorten the cruelly empty hours between dusk and bed-time. The streets, with their summer
nonchalance and human *laissez-faire*, are absorbing, and
wonderful. Like old poet Herrick in Devonshire, who

'Ne'er endited such
Ennobled numbers for the press,
As where I loathed so much'

[203]

it seems to me I never loved and understood this amazing city as well as now when I am so loathly lonesome in it.

If you see Lovett tell him that Lord, and incidentally I, would like to know when he is going to show up with his manuscript.

(Postmarked New York, Sept. 5, 1904)

I send you under another cover a piece [1] I have just finished, suggested by an experience I had in Greece of which I think I wrote you. Don't blame me for sending these things if they seem to you poor. You know you made me promise to send whatever I happened to do, and it gives me a feeling of home and nearness to share them with you immediately. I have already rewritten the opening and close, to the thing's advantage.

My life here is absolutely eventless, so far as any external or describable happening is concerned. The city lies jaded and nerveless under the long heat, only reviving enough in the evening to show that it still possesses a latent capacity to be alive. My room, however, with its northern exposure and two big windows, is usually cool, and I am enjoying myself in a subterranean sort of way pretty thoroughly.

The hot weather brings queer types of people out of their holes, as it brings cockroaches and waterbugs out of wood-work; I have encountered several such, at pick-me-up table d'hôtes, who are stranger than caricature could make them. One of them, a peak-headed advertising agent, music-hall pianist, and all-round littérateur, just now dropped in to borrow a dollar, and confided to me incidentally that he had spent so large a portion of his time

[1] *Second Coming.*

in an insane asylum, where library facilities were poor that he had got permanently rusty, and practically lost his style. When I politely inquired in what capacity he was there, he replied, without any embarrassment, and with even a touch of pride, 'As patient.'

NEW YORK, *Sept.* 8, 1904

Your last two little notes have been a pure delight to me, so full and fresh seems the happy spirit that they breathe, so filled with sweet assurance of the goodness of our past and the loveliness of our future. I love to think of you living alone in the house, ordering your day and indulging your mood as you will, without disturbing influences. I am even glad, for a time, not to be myself a disturbing influence, so precious to me is the clear stream of your individuality, with its eddies of bright whim and its wave-crests of flashing contradiction. I seem to see you these days with a vividness unknown till now, and to love you therefore with a love that reaches through vision to divination. My life floats in a golden medium of pleasure which is the thought and knowledge of you, and thankfulness that there has been given me for a life-friend a spirit so large and radiant and fruitful, so tender and swift to respond along all the farflung lines of our communicating natures. Give me more notes from the workroom. I like them.

NEW YORK, *Sept.* 13 (1904)

I have been at work for the past few days on a longish affair which has kept me going about rather in a trance than responsibly awake, so that, though never nearer to you, I seem to have neglected you in the terms of that world where the post-office serves for communication. Meanwhile two notes from you have floated into my consciousness, and left a radiance there which surprises me when I see it by chance, having forgotten the cause.

The play which derives its title from the Duke of Killikrankie is, by the way, a good deal of a joy, though excellently ill-played by the ligneous J. Drew. Pinero has a new play on here, *Letty*, which I see tonight. Zangwill's *Serio-comic Governess* with Cissy Loftus, also promises capable entertainment. You must come and see these while they are fresh.

Lovett's manuscript turned up at last, and I threw it at Lord without looking at it. In three weeks or so the proof will begin to roll its world-suffocating folds from the window of Charles Scribner's Sons.

NEW YORK, *Sept.* 18 (1904)

I want very much to write to you just now, but I haven't anything that I want to say. The fact is that our most real communion with each other, and most real significance for each other, operate in a region where language has not yet penetrated to create the loose and easy symbols by which our ordinary empiric life explains itself to itself and others. Perhaps this is the source of the feeling you often give voice to, of being about to perceive and make known some beautiful world-secret. If you and I could ever say Good-morning in such a manner as to really express our meaning, we should go straight on to glory, towing the astonished universe after us. 'Is it not so?' 'Good-morning,' 'Good night,' 'I am happy,' 'Did you rest well?' 'Is it becoming?' — over what gulfs of meaning we walk on these little bridges, what loads of cosmic matter we lift and swing into place with these frail levers! I wish you would make a poem about it.

I have been at work (rather feverishly) for some days on a blank verse study of the old 'Fountain of Youth' theme, the idea being (as you perhaps remember my exploiting it once in conversation) that there actually is such a thing and that some people find it. I have used the legendary setting of the old Spanish story. I will send you the new piece as soon as I have copied it. My chief fear about it is that it is too 'picturesque,' that the reader will take it at its face value and feel no uneasiness. Please tell me what you think. Let the embargo on comment for this time be raised.

NEW YORK, *Sept.* 23, 1904

I am glad you are to see Aiken. If he is half as good as a rank and file American as he was as a wild-eyed Navajo, you will be delighted with him. I hope he is coming on here afterwards.

Your metaphor about the star-ship is so much better than the verses which, being still in the grand realm of possibility, evoked it, that there is no justice in the exchange. I thought the *Fountain of Youth* piece really good when I sent it to you, but as usual it has shrunk in the wash. Still the idea is good, if that's any comfort! I shall be interested in the book about 'insufficient knowing.' Of course that is all that is the matter with anything, in the last resort.

It is so dark that I must stop writing or get a new pair of eyes. A compromise course would be to get a gallon of coal oil, and this shall be my earliest care.

NEW YORK, *Sept.* 25 (1904)

That is indeed very wonderful, the double coincidence of your mood with mine while I was at work on the *Fountain*. As for the verse-form, I tried to write, as you see, from the point of view of one who had not found, was in fact almost despairingly far from finding, but who surmised wistfully from observation. I thought such an approach would be more poignant, or at least more conceivable and 'convincing.' I dare say I was wrong. At any rate the poem which you suggest is an entirely different and finer one and must sometime be written; but even when it is, I think it will be better for having this one — written from the outside and therefore not 'light' — as a companion, don't you? I was much out of conceit with it for a day or two, but begin to pluck up a little faith in it again.

I am having fun now with something which you will have to excuse, and like, as a mere doggerel skit, called *Old Pourquoi*. It is a free and easy recital of an experience I once related to you, of meeting an old man on a Norman road, singing over and over to a weird tune, '*Pourquoi? Pourquoi?*'

I know that I am writing too fast, and that much of this stuff — or all of it — will have to go into the stove: but I can't seem to do anything about it.

NEW YORK, *Sept.* 30, 1904

McComas's [1] report of Thompson's [2] words is very interesting. But if he said that I am doing the same thing that he is and doing it better, he is doubly wrong. I am not doing the same thing, and I have never done anything as good as his *Hound of Heaven*.

[1] Francis McComas.　　　[2] Francis Thompson.

I have just been reading Maeterlinck's *Double Garden*, and I want to say in sackcloth and ashes that all you have claimed for him is true, and more. I have not been so stirred and stung by any book for a decade. He is a great, sincere, prophetic soul; and I envy him with that kind of envy which between men is the keenest variant of love. I could have sworn that no man who had not been blessed with a knowledge of you could have written the essay called *Portrait of a Lady*. *Our Friend the Dog*, and *A Leaf of Olive* are the other two pieces which most completely bowled me over, unless *Sincerity* did it to me worse. There is also a superb piece on the *Automobile*, and another on the *Wrath of the Bee*, and still another on the *Temple of Chance* at Monte Carlo. An imperishable book.

NEW YORK, *Oct.* 26 (1904)

When I telegraphed you I expected to get off today, but have decided to stay until tomorrow, partly to see dear old Mrs. Gilbert tonight in a play called *Granny*, written especially for her farewell tour, where she finds herself a 'star' for the first time now after sixty years of stage life. She is eighty-three years old, and a better artist today than she ever was. Talk about the fountain of youth! Last night I saw *Romeo and Juliet* — on the whole with deep satisfaction, though it is jolly raw here and there — just for a moment, however. Julia Marlowe has 'grown' remarkably, and while she hasn't got the rich alluvial nature which breeds the caprice and wild, apt invention of the true actress, she is often so near the real thing as to make the spirit groan. Sothern rose astonishingly at the crisis of the play, I thought. I mean after the news of Juliet's

[209]

death. I took your advice and bought a front seat; it is one of earth's best luxuries.

I send you Mrs. Toy's letter — partly for the curious repetition of the Thompson-Meynell legend, partly for her mention of Joe as he was when she last saw him. She is a kind of Cambridge Egeria, who was awfully kind to me when I was an undergraduate, as she was to the rest of us in our budding greatness.

NEW YORK, *Oct.* 29 (1904)

The theatre is my grand resource. There are several things here which you ought to see. One is David Warfield in a play called *The Music-Master*, dealing with life on the East Side. The play is poor enough, but Warfield is an authentic genius if one ever trod the stage, and he lifts the thing from moment to moment into greatness. It is the most richly human piece of acting I have seen in years. Réjane comes next week, and will doubtless later penetrate as far as Chicago. If she comes read the play beforehand, and sit near; you will have a feast, I think, though she may not satisfy your demand in comedy: who indeed can do that? We are to have two *Parsifals* this winter, one in German and one in English. This time I shall give myself a chance to really hear it.

NEW YORK, *Nov.* 8 (1904)

This is election day, quiet here in my den as a safe-deposit vault, but the air is full of subtle excitement. Portentous issues for each one of us, for the country and the world, are being decided by that silent snow of white ballots, falling by millions and millions all over the land. My imagination is strangely possessed by the continual downdrift of assent to or negation of the new policies. If the verdict is one of assent, I believe that the vision in the light of which our country was created and has grown great, will soon fade, and one more world-dream will have been found impossible to live out. Our different destiny may be greater, but the America that we have known and passionately believed in, will be no more. This I know you don't agree to, and think me a bit narrow and vehement in the spirit with which I contemplate the facts. I pray God it may be proved to be so, and that all which seems to me a reversion to discredited ideals in government and national spirit, may be found to be an advance toward a new and more generous order. Anyhow it will be good fun to watch the returns, which, in company with Robinson and some odd millions of noble Romans, I propose to do till daylight.

What do you mean by the cryptic allusion to the 'hero of my potential drama'? The — case [1]? Be sure and send me everything you find out about that.

Réjane is here — the most extraordinary creature — all pure genius except what is pure *cocotte*.

Write me as often as you can — your letters do me a world of good; I am working in slate like a hardluck miner and need all your beautiful lightness of spirit.

W.

(Postmarked Nov. 14, 1904)

The 'undertone of restlessness' which you say you notice in my letters is due to the fact that I find myself rather low-keyed in energy, rather lazy and sluggish. I am

---

[1] The first reference to the occurrence on which his play, *The Great Divide*, was based.

perfectly well, but the abundance and overplus of vitality which I need to do the work I want to do, visits me capriciously or not at all. It will return again any day, but I always find it hard to tide over these low places. Formerly, when my periods of freedom were hard-earned and strictly bounded, my impatience magnified a few weeks or even days of dulness, into Gehennah and the Last Trump. But now I can afford, humanly speaking, to wait. If I don't pick up my elasticity by the end of the month, I will go down to the Gulf and lie around in the sand.

I got hold of the Hauptmann play,[1] and shall send it to you tomorrow. It has taken me sometime to read it, for it is in an almost undecipherable dialect. It is undeniably strong, and undeniably brutal, though I guess the brutality is *versöhnt* in the end. I hear Réjane tonight in *La Robe Rouge*, a Tendenz-play, an attack on French legal procedure.

If you worry about me on account of what I have told you of my sluggish fit, it will be a very uncomradely return for frankness. I am perfectly well, and shall any day enter into a zone of fresh energy somewhere along my orbit.

NEW YORK, *Nov.* 18 (1904)

I send you the new version of the *Fountain*. I'm afraid you won't stand for it even yet, but it is certainly nearer right than it was before, and the second of the four lyrics is a beauty, if I do say it.

I have been knocking the *caput mortuum* of the unfinished play about the mazard with the spade of revision, but not to much purpose. Still, I think I will work it over and finish it, just for luck. When I bang it hard enough it

---

[1] *Die Waber* (*The Weavers*), by Gerhardt Hauptmann.

[212]

wags its mouldy jaws in semblance of life. I await with
immense interest the further facts of the —— case.[1] But
the kind of play I itch to write is something quite different
from anything that could be made out of that story. I saw
Sothern's Hamlet, and was forced to wonder once more
at your superhuman generosity and tolerance. Our own
Isaiah would do it nearer the modesty of nature. Marlowe's Ophelia, however, I thought astonishingly good,
considering.

I have a letter from Lodge [2] saying that he has found
among Joe Stickney's papers, besides the poems which we
both knew to exist, a prose account of his trip to Greece.
He went the year after I did, and at my urgence. He went
all over much of my line of travel; the account ought to
be wonderfully interesting, as he knew so much about
Greece before he went. He also left a translation of one of
the Hindoo religious books, in French, done in collaboration with his Sanskrit teacher at the University of Paris.
This is to be published in Paris, as a memorial to him, by
his friends there.

This morning Phillips's new play was advertised. I got
it at once and read it, and send it to you in the hope of
forestalling McClurg in his unemotional ministrations.
It is — but I will not tell you what I think of it until you
have read it in peace — then you can tell me.

I think now that I shall go south about the first of
December with the idea of staying down there a month.

On second thought I am keeping the *Fountain* by me for
a while longer, to ascertain if the flow is permanent and of
standard quality.

[1] The *Great Divide* story.
[2] George Cabot Lodge.

(Postmarked Nov. 24, 1904)

The proof of the *His. of Lit.* is rolling in day by day in huge bundles. There are several cart-loads of it stowed away about the room. I haven't had the courage to investigate closely, but it must be nearly all in type now. I shall take it south with me when I go, about the end of next week, but shall not try to do much with it until I get to Chicago.

(Postmarked Charleston, S.C., Dec. 4, 1904)
SS. Apache
Off Charleston, Sunday

We have had thus far a dark and stormy passage, and I should have done better to take the train. Still, my fellow-passengers have given me a good deal of interesting information about Florida, which will be of value. From all that I can hear St. Augustine is not a first-rate place to stay. The places recommended are much farther south, on the coast — Palm Beach and Miami. From the latter place steamers run to the Bahamas and to Cuba.... I feel very much like a vagabond and a loafer to be knocking about at this season of the year which is, by all the laws, dedicated to work; but for some reason I am in poor tone, and must perforce lie *perdu* for a while. You must not worry about me in the least. I am perfectly well, though quite good for nothing. A couple of weeks loafing in the sun will taut my strings again and put music in me.

I had to leave some juicy bits of entertainment in New York: Nance O'Neill is about to give a verse-play by T. B. Aldrich on the Judith theme, and later an English version of the *Medea* of Euripides. I saw her in Sudermann's *Johannisfeuer* — a capital thing. She is not as much of an actress as I took her to be, when I saw her in *Hedda*: her style is rather hard, and her passages of sentiment — where she forces herself to take the note — excruciatingly falsetto. The night before I left I heard *Parsifal* sung. Behind me sat of course ——, who smiled and nodded in evident relish of this new version of the old joke, and kept a sharp lookout for you under my coat.

Milton Sills going on the stage! One more matinee idol, and — I fear — one more poor actor. But his great intelligence will help him, perhaps save him. At any rate, it is a beautiful sign of the times that a youth of his equipment should care to dedicate himself to that career.

I did not think that you treated poor Phillips's play too harshly, unless to say anything at all is in such a case to be unkind. Thin it is, and while you may be right in saying it is honest in intention, it is not honest in result, in effect. Quite dishonest. 'Good things about it,' of course, but let us not do him the discourtesy to mention them, since nothing wounds and impoverishes like such sorry amends made to failure. I speak who know.

FLORIDA HOUSE
ST. AUGUSTINE, FLA., *Dec.* 7, 1904

This proves to be a very sympathetic little town, quaint and mellow, not at all touristy, at least not yet, a month before the season. I have partly explored the country round about, and found many rewarding bits. The negroes are a joy forever. The hotel where I have taken up my quarters is quiet, comfortable, and clean. Altogether I am well satisfied, and shall doubtless stay on here.... The weather, I am grieved to say, is rather cold for out-of-door life, and is reported so all over. This does not especially affect me, because when I am out I am exercising.... Though shorn of some of its strenuousness, winter is still winter here in the South, and short of Cuba or Bermuda I guess it can't be persuaded to be anything else, before the end of February anyhow.

I witnessed last night, at the 'Opera House,' a dramatic composition entitled *A Daughter of Satan*, described as an 'opera' by the local press, but that it appears, is a generic term for all works produced in the Opera House. It was a most wondrous piece written and played by romanticists of the vividest. The audience, which was about one-half darky, accompanied the action with a commentary the naïve passion and unconsciousness of which I have never seen approached, even in Italy, and that is saying much. We dispersed at the end in an exhausted condition but treading the air and uttering hoarse whispers of exaltation. If that kind of appreciation could only be got for developed art, which is lavished upon the primitive! I mean if we could get the same intensity, the same self-forgetting generosity and beautiful ardor. Instead of that, comparison and the lack-lustre eye. *Basta*.

(M. V. M. seems to have returned to New York by way of Chicago.)

(Postmarked New York, Jan. 17, 1905)

Here I am back in my den, which looks a little shabby, dull, and discouraged, as if it had resigned itself to not being cared for and lived in. I feel immeasurably better than when I left New York. I shall settle down to my winter's work with a good heart.

I send back *The Bowl* at once, to let you see how right

was your divination as to its outcome. It is a great story. I got so absorbed in the last chapter that I did not know when we reached Jersey City, and had to be thrown off by the porter, my bag on top of me. I don't quite reconcile myself to the Bowl's being smashed, in spite of the bully '*scène à faire*' which it makes — the fascinating Hawthornesque 'lead' seems to end in an inconsequence. But I remember that you were disdainful of the thing as a mere symbol, and perhaps its destruction follows a higher logic than that of mere symbolism. However, as for me, I like my toys.

I must stop in order to be in time for a ticket to the *Winter's Tale*, which is being played tonight, and which I have never seen.

NEW YORK, *Jan.* 21 (1905)

These last days have been rather uneventful and unprofitable, having been consumed chiefly in chasing down the pictures for the *History of Lit.* I have at least the satisfaction of knowing that I have got good ones. There is a preface to be written and two more proofs (a 'revise' and a page proof) to be read — then so help me God I will never touch the blooming business again.

Today, all unexpected and undeserved, the Muse walked in at my window, and gave me a few blissful hours. With soiled hands I took her, and she never minded them. Man is not saved by his works, but by grace.

The *Winter's Tale* was pretty badly butchered, but as I had never seen it before I was held spell-bound at the same time that I was acutely irritated — a sort of combination of cocktails and black coffee, so far as the nervous wreckage went. The Autolycus was a crime which, in any reasonable society, would have had to be expiated at the whipping post; but Viola Allen's Hermione and Perdita have elements of charm, of course nothing to hurt.

Torrence turned up the other day, just back from his native Ohio village where he has been attempting to regain his vagrom faculties. We went to Bossi's, my McDougal Street pirate's, to lunch, and had an amusing afternoon. It will interest you sometime to meet him (Torrence). He told me of an old lady of seventy-five whom he met in a North-Wisconsin town, who had my immortal works at her fingers' ends. I should think this a fable but that flattery is not his lay. He is staying with Stedman out at Bronxville; I have it in mind to go out there to see the dear old boy, perhaps tomorrow afternoon. Torrence tells me that Edwin Markham (*The Man with the Hoe*) has written a long poem on the search for the Fountain of Youth, which is to appear serially in the *Century*, in five parts. He was unable to say whether it was written with the hoe, or with some less strenuous and epic instrument.

Well, here is a deal of words which no woman could be grateful for, especially one with intolerant views on letters in general and my letters in especial. There is only one thing really to say, that I am dreadfully alone without my gay and disquieting and ever incalculable companion, upon whose shifting moods I have learned to build from hour to hour my house of life.

NEW YORK, *Jan.* 25 (1905)

We are having a very devil of a blizzard here. I have just floundered out to dinner and back again through snowdrifts five feet deep, and am trying in vain to keep warm by a red-hot stove. Gales shake the old house to its centre, and drive the fine snow through the loose-fitting windows in most comfortless little heaps. A storm is so excellent a thing to envelop two, and so dreary when it howls round a companionless human unit, deprived of his gumption by insistent memories. The situation cries out upon you for a supreme bungler in life, that you are not here, or do not instantly transport yourself hither. Never set yourself up again as an artist in this province, for it is the first duty of an actress to take her cue. The stage is set, the lights are up, the entrance has been delicately led up to, and Madame L'Etoile is — asleep in the greenroom, to wit making a rarebit for Henderson or reading German to Ferd, in blatant negation of her own thesis that life is short.

Sunday afternoon I journeyed out to Bronxville to pay my respects to Stedman, and stayed to supper with him. The old fellow was vastly interesting, especially in his reminiscences of Whitman, whom he knew for many years. His excitement over things, his immense flow of spirits and of talk, in the midst of manifest physical weakness, filled me with humility before the wonderful little man, which his pathos and humanity turned into complete surrender.

Next Sunday Torrence is going to take me over to Staten Island to see Markham — a very different pair of sleeves. Which reminds me that H. James is probably by this time in Chicago, certainly is, in fact, and that, as I suddenly perceive, is the reason why you no longer take the trouble to write to me.

Aiken called the other day, and left his card, but I have not seen him yet. Arnold Daly is giving a new Shaw stunt (new to me) called *You Never Can Tell*, vastly amusing and *méchant*. As you say, he is dangerously intelligent, the danger being of course chiefly to himself, and he'll be damned if he's afraid.

The Muse seems inclined to give me about one good day in five. Perhaps that is all one could expect from a person of her sex, and spoiled as she is by too many lovers.

NEW YORK, *Jan.* 31 (1905)

What do you think of this, the latest lyric outpouring of the sweet singer of the Wabash?

ODE TO A SAW-MILL

'All hail to thee, most terrible invention,
Which chews up trees to any wished dimension,
And when Man doesn't pay attention,
Will chop him up so that a Government pension
Won't do him any good —
O fell destroyer thou of men and wood!'

I shall write again tomorrow to make up for this scrawl.

Yours,

W—

(Postmarked Feb. 1, 1905)

Joe Stickney's [1] papers reached me today, and I have spent the afternoon with them. Lovely, lovely things are here, precious above rubies. He left an astonishing amount of verse, though a large part of it, alas, is fragmentary. But there is enough for a good volume of perfect work, thrice refined. His dear spirit has been strangely near me while I read, and seemed to know, what was apparent to me as if breathed from angelic trumpets, that his life was gathered up, completed, and immortally justified. Some of the love-poems are of a poignancy unequalled in English

[1] Joseph Trumbull Stickney, who died in October, 1904.

verse, I verily believe. I shall copy out some of them to send to you. Many of the later lyrics seem to show a premonition of death, but of course it is easy to read the event back into them.

(Postmarked Feb. 10, 1905)

What you say of the 'glorious sleigh-ride' is worth its weight in gold as an illustration of the divine gift you have for making over any old situation into happiness and fun.

Louis Aiken came in at this point to tell me that Fred Volz, the Indian trader at Cañon Diablo who was so kind to me and Ferd, is in town, and to suggest that we combine forces in making the stock of recollections which he shall take back to the desert, as large and luscious as possible. We shall start in at Chinatown and come up the Bowery, then negotiate as much of Broadway as our heads and purses permit. You can picture me for some ensuing days as living on the proceeds of my pawned jewelry, and wishing that the Croton Aqueduct held nothing but soda water.

(Postmarked New York, Feb. 15, 1905)

Aiken and our wild friend from the bush turned up here last night, with vineleaves in their hair and saturnalia in their eyes. I wreathed a few preliminary strands for my own brows, and forth we sallied on the loose and misty. Now, at six P.M. of the next day, I am beginning to wonder whether after all it won't be possible in another twenty-four hours to begin to distinguish between the revolution of the earth and the revolution of my head on their respective axes, and to calculate with something like accuracy the respective diameters of the same. I already can state with inexpressible relief that, of the two, head is perceptibly the smaller, and that the cosmic business of revolving cannot therefore be held to rest upon it alone to the exclusion of the neighboring ball so clearly adapted by its contour to discharge this simple mission. It was vastly amusing to watch (so long as watching anything was in question) the grim and contained delight with which the old scamp, gnarled and hardened by thirty-odd years of pioneer life in the hardest country in the world, sat down to his meal of metropolitan dissipation. He will be in Chicago from Thursday on for a few days. It would pay you to have him to dinner, if he would talk, for he is a mine of thrilling reminiscence. He would probably be too ill at ease to open his head, but possibly not, and anyhow you would be interested in him as a type.

Aiken has a very beguiling studio, embracing the whole attic floor of a house on 20th St., with an open fireplace, bath, kitchen, and bedroom, for all of which he pays but five hundred dollars. It has quite put me out of conceit with my own quarters. He knows he is lucky; it is the sort of bargain which can be picked up only once in a lifetime, but I am going to keep my weather eye out for another such all the same.

Joe Stickney's sister Lucy, his favorite sister and devoted friend, is in New York to study painting. I called on her Saturday, and she told me a great deal about the last months of Joe's life. She said he was about to join me out west (I had written him from Arizona to come) when he was taken ill. He worked at his poetry almost up to the very end, in spite of severe pain in his head.

I am re-reading the *Vita Nuova* with the greatest delight.

Have you read it lately? If not, begin it now, and we will read it by stages together. If the Italian is too hard, use Rossetti's or Norton's translation.

NEW YORK, *Feb.* 22 (1905)

You are a complete and wistful brick to have done the honors for him (Volz) so gloriously. I would have given my head to be there. He was doubtless no flatterer at all when he said he had passed the happiest evening in forty years. You are probably the first real Woman he ever saw, and he has got nature enough to realize what a portent it was that had risen upon him.

Yeats's plays are being given here this week — *Land of Heart's Desire, Cathleen ni Houlihan,* and *The Hour-Glass.* I shall see them Friday, but I know already just how thin they are — and just how thick, too, mind you, so don't lecture me. There is something exquisitely false about that Irish business, and it comes so near being exquisitely true. There is more strong meat of suggestion for me as to what the stage ought to be, in one good opera than in all the plays I have seen this winter put together and raised to the nth. And I don't care much for the opera as such, either.

NEW YORK, *Feb.* 24 (1905)

I heard the Yeats plays this afternoon, and am bound to say that my opinion of them has been raised not a little by seeing them on the stage. They had the unspeakable advantage of an actress — Margaret Wycherley — who, besides being enchanting to look at, is wonderfully permeated with the poetic spirit. Her impersonation of the Fool in the little morality-play *The Hour-Glass* was as touching a piece of histrionic lyricism as I ever saw on the stage. The most ambitious of the three plays — the *Land of Heart's Desire* — was much the least effective.

(Postmarked Feb. 28, 1905)

Today is springlike and warm here, full of adorable promise, and amounting, like all promises that are rich enough, almost to realization, if not quite. Tomorrow we shall be wading in a foot of snow, but for all that the secret is out, and spring is irrefutably on the way.

A man named Keenan [1] has inaugurated a novel and promising dramatic enterprise here at the Berkeley Lyceum, a tiny theatre about the size of a parrot cage, but just the right size for his scheme. It is to give small plays, mostly one-acters, in groups of two or three, on the plan of the Théâtre Antoine at Paris. I saw his opening exhibit last night — three little plays, one from the French, one an adaptation of a tale of Poe (capital fun) and the other a simplehearted but taking melodramatic skit by some Western newspaper man. Keenan himself proves to be an accomplished actor. Altogether, there is sap in it.

(Postmarked March 17, 1905)
NEW YORK, *Friday*

True to its waking promises, the day has given me some beautiful creative hours — all in the mist, of course, but darkening and spangling here and there into the semblance of excellent shapes. As if to set a seal on my renewed hope and confidence comes in the morning mail a letter from Richard Watson Gilder, saying all sorts of hyperbolical

[1] Frank Keenan.

things, and enclosing a sonnet made to my poetical eye-brows. It seems that after I left him Sunday evening he began to read my works (I take it for the first time, seriously) and was moved before going to bed to record his feelings. I send the verses, to show you what generous impulses can survive — in certain human breasts — after thirty years of magazine editing. As coming from an elderly and much-immersed man, himself a disappointed poet and compelled by his profession to hold a gently skeptical position toward the whole subject, I call that little copy of verses a remarkable human document, giving all sorts of pledges for our common human nature.

I am taking my stunning little niece tonight to see *Hamlet,* and have half an hour to dress and make the Waldorf.

(Postmarked March 18, 1905)
NEW YORK, *Saturday*

This is your birthday, and in honor of it the Spring is here, not grudging or tentative but giving all at once in an ecstasy of surrender. It is divinely warm, and the people go 'delicately walking in most pellucid air.'

Everything — town, river, sky, and the multitude of human faces — shines as with a kind of sacred ointment, the Biblical oil of joy. I have been wandering about in a trance, finding myself in the most unexpected places, and feeling in each case that was the one place on the earth to be.

I had a delightful evening with my little niece. We went down to 'Little Hungary,' which proved to have St. Patrick for its saint and uproar for its creed. We were so entertained that we stayed all evening, and let *Hamlet* slide.

[225]

(Postmarked March 19, 1905)

By virtue of the jealousy of God, which fears that we humans, if too favored, might rise up and dispute his throne, today is as dark, damp, and uncharitable as yesterday was divinely bright and bestowing. Internal weather conditions equally poor, absurd barometer that I am. I have been sulking about all day, picking up and laying down, scratching in and scratching out, doing and undoing with a feverish persistence. Lamplight, and you at the other end of this sheet of paper, bring again the taste of life and belief in the reality of things.

I saw Robertson's [1] Hamlet last night, and am jolly glad I did. His reading of the character was wonderfully 'high-bred,' and that is one of the qualities urgently demanded and pitiably lacking in the performance of the ordinary romantic yokel who tackles the part. The subtlety, grace, controlled and responsive energy, alertness, humor, quick divining affection and imperial scorn — all these and a hundred other qualities of the character he gave with beautiful truth. Where he failed was in the moments of intense excitement, of volatilized and whirling passion, and he failed there signally, but there was something about the failure which made you feel that it was due to a wrong theory of the character rather than to lack of innate power. Certainly there has been nothing to touch this performance since Booth.

(*March* 21, 1905)

I am a good deal excited over the prospect of seeing *Richard III* tonight, having never seen it. I wish that it were to be given by some one besides the pig-headed and

[1] Forbes-Robertson.

automatic Mansfield. His engagement here includes Molière's *Misanthrope* for which we must give him credit.

I have got an idea buzzing in my head which keeps me awake nights. It looks tremendously good, but whether it will prove fruitful 'you never can tell, sir, you never can tell.' I shall keep it to myself until I find out, and then, if it is really good, for a year and a day after that.

(During this interval W. V. M. was probably in Chicago some part of the time.)

(Postmarked April 18, 1905)
NEW YORK, *Tuesday*

Charlotte met me with a face set like a flint against taking any steps without consultation with Dr. Janeway. She has a wholesome dread of surgeons and surgery, and says she will not consent to an operation until it is pronounced for by a physician — I mean a non-surgical practitioner. We went at once to see Janeway, who is no doubt the greatest diagnostician we have, but he had no hour free until Wednesday morning. At half-past ten tomorrow we shall know what he says. Our further action will be determined by his advice. You may have confidence in its being nothing rash, for Charlotte is a determined little conservative in such matters.

On the train was Faversham and his company, twelve in all, having just 'broken training' at Cleveland and being en route for London. They were of all ages and estates, but all alike in the charming abandon with which they delivered themselves to the spirit of holiday. A more beguiling set of great overgrown children I never coped withal. Faversham himself the most boyish and awkwardly frank of celebrities, manifestly a little discomfited by the overwhelming elegancies of his third-form confederates, who — whether as a customary and diurnal glory or in celebration of their liberty regained — sported a collection of shirts, neckties, waistcoats and socks not matched since Beau Brummel gave the snub to Wales. The element in which we swam, and in which these rainbow accoutrements displayed themselves to incredible advantage, was whiskey and soda. Especially native to this element was the heavy man who played the sheeny lover to Letty, who so horribly resembled his stage counterfeit that his mildest order to the waiter threw that functionary into a catalepsy of awe and terror. They were all good fellows and children of light, though perhaps a little over-prone to box-office receipts as a theme of rhapsody, instead of Apollo and the Muses.

I did not misunderstand your praise of my lyrics to mean any derogation from my dramatic powers. Both the one and the other you set only too high value on — a value representing, let me hope, some hint that is in them, of the not yet attained but attainable beauty.

(Postmarked New York, April 20, 1905)

Janeway made a very careful examination. He was unwilling to commit himself to any definite diagnosis, except that the case was plainly surgical, and that there was nothing which medicine could do for it; upon my asking him to recommend a conservative surgeon he sent me to Dr. Bull. Bull is at the head of his profession here, and has the reputation for great brilliancy combined with great caution and unwillingness to operate when less drastic measures are possible. Bull, though confessing himself unable to say exactly what the trouble was, pronounced unhesitatingly as to the necessity of operating. His view was on the whole optimistic. He feels sure that (unless unforeseen and improbable difficulties arise) I will be out of the hospital and well on the way to recovery in a fortnight. The hospital is his own private one, very comfortable and bright.

(An operation was performed April 21 for some kind of growth on the leg.)

(Postmarked May 2, 1905)

The formalities have been longer and more tedious than usual today, but the wave of hospital routine has at last rolled by, taking the lunch tray with it.

I tried to pin Dr. Bull down to a date, but he refused to emerge from the official region of vague optimism. The visual aspect of the 'wound' gives me little encouragement. It is as deep as a well and as broad as a church door, and looks as if it would serve for any end of diabolical and unbearable detention.

I began today and am reading with huge interest Villari's *Life of Savonarola*. It contains a good deal of padding — Italian politics, Florentine constitution, contemporary systems of philosophy, etc. — which might render the whole distasteful to you, but the life-story is a most thrilling one, and I think you agree with me that next to the highest imaginative writing biography is the best thing going.

I am sitting up today as large as life, revelling in the view of an exciting strip of street wherein the children of men, under their quaint delusion of reality, are hurrying up and down, fantastically preoccupied with their dream-errands. Street, house-fronts, and strip of sky are bathed in a liquid freshness. The roar that comes up from the city is more buoyant, higher in key, and more suggestive of musical rhythms than I ever heard it before. It is wonderful how the diminution of physical energy and of egotistic purpose which sickness brings, vivifies and clarifies the finer senses. It seems almost to amount to a demonstration of the ascetic doctrines which I have spent a large part of my time detesting as false and mischievous. Thus by devious ways are we instructed. Thus are we brought step by step into the Pantheon, and learn to worship all the gods without dogma or division of heart.

Dr. Bull yesterday evaded my questions as to the probable length of time I shall have to remain in the hospital. Today, however, he volunteered the opinion that in case everything goes as well as at present, I ought to get out by the end of next week — i.e., about the twelfth.

MacKaye called on me yesterday, bearing messages from Saint-Gaudens and others of the Cornish colony to the effect that I must without fail visit their neighborhood. In case I go to Newton I will run up to Cornish for a few days.

After re-reading MacKaye's poem, I have come to the conclusion that the great trouble with it is that he really evades the theme, so splendidly given out in the prologue. Fenris, instead of working out his regeneration and

achieving a new plane of being, through his first fierce ap-
propriation of Frejya's love, never really comes to grapple
with her. The relation between them remains intellectual,
hortatory, and renunciative, therefore barren of vital results, in spite of all that the poet would have us believe.
Then, too, the influence upon Fenris of Baldur, the god of
music, the spirit of beauty, never becomes immediate. I
tried to tell MacKaye something of this yesterday, but I
fear that I only succeeded in damping his spirits, which is
the last thing in the world I wanted to do. Happily I was
able to give praise too in substantial measure. He is
beautifully in earnest, and will go far.

33 East 33rd St.
New York, *May* 7

This is a Sunday morning of the brightest, and marks an
epoch for me. I am sitting by the window, clothed and in
my right mind, even to collar and tie, to say nothing of
shoes. It is astonishing what a tower of strength clothes
are, in the world as we have seen fit to constitute it. This
collar and tie have put more iron into my blood than it
seemed would ever bless me again. With the aid of a stout
cane and adventitious articles of furniture I have made a
voyage about my room, and down the corridor to visit
some of my neighbors with whose hypothetical selves I
have been for two weeks exchanging courtesies in the shape
of wine-jelly, tobacco, and newspapers. In some mysterious fashion the news of my state and whereabouts has
reached my New York friends (by way of Cambridge and
Boston, it appears, though bless me if I know how), and
the tedious hours are enlivened by frequent calls. These I
welcome with a childish eagerness, no matter how dull the

visitor might — in a state of health — have been judged. Illness is certainly a very humanizing affair, and gives one a perception of and relish for the 'low values' in personality as keenly surprising and delightful as is the corresponding insight it brings into the world of beauty in natural things which lies below the surface of coarse everyday perception. This must have been the source of Stevenson's heroic gladness. I hope to be able to persuade the doctor to let me leave the hospital Thursday, though I may have to come back again each day for a while to have the wound dressed.

Your humorous account of the strike, as it affects you individually, is excellent copy, but only faintly reassuring with regard to your personal safety. Under the sway of these passions men lose their human susceptibilities; even your power of appeal would not avail. As compared with Joan of Arc or Penthesilea I would back you with my last dollar, but these ladies, facing a State Street mob, would lose much of their historic brilliancy. Be careful.

(Postmarked May 12, 1905)
51 WEST 10TH ST. *Friday*

I left the hospital yesterday. They were rather averse to letting me out 'so soon' — as they sarcastically phrased it — but my impatience of the deadly routine and my detestation of the blank walls and hours had reached such a pitch that I was not to be denied. The drive down town — especially the sight of Madison Square dressed in unimaginable green, such vital vocal green as I never saw before — was an experience. I did not know how fond I was of the old room until I saw it again after this blank absence. I have been congratulating myself ever since yesterday that it is still in my possession, a quiet citadel of retreat.

The crutches turned up in due order, and by means of one of them, supplemented by a cane, I manage to navigate with tolerable effect to the beholding eye, though not without a good deal of effort and some pain. Bull seems to think well of my moving about somewhat, but indicates (with distressing vagueness) a danger line which must not be passed. I let my own sensations counsel me, stopping when the limb begins to feel irritable and rebellious. Last night, with Torrence for escort, I hobbled over to Guffanti's and renewed my acquaintance with real food. A bowl of G.'s *minestrone* seems to have done more toward establishing the lost nexus with reality than would be thought decent by the spiritually minded.

(Postmarked May 16, 1905)
NEW YORK, *Tuesday*

Here I am poking away in this muggy town still, with the prospect of not getting out of it before the end of the week. My 'wound' is not yet closed, and Dr. B. conspires with Charlotte in keeping me here until that process is accomplished. It seems that said wound has begun to throw out 'extra granulations' — a line of conduct which draws after it an elaborate ritual of burning, scraping, and clipping with shears, indignities which you would think self-respecting human flesh would scorn, but which as a matter of fact it suffers with the nonchalance of so much india-rubber. Fortunately I get about better each day, being now able to walk quite well with a single cane; and this visible sign of progress keeps my impatience from overleaping all continents.

[233]

Your various remembrances have punctuated the days with bright suggestions of the companionship which awaits me out there in the west, so soon as I have paid my double debt to nature, and am free to sleep on the wind which blows night and day toward those pleasant kingdoms.

Yesterday I got out my pastels and began to tinker with that crude old painting of my mother. With the help of a daguerreotype and another photograph, which my sister had, I corrected the drawing, and in a lucky hour succeeded in getting an excellent likeness and a charming old-fashioned effect. I think you will be pleased when you see it. It represents her as older than the little picture you know — perhaps twenty-five or six — not much different from the way I remember her in my childhood.

The Stickneys insist on my visiting them at their summer place in Dublin, N.H. If I go up to Cornish I may stop there for a day on my way out of the mountains. Mr. Gilder has just sent me a nice note from Saint-Gaudens about me. Saint-Gaudens is a valid reason for going to Cornish, I think.

New York, *May* 22 (1905)

My 'wound' has been acting up a little bit the last few days — due, the doctor thinks, to too much gallivanting on my part, but as I well know, to the direct intervention of the devil. Under the circumstances to go to Newton is out of the question, where there is no surgeon and only second-rate country doctors.

Saturday, May 27 (1905)

My leg, after two weeks of the most cantankerous conduct, seems at last to have decided to heal, and unless something untoward develops, I shall be able to get off to Newton in a few days. Henrietta has just returned thither, after extracting from my helpless breast such deep vows to follow her that it would be worth my immortal soul to break them. The fatted calf has already been killed nine several times in anticipation of my immediate coming.

Last night, at a Social Settlement dinner, I met Markham, of *The Man with the Hoe*, and of other things vastly better. He is a splendid leonine head, one of the most beautiful of men, and I believe — after hearing him recite a half-dozen of his less-known things — a real poet. He had recently read my things, and was unstintedly cordial about them. He said that the *Fire-Bringer* and the *Masque* were the finest things done in the dramatic form since Shelley. He did not limit his statement to the lyric drama, but by his selection of Shelley as a *terminus de quo* he doubtless meant that. His unworldliness, simplicity, and more than youthful ardor were a great delight to me, and a big lesson in life. I also ate the other night my maiden dinner with the gentlemen of the American Institute of Arts and Letters, and was decorated with a purple ribbon, *à la* the French Institute. It was very dull.

NEW YORK, *June* 4 (1905)

My 'wound' is not yet closed, and still requires close attention. There has of course been progress, else my impatience would have reached a suicidal pitch; but it has been desperately slow. The end at last seems to be in sight, but I knock on all the mahogany trees of Senegambia with all the knuckles of the Celestial Empire as I say it. Barring unforeseen impishness in nature the thing must be by the end of this week in a state which will allow me to leave, with a pot of zinc-oxide, and a roll of bandages, and work out my further destiny alone. There is a possibility that I can postpone the Newton visit until the late summer without wounding sensibilities. I think this would be better in many ways, as I could combine it then with a week at Cornish, whereas now I am too one-legged to make the mountains feasible.

What you say about Robertson's [1] leasing the hall — with a real 'fairy' to foot the bills, is simply smashing. It looks like a real beginning, and once fairly started the thing is bound to go. More power be to his elbow; and to yours, which is more important, more leverage on which to bring to bear the power already there in abundance. The Progressive Stage Society of this city is going to give the great Hindoo play *Sakuntala* two weeks from today. If anything earthly could keep me here so long, it would be that. But nothing earthly can. The Russian players (here now) are wonders. You can follow their performance with rapture without knowing a word of the play. I am not sure that this is a proof of their powers histrionical, but it constitutes an absorbing characteristic.

(The next letter shows W. V. M. in Chicago, writing to Harriet, who was visiting her aunt in Parkman, Ohio. Most of September and October of that year he spent in a cottage at Highland Park, across the lake from Chicago.)

(Postmarked July 28, 1905)
CHICAGO, *Friday*, 11 A.M.

Today the gods are taking revenge for divine yesterday by a black and savage rain. I have had to work by

[1] Donald Robertson.

lamplight until a little while ago. Now it is lightening up a bit, and there is a hint of sun somewhere behind the enormous curtains of darkness which wave across the sky. I hope this sinister weather is not interfering with your little glimpse of country.

The cheer of the situation has not been particularly increased by a memorandum which came today from Dr. Bull. The charge which he makes for his services is less than he is accustomed to ask, I am sure, and less than they are worth, but the amount is nevertheless distinctly appalling. I shall pay what I can, and leave the rest as a pious obligation to my heirs, as I am in the mind to write him.

Your note has this minute arrived, with its breath of healing. I am sorry to have put down the above temporary discouragements, but I will let them stand, knowing that you will see how trivial after all they are, and everything else in comparison with our great happifying permanences. Sieg defends your couch with augmented jealousy, and droops in your absence. The play [1] is going fast but rather leery.

(Postmarked Grand Haven, Mich., Sept. 24, 1905)
HIGHLAND PARK, *Sunday*

Your pup is beseeching me, by all the humanity I retain after persistently disregarding his interests since morning, to abandon the sedentary life and to accept the invitation of wind and sun for a royal scamper.... The weather holds superb, the lake streaked and pied with impossible tints and raced over by great whitecaps which seem to have no relation to the wind, but to arise out of

[1] Perhaps the play that became *The Great Divide*.

[237]

their own exultation. The charm of the place takes more hold on me every day. It will be one of my most blessed memories later, and now a present joy and recuperation. I find myself in a golden drowse. Effort, accomplishment, even the least strenuous entering into one's self to behold and possess, are far too strident to be thought of. I read a little and walk a little and drowse the rest of the time, in a more than lotus-eating abatement of will. If I may judge by myself these last two days, this place will prove unexampled as a letter-down of your overspanned nerves. Come soon, and sink your being into boundless rest.

Be of good cheer, and remember in the midst of your labors and difficulties that there is peace across the lake.

(Grand Haven, Sept. 25, 1905)

Sieg is in great feather, frolicking like mad after supper in the manner of his puppy days at Mackinac. One trait of his conduct since you left is very charming. He always goes to sleep on your bed, stays there until the loneliness gets too much for him, and then comes padding in to me. Several times also each day he goes upstairs as if struck by a sudden thought, makes an examination of your quarters and Bessie's, poking into every cranny and closet to make sure you are not concealed there. That he makes a rigid inspection, visual and nasal, of all the female passengers on the trolley cars, goes without saying, as also that no wheeled vehicle conveying members of your sex passes without throwing him into absurd antics of expectation.

The weather holds superb, crisp and gay without any cold.

(Postmarked Grand Haven, Oct. 12, 1905)

I drove the team back from G. R. yesterday. We left about noon in cold but clearing weather, but after an hour the wind shifted to the northwest and blew a sixty mile gale, the sky darkened portentously, and there followed during the next five hours of the journey the most disgusting combination of driving rain, sleet, and snow, which I ever faced. The horses came through the unspeakable roads at a fast pace and in excellent condition, but Willie and his pet dog weren't fit to be put in a rummage sale when they arrived, and I am afraid to look at what remains of that glossy trap. Aside from the physical discomfort (largely my own fault in not going warmly enough clad) the ride was exciting and memorable, for the horses, spurred on and frightened by the storm, ran like demons; my arms are still lame and numb from the effort of holding them — or rather of keeping them in the road, for that was about all my government amounted to. Sieg this morning walks about stiff-legged and drops asleep whenever and wherever he stops deliberate functioning. He disgraced himself on the journey by running amuck among chickens and turkeys, two of which he killed outright, dancing like a mad Apache on their carcasses, and waving mouthfuls of feathers in the wind as a sign of his everlasting release from superstition. My efforts to restrain him and punish him drove the horses crazy with fear and excitement, and after each attempt on my part at discipline they played jackstraws with me and the rig. These are a few incoherent lines from the Iliad of the day, which was really magnificent in its way.

(Postmarked New York, Nov. 12, 1905)

When I came back I found the plasterers, painters, and glaziers in possession of my room, and this is the first hour I have found to sit quiet in an interior even primarily organized.

The Scribner news was nothing very epoch-making — merely that the textbook was making its way with all to be wished for speed, and that in their manager's sober opinion, its reception by the high school public was certain to be cordial. They showed me thirty or forty personal letters from teachers commending the book in very practical terms and promising to work for its adoption in their classes. At the same time the sales of the previous book have not fallen off but substantially increased. This is of course matter of mint and cumin, but it has its value in the large scheme.

By telepathic process, New York has got wind of our Chicago theatre project and this morning puts out a gigantic counterpart to save its own metropolitan reputation. It appears that the ground has been secured on Central Park west, a whole block front costing a million, and plans for the National Theatre have been drawn. Building and decorations to cost two millions are to be raised by the sale of thirty box-stalls, at a hundred thousand dollars each, the owners to possess them in perpetuity — two nights a week to be devoted to 'Opera Comique' (not Comic Opera, thank heaven!) and the remainder to standard drama, native and foreign — I rather guess especially *foreign*! Conried, the man who so successfully built up the German theatre here and who for two years has run the Grand Opera, is to be Manager. The thing has a rank money smell and seems built on the presumption that anything earthly or heavenly can be quickly bought for money down, but it may get into better hands and develop into the consummation we have been sighing for so long. But I think our modest plan more hopeful for sound results.

Joe's book [1] is out — at least I have an advanced copy — very beautifully printed, and an unspeakable treasure of the music which is truth and glory and the soul's salvation. I wish I could send you this copy at once, but I must keep it until I get my article written. The book will doubtless be on sale in Chicago in a few days. You will be glad to hear that Scribner has taken up Robinson, reprinted his first volume (the one upon which the President practised criticism by ukase), bought several of his poems, and is prepared to stand behind him to the editorial *n*th.

NEW YORK, *Thursday, Nov.* 16 (1905)

The plastering and calcimining gentry have at last ceased from their labors, and I have got pretty comfortably settled. I have not found a convenient sleeping room outside yet, but I am very cosy as it is.

Friday — At this point Mr. Gilder came in, and stayed until after midnight.

I am writing a review [2] of Joe's book. It is not easy to say anything, much less the right thing, in the cramped space at my disposal and for a magazine audience. However, insufficient as it will be, it will do some good in getting the attention of the public called to the book. Lodge has a new volume out called *The Great Adventure*, containing a series of twenty-six sonnets in Joe's memory. I have not

[1] *The Poems of Trumbull Stickney*. Edited by George Cabot Lodge, William Vaughn Moody, and John Ellerton Lodge. Houghton Mifflin Company, 1905.
[2] 'The Poems of Trumbull Stickney,' by William Vaughn Moody, published in the *North American Review*, November 16, 1906.

yet seen them, but will send you the book when I get it.

The *Divine Fire* lady [1] is here, a queer little papery, prim, cricket-piping yet beguiling old maid. Also the Pawpaw poet, Madison Cawein. Barrie's *Peter Pan* is a delicious trifle; I am saving up my second view of it until the holiday season.

NEW YORK, *Nov.* 20 (1905)

MacKaye is in town, and we are to dine together Thursday. I hear he has plays up both sleeves and shakes them out of his boots when he goes upstairs.

NEW YORK, *Nov.* 28 (1905)

What with the repairs to my room, my sister's illness (over now), the writing of the little article on Stickney, and a picture which I was seized with a perverse impulse to paint (the Mackinac one — the road to the Cathedral Woods, and quite a little beauty), I am only just getting settled down to real work. I have been seeing something of MacKaye, and like him better all the time. He is a splendid human being, and he has got the goods to the *n*th *in alt*. A few evenings ago he read to a little gathering of the elect in my room his new play, on Joan of Arc. It is superb, far and away ahead of the *Fenris* — a kind of miracle-play on an epic scale, full of exquisite poetry and showing a stage-craft — a 'technique' — which quite takes the breath away for its audacity and verve. It is bespoken by Mrs. Pat Campbell; we may have a chance to see it before the year is out. While the rest of us have been dawdling and mooning, he has done the thing — or something precious near it. The only criticism that on a first

[1] May Sinclair, author of *The Divine Fire*.

[242]

hearing I can find to make against it, is that it is a bit over-spectacular, a little bit over-ingenious, and that it falls down rather badly at the end. But all the same it is a masterly and enviable piece of work. He has got a magnificent start for the goal toward which we are all striving, and let us all say God-speed and Heaven be praised.

The illustration to the *Century* poem [1] was an unspeakable horror, wasn't it? Since the first sick glance at the page I haven't looked at it, but the recollection still lingers icy in my spinal cord. MacKaye tells of finding the *Thammuz* in the hands of an accomplished illustrator of automobile stories, who was going about with an air of bewildered injury cursing the assignment, and calling upon the wayfarer in Zion to tell him who in the name of non-sense Thammuz was. That will be another bad quarter of a minute to live through, when his belabored brain brings forth its fruit and the same is published to an accepting world.

(Postmarked Dec. 3, 1905)

I am afraid you spent some anxious hours before the belated arrival of my telegram. The fact is that when I am absorbed I take no account of time. A week passes like a day in a kind of trance-like routine without visible punctuation of incident or hours. Then, to write in such a state and not to write about the matter which is in my mind (which is often by the inchoate nature of the matter perilous or impossible) seems like a kind of disingenuousness — a kind of negation of that absolute intimacy which is the sweet of friendship. Besides, I have not been so

[1] *Second Coming*, published in the *Century* magazine of December, 1905.

dreadfully absorbed, worse luck, except by external incidents of a more or less meaningless kind, and though I were drowned forty fathoms deep in the authentic Pierian flood, I ought to know when you are in need of a word from me, and speak it.

The theatres have been poor here so far this autumn. The Russian players and the German are the only ones that have given me much satisfaction.

I hope by this time you have got Stickney's volume. I had my copy all done up to send you when I got a note from the editor of the *North American Review*, to whom I had submitted my little article, saying that he would like to see the volume. I hope the *Review* will print it; it is the most dignified organ on this side of the Atlantic, and will do a good deal for the book by admitting an account of it to its columns. Did you see Josephine Peabody's group of child poems in the December *Harper*?

I have no account of myself to give, except that the Zona play[1] seems to be slowly taking on something like organic form and feature. I am not sure there is enough in it to justify the time I am putting on it, but it rather seems necessary to lay the ghost of it anyhow by getting the thing down on paper. The second act, which I have now outlined, gives the development a more energetic curve and the underlying thought more body. At least, I think so. *Aspettiamo!*

We have got a man here named Wallace Irwin who writes stuff as good as the *Bab Ballads*, and does it again and again.

[1] Zona was the name of the heroine in *A Sabine Woman* — the play that became *The Great Divide*. The name 'Zona' was afterwards changed to 'Ruth.'

Here is his latest:

> O sailor coming from your cruise,
> I represent the Daily News;
> What tidings do you bring? —
> O, nothing that the like of youse
> Would think was anything.
>
> Our ship was broke in two by squalls,
> Our crew was et by can-ni-balls,
> Our passengers was drowned;
> Our capting sank with piteous calls,
> And never more was found;
>
> Three months I lived upon a bun,
> And thus survived, the only one;
> But otherwise we made
> A quiet uneventful run
> From Tyre to Adelaide.

NEW YORK, *Dec.* 6 (1905)

The only piece of experience I have to relate is that of dining at the elbow of the *Divine Fire* lady. She is a drab and angular little lady, somewhere between thirty and forty by the almanac but in reality quite undated — without a single feather to flaunt, meek-spoken, naïve, wholly unworldly and without guile, *habitat* Cranford. But her words are full of meaning and charm. She says (notice the logical transition) that she is writing an article for *Blackwood's* on me, and she volunteered the comment, 'Your work is like what I imagined Rickman's to be.' You remember Rickman — the somewhat dubiously starry youth in her novel. It appears she had written two or three others, earlier. She said, 'They do not reach the level of *The Divine Fire*,' with a little quaver of awe at the suggested level, which was really delicious. She has taken

[245]

tremendously to Robinson, who consents for her sake to sit in the drawing-rooms of Philistia. There is a story of their having been seen at 2 A.M. leaning over the railing in the middle of Brooklyn Bridge, entirely incommunicative and at one.

The little Zona play is in a state where I don't dare to leave it. By staying by it now I can probably finish it — the first draft — by the end of the month or the first week in January, whereas if I drop it I'm afraid I shall never pick it up again.

NEW YORK, *Dec.* 12 (1905)

A stupid luncheon which I could not avoid has pied my day, and I must borrow some hours of lamplight to make it good. The New York habit of seeing people at luncheon is ingrained in the manners of the place, and is most pernicious. I intend to establish an iron rule against it for my own part, in future. I have just had a note from your friend Boardman Robinson (the chap who made the little pencil sketch of me and whose letter you liked so much) proposing a luncheon for next week. I guess I shall have to bend the iron of my resolve in his case.

The function today was a 'literary luncheon,' and I am prepared to subscribe with deepest oaths to Keats's dictum that of all 'sets' the literary set is the vulgarest and vapidest.

NEW YORK, *Dec.* 19 (1905)

I sent you today a copy of Stickney's book, which you should have had long ago if I had realized that the Chicago bookstores did not contain it. The sentence on the flyleaf is the one which you spoke to me as a message

for him, and which I gave him on one of the last evenings
we spent together. I shall never forget the strange flush
which overspread his face, and the sudden dilation and
scintillation of his eyes at the words. The book contains
too much imperfect work, but the good things are beyond
price. The *North American Review* is going to print my
article, which is merely a brief biographical sketch and review of the book. It will probably not appear for a couple
of months, as their columns are very crowded — the editor
tells me — with matter demanding immediate publication.
Still, I am rejoiced that I have got a hearing for the
volume in a quarter so dignified and authoritative.

Lear is being given here now by Robert Mantell. The
company knocks it cold, and whenever they can't, the
orchestra can and does. The heath scenes and the Dover
Cliff scene are *impayable*, especially — in the latter scene,
the stage-direction 'Exit Lear, running,' is the occasion for
a moment miraculously comic.

I saw Aiken on the Street the other day, as 'like himself' (to borrow your phrase) as it is possible to conceive,
and in glowing spirits.

NEW YORK, *Dec.* 27 (1905)

The jolly Christmas box came ship-shape and Bristol
fashion, and was the occasion of an impromptu celebration
in which Charlotte, a friend of hers, and myself took part
on Christmas night. We had intended to go out to some
pot-house to dinner, but when the girls saw the box they
would hear of nothing of the sort. Instead they proceeded
to organize a most complete Christmas feast, out of the
contents. With some trifling aid from my permanent
stores the thing was done, beginning with cocktails and

soup, and ending with bonbons and benedictine. The only toast of the evening was your name, which Charlotte proposed and which was drunk standing.

The play is not done by a long shot, but I have reached a 'node,' where I can drop it for a little while without danger of loss. On the other hand, I can summon up my reserves of patience, and push it to completion. I can probably finish it by the middle of January, but it may take until the end.

NEW YORK, *Jan.* 2, 1906

The self-denying ordinance which I passed upon myself Saturday and communicated to you by telegraph, was the result of a conviction that I had better push the play [1] through while it was fluid, and not run the risk of letting it harden and fade the way the other [2] did when I stopped it in an inchoate state. I am sure this will be the happiest course in the long run. I could not frolic yet with a good conscience. At the rate it is going, it will not be very long before the job is finished.

Yesterday I ran out with Torrence to Cos Cob, hoping to find it good prospecting ground for a summer home. We had a fine time tramping over the hills and along the sound, but the place itself — I mean the inhabited part — is disappointing, as it lies back from the water, separated from it by a four-track railroad.

Have you read Mrs. Wharton's *House of Mirth*? I know you have passed Edith up, but you had better give her one more trial. The thing is worth reading. Everybody is talking about it here, including the newspapers and the

[1] *The Great Divide*, unnamed yet.

[2] The play of modern theme, in verse, never completed. Cf. his letters of Feb. 6, 15, 24, 1904.

pulpits; I read it with my expectations too high pitched and was disappointed, but I can see in retrospect that if I had approached it without advertisement I should have carried away the opposite impression.

I have been re-reading Ibsen's romantic dramas, being spurred thereto by the recollection of your high regard for them. The *Vikings of Helgeland* is superb, but the other two seem to me much less good, especially *Lady Inger of Östrât* strikes me as wooden and labored (except the opening scene, which is bully). I fancy your judgment was based on the *Vikings*, with perhaps some scenes from the *Pretenders*. I think the truth is, it took the old boy a good while to strike his pace. I have been looking in vain for Maeterlinck's essay on Immortality. Where did it appear? What you said about it interested me immensely.

Do not be surprised to hear any day that the props of my heroism have sunk in the sandy soil of my character, and that I must see you, play or no play.

NEW YORK, *Feb.* 6 (1906)

I saw my doctor and had a final examination today. He reports, as I knew he would, that I am as sound as a dollar, and all my organs examples of their kind. He says my 'system' is a bit rundown, needs a little tonic-ing, exercise, and fresh air, but that it is inherently and essentially a bully system, and only needs knocking about a little to resume concert pitch. It shall be knocked about, and more than a little.

Apropos, Percy MacKaye is here, and wants me to go up to Cornish with him at the end of this week, for some snowshoeing and a look at the country. I think I will go.

It is bitter cold, but I have not tasted the male joys of a country winter for years, and am keen for them. He promises to show me places to locate, near enough to Cornish for companionship and far enough away for seclusion at need. The mountains are much, and there is the river — two hundred miles of it — for canoeing.

Miss Jeannette Gilder (Our Own Jen) who, it appears, is a dramatic *entrepreneuse* making it her duty and pleasure to mediate between playwright and manager, has heard in some way that I have a play on hand and wants to see it with an eye severely to business. I don't know whether to let her loose on it or not. I feel that Robertson's [1] claim to it is prior, if he wants it; on the other hand, he can't afford to load up his first-year's repertory with more than one of my works, and he already has a possible two. If she took hold of it she might get it placed for this spring, which would have advantages. What do you think? The question is largely metaphysical, for I don't expect her to see anything in it but the reprehensible, or to be willing to push it with her maiden hands into a censorious publicity.

Josephine Peabody tells me she has arranged to let her light shine before the Fortnightly [2] this month. I have been gently hinting that she might use the intervening period in reading a play or two of Björnson and of Strindberg, of whom she professes a total ignorance, and against whose claims to attention she turns a sweetly stony face. She is to spend this ensuing week visiting up-country, and will I suppose lift Chicago lighthouse about the tenth or so — perhaps later. Be sure to give me a full report of the proceedings.

[1] Donald Robertson.
[2] The Fortnightly of Chicago — a women's club.

New York, *Feb.* 13 (1906)

I am just back from Cornish, which turned out to be a most enchanting spot, at least in its winter dress. From the wooded river wind deeply wooded roads slowly upward through high-hung pastures to broad acclivities of woodland and rocky open, with wide prospects unfolding on every side, and across the river the delicately majestic blue figure of Mount Ascutney — one of the most lovable mountain-forms it has ever been my lot to behold. The place combines intimate loveliness with a sense of large freedom in a remarkable way, and the distinction of the landscape is carried out with rare harmony in the human beings which inhabit it. I saw of course only the winter colony — Maxfield Parrish and Saint-Gaudens being the chief figures — but I saw also a dozen houses and gardens belonging to absentees, of such faultless taste and pure charm that they proclaimed aloud their possessors as people worth knowing. Torrence and I were given a royal welcome. The first night there was a snowshoe and sleighing party in our honor, the supper cooked over bonfires in the woods. The next night there was a small party and supper at Saint-Gaudens', and the third night brought forth a larger festivity at the Parrish's. Saint-Gaudens was a pure delight. MacKaye's little home is a very sweet place. He has two adorable children, a boy of six and a girl of four, and a very pretty wife. The weather was prime, crisp and clear, with an unspeakable moon.

Thursday

I got this far two days ago, when I was interrupted. Soon after came word from Sothern (whom MacKaye had meanwhile seen in Baltimore and spoken to him about my play) that he wanted to see it at once, with a view to production by his wife (Virginia Harned) who needs a new play immediately. I thought it worth while to let him see it anyhow, reserving definite decision, so have been working day and night to get it into presentable shape and typewritten. I shall send it to him tomorrow, but shall take no definite action until I hear further from you and Robertson.

I will write a better letter than this when I have got off the manuscript to Sothern.

Are they really going to call it the Permanent Theatre? This is to invite practical jokes at the hands of the sportive gods and the sportive reporters. Head them off, if possible. Permanent, please Heaven, but not so nominated on the bill-boards of a world in flux.

(Postmarked New York, Feb. 17, 1906)

I dare say Robertson is right in what he says about Virginia Harned. The idea of her taking the play has never appealed to me much, and I should refrain from showing it to her at all, except that that would mean giving mortal offence to Sothern. He and Marlowe are going to put on one of MacKaye's plays (possibly two of them) next year, and such as he (Sothern) is, he constitutes one of the few hopes we have of a decent theatre. So I will let him have the ms. for inspection, though quite confident nothing will come of it on either side.

New York, *Feb.* 22 (1906)

I was glad to get your telegram and note assuring me that you were serene of mind again, for I have been going through a period of depression where the thought of your distress seemed more than I could endure. This (on my part) has been nothing to worry about, merely one of my periodic visitations, causeless, impersonal, and 'cosmic,' but for just that reason as mean a thing to live through as ever you saw, since I can no more 'see out' of such a mood than if I were a frog in a well — with the lid on; nor does all my philosophy and experience of its evanescence afford me the least assistance in combating its intangible horrors. There would be no point in speaking of this except for the heartening circumstances — of which this is only one of several examples in my history — that out of the depths I have brought up a big 'inspiration' — at least it looks big to me in the first flush of recovery and ecstatic reaction of spirit and imagination consequent thereon. It is an idea for a play — but a play of a kind that there never was yet, I verily believe. However it is the merest floating protoplasm of an idea, if it is even that much, and I don't dare to talk about it for fear of puffing it out of existence with my more raw breath.

I shall send you tomorrow — or very soon — a typewritten copy of the play, for Robertson to look at. Perhaps when he reads it in the cold grey light of actuality, without the rainbow medium of your interpretive genius, he won't want it himself. The title is tentative (*A Sabine Woman*), but I am inclined on reflection to think it will do. What do you think?

(Postmarked New York)
Tuesday, Feb. 27 (1906)

The enclosed letter came this morning from Mrs. MacKaye. It tells pretty much the whole story, as far as I know it, except the surpassing beauty of the country thereabouts. I haven't seen the house, but understand it is an old farm house, with open fireplaces, and built in the solid and distinguished style of the old-fashioned New England architect. There may be a great deal to say for it and for Cornish as a place to settle — at least for the years just ahead. The settlement of city people, which I dreaded before seeing the place, I don't believe would prove objectionable even in summer, for the houses are far apart, and this particular one is especially remote. In winter of course the few people who stay there would be a priceless blessing. I don't think I could stand the loneliness of a country winter without congenial neighbors.

I have no new developments to report in the Virginia Harned complication. I wrote her yesterday to ask for some enlightenment, as she has had the manuscript now for over a week without so much as acknowledging its receipt. Did you ever see Margaret Anglin? I never have, but several persons have recommended her as a likely creatrix of the rôle.

This morning comes an enthusiastic telegram from Robertson, sent after reading the play with you. I'm afraid from the inebriated tone of it that you hypnotized him again, and that he hasn't yet seen the poor little work in its native colors. By poor I don't mean absolutely so, for I don't think it is quite that, but poor and shabby by comparison with the glorified poem you made of it.

I am going to hear the *Rheingold* tonight, having blown myself in to a ticket for the whole cycle. Ah, if you were here, and we might wander through these forest aisles and sea-caverns of melody together. I have much more to say, but in my capacity of Pig I must knock off so as to get the

Rheingold book read through in preparation for a lazy debauch tonight with the mere music and pictures.

(Postmarked March 6, 1906)

I have been struggling for two days with nervous sick headache — a most infernal case. Of all the little ills this is certainly the worst, for it poisons the very sources of pleasure and even of perception. For about twenty minutes in the middle of it I was really scared, beholding myself on the Avernian slope.... I am all right again now, and mention it for posthumous consolation (in my state of bruised and battered convalescence I crave coddling).

Your account of Robertson's reception of the play gave me much earnest pleasure, and still more your quiet ratification of the thing after a third hearing and time for reflection. Virginia has sent back her copy, protesting that she finds it very interesting and dramatic, but alas! it is a problem play, and she is afraid of problem plays. *Is* it a problem play? Perhaps. I don't know just what is covered by the term, nowadays. I shall try to get the ear of Margaret Anglin next, but I understand she is still on tour. By all means let Ferd hear it, if he really wants to.

NEW YORK, March 8 (1906)

What you say about Kreider and his possible setting of the *Fire-Bringer* songs interests me immensely. I have been feeling of late more than ever that music is an indispensable adjunct of the stage as I hope to live to see it. I tear my hair (of course very metaphorically, for economic reasons) at the thought of not having been trained in

[255]

music myself, at the proper age. If it were not utterly hopeless, I would undergo any labor even now to equip myself for musical composition. The next best thing, and the only thing now possible, is to gather together a little 'school' of young musicians who shall have the sense of dramatic values and be willing to work in strict and loyal subordination to the drama itself — for it is almost as easy for music to do harm, as I see it, as to do good, to the new stage. The problem is to reverse the Wagnerian proportion, keeping the dialogue as the backbone and nervous system of the whole, and using music as a heightening and merging medium, where the action takes on a lyric cast. (I know you understand this better than I do myself, but it is such fun to talk about it that I go on now, as often before, as if I were announcing a novel and world-shaking aesthetic, extempore.)

The suggestion you make about Margaret Anglin strikes me as capital. By all means get hold of her, you and Robertson. In case you want me to visit you in Chicago, I could time my coming so as to be present at the séance, could I not? As I said perhaps in my last letter, the best time for me to go is between the middle and the end of the month, as I want to have a full month here, to make a start on a new job, before I have to break up, the first of May. (I have practically decided to give up the studio, though perhaps when we meet you can persuade me against such a resolution.) Also, I want to talk with you, and incidentally with Robertson, about this new job before I begin it, or rather before I decide whether I want to begin it, in view of the time and labor it will involve. So retire into yourself, and having taken counsel tell me what you elect to have me do.

I have not gone up to Cornish yet. I think I can judge the place better when the snow is off the ground and the spring has made a little more headway.

Scribner has justified, in satisfactory manner, his prophecies of the autumn. I received today a statement of half-yearly sales of the two books.

(Postmarked, New York, March 23, 1906)

The first person I ran into, when I boarded my train, was Borglum. He had been out west, in Nevada, to get up material for a statue he has a commission for — a statue of Mackay the mining king (God bless us!) in pioneer duds, for the state capitol of Nevada, whatever that may be. He was brown as a berry, and full of music about the time he'd had and the sights he'd seen. Made me think twice whether Nevada hasn't attractions to offer over Spain — this incidentally, his main blessed office to me being to lighten the dreariness of the journey back.

Since my return I have bought a Spanish grammar and lexicon, a guidebook, and a history in two volumes, all of which I am absorbing. Today I wrote to Ferd urging him to take three months off before tackling his book again, but I haven't much notion that he will consider himself able to do so. Torrence is crazy to go — to Spain, Norway, or the moon — but doesn't yet clearly visualize his necessary source of income (*The Cosmopolitan*) begging him to forego his duties in the interests of the higher life. All this means that I myself feel the *Wanderlust* mounting in my veins and the East a-calling, but also that other voices still call too loudly for me to know for sure what I am going to do. It does look so colossally hoggish, but we won't go into that again, will we? I know that your view of this aspect of the question is the only large and right one, but I could act upon it with more zest and grace if it didn't seem *always* to point out to exactly me the flowery path and to just you (and incidentally one or two others in a minor sense) the dusty one! There is not so much need for haste as there would be if the season were not so cold and backward, and the Atlantic in such a state of temper. The worst storms of the winter have occurred within the last few days.

I have been thinking much about the suggestion you threw out for strengthening the action of the *Eve* play. I can't quite see it yet, but I shouldn't wonder if it were there. It raises a host of difficulties, but of a kind to pique and challenge. We shall see what we shall see.

(Postmarked March 29, 1906)

Your reckless proposal anent Torrence is characteristic of you in its impulsiveness and splendor, so much so that it almost renders itself invulnerable from criticism in the act of utterance. But it seems now he can't go under any circumstances without resigning his post on the *Cosmopolitan* staff, and he is unwilling to do that, as it constitutes the only material future he has in sight. It would be jolly to have him, but as that is out of the question I shall go alone with a light heart. At this season there will be plenty of travelling companions to be picked up on the road, who can be dropped if they prove to be bores or cleaved to as brothers in the happier alternative. Besides I do not intend to stay long, only long enough to get good and homesick, which can be accomplished to excellent purpose *mutterseelenallein*, in case the chances of the road so decree. As for the date of my departure, that will have to be conditioned by the promptitude with which D —— shows up his two hundred. There is a ship sailing on the seventh, others on the tenth and fourteenth. I should like to take the first of these if possible.

The Cape Henry clipping wrought its due work of havoc in my heart. These are among the grimmest of earth's tragedies. It puts a keen personal sting into the dull resentment which has been growing in me for a long time, against some of the more shocking aspects of our national madness. It will do me good to get away from it for a while, and cool my jaundiced eye by letting it rest on the face of a past beautiful and dead. My heart rises up in dreadful protest against a fate which stays you behind, your exquisite vital spirit exposed a thousand fold more than mine has ever been, to the corroding influences of this acid atmosphere.

Telegram:

April 2, 1906

SAILING PROBABLY FOURTEENTH

NEW YORK, *April 4 (1906)*

I have at last and this time finally decided to give up my room here, in case any one wants it, and shall use some of the spare days in bestowing my effects so as to leave a clear field for the hypothetical occupant. It is rather a wrench to part with the old eyrie, but I am sure that for the few winter months when I want to be here I can find for less money quarters more comfortable and hygienic, though hardly so sympathetic.

[259]

Telegram:

April 8, 1906

WHAT ABOUT ANGLIN   ROBERTSON TELEGRAPHS
COME   WIRE INFORMATION AND ADVICE

W V M

(W. V. M. did not go to Europe at this time, but went to Chicago where a few performances of *A Sabine Woman* were given by Margaret Anglin.)

NEW YORK, *May* 2, 1906

I arrived this morning in a drizzle, and have spent a sloppy dark day paddling about with some millions more aimless human beings, laboriously doing nothing. It is now a quarter to twelve midnight, and your friend is a rag.

I wrote Margaret this P.M. requesting an audience, if convenient — very diplomatic phrases, an 'approach' too soft to sit up on a plate without gelatine.

(Postmarked May 3, 1906)
NEW YORK, *Thursday morning*

Here is a letter from Margaret, very gracious, asking me to drink a cup of tea with her and Miller this afternoon. Manifestly the tone of our encounter is to be high.

I will send you a full report this evening.

Thursday, May 3 (1906)

A headache with which I got up this morning, and which has grown gradually worse until it has reached the 'blind' stage, makes it impossible for me to give you the exciting news of the day as I should like to do. The gist in a nutshell will suffice tonight. I met Miss Anglin by appointment at her flat at half-past five, and we talked for two solid hours about the play. The business end of the matter did not come up at all, our attention being concentrated upon the play itself and its fitness for her use.

The fact is as we have more than suspected: she is still in love with the play and loath to give it up, but she realizes (as we did) that her rôle, as it stands now, is unmistakably subordinate to that of the man. As she is a *Star*, and makes her daily bread solely by dint of being one, this settles the matter for her professionally. Two possibilities still exist: first, to rewrite the play, with an eye to opening up her rôle; second, to admit frankly that it is a man's play — in which case Henry Miller may want to star in it, and probably, alas! will also want the thing rewritten in *his* sense. Ah, well-a-day, I am to lunch with her and Miller tomorrow, when I shall get his side of the question. M. A. is very cordial, and I believe on the square.

(Postmarked May 4, 1906)
Friday

I am just back from my visit with Henry Miller, and must snatch the few minutes intervening before a dinner appointment with Charlotte to send you the gist of the matter.

I met Miller at lunch, and had several hours' talk with him afterwards at his rooms. He impressed me in everything most favorably. He is not only a thorough gentleman with the unmistakable and indescribable hall mark of the species, which sets one at ease at once and makes real converse possible, but he is alert to the higher aspects of his profession, and unselfishly devoted to the furtherance of them, to a degree for which I was totally unprepared.

His appreciation of the play is whole-souled, and his discussion of it exhibited an understanding both of its strong
points and its weak, far beyond anything Miss A. has ever
shown. He is anxious to play it himself, but declares his
first desire to be to have me make of it a thoroughly well-
rounded and self-sufficing piece of dramatic art, without
regard to his own *particular rôle*. This is like water in a
thirsty land, after Miss A.'s feverish suggestions yesterday
as to how her rôle might be made to dominate the whole
play, and herself enabled to snatch the honors of popular
sympathy from the brows of the prospective personator of
'Stephen.' Miller had many flattering and encouraging
things to say about my dramatic endowments and oppor-
tunities. He mentioned the business aspect of the present
venture in a way which makes me sure that he intends to
do the square thing when it comes to drawing up the contract. This will all — I am sure — be pleasant news to
you. He goes to Washington tonight, but is to return on
Sunday, when we are to meet for a detailed going-over of
the text. Tonight I am going to *Zira*, and to supper with
Miss A. and others afterward. Which means I must dress,
which means I must stop talking to you. I wonder if you
like these brief and hasty scribblings? I think it is a very
jolly way to keep the mystic channels open and the red
blood flowing between.

NEW YORK, *May 5*, 1906

Last night I saw Miss A. in *Zira* — a machine-made
affair which gives her little chance, but unless I was
verstimmt and prone to unliberal judgment she didn't take
what little chance she had. Her 'intensity' was much in
evidence, but was of the same unrelieved and in the end

annoying kind which she displayed in the *Sabine Woman*. I took supper with her afterward, and there was more and still more talk of what shall we do with it, much reminiscential reckoning over the number of 'hands' which this or that speech and situation evoked. Applause is the actor's currency and abacus by which all is reckoned.

NEW YORK, *May* 7, 1906

Yesterday was so crowded that I put off writing my little diary letter until I got back to the hotel at night — and that event found itself postponed until two o'clock this morning. One of the chief occurrences has been the annual dinner tendered by the old editors of the *Harvard Monthly* to the undergraduate editors. It was given this year in New York for the first time, and the occasion was a gala one. Many old friends, whom I had not seen for years, were there, and there was a memorable outpouring of the spirit, much genial reminiscence, and a general casting up of both sweet and sad accounts, to say nothing of the humorous, a column-full.

Also there has been decided progress in the business arrangements with regard to the play. Miller has showed himself a perfect brick in the whole delicate negotiation, standing between me and Shubert at every point. The net result is that I have a contract being drawn up by Miss Marbury on entirely equitable lines, to which Miller has agreed beforehand in the main features. I shall have a final discussion of it with him tomorrow, and then this vexatious episode will be fortunately concluded. Miller's conduct in the matter (and incidentally Miss A.'s as well) has restored my pristine trust in human kind, somewhat impaired by the Chicago mix-up.

I telegraphed you late last night about the *contretemps* which has arisen over the clause in the contract granting Robertson [1] the right to produce the play in Chicago in the Players Theatre. Miller, it seems, did not know of this reservation at all until I told him of it last night, after all the provisions of the agreement had been settled and the job of drawing up the paper put in Miss Marbury's hands. I had not spoken of it because I took for granted that he had seen the paper which Miss A. holds, and that this clause, not being objected to, was tacitly granted. When the matter came up, almost by accident, he was terribly disturbed, saying that the production of the play in Chicago before the appearance there of his company would 'kill' for him not only Chicago itself but a large surrounding territory, that he could not get from Shubert a good Western route if the clause were enforced, etc., etc., and that in the latter event he should be compelled reluctantly to abandon the entire project. That his balking is due to a genuine and serious difficulty in the business situation which the clause creates for him I am forced to believe, because his treatment of the whole matter up to this point has been most liberal, involving the voluntary surrender of various points of vantage, and a repeatedly demonstrated desire to stand between me and the possible results of my own ignorance and carelessness. On the other hand the safeguarding of Robertson's interests is, as neither he nor you need to be told, a matter which concerns me very deeply. I am quite broken up over the matter. I have exhausted my powers of persuasion on Miller. He speaks with great friendliness and admiration

[1] Donald Robertson.

[264]

of Robertson, and is not at all, at least not personally,
inimical to the independent theatre scheme; but he stands
like a stone wall against the prospect of giving up the
Chicago rights, which he says represent, after New York,
the most considerable portion of the 'field,' already much
restricted by the California cataclysm. Of course after the
play has had its run under the star system, it would be
open to the Players Theatre as a 'repertory house'; but
that is small comfort for us. A meliorating circumstance
of course is that Robertson is really more interested in and
has more faith in *The Faith-Healer* than in the present
play, and he understands that *The Faith-Healer* is his to
do what he likes with before anybody gets a crack at it.
Nevertheless I hate inexpressibly to bring to his knowledge the *impasse* in which I now stand with regard to
the *Sabine Woman*, which would perhaps never have been
written except for his encouragement and suggestion —
and which at any rate owes much to him on both these
scores.

Please show or send this letter to him. I would write
him personally if I knew his address; but at any rate the
whole case is stated here. The negotiations are at a stand-
still here, and I shall take no further step until I hear from
both of you at length.

NEW YORK, *Wednesday, May 9* (1906)

Am anxious to know just how he (Robertson) takes this
matter. Of course, as you say in your telegram and as he
says (with an accent of involuntary grudge, I feel) in his,
he will acquiesce in any arrangement, since his own prospects are so remote. But it is exactly because they *are*
so remote and precarious that I hate to be a party, even

passively, to any action which he would view as lessening by little or much his chance of winning out with the theatre scheme. Accordingly I have stood out for this clause of the contract until the last limit of Miller's patience has, I fear, been reached, and he is ready to chuck the whole business. The only concession I can wring from him is that Robertson may have the right to produce the play in Chicago after Miller's company has played one full engagement there. Really, leaving the personal equation aside, this is a liberal arrangement, since it gets the play into Robertson's hands a good while in advance of other repertory theatres. I hope he will understand that I have done everything I could to protect his interests, short of shipwrecking altogether the present plans, which in view of Miss Anglin's heroic exertions and Miller's liberal-minded co-operation would be very hard to justify, even if Robertson's chance of using the play were substantial instead of being, as it is, very shadowy.

I expect to get away tomorrow or next day to Cornish. The enclosed note from Percy will give you some notion of how I shall be housed.

NEW YORK, *Thursday, May* 10 (1906)

I was relieved to get your letter and Robertson's telegram giving his final attitude in the matter of the contract, for it seemed, at the last, to be quite ungrudging and hearty. I did the very best I could for him, anyhow. The negotiations still drag on and the historic document will not be signed before tomorrow or next day. The transfer of the seat of World Empire from Rome to Byzantium was an unconsidered trifle in comparison. I am, as you suspect, a bit jaded by the week long fussing over options, forfeits, royalties, 'long-run,' 'tour,' and 'stock' rights, and all the thousand and one strange considerations which it appears the vendor of a play, however unpretending it be, must take into his ken.

(Postmarked New York, May 11, 1906)

I had hoped to get off to the country today, but the momentous document was not signed, in all its eighteen imposing clauses, until four o'clock, too late to start. So I have gathered in Robinson and Torrence for a celebration, and if I can find a bird and a bottle in the old village worthy to express my sense of relief and satisfaction at the conclusion of this matter it shall be theirs. Every toast, whatever its ostensible purport, will be drunk to your eyebrows by at least one of the company. How I wish you were here, that we might rejoice together over the situation as only *we* could. If there is anything in the philosophy not dreamed of by Horatio, you will not be absent from the feast.

They are going to give the *Agamemnon* of Aeschylus (in Greek) at Cambridge about the middle of June. Can't you come to that?

(Postmarked Windsor, Vt., May 14, 1906)
CORNISH, Monday

The last two days have gone *perdu* so far as letters are concerned. Saturday I spent in a mad rush to get ready for the country, and I tumbled on to the train at four in the afternoon with half my errands undone and more dead than alive from an influenza which had been the unpleasant sequel of the jollification ceremonies of the night before. Yesterday I was in the full grip of it, unable to smell,

[267]

taste, see, or otherwise perceive, except through a sour veil of illness, the delicious country, wrapped in a grey dream of spring. This morning I am much better and shall be all right in another twenty-four hours.

The place is as lovely as I had remembered it, and everybody vastly hospitable and kind. I am not at all confident, however, of being able to locate myself in a way advantageous for the job I have on hand. The boarding facilities of the place seem very meagre. Shall write at length tomorrow, but will hasten this word off so that you may not worry at the unexplained lacuna in my correspondence. How I wish you were here this morning, to look on these delectable hills and drink the virginal sunshine. The spring is brand-new here — in the pussy-willow stage, so that I shall get it *da capo*, and must send it to you in assorted parcels by mail.

(Postmarked May 16, 1906)
CORNISH, NEW HAMPSHIRE
Postoffice: WINDSOR, VERMONT
Tuesday

This morning finds me measurably restored from the influenza visitation, and able for the first time to receive the sweet influences of the country through unblurred senses. The spring is very late, about in the mid-April stage. I shall be able to see it all from the beginning, as once before in dear old Mackinac. This is, however, conditional on my getting a liveable place to stay, which is still a bit doubtful. Today solemn deputations are to be made to various goodwives and spinsters who have been wavering in their minds, and a concerted attempt will be made to break down their hostility toward me as a stranger and a city-chap. The country people are as conservative here as if no 'colony' had ever troubled their world-old scheme of life.

Later — At this point Mrs. MacKaye asked me to go driving with her. We did not get back till two o'clock lunch-time. The stage had gone long ago, so this can't be mailed until tomorrow. On our drive we passed through the village and I bought the children a beautiful little music-box, which plays three tunes. Arvia, the little girl, after looking at it and listening to it in rapt silence, murmured to herself, 'Pretty! Pretty!' and a little while afterward brought it to me and said 'Please make it sing.' Here is Percy after me to go on our tour of persuasion.

CORNISH, *May* 16 (1906)

Our prayers (Percy's and mine) to the dames of the neighborhood were not in vain, and here I am, established in a big cool room, under the care of a motherly New England woman, whose dialect and view of life are alone worth twice per week what in her utmost stretch of thrift she has had the courage to charge me. I have four windows, two opening on a leafy road and the sunset, two northward on growing fields, a sheep-pasture, and distant hills, at this hour of five in the afternoon as blue as the hills of Beulah. On the other side of the road is a house belonging to one Harry Fuller, a landscape painter, rented for the summer to Ethel Barrymore. I expect to enjoy her, but I rather dread the crowd she will have about her. Still, they will doubtless be chiefly theatre-folk, and I am new enough to that world to entertain a lively curiosity concerning each and every denizen thereof. I note with satisfaction that there is a goodly tennis-court appertaining to her domain, and when one can't talk to her guests one can doubtless return balls over the net to them. The

MacKayes are about a mile away, and when they move at the end of this month they will be still more distant. This is an advantage, both as ministering to exercise, and as making our intercourse heartily elective.

As for your own blessed self, the thought of you in the toil and trouble, the grime and heat, takes the sunlight out of the day for me, or would if you had not conjured me not to let it do so. Since I have sat writing here at the window, a mighty thunderstorm has rolled up from the West, and now there is a glorious march and counter-march of battalioned clouds, and earthshaking thunderbursts, and leaping of lightning among the hills. By some curious freak of psychology, this brings me strangely and suddenly near to you, and I can hardly persuade myself that if I look round you will not be standing there at the other window, watching the elemental uproar, and wondering why I am so dull as to be writing letters instead of watching — and so I am. Dull, dull!

CORNISH, *May* 17 (1906)

By some unaccountable lapse of memory I forgot yesterday that it was the anniversary of our sacred day, forever to be remembered with hymns and trances of the spirit. As some slight atonement (to myself) I am going to copy out and send you the little poem which you know. I have given it, provisionally, the title of *The Three Angels*, which may be too fantastic and perhaps self-conscious. The only other I can think of is *Dies Angelica*, and Latin titles always seem like a subterfuge, somehow. Tell me what you think.

(In this letter was enclosed a copy of *The Three Angels*.)

May 19 (1906)

It has leaped here at one bound from timid and chilly spring to flamboyant summer. The calenture of the past two days gives me dark suspicions about this being the cool place MacKaye thinks it is.

I am writing to Cambridge for two tickets to the *Agamemnon*, June 19. I hope you will be the one to sit beside me and hear Cassandra's prophetic screams.

(Postmarked Windsor, Vt., May 22, 1906)

Letter from Ferd today calling loudly for the Fulda, which I had already mailed. Delighted to hear he has got to work again on the *Siena*. Did I tell you that Miss Anglin wants me to write her a Medea? Here you see the beginning of my downfall, in that I find myself seriously considering it! I suppose the real reason why I feel tempted is that I had such a great time at Corinth, the seat of the Medea legend in its later phases. They were excavating the ancient city when I was there, and had just uncovered, among other things, the well of Pirene, which Euripides (in his *Medea*) mentions in one of his wonderful choruses immortally.

Here is a gem notable for its fresh grasp of an old situation. Let me say in preface that I did not write it, and suspect the soundness of its point of view.

'Of all the women doubly blest
The sailor's wife's the happiest.
She only has to sit at home
And knit, and knit, and let him roam.

'Of all the husbands on the earth
The sailor has the finest berth,
For in his cabin he can sit
And sail, and sail, and let her knit!'

God forgive the man who wrote it. He was a bad man.

CORNISH, *May* 22 (1906)

The poem [1] in the *Reader* was written about nobody in particular, though I had in mind I forget which one of the many who have made shipwreck on the 'Art for Art's sake' fallacy. I thought I had told you about sending the poem to the *Reader*.

My arrangements with Miller, about which you ask, fill some nine pages of foolscap with typewritten clauses, but I can give you a brief summary. In the first place I agree to revise the play, and turn it over to him by July 15th. If then it is formally accepted, he agrees to produce it by Oct. 1st or forfeit $250; if it is not produced by Jan. 1 he forfeits $500 more, by May 1st $500 more; and failing production by Oct. 1st, 1907, he resigns his rights. In case of production, any or all of these sums count as advance royalties, reckoned on a basis of from 5 to 10 per cent of gross receipt, according to the weekly business. After a year's production, he has the privilege of renewing his rights for another year, by guaranteeing royalty returns of $1000 for that year, and so on as long as he desires to keep the play in his control. If he puts the play into the 'stock houses,' he shares in equal parts whatever it brings in to him. All rights of *publication* are reserved to me. No changes of text can be made without my consent. Robertson has the right to use the play in the Players Theatre any time after Miller has ended his first Chicago engagement. In case Miller decides to take up the English rights, he pays me $500 a year so long as the play is unproduced in London; in case he fails to produce, this money is mine unconditionally; in case of production it counts as advance royalties. The same for Canada and Australia.

[1] *Musa Meretrix.*

You probably stopped reading this sometime ago and have been letting your eye drift ahead for something of interest. I enjoyed the account of your morning walk with Bimbles immensely. As I asked once before, did you ever think of embracing the profession of literature?

The country here is at this moment wholly divine, warm sun and crisp breezes, shad-bushes and apple trees in their glory, more birds with more song in their gullets than I ever saw in all my life together. Blow-me-down Brook (that's its real name!) singing through miles of yellow willow between fresh ploughed fields, pine woods, and rocky sheep pastures, the whole country rolling into hill-forms of almost Tuscan grace, from any of which the climber can command leagues of delicious misty blue distance! You see I have fallen in love with it.

I am pegging away at revising the play. Have about finished the first act. It's going to be a whole lot stronger, but all the same it seems like a waste of time, when I might be doing something new and really interesting.

It is late, and I am tired from a long ramble in the hills. I wish you were breathing with me this odorous night air.

CORNISH, *May* 23 (1906)

About the *Agamemnon*. It is to be a notable performance, which I don't think I can afford to have you miss. The performance is on the 19th of June, in the open-air stone stadium of the Harvard athletic field. The conditions will approximate more closely than is usual the ancient ones. The play will be given with tragic masques, cothurni, choral dancing, and music specially written after the antique pattern. It ought all to be very impressive and suggestive. I feel that it will be a thing to remember all one's life, and I can't bear to think of your missing it. Besides, I want to show you some of my old stamping-grounds about Boston, and above all take you canoeing on the Charles for a long summer's day. Think about it, and let me have the benefit of your lucubrations.

Dark moist day here — birds singing small — frogs crazy with delight. Your little friend rather dark and moist, inclining to the bird's view of it.

CORNISH, *May 25* (1906)

Home late, after an afternoon and evening on the road with — guess whom? — No other than M—— and her Jeems. About noon she called me up from Windsor on the telephone. I had no idea she was in this region of the globe, and was naturally surprised. She explained that she and James were on a walking tour through New England, had heard that I was at Cornish, and thought they would 'demonstrate' me. I walked to meet them on the Cornish road, and we spent most of the afternoon, which was showery through sun, in the little MacKaye cottage and up on the hill watching the great panorama from Maxfield Parrish's porch. M—— was looking well, brown as a berry, and taking her twenty-five miles a day without a whimper. James pleased me a good deal more than I expected from your accounts — seems to me vitalized much above the average of his class and type, and with a temper genuinely poetic, though cramped into a mould such as one can buy at any ethical tin-shop. But the temper is there, I believe — at any rate I found myself attracted rather than repelled, which is an argument, for the person affected, unanswerable. We walked together to Windsor, crossing the river on an old-time cable ferry-barge and down the Vermont side through milking-time, frog-time, and rainy evening fragrances. I supped with them, they meanwhile persuading me to walk on with them for two days to Dorset, the highest village in Vermont, a proposition which I, not without some small heart-burnings, declined.

CORNISH, *May 25* (1906)

I am afraid you are worrying too much over Robertson's trouble, and taking the dishonesties of his opponents too much to heart. I seem to detect a flavor of misanthropy in your comments alien from your customary philosophic view of such things. This will make you smile — from choleric me to compassionate you. Smile if you will, but don't let them put henbane in your cup.

CORNISH, *May 26* (1906)

I have been helping the MacKayes to move, all afternoon. They are driven from their little nest by the choleric Admiral, who wants the house for a Swiss gardener. Fortunately, they only have to flutter a few rods up the road, and deposit the necessary feathers in the crotch of a new tree. I am carrying on a tremendous love-affair with Arvia, aged four. Yesterday she gave me a cherished green stone, carefully wrapped in the lace-and-satin skirt of her second-best doll. Today the feather of a dove which she found in the woods last fall, and had cherished with mystical rites for half a year. She is somewhat thrifty, even in her downright violence and storm of fortunes, for she ascertained by delicate circumlocutory questions what I had done with the stone, before she confided the precious feather to my keeping.

I am asked to supper at the Hapgoods', so must stop. They have a wonderful place, hung high in the face of mountain and river, the landscape, the garden in the foreground, and the house itself, subtly suggestive of Tuscany, but still with the good Yankee flavor.

Cornish, *May* 29 (1906)

I have been spending the night at the Herrick house, where I was employed until late helping Lovett get Mrs. H. and young Philip settled. Home now, only a few minutes before stage-time — hence this scribble. You need not be afraid that I will compromise with myself in rewriting the play. I have listened to what Miss A. and Miller had to say, and to what everybody else had, and shall of course take from the criticism what ever I can use. But I shall make no essential changes. What I am trying to do is to let air into the dialogue — make explicit what (for the stage) proved to be too implicit; and particularly to follow a line of reaction in Zona's case which shall keep the spectator enlisted for her, and make it possible to follow her struggle with understanding. It was certainly a great weakness of the play as it stood (tho' I think the acting was partly at fault) that she lost the sympathy of the audience, her final surrender therefore being robbed of its emotional interest. The dialogue was too suggestive and elliptical for the stage, and about all I am trying to do is to remedy this defect. Both Miller and Miss A....

Stage!

Cornish, *May* 30 (1906)

As I was saying, when the stage-driver so unceremoniously cut me short yesterday, Miller wanted me to make

[276]

some changes in the play which, tho' apparently slight, would really alter it organically. These I shall not even consider. I shall rewrite it along the lines I suggested yesterday, and if he and Miss A. do not want it, they can let it alone. *Ecco!* Such an outcome is not unlikely, nor would it particularly grieve me.

CORNISH, *May* 31 (1906)

When I get through the play (if ever that time comes) I am going to do a little spying-out of the land, in accordance with some lines I've got on abandoned farms. Your friend's remark about the 'discovery' of old age is suggestive, in connection with what has certainly been done by the modern poets of psychology for youth. The ancients seem to have studied age more lovingly and closely than youth: witness *Oedipus* and *Lear*. The moderns certainly the reverse.

CORNISH, *June* 1 (1906)

Percy has not been here for some time; he is in New York getting the elaborate stage-arrangements [1] for his *Joan of Arc* ready — stained glass windows that come to life, and bushes that turn into fairy Ladies of Lorraine, and what-not. I wish he were not so preoccupied with these paltry stage-osities. Sothern is just twice as bad as he is, and they spur one another on. However, it's a kind of dramatic measles, I guess, which everybody must have after his kind.

This is a transfigured night. It has been a sultry day, with huge high-built clouds and Jacob's ladders drifting

---

[1] These included new experiments in stage lighting and mechanics conducted by Abbott H. Thayer, assisted by Rockwell Kent and Barry Faulkner, based on Thayer's discoveries in protective coloration.

over the hills. Just before dark there was a smashing rain, then clear and cool till the moon came, bringing with her a wonderful diaphanous silver mist, which began playing tricks like those Chippewa River Phantasmagoria. My landlady's meadow is the Land of Heart's Desire, and Mr. Smoot's woods are Broceliande. And such odors — almost tangible and visible troops of incantation-weaving presences. Spicy pungencies 'in argosy transferred from Fez,' with the chill and homely tang of the New England hill-night.

Since I lit my lamp the June-bugs have been coming from this and surrounding counties to buzz and bump their protesting astonishment. It is only a question of time when they will put out the light, or me. One I have imprisoned in an empty matchbox, one under a glass, and one in my waistcoat pocket, where he demands constant reinsertion.

CORNISH, *June* 2 (1906)

The Barrymore arrived this morning, with a full complement of sensations, including a railroad wreck. My afternoon walk has intersected at various points her triumphal progress from villa to villa, as she takes a preliminary survey of her dominions. I am invited to meet her at dinner this evening, together with doubtless the entire male summer population. She is not expected to stay, by reason of Cornish's 'dulness'; accordingly all work has been suspended, and the amusement of Ethel is to be the one great communistic aim. Maxfield Parrish has laid aside his Dinkey Birds, Norman Hapgood his reforming of the national morals and manners, MacKaye his dreams, and I my contracts, to swim as goldfish in

Ethel's parlor jar. This is more than a metaphor. Her premises include a marble swimming pool, under a vine-covered pergola, with Greek pillars from which she is said to rejoice to dive. Bathing suits are furnished by rotation of peg, and the fit shall be as God wills.

As a preliminary ingratiation I have been feeding her cat (hers by virtue of having been left in the lurch by the owners of the house she is to occupy) with the choicest morsels from my plate, smuggled out under the very guns of my landlady's thrift. You will be pleased to learn that I like the cat, and faintly trust that it likes me. It is a beautiful tortoise-shell with a wild, wild, waving tail. Whether from responsive affection or with an eye to the main chance I don't dare to say, but the creature follows me about like a dog, and looks at me as it did love. Probably it is always hungry.

CORNISH, *June* 3 (1906)

The dinner proved to be of the *klein* and *gemütlich* order, myself and Maxfield Parrish the only male guests. Ethel, as one might postulate *a priori* would be the case, is exactly the same person over the soup as over the footlights, voice between a drawl and a coo, eyes *gamin* and questing, attitudes free-ish and piquant, no 'conversation' (as Jane Austen would say) but amusing little jabs at the passing subject, cigarettes ad lib. — inhaled. On the whole formidable, I should say, only to the *Weltmensch* or the fermenting boy.

What you say of Edith Flint and the little song [1] cannot but touch me. It is worth a good many dark days and disappointments to know that a word of mine has

[1] The song beginning, 'Of wounds and sore defeat,' in *The Fire-Bringer*.

entered for solace into that large and greatly afflicted heart.

After hammering at the thing in the back regions of my head for days and weeks, today I had the felicity to see pop into the front regions the right kind of ending for the play. It looks right today anyhow, whatever it may look tomorrow. It seems to me to preserve everything vital in the first, the violent, ending, and it brings the play to a close in an upswinging mood of lightness, going towards comedy — an immense advantage of course. Moreover, it makes Zona herself and not the brute catastrophe the *Erlösungselement* (such a word?) with only a fillip of the nerves to help her; and it brings in the family again, instead of leaving them hanging in the air with all their yarn unravelling, as in the makeshift Chicago version. Hoopla! Also, it makes Zona the active petitioner and pleader for the thing she has rejected many times from the hands of her lover, and makes him — through incredulity — the withholder. This last, though it may not be spotless gallantry on the author's part, is good drama. Supply yodel. I walk about comparing my fate after the Chicago mixup with that of a tragedian of the current vaudeville, who sings:

> When I got in a railroad wreck,
> An' los' my hat an' los' my check,
> *Who took dat ingine off my neck?*

For instead of the lugubrious answer 'NOBODY!' I say, 'The chap in the little back regions of me headpiece — see? He took that ingine off my neck, bless his heart for a good little chap in the little back regions!' Yodel. Blessed is he who rejoiceth while it is called today, for tomorrow he wakes up and sees what a fool he's been.

/ Arvia derives a mystic pleasure from contemplating the candies, which her mother — who is a fanatic on hygiene — won't let her eat. I told her they came from a pretty lady who loved her and therefore knew about her just naturally, without having ever seen her.

CORNISH, *June* 7 (1906)

What you suggest in the way of a newer and more vital presentation of old age in literature gives me, as the French say, horribly to think. But has not the corresponding presentation of youth in modern times been based on first-hand subjective knowledge on the writer's part, i.e. on his own youth as actually lived? What substitute for such knowledge is there in the other case, since old age has neither the power nor the desire to express itself. Answer me, O wise Sybil and Utterer of immortal thoughts.

Day before yesterday's jubilant mood, induced by what seemed to me a successful solution of the closing-scene problem of the play, has suffered from the inevitable day-after criticism; but I still believe it will do. The whole character of the girl has undergone a change as I rewrote, the soft, ample, and specifically 'feminine' elements gaining on the more robust and salient of my first conception. Less of the granite rib-rock of the New England hills and more of the velvety covering thereof. I think of changing the name to one more suggestive of these two qualities — I mean the inherited New England Puritanism and the soft covering which has grown over it. I once met a New England girl named 'Harmony' — what do you think of this — with a distinctive New England patronymic?

'Harmony Wentworth' or so-so? 'Zona' — altho' picturesque enough — carries no associations. As I see it now the girl's whole struggle is for 'harmony' between her love-life and that of her inherited codes and girlish predilections. The association between name and character would not be of course so blatantly obvious as I make it here. What do you think? But you can't know very well until you hear the new version.

CORNISH, *June* 9 (1906)

Being for some reason restless and sleepless last night I got up about three, just as the sky was brightening and the moon paling, and struck off over the hills. The coming on of day was so divine that I have been trying ever since to think of some plan of life which would make it possible to enjoy habitually this sincere and tender miracle of sunrise, and to utilize the more garish hours for rest.

(Postmarked Windsor, Vt., June 12, 1906)
CORNISH, *Friday*

Ethel is installing herself across the road, painting, polishing, and upholstering with her own fair hands and those of her volunteer corps, of which I am a humble but enormously efficient member. She is the best fun in the world, quite unspoiled, and a first-rate fellow. An exhaustless energy and a thirst for excitement almost comparable to yours, though in her case the limits of excitement are nearly coterminous with those of fun.

What you write as to your revised view of Zona's as the 'star' part in the play pleases me greatly. The rewriting will tend, I hope, to increase the power of the part to assert itself on the stage for what it essentially is. I have found for her, I believe, the 'dissolving word,' by which she brings her struggle and the man's refusal to see any need for anything but whole-hearted acceptance of their fate into a common focus, showing them both to have been forms of the 'expiation' her nature demanded: hers traditional, negative, self-conscious, gloomily purgatorial; his natural, positive, spontaneous, and cleansing through joy and life instead of through grief and refusal to live. This sounds very schematic and doctrinal, but of course it is not so much so when floated out on waves of feeling in the ebb and flow of dialogue. More of this later, for I see your face expressing vague disapproval.

(Postmarked June 14, 1906)
Wednesday

What you say about the essential meaning of the *Sabine Woman* is quite true. It is what I meant, but my phrasing of it, as usual, was drier, more formal than yours. Still, your words will help me in the final revision to give the cutting edge of the play a keener temper. As it takes ultimate shape I feel more encouraged about it. The letting-in of air which I have been doing has not, I think, thinned the thing, but made it a more inhabitable structure, and the recasting of foundations and rebuilding of arches has certainly made the form more solid and spacious. The new ending stands the test of time and criticism better than I hoped. I feel ready now to take a stand — with Miller — of No-compromise. If he wants it he must take it without disturbing a hair-line.

MacKaye read his *Nereida* [1] at his house last night to the small gathering, including Ethel. She was delighted

---

[1] Published, as *The Cat Boat*, in MacKaye's *Yankee Fantasies*, 1912.

with it, and there is a plan for her to stage it — in her studio — with herself as the boy (Nico), and Percy's sister, Hazel, as Nereida.

I go to Boston day after tomorrow.[1]

Mr. Gilder has asked me again to visit him at his Berkshire farm, and I have decided to go there for a few days after the Greek play.

FOUR-BROOKS FARM
TYRINGHAM, LEE, MASS. (*June* 27, 1906)

Four-Brooks Farm is a beautiful place, rising on terraces from creek and willow lowlands, through belts of grain and woodland, up to magnificent rocky pastures overlooking all, and covered at this moment with mountain laurel in extravagant flower. The farm is two hundred and fifty acres; a kingdom. The rich variety and royal extent of these said acres has made me revise my standards somewhat and hunger after two hundred and fifty myself, as the minimum with which a country gentleman can content himself or even contrive to get a good breath in.

I had expected to stay here only a day, or two at most, but they have made plans for me which will make it impossible to get away before Saturday. They are immensely kind and I am enjoying myself as well as I can in a state of impatience about the play.

(June 28, 1906)

They are waiting for me to join in a long drive somewhere — I believe to 'Lost Lake Farm' which Mr. Gilder owns and wants me to occupy. Life in this unworldly

---

[1] On Friday, June 15, 1906, Moody and MacKaye — en route to attend the Harvard Stadium performance of *Agamemnon* and the wedding of Josephine Peabody, at Cambridge — visited MacKaye's boyhood home at Shirley Center, Mass. Cf. note at back, under XX.

corner of the hills — now that I have resigned myself to the delay it involves — has a rare sweetness and charm. Mr. Gilder's character impresses me every day more deeply. There is something at once heroic and touching in the way he has conserved his boyish enthusiasms and ideals, the naïve ardencies and bashfulnesses of youth, its swift dartings and awkward stumblings, its obvious gaucheries and wild timid graces. He is a living confutation of the time-illusion. He has recently been to Cornell and consorted — to his delight — with your Corson.[1] Corson — he reports — is deep in spiritualism, talks daily with Tennyson, Browning and Milton, and lives on the most intimate terms of familiarity with his dead wife. You ought to go back and see Corson.

(Postmarked Pittsfield, Mass., June 30, 1906)

I have enjoyed my visit to Four-Brooks Farm, in spite of my restlessness to finish the play. Yesterday we made an all-day excursion to a farm which Gilder owns far up in the hills. It is a most romantic place, with a little old house reputed to be a hundred and seventy-five years old, and a hundred acres of woodland and rocky meadows — the meadows covered with brake and *wild thyme*, the latter in incredible quantity, giving a strange spiciness to the air. Except that the house lies rather low, and that the farm nowhere overtops the surrounding hills, it would be a fine place to live. He offers to sell it to me for a thousand, just what it stood him in for the original purchase money ($200) and what he has spent on the house. If it had an outlook I should be tempted to take up the offer. But there is no big escape for the eye, and that is fatal.

[1] Professor Hiram Corson, of Cornell University.

I have seen the illustration for the *Death of Eve*, and am on the whole pleased. Perhaps too naturalistic, but very strong, and without any suspicion of sentimentality. The poem is to appear in the Christmas number [1] — why, O why?

I have gone over the play in detail, with your criticisms in mind. Surely you are right. At first I was considerably discouraged and inclined to chuck the whole enterprise as an irrevocable failure; but after a closer examination I am led to believe that I can meet your objections without great difficulty and without very sweeping change. 'Whining metaphysician' rather sticks in my crop. I don't think the poor girl is quite as bad as that, though she is certainly over-anxious to vindicate herself. Rather a human failing, you must admit. Well, it will soon be up to Miller. If he is still dissatisfied, that will settle it, and the incident be closed.

Read the article 'A Swimming Pool at Cornish' in *Country Life* for July. It (the pool) is the one in which I am wont to disport myself after tennis on Ethel's court. There is an article on the Greek play in the *Theatre Magazine* for July — perhaps worth reading.

(Postmarked July 1 (?) 1906)
CORNISH, *Sunday*

I got back last night to find a letter from Miller clamoring for news of the play, and saying that in case everything was all right he wanted to open his season with it in the middle of September. I have written him asking for another week in which to finish it. With what there is still to do, and the recopying, this will be a strenuous week.

---

[1] Of the *Century Magazine*.

When the manuscript is ready I shall try to get him to come up here to read it, for I dread a trip to New York in this weather.

CORNISH, *July* 2 (1906)

I am working with teeth and toe-nails to get the play in shape to show to Miller, for if he carries out his proposed plan to open the season with it the eleventh hour for its completion has already struck. I have been at my desk all day and am too pen-fagged to write more than a line.

Cornish is very gay — for Cornish. I am refusing everything but dinner-invitations, of which I have seven at least to the week. After the day's work in seclusion it is refreshing to meet people in the informal way practiced here, and to eat a good dinner in witty company. I fear I could easily contract the dining-out habit, which has killed so many good poets. Lend me your prayers against the threatened disintegration.

CORNISH, *July* 4, 1906

I am copying the play — a long tedious job. I expect to get it off my hands, thank the Lord, this week, and hope I may never hear tell of it again.

CORNISH, *July* 6 (1906)

Your letters about A—— and her operation constituted a little masterpiece. They convince me anew that unless you turn your gifts of expression to some overt use the world will be the poorer by one great and delightful talent. Buy a graphophone and talk into it. Hire a stenographer to follow you about and surreptitiously transcribe you. Meanwhile write me about all the characters which,

[287]

coming under your observation and warmed by your benign presence, expand into something I ought to hear of.

CORNISH, July 7 (1906)

I was overwhelmed last night with a visitation of sickness which has kept me in bed all day. I am now (6:30 P.M.) — somewhat uncertainly — 'up and dressed.' I had dined at Arthur Whiting's, with music galore afterwards in a big dark room looking out on moonlit river and mountain, and had enjoyed myself deeply. Miss Barrymore gave me a lift home in her trap, and I went to bed feeling as fine as a fiddle, only to awaken in a couple of hours with the most dreadful headache and deadly nausea I have ever experienced. From then until the approach of breakfast time roused the house, was ages of misery, and the daylight hours (nominally such) have been little better, until an hour ago, when the ptomaines or other intestinal enemies gave me up as too tough to kill and withdrew discomfited. Now I am all right, or soon shall be. The feeling of ghostly lightness, insubstantiality, and eerie fecklessness, now that I am sufficiently released from pain to observe it, constitutes a curious charm. Myself, the world, time, history, memory, are stretched out as fine as tissue paper around me, and it is odds but I take an idle forefinger and puncture them into absurdity and shred them down the wind forever. Except that you are flattened and bleached out there somewhere in the papery expanse, and by a miracle of patience perhaps recoverable, I would do it.

CORNISH, July 8 (1906)

I shall probably have to go to New York tomorrow or next day to see Miller. He telegraphed me yesterday that he should be unable to come up here, and was writing. His letter will probably necessitate my making a rapid slide to the city, where we shall probably have a battle royal and shake hands over the corpse of my ambition as a 'practical' playwright.

(Postmarked Windsor, Vt., July 12, 1906)
CORNISH, Thursday

I have been in a state of (artistic?) irritability over the finishing of the play, and have let several days go by without writing, so loathly was the sight of pen and paper after I had finished fussing with my manuscript for the day.

A letter from Miller yesterday announces that he is unable to come up to Cornish as he had hoped, and wants me to come down. He says there is considerable interest in the New York theatrical world about the play, and he seems sanguine about the prospects. I have followed your advice as to condensing the dialogue at the two critical points, and it seems to me now to move swiftly enough. I think Robertson is wrong about the pistol-shot. It is a matter of nervous reaction on the part of the audience — almost mathematically calculable. I am sure that the present ending is better, though I don't believe you thought so after a hurried reading of it. The third act is weaker than the other two by the logic of the piece, and must remain so; but perhaps that won't prove disastrous. If it does, what matter? I am sure the second act is better without Mexican. He is sufficiently accounted for by the dialogue and acting.

I leave for New York, either at noon today or midnight.

[289]

CORNISH, *Friday* (May 13, 1906)

I wasn't able to get off yesterday, but am going at noon today. Miller has asked me to be his guest, and I suppose he will put me up at the Lambs' Club or the Players.

I think Robertson is wrong about retaining the original title of the play. It is true we shall lose some advance advertising by the change, but this seems to me a small consideration beside the value of a really appropriate and satisfactory title, which I feel *The Great Divide* to be. MacKaye is enthusiastic for it, and also for the new ending. Since you heard it I have pruned and polished to great purpose, and I feel reasonably satisfied now that it will do. How long a stay I shall have to make in town I don't know; Miller is to take me to White Plains, where Miss Anglin is staying, for a day, and a day or two more ought to finish it.

THE PLAYERS, NEW YORK, *July* 15 (1906)

I came down day before yesterday, arriving in time to dine with Miller and have a drive in the park before I read him the play. We began at eleven and finished at four in the morning. I did not get to sleep — what with smoke and excitement — until eight. He came to breakfast with me at eleven, then we had a couple of hours in the Princess Theatre, discussing stage-setting, from which I had to rush for a White Plains train to reach Miss Anglin's summer place by four. Reading the play to her, with dinner and other interruptions, kept me there until ten thirty, and I got back to N.Y., and tumbled into bed, more dead than alive, at midnight.

Miller is delighted with the new version, and intends to open the season with it here. Whether Miss A. will play the heroine or not is still uncertain. She balks at several points which are essential to the integrity of the idea, and which I have refused, unconditionally, to change. She hasn't now, and I think never has had, any conception of the play as a whole, or any interest in it. She is solely intent on getting a 'part,' but is not willing to lend herself to one when she gets it — the part must conform itself to her desire to score once every so often. Like ringing up fares in a street-car.

I am very pleasantly installed here at the Players Club, where I shall be for a day or two longer.

THE PLAYERS, NEW YORK, *July* 16 (1906)

I leave tonight (for Cornish) after a strenuous three days — so strenuous, plus the terrific heat, that I am a mere pulp physically and morally. I wrote you yesterday of Miller's hospitable reception of the play. It looks today as if Miss Anglin would insist on her right to play the rôle and there will have to be some more weary argument over certain points which affect her *amour propre*. I am determined not to yield anything essential, but I can't break off negotiations altogether, since the differences between us are small, and she has of course established a claim upon the play by her initial acceptance of it. Miller thinks I shall have to be here for a couple of weeks or so before the opening — that is to say, from about the seventh of September on.

CORNISH, *July* 18 (1906)

I got back to the country yesterday, rather the worse for wear, having hardly closed my eyes in slumber since I left. I have found a translation of some of the great Greek plays which I believe will please and profit you as much as — on a preliminary examination — they do me. They are in three volumes (one for each of the great tragedians), the series is known as *The Athenian Drama*, and is published by Longmans, Green & Co., New York. The Euripides is translated in uncommonly acceptable verse, by Gilbert Murray; the others I have not examined. You had better get them to read.

CORNISH, *July* 19 (1906)

It is blazingly, or rather smotheringly hot here. Hotter than it was in town. Of course it is unprecedented in the experience of the oldest inhabitant. MacKaye and I, with perhaps two other men, are waiting for a cool spell in order to climb Mount Ascutney. We expect to spend the night up there in an abandoned stone house, and come back the next morning. Aside from the prostrating heat the country is lovely. I have never seen such color — in New England — as these glowing days bring out in hills and woods and river, and the nights are beyond words wonderful — stars twice as big as they ought to be. Yesterday I saw a deer in the road near Parrish's. It was a full-grown doe, nearly as tall as a man. It watched me approach until I was scarcely fifty feet away, and then, apparently without fear, merely from a sense of bashfulness, dropped into the bushes and *floated off* (literally) across a field of high grass, moving like a swallow. There has been no 'open season' now for three years, and the gentle creatures have two more years respite. Then the ghastly business of extermination will begin again. — *Apollōn! Apollōn!*

Imagine me lying on my back in shady places, reading Euripides.

[292]

CORNISH, *July* 21 (1906)

The weather has been oppressively hot until this morning, when the heat broke in a tremendous thunderstorm and torrential rains, which still continue, turning the valleys into lakes, and even the roads into headlong rivers. The Biblical phrase, used to describe the rains of Noah, 'the heavens were opened,' never appealed to me as literally descriptive before. For half an hour this morning the water seemed to descend not in drops nor in sheets, but in a solid mass, as if the bottom had dropped out of the sky, and the 'waters which be above the heavens' were precipitating themselves bodily upon the groaning earth, loosening the mortised frame of nature with their impact. Incidentally, the roof over my personal head gave way, and my room became absorbed in the drowned landscape. I am writing in the stuffy farmhouse 'parlor,' and wondering where I shall sleep tonight.

I give ear to your advice as to knocking about New England for a time before beginning another job. MacKaye is very much used up from working — or trying to work — through the heated term, and I think perhaps I will drag him away from his inkpot by force, for a walk in the White Mountains. If so, I shall keep my eyes open for a mountain home.

(Postmarked, Windsor, Vt.; July 26, 1906)

It has just occurred to my dull wit, what it was which caused you to feel anxious about my condition — the exaggerated account which I gave of the rainstorm and its ravages. It *was* a terrific deluge, and it is true that the roof of this old farmhouse failed to stand the strain, making my room for a time decidedly damp. But a few shingles fixed all that, or will, when the proprietor 'gets round to it,' a process which has already, I understand, consumed all his effective energies for some six months. Meanwhile, the weather has come off dry and clear — and what is better, cool.

In consequence I have plucked up heart, and begin to feel within me the stirrings of something which may under a continued application of the same reviving agency prove to be a soul. The plan for the *Eve* drama, fished from the bottom of my trunk and the refuse-heap of my mind, takes on allurement. It seems to me, on coming back to it after giving time for the decomposing process to strip it bare of its more perishable integuments, that the idea has dramatic vitality, and is worth fussing with. I fancy you are a bit sceptical (probably my own reflected scepticism) and perhaps you are right; but I am going to give it the benefit of the doubt, and sit on the problematic-looking egg until convinced that it is addled.

(In August W. V. M. went to New Mexico to get properties for the stage-set of *The Great Divide*.)

ALBUQUERQUE, N.M., *Thursday*
(Late in August, 1906)

My train was several hours late, and I have had time for only a brief survey of the Indian and Mexican goods on exhibition here; but from what I have seen I anticipate no difficulty in getting together the necessary articles, though it seems probable that I shall have to make a trip up country into the reservation, in order to get the loom. There is no word from Miller yet, which means he has written instead of telegraphing.

I wish you could have watched with me the light fade on the mountains just now. This is a great and inspiring country. Before long we must both know it better.

ALBUQUERQUE, N.M.

I have time only for a word, as I have heard at the eleventh hour of an Indian 'harvest dance' tomorrow at the famous pueblo of Acoma, and am making a rush to see it. I go to a little hole called Laguna tonight, where I shall sleep under a cactus bush if I am lucky, if not, on top of same. Tomorrow morning ride eighteen miles into the desert — if I am lucky enough to get a pony, for I hear that the expected crowd will tax and probably exhaust the resources of Laguna for transportation.

Everything going smoothly here. Probably leave Monday for Chicago. Miller telegraphs that I must *positively* be in New York — with my stuff — by Friday.

Telegram:

ALBUQUERQUE, N.M., *Sept.* 3 (1906)

REACH CHICAGO WEDNESDAY AFTERNOON
MUST BE IN NEW YORK FRIDAY NIGHT

W

(Postmarked New York, Sept. 8, 1906)

Arriving here this morning I found everything in commotion at the Princess, stage-carpenters, scene-painters, property-men, advance-agents, *et al.*, feverishly struggling to get ready to go to Albany tonight — the plan being to open Monday. I came, you see, in the nick of time; in a few more hours Miller would have given me up and duplicated, the best he could, my bringings. He has attacked the play with magnificent energy, enthusiasm, and understanding; says that in his career of twenty-six years as an actor he has never been so interested. The changes he wants me to make are no-way vital, and can be made with no difficulty or heart-burning on my part. I go up to Albany at noon tomorrow, to be present at the dress-rehearsal Sunday night, and shall travel with the company until everything is shipshape.

(Postmarked Albany, Sept. 10, 1906)

The Miller-Anglin aggregation, with a carload of scenery, hit the town early this afternoon. We are in for a week of one-night stands between here and New Haven. I expect to have a good deal of fun watching the humors of the road. The opening performance, tomorrow night, is to be given in a vast affair which resembles nothing so much as a stock exchange except a skating-rink. I shall see rehearsal tonight and be able to judge of the company; as Miller himself is in a state of gloom over them, I hardly anticipate for myself an undiluted rapture.

Monday noon

Dress rehearsal last night from 7 until 5 — ten hours of horrors. This morning I am ready to swear on a pile of Bibles as high as Chimborazo that if I emerge from this venture with a rag of artistic reputation I will never write another line for the stage as it exists today. The company is indescribably bad, the vulgarizing process sickeningly complete. Even Miller, though he understands the part, cannot play it. The minor parts have been mis-mated to their would-be interpreters until the unholy cohabitation cries to heaven. The stage-setting, for all the money and pains that has been spent on it, isn't within ear-shot to our improvised affair of last spring. *O tò tò tò — tò po-poidá — Apollōn! Apollōn!* Give me a cave and a cup of water on the mountain of the muses, and let me die un-produced!

I shall stick at the nauseating business for a few days, and try to suppress some of the more monstrous features, then for a place to hide my head until the thing is over and forgotten, which fortunately will not be long. Your prayers, your pity, your forgiveness! I don't want to be a playwright. If I must write plays, buy me a burglar-proof safe, with a time lock set for A.D. 2006, to keep them in.

Yours in despair

W—

(Postmarked Sept. 11, 1906)
ALBANY, Tuesday

I must sing a palinode and recantation to my jeremiad of yesterday. The company pulled itself together for the first night, which I had dreaded so much, in a most wonderful way. The house was large and enthusiastic, which of course may have tended to flush my eye-glasses with *couleur de rose*; but when all deduction is made I believe even you, who are so much more jealous for me than I am for myself, would have found matter for approval in the work of the company. At any rate it was impossible to recognize in it the barbarous aggregation of that night-mare dress-rehearsal. I enclose a clipping from the local newspaper. We go to Amsterdam today, wherever Amsterdam may be. There is something, to me, touching and old-worldly in this strolling players' existence, even when carried on under the modern methods. I am so groggy I can hardly see to write, having been up again last night until four, at an impromptu champagne supper given by Miss Anglin.

NEW HAVEN, CONN., *Sept.* 13, 1906

The last two days have been a wild scramble of rehearsals, performances, rushing to and from hotels, catching and missing trains, chartering automobiles and trolley-cars for cross-country dashes to make good a missed connection, with bickerings over text and 'business' filling every cranny of time not consumed by more overt violence. Heigh-ho! But after all it is amusing.

I have been up so late every night and so early every morning that by now I am quite light-headed, and can't see the words on the paper. We shall settle down for a week at Washington, when you may again begin to prize me as a correspondent. At present I know you can't.

ATLANTIC CITY, N.J., *Sept.* 15, 1906

We came here last night for a fearfully delayed performance, ending somewhere between midnight and morning, the delay being due to a stalled baggage-car plus a wrecked passenger train (not ours), to get around which the company had to resort to trolley, team and automobile, in a crazy scramble cross-country. The theatre, when reached at last, proved to be on a pier out in the ocean, with breakers thundering a majestic accompaniment to my puny lines (they were once mine, and even these changelings claim a vague parentage in me!), dwarfing the little feverish action on the stage quite comically. But there was a big crowd ('the largest advance sale in the history of Atlantic City,' the manager grandly announced) and the people seemed interested. After it was over, I went out on the beach, and walked in the darkness and booming wind.

America — 1906

ATLANTIC CITY, N.J., *Sunday*

I have just returned from a five-mile tramp up the beach, and a sail, and feel like a human being again, the first time in days. We ended our first vagabond week last night, with a big 'house,' including the Czar of all the theatrical Russians, the magnipotent Shubert himself, to whom I was tremblingly presented, receiving some dubious curt praises and indubitable loquacious warnings not to be rejoiced before the time, since 'Proadway' was a monster of great incalculability of taste, wont to eat alive a playwright a day. There was that in the little man's salacious eye which said he deemed me the merest spoon-food for the animal in question, salvable but by some quaintest freak of humor. Still, there was the hard fact that we had 'played to' over six thousand dollars in a week of one-night stands, and that men breathe and walk on mystery.

We go to Washington tomorrow for a week. I shall stay with the company probably until the end of it, for there are still an infinitude of matters in the presentation which try my very soul. Many of them are ineradicable, but I must keep busy until what can be done is done. You mustn't feel that the 'first night' is over. These performances on the road are regarded by us as mere public rehearsals. The real opening will be in New York, Oct. 3rd, and you must be there to see it — that is, if by that time I think you can stand the performance.

WASHINGTON, D.C., *Monday*
(Postmarked Sept. 17, 1906)

We open tonight for a week's run at the 'Belasco Theatre,' quite a grand affair opposite the entrance to the

White House Grounds. The last two days of strenuous
rehearsals have made some impression upon the crudities
of the company, and the poetry of the play (if you'll admit
it has any of that) begins faintly to emerge. I have some
hope now that by the time we reach New York it won't be
utterly bad. Louis Shipman (one of my Cornish friends)
has his opening tonight — a play of the Civil War from
the southern point of view. — His wife is a Southerner (I
mean Shipman's) and I judge from the rehearsal I saw this
afternoon that she has enabled him to assume the Southern standpoint in a way which will be novel and charming.
She is a daughter of an army officer and a native of Washington, and the whole town is expected to turn out to
whoop it up for Louis. I shall be among them, leaving my
own bantling to scratch worms for itself. I'm afraid it will
be pretty hard scratching; we shall be lucky to get half a
houseful under the circumstances.

WASHINGTON, D.C., Tuesday
(Postmarked Sept. 18, 1906)

Today has brought almost a repetition of that ghastly
morning which followed the first night of the play in
Chicago. Last night was our opening here, and everything
seemed auspicious; there was a big audience and hearty
applause. This morning, however, the Washington Star
(the leading — in fact only — morning paper) contained
a most brutal and blackguardly onslaught upon both play
and performers, a thing so shamelessly unfair that we were
at a loss to find a motive for it, until, in the course of the
day, it has come out pretty clearly as the work of the
Syndicate, who hired a wretched scribbler to stab us in the
back. He did his work thoroughly, for it appeared when

the New York papers arrived that he had telegraphed his article *in extenso* to them. There is general indignation among the other newspaper men in Washington, and they will do what they can to repair the damage, but our sales for the week are, Miller thinks, knocked in the head, and that, together with the prejudice to New York opinion, is a pretty serious thing. The days of guerilla warfare are not over, nor is the trade of the bravo obsolete. Will write further particulars tomorrow, with clippings, when the situation shall have developed further.

(Postmarked Sept. 19, 1906)
WASHINGTON, D.C., *Wednesday*

The delayed letters reached me today. Your buoyancy of spirit cheers me like a cordial. I am not without need of such cheer, for the situation here is strained. The blackguardly newspaper onslaught, engineered and carried out to its legitimate consequences by the 'interests' opposed to us, has co-operated with the smothering heat to reduce our audiences to a handful. The expenses even of a modest company like ours are crushing, when there is practically no in-take to counter-balance them, and it hangs on a hair whether or not we will survive the ordeal. Of course, in the large purview, it matters microscopically little whether we do or not, but there is a kind of dogged instinct for 'success' in me that clinches my teeth over-hard in this crisis. Your lovely letters come as an emollient to my chafed spirit, and admonish me of the realities. My astonishment and awe grow hourly, that you, immersed for months and years in this acid bath, nevertheless keep your instincts keenly true.

Thursday

The force of the Syndicate attack seems to have about spent itself, but the weather is the most awful I have ever experienced, and the best the company can do is to drag listlessly through their parts to practically empty benches, since none but theatre-maniacs will subject themselves to three hours' imprisonment. For our sins, there exists under the stage an establishment of Turkish baths, in full blast; you may imagine what this means, with the weather conditions given. I enclose a specimen of the kind of criticism we have been getting, just to show you what the Trust can do when it tries. The only solace in the situation is that they should deem us formidable enough to call for such methods. This little tidbit was telegraphed, by the local paper which printed it, to the *New York Herald*, and from that as a centre has doubtless been sent broadcast. These are among the amenities of the profession, I suppose, and to be accepted as such. Mrs. Le Moine (you remember the lady who did *In a Balcony* in Chicago, and *Blot in the 'Scutcheon* in New York) is holding Miss Anglin's hand through the crisis; she is a homely, vital, eloquent, and thoroughly crazy person; you would delight in her, unless you found she talked too much.

We go to Pittsburgh Sunday.

WASHINGTON, D.C., *Sept.* 22, 1906

I didn't write yesterday, being in a state of profound depression from the weather and the sweeping effects of the newspaper war which is being waged against us. Our 'business,' which up to the time the cyclone struck us had been nearly a thousand dollars a night, fell off immediately to less than three hundred and has not recovered. This of course means ruin, if very long continued, and the ghastly and prankish injustice of the thing makes me ill, on the speculative plane, quite apart from its practical bearing. If the play were shelved tomorrow I should still feel that I had found my account in it, and had no cause to repine. But the fact that an ignorant malicious reporter can carelessly sandbag and throw into a corner an enterprise which has cost numbers of worthy people endless thought and labor, is really a thing to make one sick with disgust. Tonight it is a shade cooler, with a blessed hint of rain somewhere within a hundred miles, and I feel my spirits beginning to revive. Miller has been a brick throughout the trouble. His faith in the play is unshaken, and that is saying a good deal for him, when he is paying for his faith in hard dollars to the tune of thousands a week. We go to Pittsburgh tomorrow.

PITTSBURGH, PA., *Sunday night*

Here we are in Pittsburgh, after a hot day in the cars, to find it heavenly cool, an inexpressible relief after the awful heat of Washington. Our experience there was one of mingled tragedy and comedy. The newspaper which took a particular aversion to us manhandled us all week, and pursued us out of town with a column of variegated abuse in the Sunday edition. We relieved our feelings from time to time by offering five hundred dollars to any charity if the managing editor would put us for five minutes in the same room with the anonymous author of our woes, and lock the door. The man. ed. was all compassion and condolence, finally declaring that he knew exactly how we felt, having himself once put thirty thousand dollars into a burlesque, only to have it sand-bagged into thirty cents, by the papers. We pressed the point of veracity, of critical probity. It was like climbing a mountain of plate glass. He understood our feelings and mingled his tears with ours, and the next morning printed a more outrageous libel than ever. *Basta!* I am going to the mountains of Estremadura and enter a Trappist monastery. I am inclined to think that the Syndicate had nothing to do with it — that it was personal righteousness and the moral code, on the part of some glad-eyed young Southern knight of the pen. Who-ever it was, I respect him, for he certainly did do it to us a plenty.

We have one week here, then go back to New York, to open at the Princess on Wednesday, Oct. 3rd. We shall need the two odd days to rehearse with the new set, in the second act, which is so different that the timing of the cues will all have to be done over again. I am taking it for granted that you are coming on, though I tremble too.

PITTSBURGH, PA., *Tuesday*
(Postmarked Sept. 25, 1906)

We opened here last night and woke up this morning to find ourselves still in the critical storm-belt. All the morn-ing papers except one attack the play savagely, on moral grounds, seeing only the shell of it and utterly ignoring its inner sense. To them it means an attempted rape, a re-volting case of forced marriage, and the final surrender of the woman to a moral monster. *Eheu!* I guess the meat we are trying to get them to taste is too strong for them. I feel pretty thoroughly convinced that they won't have the play on any terms. But we are not going to give up the fight until we are sure. Sometime or other they have got to take it. It is right.

Lend me your prayers. We maybe won't weather the storm, but we want to go down gallantly. In this time of misunderstanding my heart turns to your nature and your mind as a sunflower to the sun.

PITTSBURGH, PA., *Wednesday*

The newspaper hammering which we got here has not materially hurt 'the business,' and unless something quite cataclysmic occurs we shall open as brash as you please in New York on Wednesday of next week. I am torn between eagerness to have you there, and fear that the whole thing will seem to you — and will really be — a dismal failure. Nothing about play or players satisfies me or gives me any rest from the fretful desire to make it quite over; but it may be that I have watched it all too closely and too long, and have got it on my nerves. I'm not going to accept your not coming, even as a remote possibility, though Heaven knows, after you are in New York, I shall probably lock you up, and prevent your going near the theatre, in sheer shame-facedness and panic. The things which have been written about the play by the guardians of public morality have given me a vaguely criminal feeling, so that I begin to skulk and look behind me.

(Harriet did go to New York for the opening night of *The Great Divide*. On her way back she stopped at Parkman, Ohio. From there she was called home by the news of a fire in the workroom of her business.)

NEW YORK, *Oct.* 7 (1906)

I have been wandering about in rather a daze today, chewing the cud of recollection, and trying to assemble my parts after the late disrupting excitements. Saturday night I timidly suggested to Miller that I wanted to make a few trifling changes in the play, but he threw up his hands to heaven and declared me a Nihilist, a man of no bowels, and a damn fool who didn't know when he'd got a good thing. Nevertheless I am going to rewrite the act along the lines we talked over, and spring it on him by stratagem. The Bubble, if anything, continues to swell; the house sold last night seventy dollars above 'capacity,' and tickets have been put on sale *twelve weeks in advance!* This last is an un-heard-of piece of braggadocio, and ought to be visited by an avenging Heaven with catastrophe and collapse.

This afternoon I saw Mrs. Le Moine, and told her something about the *Eve.* She listened attentively, and then asked if I couldn't transfer the story to modern life. I told her that's just where it was already, and I didn't in-tend to expose it to cobwebs and museum shelves by put-ting Adam in creased trousers and Eve into glove-fitting etcetera. She affected to understand the play as out-lined, and to like it, but she did neither the one or the other.

I have been seeing you today against the green Parkman woods, just ripening to autumn. I hope you got a little heartsease out of your hours there, and a little strength to take up the battle.

NEW YORK, *Oct.* 8, 1906

Your telegram about the fire gave me a great shock, and in spite of your reassuring braveries, I fear that the blow to your worldly prosperity will prove to be serious. Will you be able to go on with the manufacturing during re-pairs?

The Great Divide continues its triumphal career. Mrs.

Davidge — a daughter of Bishop Potter — in a note just received, says, 'I was there the second night, and it was a great blessing that I was able to be as orderly as I was in a moment of such glory and triumph as you have brought to our time and our country. To feel that stupid common audience become alive and sentient in spite of itself, groping round for conventional ropes to grasp when puzzled because it had to face God and Nature, was a great and grand experience,' etc. etc.

I was marched, at the point of a pistol, to Sarony yesterday, by the business manager of the Princess, and made to sit for my picture.

(Postmarked Oct. 13, 1906)
NEW YORK, *Thursday*

The play still rides the comb of the wave. I enclose a couple of fool newspaper clippings; they are not worth reading, except for the fact that the managing editors of the respective sheets think the play of sufficient public interest to waste space on still.

NEW YORK, *Oct.* 13, 1906

The buoyant tone of your letter gave me great pleasure and relief. You wretched creature, I believe you positively enjoy being burned and drowned out of existence, for the zestful excitement those exceptional processes add to the same.

The large iridescent bubble of our luck here refuses to burst, and we are beginning to believe that — at the worst — it is of good tough rubber, guaranteed not to leak for several weeks anyhow, and to collapse by gentle degrees when it does. I find managers and dramatic agents waiting under every lamp-post with contracts in their hands. Daniel Frohman offers vague but glittering terms for a play for his wife — Margaret Illington — now starring in Pinero's *House in Order*. Against all this of course in sheer self-defence — to say nothing of self-respect — I set my face as a flint. Shubert's 'publicity man' the other day beguiled me by treacherous means into Sarony's studio, and had me photographed before I knew it. I send two pictures representing the least regrettable results. The one bending forward is perhaps not so very bad. The other — and perhaps both — I am afraid you will deplore. However, 'done is done and lost is lost and smashed to hell is smashed to hell.'[1]

NEW YORK, *Oct.* 14 (1906)

Here are some clippings which may amuse you. The (John) Corbin one is interesting and acute, tho' he leaves the poems little to say for themselves. The 'deadly parallel' which he established between the play and the Philippine poems will (I fear) strike a responsive chord in your imperialistic bosom, though of course the parable will not hold water, nor are the two cases in the least analogous, essentially. However, the retort is so neat that I can't help rejoicing in it, as a stroke of art, as I wrote Corbin after I read it. It is hard to be told at this late day that one is a mere echo and ape of former men; but it is all in a day's work, and I dare say there is a good deal, superficially, to warrant the charge. I have been too careless in the matter of expunging chance traces of 'influence' — a thing which would have cost me no pains, and would have aided the weaker brothers by removing a stone of stumbling.

[1] Quoted from lines of the hero in *The Great Divide*.

If my engagements here are not too pressing, I go to Philadelphia tomorrow to hear Percy's *Jeanne d'Arc*.

THE ST. JAMES (Hotel)
PHILADELPHIA (Oct. 16, 1908)

Last night the audience was cordial and today's newspapers are very complimentary, though the performance dragged and the many lovely passages of poetry went for next to nothing, being badly rendered and lost in the vast spaces of the theatre. Poor Percy is going about haggard, listening to a thousand conflicting counsels as to cuts and changes. I am hoping they will give him time to cut it properly. Miss Marlowe is enthusiastic over her part and Sothern is loyal. I send you the morning press notices. This has given me to think — I mean about the problem of the verse-play on our stage. I go back to New York this afternoon, and shall probably stay there another week, then I join you. Philadelphia wears the same benign aspect we remember. I have saluted our holy places.

Yours —

W—

(Postmarked New York, Oct. 19, 1906)

The last two days have been full of business and turmoil — a mad round of reporters, cartoonists, literary and dramatic agents, with plans to propose and contracts to be signed, with Brother Douty (the agent for the studio building) weaving an embroidery of legal threatenings and slaughter over all. I shall have to pay for the studio during the six months it has been vacant. I tried to get it back but unsuccessfully. I realize now my folly in letting it go, for it is the only livable place in New York at all within my means, and I suppose I shall want to be here off and on, shall have to be in fact, if my high dive into theatrics does not prove a final and fatal header. The town seems to have gone completely daft about the play, so much so that I begin to feel concerning it a kind of distressing aversion and shame.

MacKaye is here today, from Philadelphia, where it appears that his prospects — for which I feared — are good. His play has been cut and otherwise quickened, and is now going excellently, according to his own and newspaper reports.

I ran across Nordfelt here today, and expect to dine with him tonight, in company with some other chosen spirits.

NEW YORK, *Oct.* 20, 1906

Everything is all right here, though I am getting tired of the round of excitement in which I am kept perforce, day succeeding day with nothing done, nor even a quiet hour to think or read. Yesterday I was approached with elaborate diplomacy, by an agent of Charles Frohman (the main guy of the Syndicate, as you know) offering the most alluring terms and conditions in case I would give him an option on my next play. The offer was fifteen hundred dollars advance payment, and royalty percentages nearly twice as large as I am getting on *The Great Divide.* I turned him down, of course, but I confess to feeling a twinge of temptation to accept, in view of the fact that everything (I mean as to time, stars, etc.) was left so alluringly vague. Still, I know that the feeling of being under contract would paralyze my effort, and I did not seriously consider the proposition even for a moment. The jubilee dinner which Miller is giving comes off on Tuesday night. After that I want to go up to Dan Mason's joint in the Connecticut hills and get a sniff of autumn air.

(Postmarked Oct. 22)

I go out this afternoon with Dan Mason to his country place in Washington, Conn. From what he says I am prepared to like it. It is a thousand feet above sea-level, on the watershed of the Housatonic River, perfectly country-like and unspoiled, and only two hours from New York. I worry a good deal about you these days. I fear that the complications resulting from the fire, added to those already existing, must be dreadfully wearing.

WASHINGTON, CONN., *Tuesday*

This country hereabouts is almost *almost* good enough to make one exclaim 'I will search no farther' and begin at last to live. What it lacks is the chance for the spirit to escape exultingly into vast distances; but it possesses every intimate beauty and charm. We have just had a great bonfire of maple-leaves, and how I wish you could smell the smoke and watch the quivering embers, changing like watered silk in the crisp evening breeze. The Masons are hanging on as long as the weather will let them, like the wise people they are, hoarding every minute, and dreading the hour which shall knell them to their hundred-and-'leventh-street flat.

NEW YORK, *Oct. 25, 1906*

The old studio has slipped through my fingers irrevocably, by virtue of my dilatoriness, but today I found another which — apart from its comparative expensiveness — is very tempting. It is at the top of a new studio

[311]

building just erected by the Arts Club on Twentieth Street. The building is a very tall one, and from the windows of the rooms I have an option on you can see all over the city and the East River, an inspiring view. Besides the studio there is a bedroom and a bathroom — everything in good taste and excellently furnished. If the price were less I should snatch at it, for I could not be better situated at such recurrent periods as I want to be or have to be in New York. The studio building is connected with the club, making the meal problem easy, and it fronts on Gramercy Park, one of the few quiet corners of the city. The hotel and lodging-house existence which I have been leading renders the prospect of a livable place as a *pied-à-terre* in time of need very enticing, but the price (eight hundred) seems extravagant, for a person of my tastes and resources.

NEW YORK, *Oct.* 27, 1906

I meant to write you yesterday from Cos Cob, where I spent the day with Torrence, but I couldn't get away from people long enough. There is a charming place to stay at Cos Cob, an old Revolutionary-times house, on a quaint village street (or rather road), kept by a nice young couple, gentle folk, in unconventional family style. A rocky, hilly country is at hand, and the Sound not far off (walking distance). I believe it will be a great resource as a place to run to, when I am in New York and want a breath of country. Upon mature consideration I have decided not to take the studio. The club aspect of it threatens to be too pronounced, and the price is high, very high considering the amount of use I should get out of it. Saturday night was the long-talked-of dinner at the

Players Club. There were notabilities present, and 'a good time was had.' I went home by daylight leaving a few old inveterates still talking theatre over the demolished table.

NEW YORK, Nov. 2 (1906)

Have been struggling with the blue devils all day and yesterday — perhaps the back-wash of your 'poetry-letter,' which sent its first wave by me so innocuously. I keep starting up in a terror of haste, hearing a dreadful Voice cry that life is going or gone and nothing done. And then another, thin and satiric, inquiring in a level tone what this so important business is which isn't done, and exactly what *my* part in it would seem to be, anyhow! Disturbing gentry, both. Perhaps their hanging-about is partly due to reading over the proofs of my North American article on Joe, which will now be out soon.

(Postmarked New York, Nov. 4, 1906)

I can't shake off the cloud of oppression and quasi-despair which hangs over me, but I know perfectly in my inner mind that it is nothing except the revenge which Nature is taking for my too long loaf. Don't be alarmed for me; I have myself in hand and shall be all right soon.

Sunday, Nov. 11 (1906)

I blew into town last night, after one of the most amusing and exciting four days imaginable spent in the quest of an abandoned farm. The quaint and world-forgotten places I found, the delicious types! One of them, for instance, an old house standing high in rolling hill country (1000 feet elevation) overlooking a fine forest-locked lake, with eighty acres of land attached, all for two thousand dollars. When I asked the owner how old the house was, he looked up at the roof-tree, and said with unforgettable dignity and pathos: 'I have lived here for the seventy-six years of my life, and my great-grandfather left this house, with his four brothers, to join the forces of General Washington.' The house is staunch and goodly still. It seems a sacrilege even to think of buying it, and exiling the aged couple; but they (or at least the old gentleman) is anxious to sell; the old lady manifested a cold silent hostility toward me, and there is no doubt a tragic story here, in the divided will of these old friends and lovers, which has kept me awake nights thinking of it. There is also probably privation and suffering. I am going to try and smuggle a little money into their hands, if it can be done without violence to their pride, which was manifestly great. The thought of that ancestral pair alone in that mountain solitude, facing a New England winter with their meager store of strength and comforts, is one to dwarf the imaginings of Shakespeare and Sophocles.

(Postmarked Nov. 15, 1906)

I stumbled yesterday on an apartment which was so tempting as a permanent *pied-à-terre* that I took it, and am now engaged in fixing it up. It is on Waverly Place, very near Washington Square; the entire top floor of an old-fashioned house where you never see a soul or hear one squeak. There are six rooms, including a kitchen; two of the rooms have grates, and are very pleasant places, also a third smaller room with a good light. The two other rooms are darkish, but will make excellent store-houses, etc. It has just been painted and papered throughout, and is clean as a pin. There is a nice janitress, who will take care of the apartment for a consideration. The price is only ten dollars a month more than I paid for the studio, and though there is no single room which is as pleasant as that one, the possession of such realms and islands of space will be a boon, will it not? There is to me a quaintness and old-worldishness about the whole establishment which I believe you will also feel and prize.

There have been great doings here this week — a sumptuous production of *Pippa Passes* (which was damned unconditionally by a carping, narrow-minded press) and Mme. Nazimova in *Hedda Gabler*, critical opinion being sharply divided and faction running high. To my mind she was emphatically not Hedda, though greatly fascinating and artistically consistent. Tomorrow and Friday Miss Anglin and Lena Ashwell play alternate tragedy and comedy rôles in *Mrs. Dane's Defence*. Henry Arthur Jones, the author of the piece, you remember, is here to serve as arbiter of arbiters upon their performance. I hear that the New Theatre, having proved its thirst for modernity by producing *Engaged*, is now demonstrating its zeal for the high and beautiful by giving a dramatization of Rex Beach's *The Spoilers* under the mild patronizing eye of Daniel Frohman.

(Postmarked New York, Nov. 17, 1906)

I am engaged in a struggle similar to yours, trying to get my rooms in shape for future occupancy. Paper hangers, carpet-layers, plumbers, et al., are in their immortal conspiracy against even my humble plans, and the days go by without visible progress made. I am tired in my very soul of living in hotels, as to the body, and in a no-man's land of idleness and frivolity as to the mind.

Thursday night I went to a dinner given by Henry Arthur Jones to 'the Dramatists of America,' as the menu grandiloquently stated. There were some hundreds of them (the D's of A), doubtless all known to fame, but with a few exceptions profoundly unknown to me. Jones himself was delightful, and some of the old guard, like Bronson Howard, interesting to see and talk to. Sousa was there, and marched through his dinner at a stirring tempo.

Last night saw the opening of the Lew Field's burlesque of my play, under title *The Great Decide*. Parts of it are excruciatingly funny, and it contains a lot of sound criticism in the guise of travesty. You must see it before the gas is all out of the champagne.

I send you the long-delayed article on Stickney. The dreadful syntax of the opening sentence is not my fault.

NEW YORK, *Nov.* 21, 1906

We (Percy and I) went together to *The Great Decide*, of which I send a program. The burlesque is not on the whole good, though Miss Anglin's appearance and manner are caught to the life in delicious parody.

So the New Theatre is about to join the great majority of ill-considered ventures of which it was so conspicuous an example! *Absit in pace!* Of course I will do anything I can to help Robertson, even to public speaking, though the thought of that sends cold chills down my spine.

Telegram:

Nov. 27, 1906

COMING HOME FOR THANKSGIVING ANYHOW
ARRIVE FOUR WEDNESDAY AFTERNOON
PENNSYLVANIA   W

NEW YORK, *Jan.* 4, 1907

Since arriving in these blatant regions, homesickness, dreary weather, and a series of *contretemps* in connection with my rooms, have kept me from writing, lest I might break the bright circle of our understanding with my peevish distressful mood.

As for the rooms, nothing that I had left orders for had been done, or if done, so badly done that it were better left undone. My water-pipes had frozen and burst, as one detail, and as another, my grates today absolutely refused to draw and concentrated their energies upon filling the world and my lungs with infernal and unstanchable smoke. Landlord Smith promises that some revolving contraption of tin affixed to the chimney-pots will make me wonder why I ever had a fleeting doubt of him or of his works. I suspend judgment, but with a fainting heart. My gas was not turned on (another detail) and thirty-six hours of pleading and threat have not yet availed to convince the gentlemen of the gas-monopoly that, having pocketed my deposit as guarantee of good faith, they have not discharged toward me every earthly duty.

107 WAVERLY PLACE, *Jan.* 8 (1907)

I have got nearly settled by now, and am beginning to see a little meaning in life again. The chimney-cap, about which I was skeptical, seems to be all that the authorities claim for it. My grate draws like a wheel-horse; I have a fine fire in it this afternoon, which was kindled three days ago. I was instructed enough to buy a very high-grade anthracite, which burns to a white powder and makes absolutely no clinkers — so far. I have followed your instructions in fitting up the small front room as a bedroom, and a few nights have so inured my tympanum to the street noises that I only wake up when they stop, which is seldom enough in all conscience. The front rooms have begun to take on a habitable, even a cosy, air; the larger back room is a limbo into which I rarely venture.

You will be glad to know that the seat-sales at the Princess have picked up again since the holidays. Miller was not, as I had feared, discouraged by the falling-off; all the theatres shared the same fate. To my considerable relief, he has about given up his plan of going to London for the spring season. He thinks, and I have always thought, that to interrupt the run here, and hazard the future fortunes of the play on a more than doubtful London success, with its inevitable bad effect upon the next American season, in case it didn't pull off, is poor strategy. He plans now to run here through the entire season, open at Daly's next fall, and keep it on the boards there as long as the public wants it, then to tour the country with a solid New York endorsement back of him, uninvalidated by a possible 'frost' abroad.

I am re-reading Wm. James's wonderful book, *Varieties of Religious Experience*, with a view to better understanding my man Schlatka.[1] Do you know the book? The main text might not interest you, but you would be carried away by the 'documents' cited in illustration. These are numerous and amazing; and they range over all history. Already I feel a sounder grip on my theme from studying them. James's treatment is masterly. He gives the cynics and the skeptics all they ask, and then proceeds quietly to spread out the documents — chiefly autobiographical, until the mind gradually loses its resistance, and is

[1] The name first given to the Faith-Healer in W. V. M.'s play of that name.

overwhelmed and confounded by the heaped-up evidence.
Not that James has a thesis to prove; he merely investi-
gates and compares, but the conviction which emerges,
that there is a living divine spirit at work in the world,
by excluding which we are lessened and by receiving increased, seems at last inescapable.

107 WAVERLY PLACE, *Jan.* 12 (1907)

I had (I use the past tense for self-encouragement) the
devil's own time about my rooms, and after I got com-
paratively settled, and turned to my work as to a refuge,
there descended upon me the water-spouts of God in the
shape of the black melancholy which always lies in wait
for me at that threshold, after I have been too long
away. Well, you needn't worry about that; it will pass, is
already passing. It is imperative for me not to be anxious,
or in a hurry, for that spoils all. I must take example by
the large generosity with which you treat life, and use myself a little in the same spirit of tolerance. Perhaps I have
been only lonesome and homesick; it is very likely. You
have been continually in my mind, but not as a part of the
distressing foreground, rather a light behind and above.

Torrence and Robinson have the dramatic fever acutely.
Torrence has just finished a three-acter which he is to read
to me tonight. It is called *The Madstone* — certainly a
striking title, is it not? It seems the 'mad-stone' exists
among the folklore properties of his native Xenia, Ohio.
It is a small porous stone supposed to possess the property
of extracting poison from the human body, when placed
upon an envenomed wound. He uses it as a symbol of
woman. Robinson thinks the play is a big thing. He (R.)
has also one in first draught, called *Ferguson's Ivory Tower*,

the ivory tower, I believe, being Art. It would be wonderfully good luck if they both pulled it off. One could begin to think the American drama, long awaited and devoutly prayed-for babe, really about to be born.

The Faith-Healer is stodgy and sullen, but I haven't lost hope of its starting in some day to behave. If it doesn't, I know exactly what to do with it, to wit, chuck it over the moon and forget where it falls.

Jan. 13 (1907)

Your picture of the benign old madman in the snowy street, sowing mysterious seeds in the air, gave me the good shivers. It must have been Old Pourquoi, in a Christmas mood.

Don't worry about Brother What's-his-name the book collector. He is an amiable lunatic who has devoted his life and a large fortune to gathering first editions of living authors (all of them potentially dead authors) and getting them to write on the fly-leaves.

Torrence read me his play last night. It is quite a remarkable thing. I have already got Miller interested in it for Mme. Nazimova. Will tell you more about it later. Write me whatever occurs to you to say about James's *Religious Experiences* — or any part of it.

(Postmarked New York, Jan. 18, 1907)

My not writing has been due to a feeling that the Faith-Healer didn't want me to. You understand. In the conscious region I suffer from a kind of paralysis and inhibition about him, which prevents my putting pen to paper (to any purpose), but I feel also that something is going on 'inside.' It is clearer to me every day that the greater part of any real work of the imagination is done in the subterranean regions of one's personality, and that the part of wisdom is absolute passivity and patience. This is a hard lesson to learn, and a thrice hard method to put in practice, especially for one so impatient and faithless as I am. Doubtless the inability to sustain the period of incubation, the heathen yielding to the demand for something to exercise the surface faculties upon, is the secret of many tragic failures in this way of life.

Tonight I am going to see a Yiddish play in the Bowery, by one Kramer, pronounced by no less an authority than Mr. Huneker to be the 'greatest American dramatist.' As you would say, I do not know my Kramer.

107 WAVERLY PLACE
Monday, Jan. 21 (1907)

I went last night to the annual dinner of the 'American Dramatists' Club' at Delmonico's. The dinner and the wines were good, and dear old Bronson Howard presided; but here the mitigation ended. The guest of honor was Charles Klein, whose dishwater *Lion and Mouse* is just rounding its five-hundredth performance (consecutive run) in this city, with five road companies going full steam. This furnished the keynote of all the speeches, which, taken together, constituted a more naïvely blatant mumbo-jumbo ritual before the shrine of 'Success' than I would have thought possible in a civilized gathering. The idea that any other standard of judgment existed than that furnished by the box-office tally-sheet never for one instant, even by innuendo, lifted its head, throughout two hours and a half of speech-making. All plays and all playwrights were by tacit consent ranged in a hierarchy of

merit according to the amount of cash receipts they re-
presented, little Klein, with pathetic face and winking
eyes, heading the august line, in which even I, God help
me, had for the nonce my quasi-conspicuous place! O, fie
on't! Why not write a play to show up in its true colors
this success-madness? It is certainly a dreadful organic
disease in our society, an impostume that cries to heaven
to be lanced, and lanced deep. I hear you saying that no
work of art with so moralistic an origin ever got anywhere.
But I am not so sure that moral passion (if it be really
that) is not as good a motive-spring of art as any other
passion; it may include most others, if it reach the creative
tension and the apocalyptic elevation, as it certainly
sometimes does (as in the Bible).

107 WAVERLY PLACE, N.Y., *Jan.* 25 (1907)

I am making very slow progress with *The Faith-Healer.*
It is a vastly more laborious job than writing a wholly new
play would be. It is like building a new house out of the
materials of an old one, plus a lot of quite disparate
material, while a family for whom you care is occupying
the premises. This simile is expressly designed to appeal
to you. Your scattered comments are of help to me,
whenever you are moved to make them.

Percy is here and wants to be remembered affectionately to you. He is hovering about unable to make up his
mind whether to wait for the opening night of his play here
or not, on account of the way in which the Marlowe has
treated it. To stop her would make sawdust of his and
Sothern's friendship. Tonight I go to a dinner given by
that august body, the National Institute of Arts and
Letters.

107 WAVERLY PLACE, N.Y., *Jan.* 31 (1907)

I have spent rather a strenuous day, beginning with a tussle with *The Faith-Healer* (*de novo*) and ending with a lecture by William James, who is exploiting a new philosophy ('Pragmatism') destined, he thinks, to do for metaphysics what the Reformation did for theology, namely, hand it over to the laity and to practical men. The idea which he is working out would interest you, I believe, as much as it does me. In a nutshell, it is that there is no such thing as abstract truth, but that truth depends entirely upon the actual working value, or 'fruits for life' of any given proposition. Of course we all act upon this hypothesis instinctively, but we do not apply it courageously or consistently in conduct, nor do we as yet dare to follow out its vital consequences in thought. It looks to me like a very high explosive, capable in the right hands of clearing away pretty much all the century-old lumber by which our lives are encumbered.

This morning I followed your bidding in jotting down as many points as I could think of for the new play.

Robinson has written a three-acter called *Van Zorn*. I haven't yet read it, but he gave me over the coffee and cigars a full synopsis of it, and it sounds good to me. I believe we have got the ball rolling, and that the next ten years, if nothing happens to interfere, will see something done.

NEW YORK, *Feb.* 28 (1907)

I haven't anything encouraging to report about the Washington affair. Miller has got his teeth set to do it, and nothing, I'm afraid, will stop him. It is a blatant piece of advertising, combined with an equally blatant desire to 'get even' with the Washington papers for their summary treatment of us last fall. It will probably bear fruits of a like nature with the seed from which it springs, but as nothing can be done about it, the only course is not to worry over the prospect or repine at the outcome.

Meanwhile another matter has come up, which I want to submit to you for your advice. Torrence has money for a Mediterranean trip. Something of the kind he needs, for the winter is going hard with him, and unless he gets into a milder climate, his doctor won't answer for his lungs. He is wild to have me go with him. He proposes to sail next week either Wednesday or Saturday, and be gone two and a half to three months. Perhaps this is a chance which I ought to seize, to get a bracing touch of Europe with a congenial companion. What do you think? I feel stale, mentally, and a few weeks in — say — Sicily, North Africa, and Spain, seem very alluring.

It seems very low and selfish to be thinking of the Mediterranean with you bound to Chicago. Alas!

107 WAVERLY PLACE
Feb. 28 (1907)

I have been putting Torrence off until your telegram should arrive, but now that it is here, and sounds as if you were unequivocally in for the plan, I have told him I would go, and everything is in train. My heart soars at the prospect of seeing again those magic lands, and sinks at the thought that you will not be there to see them with me. Some day, Heaven send!

107 WAVERLY PLACE
March 3, 1907

Torrence has gone to Ohio to see his folks, and won't be back until Friday.

I met Stickney's younger brother last night at dinner. His resemblance to Joe, though after all not very great, was sufficient to throw me into a state of perturbation. I had seen him once before, when Joe and I spent an evening in his brother's rooms, and at that time I noticed hardly any likeness at all, but either it has grown since, or else I supplied it. Joe was very fond of him, but he seems to have none of his brother's magical quality beyond the physical resemblance. I dine tonight at the Fletchers' (Herrick's brother-in-law) to meet a friend of Joe's, who has expressed a desire to see me on that score. Nearly every week I encounter a similar example of the hold Joe had taken upon the affections of the men who knew him, and the tacit free-masonry which his memory creates among all such. That is what you call, and what I am willing to call with you, success in life.

Robertson [1] writes beseeching me to finish *The Faith-Healer* before I go, for production at Ravinia this spring. I have tried to show him how impossible that is, but doubtless he will not be convinced. Even if it were completed, it seems to me that Ravinia would be a main poor place to launch it, before a lot of summer pleaserlings eating ices.

March 10, 1907

The bay is broadening out majestically, and the Atlantic calls beyond. I shall think 'long thoughts' of you out here on the ocean.

[1] Donald Robertson.

[325]

Our little ship's company looks pretty unpromising, but I am glad there are so few, for one feels the sea much more movingly thus than in a big boat crowded with chattering humans.

My steward warns me that the mail for the pilot boat is being made up. Goodbye, and God bless you for everything.

On board SS. Romanic
March 18, 1907

Your birthday has dawned refulgent after ten days of almost uninterrupted cloud, rain, and storm. The first three or four days out we had a most terrific gale, in the midst of which our ship, though staunch, rolled and wallowed herself nearly to pieces, and reduced everybody on board to a state of pulp. I managed to keep on deck throughout, though with mingled feelings. Our ship's-company is a remarkably pleasant one, including several families of old-fashioned Southerners — Maryland and Virginia people — and they have mitigated what would otherwise have been — in view of the bad weather — rather an unrewarded crossing. They tell great stories of what is to be found down that way in farms.

We celebrated St. Patrick's Day, and I wore my green ribbon with a difference, for your sake. I wonder if you celebrated. I hope so.

We are promised Gibraltar tomorrow afternoon or evening — perhaps too late to disembark until Wednesday morning. Our plan now is to go at once to Tangier, and spend perhaps a week or ten days thereabouts. We dream of an excursion in true Oriental style, with camels and a military escort, back into the desert to the holy city of Fez.

[326]

I would certainly make it if I were alone, but I am a little afraid to risk it for Ridgely, in his present state of health. But we shall see. In case the desert trip doesn't seem practicable, we shall come back to Spain, by way of Cadiz, and spend Holy Week in Seville, where there are even greater goings-on, I hear, than in Rome, with a grand bull-fight Easter Day as a culminating splendor.

What did the Lord mean by creating the blue of this sea and sky, and not placing you in the midst to behold them? There have been porpoises, absurdly mythological, about the ship this morning, and flying fish, and a whale spouting off southward, a leviathan by the immense fountain he flung up into the dazzling air. Soon we shall see the mountain which Atlas holds on his shoulders, and then the pillars that Hercules set to mark the end of the world.

EUROPE

TANGIER, *March* 23 (1907)

I write this in a native café, in the midst of cross-legged, burnoused Moors, who look every one like an Old Testament figure, and sip coffee with the solemnity of a prophetic function. We have been only two days in this extraordinary place, but two days so full of smashing sensations that it seems more like as many years. It is hopeless to attempt to convey what it is like, you will have to come and see. We have had great luck in getting hold of a native guide (named Mustapha) who, in addition to being straight out of the *Arabian Nights*, speaks enough English of a weird type to lay the life here open to us, where otherwise it would be all pretty much a sealed book.

Yesterday in the market square there were dervishes who slashed themselves with knives as they danced to the sound of goat-skin drums; there was a snake-charmer who teased a huge reptile with his protruded tongue until it struck him again and again in the mouth; there was a story-teller intoning a Tale of the Caliphs to all who would sit to hear; and a troop of actors disputing popularity with a band of acrobats, on the equal terms of a flat scrap of earth innocent of scenic accessories; and gathered about these and other attractions was such a crowd of personages as I have never thought to see outside of a dream — on donkeys, on camels, on Arab ponies (beauties! They can be bought for a hundred and fifty dollars apiece, and I am sure would be worth a thousand on the New York dock, if they were not certain to be worth more than that on a farm). Mustapha is imploring us to go with him to Fez, and we are balancing the attraction of this proposal against Easter Week in Seville. Probably the latter will capture us, since the weather is unpropitious for camping, and caravan travel is so ruinously expensive that we should very likely have to stay in Fez as prisoners for debt. The great drawback to our pleasure thus far is the weather, which persists dark and cold. I haven't been able to get any photographs yet because of the lack of sunlight — an irritating circumstance, since alluring subjects beckon everywhere.

I think of you constantly in connection with this life out here. It is all so ripely human; the machinery so much less obvious than with us at home; you would love every inch of it, and every inch of it would love you.

GRAND HÔTEL DE PARIS
SEVILLE (Not dated)

You will see that we had to give up the camping trip in Morocco, and are started on our pilgrimage through Spain. The weather remains unpromising, and it is likely that we shall go on from Gibraltar by the boat which leaves there on the 8th of April.

Seville has been intensely interesting, chiefly for the dances, which are all they are cracked up to be, and as much more as you please. Last night there was a wonderful series of them, twenty-four in all, no two alike, and each more maddeningly good than the other. I thought of you, and seemed to understand your passion for the dance, and the loftiness of the dance as an art form, as never before. Words cannot describe or even hint at the intoxicating quality of the rhythms, mingled yet distinct, each imperiously asserting itself while luxuriously yielding to the other, of the guitars and the human forms, as they fought out their amorous and jocund battle.

Ridgely proves to be a capital travelling companion, self-supporting, good-humored, and sensitive to all the varied excitements, small and large, which make up the poetry of travel. His health is good, and there seems to be no danger that there is anything radically the matter with him.

ALHAMBRA, GRANADA
April 3, 1907

As you will see by the superscription, we are on our way south again, after a dash at Madrid and Toledo. These latter proved rather unprofitable (except for the Velasquez pictures) and we are kicking ourselves for not having made directly here from Seville. For in spite of Washington Irving and tourists and tourist-parasites, this is without question one of the most lovely places in the world, perhaps more beautiful in its decay and humiliation than it ever was in its hour of pride. There is a moon, if one stays up late enough, and everywhere and always many-voiced rills of running water, and if you are patient you will hear a nightingale or two for sure.

I have had no word from you yet. I am hoping confidently for a word at Gibraltar, where we go Sunday to take the boat for Naples. Personally I should be glad to stay longer in Spain, but Torrence is anxious to see the worlds ahead which are still to conquer. I can't quite say that I go unwillingly, for Italy is always Italy, and Spain is hard in key and a bit barren in comparison. Either that, or

[330]

else I haven't the same voracious appetite for these things as in the past. I keep thinking of America and home-matters even when the sights about me are most absorbing. I am in fact, I suppose, a little homesick, and certainly a little restless, and not able to give myself up, as I want to, to these half-alien beauties and diversions. This I take to be a symptom, warning me that I have got into a rut, or is it rather a sign that my centre of curiosity, of excitement, has permanently shifted from the outer to the inner world, and from what you call 'scenery' to life, and of course therefore to life as I know it best, as I know it only, which is at home? Whichever it is, I am going to go on until I feel the rejuvenation of which I feel in need, unless the fact of wanting and expecting it keeps it away. All of this is more or less morbid self-scrutiny, of course, and to be chucked forthwith. I am reading the Spanish drama assiduously, chiefly Echegaray and Galdos. It strikes me as awfully thin. Galdos had a wonderful lead in his *Electra* (which get and read if you can find a translation) but he fooled it away in a most childish fashion. Echegaray's *Gran Galeoto* is also stunning in its initial idea, but worked out in a vein of flabby sentimentality which is hard to bear in the orotund original and must be quite unbearable in English. These two plays seem to be about as good things as they have to show; in the mass, however, the product is striking, for all the short-comings of each work individually.

We go from here to Ronda, and thence to Gibraltar and Naples, where we are due on the eleventh. I hope for quite a harvest of letters there. The stupidity of space and time are painfully emphasized by the international postal system.

Le SAVOY
NAPLES, *April* 16, 1907

The three days sail through the Mediterranean was delightful, but the fiend's own weather reigns in Naples, storm and cold and rain implacable. It seems I shall never learn, in spite of many bitter lessons, that Italy in spring is a delusion.

The rain has ceased, the clouds seem to be breaking, and Ridgely is at my elbow suggesting his desires as to sightseeing.

R. PALUMBO HOTEL CESARI
ROMA, *April* 23 (1907)

We are in Rome, after ten days of ineffectual waiting for winter to recede from the country south of here and allow us to renourish our shattered illusions. The most relentless weather, cold, rainy, and dark has held us in its grasp. You know how dark weather always shuts for me all the doors of hope, and dark weather in southern Italy is *worse* than anywhere else, because more hatefully unnatural. We traversed the scenes which I had known of old, but there was nothing in them to recognize, except a bald, forbidding outline. We were in Sorrento, but I refused to go and see the square where I saw the Good-Friday procession years ago. That at least I wanted to keep. By one of those tricks of chance which makes Nature seem at times possessed of personal favoritisms and grudges, the moment we gave it up for a bad job and boarded the train for Rome the sun came out in his splendor, and has shone since with a riotous and exulting brilliancy. I forgive the spiteful intention for the sake of the resultant thawing-out of mind, body, and heart, for now as always I arise as from death and rejoice aloud when the sun consents to shine.

I have a note from M——, inviting me to look in on them at their cottage near London. Our plans include a week or two in England before sailing for home. I don't know why, but I feel — still feel — rather played-out and sluggish. I keep longing for home and my desk, but know also that I should do no good there until by the grace of God I have picked up tone and vitality. There is no excuse that I can see for having lost these desirable adjuncts.

Rome is flooded with glorious sunlight.

FLORENCE, *May* 1, 1907

We reached Florence yesterday, and today I have a May-Day gift of two beautiful letters from you, one written before leaving for Parkman, the other from there. They have given me, as your words always do, new hope and strength. In return for the white violets I send you an ivy leaf from Keats's grave in Rome, plucked for you with many thoughts. The daisies which used to cover the grave are gone, but the ivy does its vigorous best to make good the loss.

The weather, with complaints about which I must already have worn you out, continues bad to the point of distraction and despair. In four weeks we have had hardly four bright days. I do not know my Italy. Yesterday, however, along with the letters, as a necessary and preordained accompaniment to their song of life, burst upon us a day of glorious brightness, of lustre altogether unworldly. I awoke with the intoxication of it in my veins, and wandered about all day as drunk as a lord, unable to look at anything but the sunlight, or to feel anything but the amorous clasp of it on body and soul. My dependence on sunlight — the mere material solar article — seems to grow greater rather than less with — in spite of — years and wisdom. In the heightened state of being to which this visitation raised me, I had a big illumination, handed out gratis by the inscrutable provider who has been so stingy of late.

To speak plainly, as I was walking along the street thinking of nothing but the good feel of the sun and the good taste of the air, suddenly something clicked inside my head, a kaleidoscopic down-rush and up-thrust and over-tumble of broken pictures and half-thoughts passed before my mind, whirled a minute, settled into place, and behold! there was the third part of my trilogy. For an hour, or a quarter of a second, or however long it lasted, it was as plain as print and as perfect as the atomic structure of a jewel. This morning it is dim and disjointed again, but that does not much discourage me, for I have seen it once, and I shall see it again, according to all the precedents in my mental history. Also according to precedent, it is nothing actually new, but a rushing into organic relation to each other of several things which I have thought of for a long time. It is the *Eve* play, combined with a continuation and culmination of the 'Judgment' theme as it is left at the end of the *Masque*. This element of the poem must lock the whole — I mean all three parts — together, but it will be brief, for I feel that the subject is one which won't stand extended handling. Also, your conviction that the theme of the third part must lie in the words of the Apocalypse, 'The old earth has passed away, and a new earth, etc.' finds a place in my present conception; it is only to be suggested, at the very end, and that too in a way that may seem to you inadequate, even trivial. But you wait and see. Finally, there is something 'big and important' to be done to the last act of *The Fire-Bringer*, as a prelude to the development of the theme in the two succeeding parts. This also was handed down to me off the pantry shelf by the same good grandam in the same quixotic spasm of generosity, after I had got tired crying for it.

I had been in the depths, debating whether it were better to get off the earth altogether or to turn reformer and useful citizen. God save us all for pagans and faithless! Among them I shall doubtless soon again be numbered. The total inability to 'see out' of a mood of discouragement, to remember, to discount, to strike a rational balance, is one of the most amazing and awful things in life. It is the suggestress of suicide and the mother of dead dogs. It lies at the root of all our pitiful bungling and waste, with regard to the real issues of our lives. At least it is so with me. You will know what I mean by this, since you have had to suffer with me the vital consequences of it; you will understand, and understand, and understand, above pity or forgiveness or regret. You will do this, and you are the only woman on earth who could.

It is quite possible, if I feel moved to work, that I will stay here, and let Torrence go on to France and England without me. I should like to get the new piece started before coming home.

HÔTEL DE ROME ET SUISSE
VENISE, *May* 16 (1907)

Your letter with the terrible news about Sieg came yesterday. I have been trembling all day for fear another would come telling of a relapse, for it seems absolutely incredible that he should have got through without fatal internal injuries. Your account of the accident was so meagre that once or twice I have thought you were only trying to break the blow, and have reread your words in that sense: only to conclude that I was wrong, chiefly because I know that is not the way you would handle a hard situation. What a dreadful moment it must have been for you, when you saw the wheels go over him, and heard his cry; and still more afterward, except that then I know your powers were all bound up as in a trance with the act of succor.

Summer has come in like a lion; the days here in wonderful Venice have been radiant beyond description. I am glad that Italy relented toward me at the last, and rewarded my constant love by investing herself in her proper glory. The change came on the very day when, as I wrote you, the fates vouchsafed me a sudden and perfect vision of the poem I want to write. Let us think it an omen. I wish you could see the lustre that bathes water and sky, and all the noble works of man between, as I sit here on a balcony beside the Grand Canal, an hour before sunset. I know nothing to compare it to, in its generosity and harmonic fullness.

We leave for Paris tomorrow, where we shall make only the briefest stay; then London, and (I hope) some quiet place in the country where I can settle down for a couple of weeks, long enough to get my poem started, and feel some beginnings of sureness take the place of the anxieties and fears which assail me when I bend my thoughts that way. It is all as clear as day, but can I find the words? And if the words, can I find the music? All creation puts on mocking forms to say No, No! and only the still small

voice, says Yes, and that falteringly. M—— writes from
her Iffley that the hedges are in blossom, and invites me
to a cup of tea. A cup of tea I think will suffice for Iffley.
I have in mind a place on the Irish Sea, or perhaps in Ire-
land, where I haven't yet been. I rather dread the prim-
ness and decorum of landscape and people in the tight
little isle. More than once I have been tempted to go to
Palestine; but I am deterred by the thought of the added
weeks of absence from home, and also by a feverish impatience to have done with gross locomotion and to revisit
myself. I have found the refreshment which I sought, the
fountains have again been unsealed, if briefly yet with
thrilling promise, and there is not much use in gadding
about longer.

I shall write from Paris. I rather dread going there, on
poor Joe's account.

SAVOY HOTEL, LONDON, *May* 27 (1907)

I have let too many days go by since my last letter, but
we have been moving rapidly from place to place, and I
have felt nervous and unsettled. To tell the truth I feel so
still. London is a very wonderful place, and sometime or
other I want to spend a long stretch of time here, but at
present the soles of my feet burn. I suppose the cold fact
is that I am homesick.

Yesterday Torrence and I went out to see Swinburne,
being armed with a letter of introduction. S. was invisible, sending excuses by his house-mate Watts-Dunton,
into whose less deaf ear we shouted our names and other
matters till the welkin rang. Not a gleam of humanity
emanated from the pursy, snuffy little man, until we
thundered an inquiry concerning his own works —*Aylwin*

and *The Coming of Love.* The transformation was miraculous. He held forth for one amazing hour upon himself, regarding the subject, systematically, from one viewpoint after another, almost visibly keeping tally of the subdivisions of his theme upon his fat little fingers. We sat frozen in a kind of ecstasy, compounded of humor and horror, for the self-concentration of it was really horrible. This will all strike you as ill-natured and inhuman and Harvardian, but that is because I cannot convey any impression of the involved and swollen egotism of the thing — the really ghastly and monstrous lack of proportion in the brain of the man. At the end he showered upon us copies of all his works, after we had shouted our names and the spelling thereof a half-dozen times into his best ear, as well as the name of poor Stedman, who had given us the introduction with the assurance that both Swinburne and Watts-Dunton were his life-long intimates.

Let me not close this letter in cynical vein, for my heart is very full of thoughts and longings that are the reverse of cynical, and reaches out to you in an appeal which there are no words to phrase, imploring you to deal rightly with our common fate, forgetting my imperfections of will, my sometime lack of trust in life, out of which flow all my sorrows, and all yours.

W—

Cable message: LONDON, *May* 29, '07
          SAILING TODAY MAJESTIC

AMERICA

SEPTEMBER 20, 1907 — APRIL 28, 1909

(On his arrival with Ridgely Torrence in New York, W. V. M. was met there by Harriet with whom he returned to Chicago. He spent the summer at 2970 Groveland Avenue and at Mackinac Island, Mich. From Chicago, Sept. 13, 1907, he wrote to P. M-K.: 'I am scheduled Cornishwards next week.')

NEW YORK, *Sept.* 20, 1907

I have spent two days here, very busy doing nothing. Not even time to get in to see Miller, and now there is no opportunity, as I have promised Percy to go with him to-night to see the husky old romantic actor, James O'Neill, do that husky old play *Virginius*, resurrected from the ashes wherein our fathers saw it entombed.

Percy gives me the news, clipped from a dramatic paper that Miss Anglin is to be succeeded in the rôle of Ruth by Miss Matthison — you remember, the lady who captured all our hearts as *Everyman*.

I go up to Cornish tomorrow with Percy and your friend, Shipman,[1] you remember, the author of the little war play whom you saw on the opening night in Chicago. I shall stay up there only a few days, then to Newton.

NEWTON, MASS., *Sept.* 27 (1907)

Here I am in Newton, after a visit of four days at Cornish. Cornish was very quiet, and therefore pleasant —

[1] Louis Evan Shipman, of Cornish, N.H., author of *D'Arcy of the Guards.*

there seems to be less social fuss and feathers than last year.

My plans are a good deal in the air. There is the Maine coast to explore, and there is Gloucester, or Annisquam, where I feel pretty sure I could work well, and there is New York, which perhaps in view of the immediate situation is wisest. I am in the air, and as uneasy as most terrestrial beings in that situation.

NEW YORK, *Sept.* 29, 1907

Everybody discourages me on the subject of the Maine coast in October, declaring that the mountains are the only thing. To judge by the darkness and rain which I found at Cornish the mountains are not much more promising. Also New York is wrapped in a London drizzle. I am keeping my spirits buoyed up with the theory that these distressful conditions are the fag-end of the equinoctial rumpus. I am not sorry to be in New York, both on the weather's account, and also because some new plays are being tried out here now; most of them — of course — will fail, commercially, and this will be the only chance to see them. Jones has a new one called *The Evangelist*. The title comes painfully near my *Faith-Healer*, but the character and story are both, I gather, entirely different from mine. I haven't yet seen Miller, or learned anything about the prospective fortunes of *The Great Divide*.

I found my rooms buried beneath a three-months' accumulation of dust, but otherwise in good shape, and not uninviting. I have tried rearranging the front room after your suggestion; I believe the table in its new situation will be more hospitable to the working mood. With curtains, some more rugs, and a few pictures, the place will begin to look habitable.

During these days in town I have gone back to *The Faith-Healer*, and am getting in so deep that it looks as if I shouldn't be able to tear myself away from it until it is finished. Perhaps this is not to be regretted, for with this long-delayed task out of the way I can go at the *Eve* with a more single mind. Also, on the side of prudence, I should like to be able to put the *F.-H.* on the stage next autumn, in case it proves playable — as to which I am in much doubt, though it gets more and more absorbing (to me) as I go on. Nazimova is playing *The Master-Builder* — amazingly interesting, or, as Hilda Wangel keeps exclaiming in the play, 'Dreadfully thrilling!' Do you know *The Master-Builder*? I wonder how Ibsen ever got the name of a realist. A very debauchee of Romance. And that is really the hold he has over people.

Miller and Miss A., whom I had a long and very friendly conference with yesterday, seem to have weathered all their storms, and to be once more in blissful accord. Miss A. hinted, though she did not positively state, that she intends to renew her contract (which expires Jan. 1st) and stick to the play for another year. At first they planned to go on the road October first, but the 'business' has remained so good that they now expect to stay at Daly's until Christmas, and then to play four weeks downtown at the Academy of Music. After that there is talk of going to England before touring the West, apparently on the theory that a plum pudding cuts richer the longer it is kept. Do plum puddings ever spoil?

Miller has bought a farm and old colonial house on high ground in Connecticut, within an hour's run or so of the city by motor-car. He promises to take me out and show me the country. Says there are still bargains to be had, and a wonderful region. But his idea of a bargain is very liberal.

NEW YORK, *Oct.* 13 (1907)

It seems a long time since I've heard from you, but I dare say that's my fault, for it's been a long time since I have written. I've been badly tangled up with *The Faith-Healer*, and still am. Heaven preserve me from ever trying again the experiment against which the holy book gives warning, of pouring new wine into old bottles. I should have done better to throw away the first play altogether, and take a fresh start. I may, indeed, have to do so still, and would gladly if these scenes hadn't somehow assumed a control of my mind — established themselves there as actual — so that I can't annihilate them completely enough to begin again. Well, we shall see.

Friday night Robinson read me a play he had just finished called *The Porcupine*. Corking title, isn't it? and a stunning play. The 'porcupine' is a woman who, fearing that she is with child (that is, as a girl, ten years before the play opens) by a boy who has meantime run away from his torturing New England home and lost himself out West, marries to protect herself, and naturally becomes a porcupine to her parson husband, who suspects nothing and accepts the child as his own, suffers for years from his wife's venomous quills, and finally runs after the rather naughty wife of a friend of the family, another case of mismating — her husband pining for liberty to take another lady to his bosom. A Robinsonian imbroglio, you see. Appears upon the scene scape-grace lover of first lady (the Porcupine) who has made a fortune in the West, and

who begins immediately and light-heartedly to untangle
things, and give every Jack his Jill. The Porcupine finally
(after his schemes are joyfully under way) tells him of his
fatherhood of the child, who has taken to him and his
fiddle as a duck to water. She does not tell him, however,
until she makes sure that he does not love her and never
has, except in a cursory boy fashion. He accepts the
situation light-heartedly, and plans to make this final
readjustment — a little scheme which is cut short by the
suicide of the Porcupine.

I have told this clumsily, but you can see the possibilities of the plot, which Robinson has abundantly taken advantage of. It is really a very strong play, and handled
with a wonderful deftness and lightness of touch. I am
going tomorrow to beard Charles Frohman in his den, with
it in my hand, and try and hypnotize him into taking it.

Saturday night there was the largest house we have yet
had, by a long shot. Pretty good for the tenth month,
isn't it?

NEW YORK, *Oct.* 16 (1907)

Your letter came just in time to inspirit me, before I
entered the den of Apollyon, i.e., the private office of the
'Syndicate,' with Robinson's play in my hand and terror
battling with disgust in my pericardiacs. The great Frohman sat at his desk, the very figure of what he should be,
like a fat black spider in his web. But — shall we ever
learn that human beings are always — or nearly always —
human, and the devil not so black as he is painted? No
sooner had the spider opened his mouth, and begun to — I
would say *sing* if that were in the spider's repertory —
than my charmed eyes closed, to open again upon a very

simple-hearted, kindly, and enthusiastic little man, full of a sort of shy pathos and unexpected wistfulness in his attitude toward all that I, by program, was glacially concealing my interest in or knowledge of. Before I knew it I was pouring out my heart to him on the subject of the stage, and what our little group dreamed of trying to do by way of crusade. He is either an actor of the first order, or else his sins are due to ignorance and necessity rather than inherent baseness or even essential vulgarity. Before I left he promised to read E. A.'s play at once, and bade me tell the other crusaders (I mentioned Percy and Ridgely, too) that whenever they wanted tickets to any of his theatres they were to be had for the asking. How was that for handsome? I swore the daylight black and blue cracking up *The Porcupine*. I somehow have a feeling in my bones that he'll take it. Add your prayers to mine. It would give the boy just the stimulus and hope he needs to bring out the best that's in him.

Have you read F. W. H. Myers' *Human Personality*? It's an astonishing book, and lives up to its sub-title, *And Its Survival of Bodily Death*, with an array of argument and evidence — especially *evidence* — which takes the breath away.

Oct. 18 (1907)

My gushing estimate of Frohman received a shock yesterday when he sent back poor Robinson's play with a scribbled line of comment, 'Not available for stage.' It was one of the hardest things I ever had to do to take it back to the old boy with this disheartening report.

I have spent two highly amused evenings with Bernard Shaw's *John Bull's Other Island* and *Major Barbara*. The second handles the Salvation Army, or rather plays skittles with it. The Irish play has one delicious passage, where an unfrocked priest talks to a grasshopper on a hill at sunset — a beautiful piece of humor and feeling which shows how sadly Shaw has wasted himself on pamphleteering. — These plays are indeed only pamphlets, though funny and human as you could wish when the author forgets his pigheadedness.

THE PLAYERS
16 GRAMERCY PARK
Oct. 22 (1907)

We are all in the dumps here. Last night *Sappho and Phaon* had its New York *première*. I had seen it in dress rehearsal, and had hopes. The hopelessness of the acting as it stood forth last night I was not prepared for — the gloom only relieved by a cat which strayed in from the right wings, sat down in the middle of the stage near the footlights, looked meditatively round on the Leucadian landscape, wiped his nose with a reflective paw, and padded solemnly out on the left. We good men in buckram, together with a large Cornish contingent, kept up alarums and excursions of applause all through, to the good end that we dragged Percy before the curtain, more dead than alive. Today the cynical crowd of newspaper critics are slaughtering him in good style, with all the cosmopolitan refinements of torture. Kalich gets her full share, and really, my dear, though I am willing to take your word for it, and go to the stake declaring that she *can* act when she wants to, last night she was beyond redemption bad. You would have said the same yourself. I am grieved to hear that your strength and buoyancy are so slow in coming back.

[345]

NEW YORK, *Tuesday, Oct.* 29 (1907)

I had an experience last night which is so much in your line that I am moved to relate it, though I can't give any of its immense 'human' value. I was walking down Fifth Avenue about midnight, after the theatre, when a shabby man of about thirty emerged from a dark doorway and asked for money. I don't usually give, being dominated by the theories of the professors of this branch of sociology, but this time something in the fellow's look or voice prompted me to forego my scientific principles and give him a small sum. He fell back, but a moment after overtook me again, murmuring confused thanks. There was a note of such tragic sincerity in these that I stopped and talked with him. He said he was a clerk, a Canadian who had come to New York last spring (he did not tell me why, glozing over his motives shyly and with trepidation), had spent all his money without finding work and had then come down with typhoid, being now only a few days out of hospital. He had gradually pawned all his clothes except the few poor rags he had on, and now, he couldn't get a job because of his seedy look. His affecting gratitude was for money to get a bare meal, for when I asked him what he expected to do for the night he pointed to a park bench, with the reflection that it was not so bad when you had eaten. (By this time a fine cold rain had begun to fall and the wind to come up.) His voice was of that unmistakable quality which denotes refinement of nature, and his speech unexceptionable; still, I have been taken in so often that I wasn't sure of him.

His persistence in making light of his misfortunes, though stating them with grim literalness, was the most persuasive sign. After getting him a bed at the Mills

Hotel (that poor man's paradise) I agreed to meet him this afternoon at the shop where his clothes were lying in pawn. Sure enough he was there, and the clothes (very good ones) producible. We spent the rest of the afternoon rescuing shoes, hat, shirts, and underclothes from widely scattered pawnshops where in the exigency of the moment he had successively deposited them. It was wonderful and touching to see his spirits rise, and hope and buoyancy and firmness present themselves in voice and manner, where before had been only a stoic uncomplaining patience, a grim yet gentle acceptance of his miserable situation, without a touch of rebelliousness or spleen, but also without any spring or grasp, any natural and perhaps salutary bitterness. The climax of this story — in fact the real point of it — is why and under what circumstances he left Montreal. I will tell you when he tells me, but that will not be yet, for any attempt to probe that subject arouses in him a kind of breathless and speechless panic, which would point to dark things if the man were not so palpably pure of heart. When he gets his job, and gets settled once more in a not-too-savage world, perhaps he will tell me. I see I have failed worse than I thought I should in conveying what was dubious and arresting, and at the same time perfectly everyday, in the man's nature and predicament.

I am working away at *The Faith-Healer*, one day tremendously encouraged and the next dashed to the nethermost pit of forlornity. I think of changing the title. Isn't it bad policy to give the man's vocation away at once, instead of letting it steal upon the reader or hearer by faint hints and indirections? What do you think of *The Pool of Bethesda*, if sufficiently supported in the text? Suggest another.

NEW YORK, *Nov. 6,* 1907

I have been out of town for a couple of days, travelling
— bless your heart — in a fifty horse power touring-car.
Herrick and his sister were of the party, and a Mrs. P——,
now of Cambridge but primitively of Texas, and what you
call a 'free soul,' was hostess — if that's what a lady is who
sets up the gasoline on such occasions. We had a glorious
two-day spin through perfect autumn weather and a
delicious country — up the Hudson to Poughkeepsie, then
northeast over the Connecticut hills to a lovely high-up
village called Sharon, then back the next day by another
route. I thought of you, with a joyful pain, knowing that
of earthly experience this of winged flight through a crisp
Indian-summer hill-world would come near ranking highest in your eyes.

I think your suggestion as to using the man's name as
a title a capital one — *Hermann Schlatka.* Looks swell,
doesn't it? But perhaps lays too much stress on the *foreign*
antecedents of the man — do you think? The title, too, is
of the kind usually associated with the German drama.
However, I sha'n't reject it in a hurry, you may be sure.

Nov. 13, 1907

I have been hard at Schlatka for a week (I mean *hard*
for a week), and have finished two acts of him. So far I
almost think he'll do, but the third act is crucial. I sit
staring at the paper, seeing the thing act itself out as plain
as day, almost *hearing* the words with my bodily ears, but
when I take up a pen, all goes to the bad. I am unable to
write a word, in fact the mere thought of writing is re-
pugnant, paralyzing. I guess I'm a bit off my chop. I will
loaf and read a novel and see then.

Miller closes here this month and goes West, I believe almost directly to Chicago, where he is to play three weeks. At the same time two hack companies start out, one north and (*absit omen!*) one south. I have exhausted my eloquence trying to persuade him against this latter piece of headlong folly. He will not admit for an instant that there is anything in his rôle to which an angel could take exception. Maybe he is right about the angel, but wait till he hears from Savannah and Mobile! He does not realize the peculiar conditions down there, and the inflamed state of public feeling on the subject. I expect there will be lively times, not of the pleasantest.

You give no news of yourself, nor whether you are still keeping up your regimen of early hours. I hope and pray that you are, and that you are beginning to get back some of your precious strength and buoyancy. They are the greatest treasures we have, and one and all we squander them as water.

NEW YORK, *Nov.* 29 (1907)

After a week of discouragement I am again feeling hopeful about it (*The Faith-Healer*). I feel now that it will surely be interesting to read, whether any mortal manager will ever have the spunk to produce it or any actor to play it. At least it is taking on *form* — a thing it has never before been able to boast among its assortment of qualities.

Augustus Thomas has just produced a 'telepathic play' here which has had an enthusiastic reception. So far so good, but I don't know how much of the critical complaisance is due to the 'psychic' theme, and how much to the melodrama and rather coarse-grained humor with which it is interlarded. I am torn between pleasure at seeing such a subject eagerly received as legitimate dramatic material, and wrath at having the public mind mussed-up with a second-rate handling thereof. There is, however, one act which is fine and true.

[During some part of this interval W. V. M. was in Chicago.]

107 WAVERLY PLACE
Jan. 10 (1908)

You can imagine me camping disconsolately on my coal-box, or next door to it, as Charlotte, in her housekeeping zeal, has taken all the keys along with her to Newton, leaving me even towel-less. The flat is unchanged — the transformation scenes which were scheduled to come off after my absence not having eventuated, in despite of Mrs. Davidge's professional threats and Charlotte's own ill-concealed eagerness to get me gone that she might begin her deadly work. But everything removable has been clapped under lock and key, even to the pictures on the wall and the soap on the washstand.

I gather from Mr. Gilder over the telephone that the dinner tonight is a large one, and in honor of some worthy or other.

107 WAVERLY PLACE
Jan. 15 — '08

The Carnegie dinner was a wonder. There were twenty-four guests, all men, personages of light and leading both domestic and foreign. There were speeches and drinking of toasts galore and mutual assurance, in all tones dulcet and martial, that we were very fine fellows indeed, and the fussy little laird the king-pin of creation. An incident of

[350]

the service that will interest you was this: after coffee, an indelible pencil was passed around, and each guest wrote his name on the tablecloth, to be afterwards embroidered in white on the cloth, as a memorial. There were other names there already, scores of them, and no few big guns among them. The cloth ought to be quite a trophy if this process goes on; and the big guns don't all get hopelessly forgotten by the world, turning out to be mere pop-guns.

I am still hard at work on the play. I thought it was as good as done when I left Chicago, but it isn't. The first and second acts have at last stopped crumbling under the file, but the third act is still full of soft places. In fact I have been on the point of despair concerning it, fearful that I had used too much of the old material and that all of that was worm-eaten and dust-corroded beyond refurbishment. Faversham, who is I believe now playing in Chicago, has somehow heard of the play and asked to see it. Picture Faversham in the part. I shall probably not be ready to read it to Miller before next week, when he will be in Washington.

107 WAVERLY PLACE
NEW YORK, *Jan.* 22 (1908)

As for the play itself, I have written *finis*. I have done for it all I can do. The verdict of the friends I have read it to is either negative or hostile, with one exception. If it were not for your conviction about it I should be greatly cast down. Mrs. Davidge, a keen critic and herself an enthusiast — not to say an active devotee — on the subject of 'divine healing,' repudiates it root and branch, and mourns over me loudly and in public for a lost soul, a star gone down in Israel. She declares that she would gladly lay down her life at the doors of the theatre where it is presented, if by so doing she could prevent people from coming to see it; and says if it is widely listened to it will keep back 'the cause' for decades. Her main objection to it is in the use which has been made of the love motive; she talks of Mariolatry, the degradation of the prophetic character to the uses of sentiment, etc., etc. In other words she repudiates the 'human' ideal which I have set up against the ascetic one, declaring that the latter is an indissoluble part of the prophetic character and mission, an inherent function of the Messianic nature. What she particularly rages against is the active part which the woman plays in the man's regeneration; declares that these two types of emotion belong to disparate worlds, etc., etc. I don't give her argument as cogently as she gives it, but you see the line of attack and that the issue is squarely joined. This might be endured easily, as a difference of philosophical position and of psychological belief, but when she charges me with degrading a saintly memory (she means Schlatter himself, the historical person) for purposes of melodramatic excitement she hits harder. Hadn't I at least better disguise the name still further? I hate to do it, and I know you will be sorry to lose the name with which we have grown familiar; but perhaps it is necessary, to avoid giving needless offense, possibly (certainly in her case) pain. The passion of her attack amazed and staggered me. It shows at any rate how vital the whole field of thought is to our generation.

I expect to run up to Cornish for a few days, for a taste of country winter. I expect to see Miller in Boston, where he begins a four-weeks engagement on the 27th. Unless he is convinced about it I sha'n't let him have it.

I left New York ten days ago, and since then have been involved in such moving accidents by flood and field that I have neglected writing too long. The second day after arriving at Cornish (with Torrence) the thermometer dropped out of sight, and the resources of the Davidge 'tavern' were taxed to the breaking point to keep the breath of life in our bodies. As soon as the intense cold moderated, the heavens opened and incredible quantities of snow buried us out of sight for several days. It was a great experience, though strenuous; both of us had gone up to Cornish quite inadequately furnished with winter clothes and wrappings.

She (Miss Anglin) leaves the cast for good (so far as now appears) at the end of this week, and Miss Matthison (of *Everyman* fame) takes her place. After seeing her rehearse I am not encouraged, but she may do better when she gets into it, and her name is worth something anyhow.

To come to the main news, I had an all-night session with Miller, reading the new play. We started in at midnight and finished our sitting at five-thirty in the morning. His understanding of Schlatka's character — and of the larger meaning of the piece as a whole — was immediate, and his judgment of both enthusiastic in the extreme. He thinks it stands a fair chance for commercial success, but says that whether that comes or not is a matter not to be seriously considered. He is sure that the play will add to his prestige as a manager and to mine as a writer sufficiently to make good even for an absolute commercial failure, which is hardly to be apprehended. He does not think best to produce it before next fall. In this I heartily concur. It is an immense satisfaction to deal with a man of such luminous intelligence and of outlook so broad and (to use again the hard driven word) so human. I need not assure you that Mrs. Davidge's outburst has not caused me to make any serious changes, though in a few minor matters I think she has shown me the way to sounder workmanship — psychologically speaking. We must discuss the advisability of a return to the next-to-the-last ending, which your last letter advocates. I don't yet feel that anything will be gained thereby, as over against what will be lost. It would not satisfy Mrs. D. (I let her stand for a type of objectors) for according to her view he is damned anyhow, and he may as well be damned living as dead. The idea of death, no matter how shadowily suggested, will (in the present state of our feeling about the matter) tend to lower the spectator's spirits, and (partially at least) destroy the 'uplift' of the final scene. Will it not?

I go back to New York tomorrow, where I stay long enough to see the new things at the theatre, and perhaps long enough to judge whether Miss Matthison is up to her job.

NEW YORK, *Feb.* 19, 1908

I went last night to see the new Ruth — Miss Matthison of *Everyman* fame — and I know you will be curious to hear how she impressed me. To put it in a word, she impressed me as perfunctory. She is really over here to play one or two of her husband's things, I imagine. (He is the man [1] who played the Herald in *Everyman*, and has since commenced playwright.) Though Miller makes a strenuous bluff at pretending that she was imported for *The Great Divide* alone, I am sure he banks upon Miss Anglin's return to the rôle as soon as she has worked off

[1] Charles Rann Kennedy.

[354]

some of her humors. She is now on the road with *The Awakening of Helena Ritchie*, a *rechauffée* of the novel. But in a few places, where Miss Matthison stopped giving a reproduction of Miss A. *à l'anglaise*, she showed a sensitiveness and understanding of the *nuances* of the part which would have delighted you, I am sure. In justice to Margaret's power over the crowd, it must be noted that since she left us the 'business' has fallen away to a quite disastrous extent. Miller, the great child, is in the depths of pessimism, ready to sell the play for a song, whereas ten days ago in Boston he was declaring that it would 'run strong' for five years, and was a gold-mine which he had only begun to work. His interest in the new play keeps at high pitch. He is going to arrange a meeting this week between me and Tyrone Power, so that, under the guise of doing something less offensive, I can give him a looking-over. As for the play itself I am again convinced that the third act must be rewritten, to purge it of the cruder matter which clings to it from the old version, and day by day put off beginning the task, not feeling any strength or spring in the muscles of my mind adequate to the same.

My sister Charlotte and my niece are coming toward the end of the week. I shall give up my quarters to them and retreat to the Players Club or the Harvard Club for a brief season. Thence I shall issue, under Miller's guidance, with a mask and a dark lantern, to watch a few actors and actorines at their unconscious gambols, with a view to sizing them up for the new play. He seems inclined to give me a much more potent voice in the selection of the cast than I had before — in fact he seems to want to have me do it all, a responsibility from which I naturally shrink. It is good to hear that you are yourself again, physically, and to catch the old brave and buoyant note in your letter.

Feb. 24 (1908)

I have taken up my abode here at the Players, in a pretty old-fashioned room at the top of the house, looking out on Gramercy Park, where in these last warm days the buds are beginning visibly to swell, or else my heart gives promptings to my eyes to deceive me. There are pussy-willows for sale on the streets. Where do they come from? I thought spring was a legend — an invention of the more fanciful school of poets. In fact, I thought I recollected inventing it myself, when I was a poet.

NEW YORK, *March* 3, 1908

Miller is arranging meetings for me with actors whom he regards as possibilities for the new cast. This — in deference to the histrion's susceptibility — has to be done with elaborate carelessness, so as to avoid the appearance of a 'look-over.' The other night I spent the evening with Tyrone Power, of whom I spoke to you disparagingly, on the strength of a recollection of him as *Ingomar* (God save the mark) and *Ulysses* in Stephen Phillips's play. On closer view I am not so sure that he will not do. He has a magnetic personality, a powerful and ascetic face, a large and shambling frame, and a glorious voice — too glorious in fact; I'm afraid it would swamp him. There is a taint of melodrama about him — of the old style longing to 'make all split' — of the magniloquent and seedy tragedian turned tramp — but Miller thinks that all this could be made valuable if subdued and chastened. Certainly it could, if the man has the requisite fineness of

grain; I'm afraid he is coarse in the fibre, and not capable
of taking an edge, but I trust I am wrong.

Miss Matthison has been very generously received, both
by press and public; and there is indeed from point to point
a fineness of perception in her playing and a delicate sense
of values for which one is mighty grateful. On the whole,
however, she is not good, partly — perhaps chiefly — because she is not interested, a state of affairs in which her
essential anaemia asserts itself to the destruction of all joy.

Last night, urged by rumors I had heard of its quality, I
went to see Debussy's operatic setting of Maeterlinck's
Pelléas et Mélisande. As a preparation I read the poem, and
arose from it with a vastly increased admiration for your
beloved Maeterlinck. I think I felt his essential quality,
and succumbed to his authentic spell, for the first time. I
am not sure but he is all right, and that this shadow world
is more real than the tangible one with which I have been
laboring. Certainly it is more ductile to the shaping hand
— a powerful fascination to the shaper and perhaps a
source of keenest pleasure to those who look on at the
shaping. I hear that in France high-souled poetical cooks
make the most marvellous creations out of puff-paste. It
is as good as marble if it looks as good, and while it keeps
its shape — a thing which not marble nor brass will do
forever. This of course is not to liken Maeterlinck to an
artist in march-pane, but there is something essentially
perishable in his method and material, I still think. But
the poem moved me immensely. The opera not so much,
very little in fact. I had heard that Debussy had sub-
ordinated the orchestra and the singing parts, and raised
the dramatic equation in something the way I should like
to do if I knew enough to write music. But he has done

little or nothing in this direction. It is all recitative, in which the delicate and spiritual suggestions of the text find little enough reflection. The orchestral accompaniment, however, is new, and strangely moving. If he had made of this merely or at any rate chiefly a background for the spoken word, he would have done the trick perhaps. Let us learn to labor and to wait.

(W. V. M. went to Chicago to see Harriet after the death of her mother, early in March.)

107 WAVERLY PLACE
NEW YORK, Mch. 20 (1908)

It is late at night, and this is my first chance to get a word with you. I do not need to tell you how much you have been in my thoughts all the way East on the creeping train. (It took a round twenty-four hours to make the distance.) I was just unwell enough to be in a kind of physical stupor which left the mind wonderfully clear, and I thought long thoughts of you — long, long thoughts. My indisposition is annoying, but you must not worry in the slightest, for Charlotte, who is very wise in these matters, says it is only a little thing.

I am dead tired, but you will make a good letter out of this, knowing that my heart goes with it. I wish I could help you better in these dark and trying days.

Telegram: NEW YORK, March 22, 1908

DOCTOR FORBIDS WRITING FOR DAY OR TWO
MAKING GOOD PROGRESS
W.

(Following this, W. V. M. was ill with typhoid fever, at 107 Waverly Place, New York.)

[358]

PORT CHESTER, N.Y.
May 25 (1908)

I am not allowed to write, but I am going to scribble you a word (rather wobbly, I fear) and try to get it smuggled out by the butcher's-boy. It seems a long, long time since I lost your dear presence, symbol and pledge of the life which I feel slowly — O so slowly! — returning. I hobble about the purlieus of the tiny island, each day a little further, except when I go too far and have to lay up for certain weary hours to repair the damage. I spend vast stretches of time — whole existences — sitting in a porch-chair in the tender spring sunlight, looking at the sky and the water, playing with the pup, and thinking about the eternal mysteries. 'O Love, O Life, O Time!' You sometimes seem very close to me, and on your lips seems hovering the answer to the everlasting riddle — the double riddle, of the world out there and the world within, at other times so hard to reconcile with itself. I hope and pray that you are strong of heart, and looking to the future as to a place where your house is to be builded fair and joyously inhabited.

Send me a line now and then. I shall soon be able to write without eluding surveillance, and an occasional word from you will go far to fill the slow days.

PORT CHESTER, N.Y.
June 5 (1908)

I have been lying low, after a little set-back, due I suppose to a too-long walk last Sunday. It is nothing serious — I only mention it as part of the news. I don't seem to get the miraculous uplift I have been promised (though I get hints of it now and then of mornings). The doctor says my mind (my *mind*, bless your heart!) has been and is too active. I try to keep it in leash, but it *will* get away, and once away will wander far. I get greatly discouraged at the slowness of my progress, but looking back to the day I came here I can see that I have no just reason for repining. I am able to get over to the shore now once in a while, and wander a little bit along the coast and through the adjacent meadows. It is lovely, in a mild way, and the gardener's collie does her best to make up for Sieg's surprising and ever-regrettable absence. The news you gave of him warmed my heart.

Miller received the manuscript, as I know from Weller, who came down the other day on an errand which has given me — in its implications — a good deal of uneasiness. It seems that Miller, on reading the play, thinks it has been in some way hurt (for his purpose) by changes made since he heard it in Boston. Practically no such changes have been made, and the real state of the case is that on closer inspection he does not see in it the kind of obvious actor's medium that he at first imagined. (His feeling is that certain 'Climaxes' have been weakened or destroyed — something of the sort.) Of course, he is right essentially. It is not the kind of play he imagined — never was and will be less so as I go on with it. I am forced to regret sending him the MS. at all, or even telling him about it, until it was wholly finished and to be firmly stood by. I am more than half inclined to ask him to return it. What do you think? I must do something at once.

It looks as if the doctor would not consent to my leaving here before the end of the month, and indeed in my soberer moments I am compelled to acknowledge that to do so would probably be unwise. The chief point of weakness seems to be my back, which remains disgustingly sore and mucilaginous, collapsing altogether under slight exertion. The doctor says this is natural. He does not regard it as in the least an alarming symptom. In fact I think he secretly welcomes it, as reinforcing his exhortation to go slow.

A shaky hand warns me to stop now — though I have not begun to say anything.

PORT CHESTER, N.Y.
June 14 (1908)

The authorities at Yale College have asked me to come to the Commencement, June 24th, to receive an honorary degree. I don't want to go, but I don't see very well how to get out of it, being so near, and able (by that time) to undergo the slight exertion involved. Will you send me, as speedily as possible, my old cap and gown? Or, if that has disappeared, will you borrow one from Ferd and send it on? In case neither of these sources prove fruitful, I shall have to send to New York, which will be a gamble.

I haven't written for too long, but you will understand that the little strength I have for writing has to be used partly for discharging my long arrears of correspondence in directions not quite negligible though at bottom unimportant. As for my condition, it is I am sure satisfactory, though I can't help fretting and fuming a bit at the slowness with which energy ebbs back again into nerves and brain. My back remains the point of greatest weakness, and dilatory beyond excuse in re-establishing itself in normal conditions.

The prospect of being able to go to California, or even of getting the play into shape to be rehearsed without me, seems remote. I have written Miller to this effect, and suggested that he send back the MS. I have made up my mind fully not to allow the play to be given until I have had time to rewrite the third act to my satisfaction, and it is very doubtful whether I can do that soon enough for him.

The books which you have sent from time to time have been a God-send, as the life here is lonely — not quite so bad now as formerly, for Ridgely is staying nearby — at Cos Cob — also Mrs. Davidge, who takes Charlotte and me on auto-rides over this beautiful Connecticut country, and yachting up and down the Sound. Yesterday she brought us over to Cos Cob (where I am writing) in an old fishing-boat, to a charming old inn dating from Revolutionary times, run by the wife of an artist who is delectably installed. Wife's father is a wonder of an old man — goes to Cuba every winter and collects rare woods which he works up into furniture — the kind that isn't made any more — beautiful joiner's work without a nail or a rivet.

I expect to leave here after the Yale commencement and a few days of recuperation. Unless some better plan occurs, I shall come to Chicago.

Don't blame me for this scrawl, full of matters of mint and cumin instead of realities. Even this has left me shaky.

(Postmarked Cos Cob, Conn., June 15, 1908)

I think it will be necessary now to let Miller go on. Before the rehearsals are over I can get the third act rewritten to my satisfaction, and can insist on his making the necessary changes. I am afraid that to stop Miller now would work an injustice, as he has probably made definite arrangements.

We go back to Port Chester today or tomorrow.

I have heard of a place for sale on the Maine coast which sounds so entrancing that I am in a state of wild excitement about it. The enclosed photograph, for which I have to thank Miss Sarah Orne Jewett, will give you an idea. It is owned by the widow of Thomas Bailey Aldrich, and was his favorite retreat. Rather than risk delay I am going to make a flying trip up there to see it. Don't worry or have any fear of my over-exerting myself. I have made rapid progress of late, and am quite equal to the journey, for which I have both Charlotte's and the Doctor's consent. I am taking Ridgely along, to carry bags and do all the heavy work, starting tomorrow or Thursday, from New Haven, after the ceremonies there. We shall be gone perhaps five or six days, after which I shall return to New York, and thence to Chicago.

Post card, MONHEGAN (ME.), *June 30* (1908)

Here we are at this wonderful little island fourteen miles off the Maine shore. The house I sent you the photograph of didn't pan out, but I am still hopeful of finding something. Am going slow, and taking things very easy. The climate is doing me an immense amount of good.

MONHEGAN, *July* 2 (1908)

Two days on this entrancing island have made me a captive for life — in fancy. It is Mackinac unspoiled, and fourteen miles out in the open sea. Am tempted to buy a piece of ground, to build on in the future sometime. Return to New York tomorrow and thence to Chicago. Picking up strength fast.

Telegram: NEW YORK, *July* 7, 1908

TAKE MACKINAC PLACE   SHALL ARRIVE
THURSDAY AFTERNOON FOUR O'CLOCK
PENNSYLVANIA
                                        W

(Postmarked Mackinac Island, Aug. 21, 1908)
MACKINAC — *Friday*

This is to report that I have taken heart of grace and
pulled the portrait sketch of you together again, so that it
is as good as new and wants only a face to make of it a
handsome lady. This is all I have done since you took
flight, except a little driving with Charlotte, and a good
deal of lying on my back — my accursed back — waiting
for my energies to rejoin me. Charlotte has taken to horse-
back riding with an amazing zest and success.   I have ridden once, without any very encouraging results.

We have had three days of tremendous high winds, the
whole island rocking and groaning on its foundations. It
seems to be the work of a remarkably gifted understanding
of the equinoctial.

Sieg, after twenty-four hours of moping for you, has
patched up some kind of a life on a basis of suspended
judgment, meanwhile getting support out of Charlotte, to
whom he seems already much attached. This will arouse
jealousy in both your breast and Bessie's, but I report the
fact as an impartial observer.

When are you coming back? It is very lonesome here —
the whole island mourns you, wringing ten thousand hands.

(Postmarked Mackinac Island, Aug. 25, 1908)
I am feeling much better the last two days, having lifted
myself by the scruff of the neck out of a slough of invalid-

ism, which was daily increasing, and decided to try a little faith-cure on myself, with amazing results. There is really something in it. We are having wonderful golden weather here. Don't delay too long, for fear it may all be gone. I am holding on to it with both hands for you.

(Postmarked Mackinac Island, Oct. 11, 1908)
Oct. — ?

Your telegram was a joy to sore eyes. Since receiving it your return has seemed so imminent that letter-writing has assumed a more than ordinarily distant and mythical character, but here is a word anyhow, at the eleventh hour. My message is only 'Return!' said in many melodious keys — 'ditties of no tone.'

The island, after a night of sharp frost, is looking her loveliest. Please, please come back before a catastrophe of rain or something occurs, to strip these paradisiacal boughs of their gold and crimson.

I have painted you a new picture, a little one but a good — at least it looks excellently good to me, in the flush of completion. It is the other view of the fort hill, with the church and the old stable — you remember? Painted with four colors. This matter of using *few colors* is the secret of painting, and also — I dare say — of writing, if one could grasp the connection. Effect brown and gold — but not at all like 'The Pond' (how is that for a title?) — the gold tones making all the difference. Also I have finished the Mission church picture — not very good, but has nice points.

107 Waverly Place, N.Y.
Nov. 4 (1908)

Since I got here I have been distractedly busy, to little purpose. Miller has done nothing toward assembling a cast, and the available material looks slim enough. I told him about Sills, with proper reservations, and he is in communication with him, trying to get him to join the Miller forces, with the idea that in case he won't do for *The Faith-Healer* he can be worked in somewhere else. It is a great opportunity for Milton. In all probability, however, he is tied up by a season's contract with his present company, and to get him released would prove too expensive.

Miller seems to have been rebuffed by the London managers, and has come back hugely disgruntled with all things English — says he will take out naturalization papers and become in fact as he is in spirit a *bona-fide* American citizen. The great sweet child! Says he tried to get Forbes-Robertson to take the play. O me, O my!

As soon as there is a lull in the present activities I intend to slip up to Maine and look at some of those farms. I am more convinced than ever (since plunging into this maelstrom) that it is 'me for the country.'

The New York, New Haven and Hartford Railroad Co.
(Postmarked Nov. 8, 1908)
En route
Thursday

Behold me flying Maine-ward, to snatch a look at a farm or two, during a lull in the preparations here. I told Miller all about Milton, and he has engaged him. We have given no promise, however, to put him in the rôle of *The Faith-Healer*. If he proves incompetent he will be otherwise provided for. The whole thing is a secret — Milton himself even does not know for what purpose he is wanted, and will not until he gets here. He will not be free for two weeks, and this will cause some delay in our plans, which I will utilize as far as possible in searching for a farm.

My explorations were cut short by the necessity of advising about the stage-set (which has been made in miniature) and I didn't have time to find anything good — nothing in fact that I would think of twice. I looked at almost all the 'shore places' advertised. They are shore places, to be sure, but being on bays and inlets, and the banks low, the water running out twice a day leaves miles of mud flats, the most dismal sight in the world. I saw one possible place in the hills, a fairly good old house, and a grand view, but the country lying between this place and the railroad was not attractive, because almost denuded of trees. This difficulty exists almost everywhere. It is a shame and a sorrow to see the way the land has been stripped of its wooding — and the devastation still goes on, shockingly. When I have recovered from my disappointment I shall sally forth again.

Miller accepts the new version of the *F.-H.* unreservedly — didn't I tell you? — considers the new third act a great improvement. There is a deal to tell about the difficulties which beset us in preparing the production; but that I will reserve for another time. Things are going — he says — as well as we could hope; but they seem to me to be going badly enough. Meanwhile I am getting the *F.-H.* and the *G. D.* ready for press. In the latter case this means work, for the MS. has got badly mixed up in the process of time.

Preparations for the production of the *F.-H.* go on slowly. Miller's plan at present is to give a trial performance at Boston when he goes there next month with the

Divide, using as many members of the present cast as he can work in. Then if the reception of the play by the Boston public seems encouraging, he will organize a full separate company and launch it upon its own independent career. He is manifestly timid about it and fears a rebuff; nevertheless his personal feeling about the play seems enthusiastic enough. He keeps recurring to Tyrone Power as a possibility for the leading rôle. Certainly his performance as the Drain-man in *The Servant in the House* is not encouraging, but Miller declares that he has capabilities which are there unrevealed. Meanwhile Sills has been engaged, without a specified agreement as to whether he will be allowed to play the rôle or not, and will appear on the scene next week. I am somewhat worried about Frohman's hostility to the play and refusal to share its fortunes, though he is Miller's partner in all his other operations. I attribute this to the fact that — as you may remember — I rejected an extraordinarily liberal offer of his, a year or so ago, to sign a contract with him. If he cherishes a personal grudge on this account, the career of the play, even if initially successful, will be greatly jeopardized.

I have been busy, since getting back from Maine, in making a fair copy of the *Divide* for the printer. My own copy is so imperfect and so many corruptions have crept into the text which Miller uses, that the task is no light one. I have had a letter from a German named Freund, who has married an Englishwoman and lives in England, proposing that he translate both the *G. D.* and the *F.-H.*, and exhibiting excellent credentials. If I can make an arrangement with the egregious Marbury, I think I will let him do the job. He has translated Kennedy's two plays (*The Servant in the House* and a new one, coming out here this

winter, called *The Winter Feast*) and seems to have intimate relations with the German theatrical world.

There is a wondrous dancing creature here called
Isadora Duncan, fresh from European triumphs, who
dances to the accompaniment of a full symphony orchestra
— renders in fact in dance the Seventh Symphony of
Beethoven and other such trifles. I saw her dance a whole
afternoon, while the orchestra played the music (or most of
it) of Glück's *Iphigenia in Aulis*, and she filled the huge
Metropolitan Opera House stage in a fashion quite incredible. Also I saw her do impromptu things in her own
studio — no less than marvellous. I hope you will have a
chance to see her. I can imagine nothing which would give
you more pleasure. She is going West, I believe, on tour.

Telegram:

NEW YORK, *Nov.* 19, 1908

MUST CHANGE HEALER'S NAME
TOO MANY PEOPLE REMEMBER
ORIGINAL   CAN YOU SUGGEST
ANYTHING   W V M

107 WAVERLY PLACE
NEW YORK, *Nov.* 22 (1908)

These have been, and are, tremendously busy days, so
crowded that I hardly know what has happened since I
wrote you last. Your zeal in hunting me up a name for
my man was wasted by the necessity I was under of sending a name at once, to stop the clamor of the printers. I
believe, however, I hit on a first-rate name — *Michaelis*
(accent on second syllable) — East European and yet not
definitely Russian. How do you like it? It is in use here in

America — I found it in the New York City Directory. For first name I think I will call him Ulrich — suggesting old German or Gothic associations, but also in contemporary use here in America — *Ulrich Michaelis.* It rather pleases me, and I hope it will you.

We have got hold of a love and a dream in the person of a ten-year-old girl to play Annie. Her performance promises to be a gem of child-acting. She already towers above the whole company in artistry — without art, at least without Art. Tyrone Power seems to be definitely decided on for the title-rôle. He does better too than you would expect from his performance as the Drain-man, and seems to have real insight into the character. The thing to be feared in him is melodramatic robustiousness, but Miller thinks we can keep him toned down. Meanwhile, the arrival of Milton, announced for tomorrow, opens up a new complication. Miller did nothing to head him off after the rôle had been otherwise filled, and I can't make out what he intends to do with him unless it is to hold him in reserve in case Power — for some reason or other — flunks it. We have got a first-rate woman for Martha. For the present Rhoda is being played by a Miss Lawton, who is the latest in the long and melancholy list of Ruths. She serves fairly well (as Rhoda — I haven't seen her Ruth) though she lacks lightness — is prone to the intense and tremulous in action and speech. The other parts are temporarily — I hope only temporarily — assumed by — our esteemed friend Wingate (the Philip of the *Divide*) and Butler (the Dr. Newbury of ditto). We haven't yet got hold of anybody who can touch Uncle Abe with a ten-foot pole, though an amiable young man is struggling dismally with the rôle. All this sounds pretty blue, but in spite of what I say — and as to the badness of the bad ones I have phrased the case with angelic mildness — I feel, quite illogically, buoyant about the outcome. This is probably due in large part to Miller's beautiful understanding of the play in all and sundry of its phases and ramifications. I am more impressed than ever — much more — with his intellect and imagination. And he has been kindness itself in mopping my fevered brow and administering anodynes to ease my tortures.

If nothing intervenes to upset the program, the play will have its première two weeks from next Thursday afternoon, in Boston. Two performances only, both in the afternoon, are scheduled to be given there. Please consider yourself engaged for the first one — the second may never be demanded by a distraught public.

It is nearly morning, and I am frightfully tired, though — as usual nowadays — far too wide awake to look forward with any relish to bed.

(Postmarked New York, Nov. 28, 1908)

I don't think *Michaelis* is Jewish — at least not obviously so, since many people to whom I have shown it have failed to perceive the fact. And even if it is? Was not Jesus a Jew? And John?

I am in a bushel of trouble about the question of copyright protection. It seems that our enlightened Congress has refused to join the Berne Convention, which makes copyright easy and automatic throughout European countries, and has ranged itself with Patagonia and her sisters. The result is that there is a mountain of red tape to untie, with no very sure chance of protection at the end. Among the details is a law compelling plays (in order to secure English copyright) to be submitted to the Lord Chamberlain of England, *in printed form* (typewriting, it seems, gives you no safeguard whatever). This functionary takes his own time to pass upon the book and grant permission for the play to be performed in England, which *then only* acquires copyright standing. The performance is of course a private one, and offers no special impediment except one of expense; but while all this is being done, here must sit our good friend Henry, with an expensive company on his hands, doing nothing except wait upon my lord's pleasure. Of course it is my fault, but the fault only of my ignorance. In the case of *The Great Divide* all this red tape was got through with during the summer before the definitive production, so that I learned nothing of the difficulties involved. God bless our Congressmen, and the book-dealers in whose favor these barbaric laws exist — unless they exist in favor of Frohman, Shubert, *et al.*, in order to provide them ampler forage upon the brains of men who are misguided enough to write plays. I am writing this in a restaurant whither I have drifted after a day of hurry, perplexity, and unconscious starvation — at this moment suddenly horribly conscious. If it is unduly tart, the conditions will excuse me.

P.S. The Boston production is probably off, for the reasons here stated.

NEW YORK, *Dec.* 7 (1908)

I got back to New York last night, after a very strenuous week in Boston struggling with the copyright tangle.

The days since I wrote have been so crowded with anxious labor and general confusion that I hardly know where to begin to tell you about it. The upshot of the whole business is that I have succeeded in saving the foreign rights of the play, though at a considerable sacrifice. The production has had to be postponed, probably until the middle or last of next month. I have lost Power, as he has had to be drafted off for *The Servant* again. This you will not regret, but I take it hard, for he made a deep impression upon me as the Faith-Healer. Worse even, I stand to lose the little girl who, as 'Annie,' delighted me beyond measure; but it is possible she may be recaptured. Miller has been kindness itself, and a great comfort, instead of being — as he had every reason to be — vexed and angry at the overthrow of his plans.

You will be delighted to hear (and it is almost a valid offset to the main catastrophe) that the third act (of *The Great Divide*) has been restored, in every respect, to its original integrity, including the final exclamation 'For us' by which you (rightly) set so much store. The new Ruth (a Miss Lawton) is in many essential respects wonderfully good. She gives a performance that comes nearer my conception of the part than has yet been given. She doesn't draw well, alas. Our people seem to love bad acting.

Telegram:

NEW YORK, *Dec.* 7, 1908

PRODUCTION OF PLAY POSTPONED
AM COMING WEST

W V M

(With the hope of re-establishing his health, which at this time seemed to be in a very precarious condition, W. V. M. went to California in February, 1909, with

William Wendt, the painter. They were detained in Los Angeles by heavy rains, but finally got settled in a cabin in San Dimas, and began to paint. After a week or ten days W. V. M. was called to St. Louis, where *The Faith-Healer* was to be tried out by Henry Miller.)

(Written on picture post cards, postmarked
Albuquerque & Ashford R.P.O., Feb. 5, 1909)

I have had a rather badish night the first out, but this bracing air (from 5000 to 7000 ft.) is pulling me up wonderfully. I should not be surprised if this country would be a better place to recuperate than the Pacific coast, especially as here horseback is one's native element. A puzzling circumstance is the apathy or even dislike which most of the passengers seem to feel for the amazing country. Perhaps it is too strange and unhomelike to appeal to the general. I take this helter-skelter means of writing, partly to show you the pictures, which I am sure you will enjoy, and partly because I can only write during stops, as the trains wobbles so as to make my communications illegible except during stops.

The lunch has been a great boon, as well as an astounding new revelation of your powers as a 'provider.' W. and I get along famously in a quiet way. I found my camera after all — sorry I worried you.

Here we are in God's country. This morning since sunrise has been a wonderful procession of sights. At 8 o'clock we crossed the Great Divide, over 7000 feet high. Now we are on the Arizona plateau, with everything in the world to see, as witness above for sample. (Picture of San Francisco Mountains, Arizona.)

Telegram: SAN DIMAS, CALIF., *Feb.* 21, 1909

FIND OUT MILLER'S ADDRESS THIS WEEK AND
WIRE HIM WILL ARRIVE ST LOUIS MARCH
EIGHTH

W V M

SAN DIMAS, *Feb.* 23, '09

As to the trip East I prefer some other road than the
Santa Fe — say the Rock Island or the so-called Salt Lake
Route. There will not be time for the Canadian or Northern Pacific. The main point is to take some road which
will land me at St. Louis by the shortest route. I shall
leave here Saturday or Sunday.

We are having a good time and a strenuous. The open
air is putting me in shape fast, I think. Wish you could
share it.

Telegram: ST. LOUIS, MO., *March* 8 (1909)

OUTLOOK   DISCOURAGING
SHALL WRITE PARTICULARS
TOMORROW

W V M

Telegram:

ST. LOUIS, MO., *March* 12, 1909

FAITH HEALER ONLY ONE WEEK TRY–OUT FOR
NEXT FALL PARTIAL CAST   DRESS REHEARSAL
PROBABLY MONDAY MORNING ELEVEN

W V M

(Postmarked March 12, 1909)
MARYLAND HOTEL
SAINT LOUIS, U.S.A.
Friday afternoon

I have been in such a whirl with the thousand and one things to be attended to that I have resorted to telegrams to keep you informed as to the state of affairs. It appears that Miller is making this production only as a preliminary experiment, intending to postpone the definitive production until next spring. He and the fair Lawton are taking the main rôles, and the rest of the company is partly new, partly patched up from the old *Divide* company. I do not expect much result from this make-shift company, especially as the rehearsals have been exceedingly inadequate in time and number. The dress rehearsal, it seems now, will take place Sunday morning (about eleven) but possibly not till Monday. I doubt if you had better come on for the rehearsal. Your impression will be calculated to increase my own dissatisfaction, and raise it to distress. At present I am taking the thing philosophically, and I don't intend to be upset by the result, which is almost certain to be poor. If, however, you are anxious to see the dress rehearsal you can come. Whenever you come, you had better stop at the Jefferson Hotel, 12th and Locust Sts. The place where I am staying is away out in the suburbs and not very good, besides being inconvenient to reach.

Miller seems enthusiastic and there is a good deal of miscellaneous interest astir in the city. There is nothing to do but pray the thing may not be an utter fiasco, and to care as little as possible if it is. The proofs arrived safely. The photographs have come out pretty nicely.

(Postmarked April 24, 1909)
HARVARD CLUB
27 WEST 44TH Street (N.Y.)
Saturday

I have spent several days at 'Sky Meadows' and am going there again tonight. When I arrived I found Miller in a fearful state. It seems that his recent theatrical losses have compelled him to heavily mortgage his farm, 'Sky Meadows,' the apple of his eye. For the first day or two after I came there was nothing to be done with him. Then he pulled up again, and soon regained his sanguine spirits. He liked the new version of the third act greatly, and was enthusiastic about the future of the play. He hopes by means of it — and the English campaign — to recoup himself for other failures. I devoutly hope he will, for if these two ventures go wrong he will be down and out. Meanwhile I have rewritten the third act again, and have at last got it in a shape that I believe will stand. I am going out to the farm tonight to give it a final reading.

As for our plans, I have not written because I thought that if I did I should probably open old questions and dilemmas which the time has come to bury. The less we talk and the more promptly we act, the better now. I prefer to sail from Canada, and as soon as I find out the necessary particulars as to that and where you are to meet me, I will telegraph, giving you a couple of days, if possible.

Telegrams will reach me here, unless I inform you of a change of address. I shall try to get this on the Twentieth Century, so must hurry.

Telegram: NEW YORK (date not clear)

NO PRODUCTION THIS FALL

FINISH HERE SATURDAY

SHALL I ENGAGE PASSAGE

W V M

HARVARD CLUB
NEW YORK, *April* 28, '09

I returned from 'Sky Meadows' yesterday to interview Milton Sills — at Miller's request. He joins Miller's forces for the summer as curate in the *Servant-in-the-House* company, and Miller now is anxious to put him into *The Faith-Healer* next fall, his own prospects as to London being so hazy. Since he sent for Sills last winter the young man's prospects have taken a decided leap. He has been flattered by Belasco and Clyde Fitch. Moreover, he is involved already in a quasi-contract for next fall — which, however, he can get out of if it seems worth his while. These matters cannot be settled for several days. In view of all this I can't sail before next week. Good boats sail from Montreal, May 7th — and weekly. Does this suit you?

Engraved Announcement:

MARRIED

in Quebec, Canada

THE SEVENTH OF MAY

nineteen hundred and nine

HARRIET TILDEN BRAINARD

to

WILLIAM VAUGHN MOODY

CONCLUSION

Harriet Moody

CONCLUSION

XXII. COMPENSATION OF 'CLEAR, LIVING HAPPINESS'

'We made no sign; we named no name.'

So, from an earlier May eight years before, from mute beginnings, the beneficent disaster of their sacred day had led on at last to the making of the sign and the naming of the new name — Harriet Moody. For this strange pragmatic fairy tale was all now to be 'happy ever after'?

'Let none be called happy, till after death has called him' was the gauge of life invoked by the old Greek dramatist at the close of his mythic tragedy. Tragic indeed were to be the last fifteen months of Moody's life, ministered to by Harriet's tremulously buoyant devotions till its end, not wholly — like Milton's — enwalled with 'spent-light ... in this dark world and wide,' but slowly merged in half-light, while the sentient Arcadian mind watched that gradual submersion with Spartan endurance. Yet after lapse of long separation, now that death has called them both, in very truth they may be called happy ever after, having substantiated for the world's blind and halt a radiance beyond eyesight and a stature above lameness.

None the less, in their fairy lore of friendship before death, it is humanly consoling to discover a momentary sequel less austerely Greek in contour and more *gemüthlich* in its compensation for long-withheld desire, in this passage from Harriet's own diary, written by her during their honeymoon, dated at Bonchurch, Isle of Wight, June 23, 1909:

A beautiful, bright morning, warm and quiet. We are entirely secluded here in a bower of greeneries of all kinds that look out on the sea. I have a dear little room just across the hall from our large room, with a wonderful great rock rising up past the window, but with much reflected sunlight coming in from the rock, and I feel strangely free from anxiety and exquisitely happy. Not even for the youth which was almost unbroached when I was here before, would I change this clear, living happiness.

XXIII. HONEYMOON IN ENGLAND, CHANNEL ISLANDS AND LAKE COUNTRY

Harriet wrote three diaries,* in 1909–1910. The first was written at moments snatched from travel and increasing anxieties withheld by her from Will — anxieties involved in his illness and in her own large business project which she was then initiating with Selfridge in London. Since her letters to Will Moody have not survived, and her diaries in England and America comprise the only immediate record of his last months of life, I have included a few excerpts, here published for the first time. The following give glimpses of their sojourn in England and the Channel Islands in 1909.

June 12, Guernsey. We left London this morning by train for Weymouth. The approach to Guernsey is very beautiful and the harbor and castle of Saint Peterport most imposing. We arrived at half-past six, walked up the Esplanade and there had our fancy captured by a delicious little garden which peeped out through a half open door, at the Bel Voir Hotel, where we found quiet rooms....There is a little maid here named Bertha, whose white cap-ribbons vibrate and whose throat trembles and swells like the throat and tail of a bobolink, in the very ecstasy and passion of the national 'thank-you.' Being a descendant and country-woman of our own Thomas Jefferson and therefore 'not to be outdone in politeness,' I responded in kind, until Will called my attention to the moment of stunned surprise, and the frightened return to the charge, with which she met my reciprocities.

June 25. Isle of Wight, Bonchurch. Another lowering day. Will feeling much depressed. After breakfast we went for a stroll to the old church and the sea. The churchyard graves were hung with roses. 'As touching a memorial of the old religious feeling as I have ever seen,' said Will. We tried to find a secluded spot by the sea, but my foot was behaving badly and suddenly my courage gave out. I tried to conceal it but did so only indifferently....After luncheon we drove to Shanklin, a very beautiful drive over the hills in the falling mist.

June 27. Winchester. Will feeling better, and we moved into a little place centuries old, called 'God-Begot-House.' Our rooms in the top story, and named 'Asser' and 'Queen Eauswitha,' are heavily cross-beamed with age-eaten oak.

June 28. I left Will at Winchester, and with a great wave of desolation came to London.

June 30. Will writes the Salisbury Cathedral is more beautiful than that at Winchester. He went up on Wednesday to Stonehenge.

July 1. I met Will at the Waterloo Station. He has had so much pain that he felt like getting near to doctors and other resources in case of need.

July 2. It seems to me Will needs to live in the open air and I long to go with him to the country. I suggest America and Mackinac, or any other country place; Sark and the cottage there, with Dr. T—— near at hand; a cart and slow driving through English by-roads. The truth is I am deeply anxious and at loss what to do.

July 9. Jersey. To Mount Orgueil. I can give no idea of the pleasure we had in wandering through the old castle. We climbed to the top of the ruins, up devious, winding stone staircases, and in imagination 'flung all the banners on the outer walls' as we were beset by the hordes of the enemy. Will gathered flowers for me going up and down, poppies first, and last the lovely rose-colored climbers for which we knew no name.

July 10. The pleasantest day of our journey. We drove over the gently undulating country until we reached the bluff coast which hangs over Bouley Bay, Will often breaking out in admiration of a beautiful tree-shaded lane, a handsome old pile of buildings, the effect of light and cloud-shadows on the landscape.

Returning to England, they proceeded via Bowness to the Lakes.

July 22. Windermere. Wonderful views of purple mist-topped mountains. Will walked about and reported the place as the thing he has been looking for.

July 25. Sunday. Ambleside. We went into the kitchen of a cottage inn and dried our damp garments. The fire was very snug indeed. Further on we came to the churchyard where Wordsworth is buried. We stood by his grave for a while in the rain while all the sorrow of all the world, that lies between the inert mass and that delicate soul, knocked at my heart; and I fell to tears for the mighty being by my side, held in the grasp of inflexible and remorseless sickness and to prayers for the passing of that sickness.

In those words of Harriet's the 'mighty beings' of great poets are strangely linked. A century earlier 'that delicate soul' Wordsworth himself had stood a pilgrim at another grave, shivering

'At thought of what I now behold:
As vapours breathed from dungeons cold
   Strike pleasure dead,
So sadness comes from out the mould
   Where Burns is laid...
               But ere
Night fell I heard, or seemed to hear
Music that sorrow comes not near...'

Moody at the grave of Wordsworth left no recording poem of his own thoughts; but Harriet's diary here records this moving analogue in the pilgrimage of poets. After leaving Ambleside, these last brief entries conclude her transcript of their stay in England.

July 28. London. Hills under heavy storm clouds coming from Ambleside to Bowness by boat. Will came on with me part way, but revoked his decision about coming to the city and went to Dartmoor.

July 29. Telegrams from Will (at Dartmoor).

Three days afterward, from 'Okehampton, Dartmoor, Aug. 1, 1909,' Will wrote to me in America:

Dear Percy, this is about the time when *The Canterbury Pilgrims* * is to have its great display at Gloucester before President Taft and the nobility and gentry.... I had hoped to be there, but we have been detained abroad. The other member of 'we' refers, of course, to Harriet. The news of our marriage has doubtless reached you, and you, who know something of her wonderful gifts of mind and heart, will have been the first to congratulate me.... English weather has been at its worst, and my health has suffered. I am looking forward with eagerness to a New England autumn, for I want to buy a little farm somewhere up there, and settle down to country life — the only one for me. I admire your wisdom in having set up your Ebenezer early and permanently on those lines.— Harriet joins with me in love to yourself and to Marion, and to those adorable children (I take the newest one * on trust as equally good with the two I know). Always your — W. V. M.

XXIV. RETURN TO AMERICA: STRICKEN: TOWARD THE GREAT WEST

This perennial yearning to set up his own 'Ebenezer' on some farm * with Harriet was never to be satisfied. On their return to America in September, he was too ill to do more than go back with her to Chicago, where they were joined by Will's sister, Charlotte. On account of increased anxiety concerning his eyesight, they went in early October to Baltimore for consultation with doctors at Johns Hopkins hospital.* There two explorative operations were performed on October 28 and November 25. About the last of November, I received a telegram thus recorded in my wife's diary (at Cornish):

Going down to Cambridge to see about the Harvard Dramatic Club rehearsals of *The Scarecrow*,* Percy received at the depot a telegram from Harriet Moody, saying, *If possible come at once to Johns Hopkins hospital, Baltimore.* So he telegraphed he would take the midnight from Boston. It is about Will Moody and I have since had letters from Baltimore. They were having a consultation of doctors as to a third and probably fatal operation on the brain. Percy saw the doctors and the verdict was no operation. He bought the railroad tickets and saw Will and Harriet off for California, Will not knowing Percy was there for fear of exciting him. Percy was often so close that he brushed Will's sleeve, but Will did not know, as his sight is permanently impaired, poor tragic fellow.

Those were some of the most poignant hours of my life, so near to my friend, whom I longed to speak to, yet dared not lest his quick intuition should sense from my presence that I had been summoned to confer upon his own mortal danger. On leaving the hospital, as he, Harriet, Charlotte and I stood by the elevator doors, Harriet asked him: 'Will you take the lift down?' He answered: 'No, let's take the stairway. I think I'd feel nobler to walk down.' I was beside him walking down and in the same cab to the station, where I helped him into the train and stood watching on the platform just outside his Pullman-car window, through which I saw a faint, glad smile light up his face under the bandaged forehead, as the train moved slowly outward toward the Great West.

XXV. DARKENING VISTAS: 'NOBLE BALANCE OF SELF-CONTROL'

About a week later, Harriet's diary begins again her record of the long, gradual sundown of Will's passing.

Dec. 9, 1909. Wed. Riverside, Cal. A rainy day. Will feeling well. No pain, even encouraged about his sight. Read in Maeterlinck's *The Life of the Bee*. Concerning the bees I said that their organization and purpose seemed almost terrifying in its completeness and he said that their sacrifice of all considerations to that of the future of the race appeared to him a limitation upon their manifestation of intellect. This, in as much as he is a strong individualist by nature, and as it went right to the pith of a reasonably abstruse matter, seemed to me well worthy of note.

Dec. 9. Still rainy. Began reading *Ramona*. He commented that *Ramona*, although charming in style was 'old fashioned,' and instanced that lack of fidelity to life in drawing the Scotchman, Angus Phail.

[387]

Dec. 10. A brighter day. Will wakened quite happy in the thought of going to Santa Barbara today.... He felt most encouraged and has spoken of things he could see: the most remarkable being the water on the coast, seen from the car-window in heavy twilight at six o'clock.

This new locale of W. V. M. on the sea-coast has been feelingly memorialized by Ridgely Torrence in his poem, *Santa Barbara Beach.**

Dec. 15. Santa Barbara. A very natural aspect of the eye was the most cheering sight of the morning. At five we went for a short drive with a lazy horse we have hired. Will got out about half a mile from the house with Charlotte and walked home.

Dec. 23. Today he began speaking of his new play.* He asked to have the manuscript read and made some valuable suggestions for changes which I noted.... We drove to the Old Mission where he tested his eyes by looking at its elevation. He was overjoyed to find he saw it quite well and without 'blurring.' This greatly raised his spirits.

Dec. 24. Went out in cart till five-thirty. He walked with Charlotte up two long hills because the horse could not pull us all through the mud. The ravine was full of mist, but he was greatly disappointed that he did not see as well as he had. Spoke with affection of Christmas Eve.

Dec. 25. Wakened with many Christmas wishes for us all. At one-thirty we sat down around our unlighted small Christmas tree. This he enjoyed with all his own sweetness of spirit. He had taken much interest in having the gifts bought for him to give, especially for the servants. He also entered into the spirit of the Christmas dinner and enjoyed it heartily. He constantly shows his old delicate solicitation for the welfare and comfort of others, and fills the atmosphere with his gentle spiritual tenderness.

Jan. 3, 1910. We were reading a paper concerning the 'Idealism' of different philosophers. In this he took great interest; and spoke fluently and well to several points.

Jan. 4. Today's period of reading was divided between philosophical essays, the Bible and *A Tale of Two Cities*.

Jan. 7. 'I can see you, your face and all with it alone,' he said. He felt much encouraged and so settled down to our reading with great interest.

Jan. 8. Read *Tale of Two Cities*. He called attention to the point in the story where the play had begun, successfully played by Henry Miller.

Moody's continuing thoughts of his 'grand resource, the theatre,' is evidenced throughout these further passages of Harriet's diary.

Jan. 14. Damp and dark. Read till eleven. Will said he was going to walk and Charlotte went with him. At twelve-thirty, I walked down the road to meet him as I had a telegram for him. As I came near he exclaimed 'Why! I see your face, clearly.'

The telegram * announced the forthcoming staging of *The Faith Healer*, together with Mr. Miller's satisfaction in the new version. This news involved the sending-off of three telegrams, one to Mr. Miller, one to Will's publishers, one to his manuscript copyist, the last two rather complicated. These he dictated with great firmness, deciding some rather involved questions entirely for himself.

He proposed to me to go to New York and watch the early staging of the play and said he could get on well now for a time. After dictating the telegrams, in response to my statement that I thought he would be foolish to let this play occupy his attention at all now, as it was the thing with which he overtaxed himself before, and he needed to be free of it, he said he guessed that was true and he wouldn't do it. He then turned on his side, composed himself and slept.

Jan. 19. Will much interested in the fact that *The Faith Healer* is being put on in New York tonight, but is also very restrained about it. I cannot commend his bearing of himself too highly, for this play has been the darling of the last few years. Read till five. About nine o'clock an enthusiastic telegraphic message * came from New York friends sent after the New York première, and gave him great pleasure. But this play has cost him so much in vital force that I am fearful of his getting excited about it now, just when he seems to be gaining; so we put this excitement resolutely aside.

Jan. 21. Will received and personally answered telegrams relative to performances of *Faith Healer* to be given soon in Cambridge and Boston. He spoke of pain in the left eye, and also that sometimes at night, he would open his eyes and the room would appear light for a minute.

Jan. 26. Will rested a little but walked about, talking of *The Faith Healer*. Went to walk. Felt some anxiety about Sunday (his dog) who had a sharp attack of sickness.

Jan. 27. I should have mentioned that he had the adverse New York newspaper clippings concerning *The Faith Healer* and that he bore all this with his usual uncomplaining acquiescence, and without allowing himself to be cast down. His is always the most noble balance of self-control in the world.

Jan. 29. A telegram came from Henry Miller * including the statement, 'I believe the play will live.' This gave him pleasure. But he had much pain before he slept.

Jan. 30. A letter from a friend in Cambridge * (E. K. Rand) full of understanding of *The Faith Healer* gave him good cheer.

Feb. 1. After breakfast we sat down to correct proof. I read the printer's page aloud while Charlotte followed with the typed manuscript and Will listened. He was never surer of what he wanted done in his life; dictated all the corrections, some of them involving nice points of judgment. We worked from nine till twelve-thirty.

Feb. 16. Read till 11.30. Then Will helped wash the dog. This he enjoyed. He felt he did not see so well today and was in a most discouraged mood. In the evening a consignment of proof of *The Faith Healer* came.

March 1. Will awakened feeling very well. During the breakfast hour we had a memorable and most uplifting talk. His old personality spoke forth fully and his whole aspect seemed changed. I went out for an hour. When I came back he met me with the word that 'something strange had happened' to his eyes. He found he could see to read parts of a letter written in a reasonably fine hand! Our day was one of great joy, too great to write of. At night he was well able to distinguish the stars and even picked out the Pleiades and described the group.

March 6. Went to drive. On the road Will read again the long sign-board he read two weeks ago, but with much more ease at a greater distance. He took out Mr. Mason's letter * and read nearly half a page of it. He is now fully assured of his complete recovery and feels himself already cured. He prefers to go to Colorado rather than to Los Angeles. This is perhaps what we shall do.

April 9. The new edition of *The Faith Healer* came. He was greatly interested, examined it most carefully and had it read aloud during the evening. His interest was alert and entirely natural. We talked the play over a bit after finishing. He went to bed with some pain.

April 10. Sunday. Talked with much hope of his future work. I got off letter for him to Macmillan concerning a typographical error, the only one in the book.

April 11. We are reading the Acts of the Apostles in which he is deeply interested.

April 18. After supper I read his own poems to him, for an hour. We enjoyed it, but it was too much for both of us, and though I read till after ten in Sudermann's *Song of Songs*, he went to bed sad.

XXVI. 'THE GROVE,' CHICAGO: SARDONIC EPILOGUE OF THE 'POETS' ONSET'

At the close of the spring, they went home to Chicago, where they passed the summer and early fall in their old haunts at 2970 Groveland Avenue,* fondly called 'the Grove' in these letters. In July, 1910, I went with my wife and Margaret Anglin to Berkeley, California, to assist Miss Anglin in staging the *Antigone* of Sophocles at the Greek Theatre there, while writing a play * for her laid in California. *En route* through Chicago, between trains, I visited 'the Grove,' and felt encouraged by an apparent rally in Will's health. As my wife and I were driving off in Harriet's carriage to the station, we caught our last glimpse of Will walking south on Groveland Avenue with his happy setter dog, Sunday, leaping about him. Of this visit I wrote a report to E. A. at Chocorua, N.H., where, on July 29th, he wrote to Harriet this letter from 'one of Will's old haunts.'

Dear Mrs. Moody, I was afraid that Percy, with his over-sanguine temperament, might be helping matters a little, but it is good to know that you bear him out substantially in your own words. You will see from this that I am in one of Will's old haunts — up here in the semi-wilderness with old Bartlett * who wishes to be remembered most violently. He is just the same as ever — only a little older. His chief excitement in life consists in killing flies during meals and swearing in a most piratical manner when he gets one. He has lost little of his old energy and none of his profanity -- for which one is to be grateful.

In spite of your veiled warning, I regret to report I have written two chapters of the novel — if it may be called one — and that I am ass enough to be rather pleased with what I have done. Of course this means that I have entered the Valley of the Shadow. If the October book of verse should by any chance amount to anything, the novel will undoubtedly knock it on the head and serve it right. I ought to be willing to be a freak forever, and not try to make money.

Won't you tell me something about the third part of W's trilogy? All I know is that it is more or less about Eve. From one point of view this is sufficient, but I can't help wishing that I knew a little more. Yours sincerely, E. A. Robinson.

The 'impossible play' of E. A. was his *Van Zorn*, and the 'two chapters' of its 'rehashment' in novel form were soon to be portion of a period of unpublished novelizations of plays; for a year later (July 17, 1911) Robinson wrote to me concerning that same *Porcupine* of his which Moody had sworn 'the daylight black and blue' cracking up to Charles Frohman in 'the den of Apollyon': — 'I am now going to try to make the *Porcupine* eat out of my hand, keep his quills down and be a novel.' This he did, completing a 75,000-word manuscript of the novel.* Thereupon, as he himself told me, he tore up his only copy of the manuscript and burnt it. So closes for this volume the sardonic epilogue to E. A.'s part in Moody's gallant championship of 'what our little group dreamed of trying to do by way of crusade for the drama.' ¹

In early October, Harriet, Will and his sister, Charlotte, went to Colorado Springs, where they rented a little cottage, surrounded by the autumn zests and splendors of the high cedared Rockies. From its porch there was a noble view of Pike's Peak, which Will's failing sight could still

¹ Cf. his letter to Harriet, Oct. 16, 1907.

faintly descry. There, two or three days before his death, he received this letter from Robinson (dated, Chocorua, N.H., Oct. 9, 1910), seeking to cheer him with early recollections of their old White Mountains pal, Bartlett,* whom Moody, ten years before, had described as 'magnificent old goat and man of God':

> Dear Moody — I am sending you a copy of my book ('The Town Down the River'), in the hope that it may not be bad enough to interfere with your rapid recovery. I say *rapid*, hoping and believing that I am using the right word. A word from you direct or from Mrs. Moody will be very acceptable.
>
> You can see from my choice of words the state that my intellect is in today. Perhaps I had better build a fire, and go down stairs and find out what *Pere* Bartlett is doing. He is making a devil of a racket and singing to himself as if he had caught another rat. He speaks of you often and wishes to be remembered when I write. You will mention that I have followed his instructions. Yours always, E. A. R.

From such 'wishes to be remembered' voiced in this last letter of his life, Will's brooding autumnal thoughts recalled perhaps that springtime of his young brave *Ode* before his 'ark of the year' had been veiled, and may have murmured aloud his own lines from it—looking off

> 'where the white Sierras call
> Unto the Rockies straightway to arise
> And dance before the unveiled ark of the year,
> Sounding their windy cedars as for shawms.'

XXVII. MOUNTAIN DEATH: THE MOMENT AND ENDURING MEMORY

At Colorado Springs, amid those far snow-capped presences, Will and Harriet continued to take their daily

walks on paths of wild nature until the seventeenth of
October. On that morning, Will awakened with cerebral
pain which caused him not to rise as usual. Throughout
the day Harriet and Charlotte attended his bedside.
Towards evening his pulse had ceased.

On that same evening, at Cornish, I received a telegram
from Harriet, asking me to inform Will's intimate friends.
I did so, and E. A. wrote again to Harriet, from Chocorua
(Oct. 17):

I have just received Percy MacKaye's telegram about Will.
I cannot possibly say anything now more than to express my
deepest sympathy for you at such a time as this. Thank God
he lived to do his work — or enough of it to place him among
the immortals. But you are not thinking of that now. Please
accept these few clumsy words as you know that I would
have them accepted and forgive my inopportune note of the
other day.

I hope that I may see you again sometime and perhaps
make you understand more clearly how fully I realize what
you, and the world, have lost. Most sincerely yours, E. A.
Robinson.

The day after sending the telegram to E. A., I wrote to
Prof. George Pierce Baker in Cambridge, proposing to him
a plan for a Harvard Theatre in Moody's memory, set
forth in a letter of which this is an excerpt:

Dear George Baker: I wrote you yesterday the news of
Moody's death. It was a shock the more keen to me that I
had seen him so greatly recovered in health last summer in
Chicago. I cannot keep out of mind the thought of him and
his splendid life-work unfinished, not simply because he was
one of my dearest friends but also my intimate fellow-worker.
I know that you also prize his memory well, and so I am
writing you this letter, in which I shall briefly set forth a
plan which came into my mind to-day in my studio, while

working on a play of my own: a plan to make perennial the inspiration of his significant work and life by correlating it permanently with the forces of dramatic renascence in our country today and tomorrow.

For the proposed plan * I suggested a committee, which I then organized. That was a quarter century ago, and still Harvard has no theatre. Hopefully the record of Moody's inspiring life and labors furnished in this volume may lead toward that consummation, newly stirred by the meanings of this twenty-fifth anniversary * of his passing, at a time when anew the majestic idea of a National Theatre is being definitely broached by our Federal Government at Washington.

For the memory of Will Moody is of more lasting stuff than governments and universities. At Colorado Springs, on October 17, 1910, there died a poet as cherishable for his *gentilesse* by our own 'Mermaid' of memories in America as another 'gentle Will' by his fellows of old London's tavern in 'Merrie England.' And fittingly for the one who invoked *The Fire-Bringer* * for his new land, his spirit was returned in fire, and his body to the elements in ashes.

XXVIII. LAST SEA-RITES; PROMETHEUS AND THE PSALMIST

The last rites, held by four loving friends beside the old Homeric 'many-syllabling sea' were imbued with the spirit elements of all timeless poets, merging the elegies of *Adonais* and *Lycidas* with the last sea-dirging lines of Walt Whitman's *Out of the Cradle Endlessly Rocking*, memorializing those same ocean-dunes of Long Island's shore,* not far from Walt's birthplace. From the nobly simple statement of Ferdinand Schevill sent to me for record here, one catches, as on tones of an ever-blowing sea-wind, the elemental reconcilement of Prometheus and Christ to which Moody's poet-mind was dedicated, in these lines from his own *Fire-Bringer* blending with the Ninety-first song of the Psalmist:

Here gather they, with mute and doubtful looks
At one-another, waiting till She comes,
Mnemosyne, mother of thought and tears,
Remembrancer, and bringer out of death
Burden of longing and sweet-fruited song...
Then... swifter than the osprey dips
Down the green slide of the sea... upon the shore
Of this our night-bound wretched earth I paused...
And lo, my vase was rended in my hands,
And all the precious substance that it held
Spread, faded, and was gone, — was quenched, was gone!
. . . .

He that dwelleth in the secret place of the Most High
Shall abide under the shadow of the Almighty...
Thou shalt not be afraid for the terror by night —
For the arrow that flieth by day...
It shall not come nigh thee.

The following is the brief historic statement of Schevill, based in his diary-notes of that date:

On the morning of Friday, October 28, 1910, I arrived from Chicago in New York with Harriet, Charlotte, and Will Tilden, Harriet's brother, with whom she was going to sail for Europe the next day. Torrence met us at the station, and as soon as we had taken Will Tilden (who was a very sick man in charge of a nurse) to the hotel, Harriet, Charlotte, Torrence and I departed for Long Island to dispose of Will Moody's ashes. (These were in an urn, wrapped in Harriet's chiffon scarf.) It was Harriet who had developed the plan we four carried out.

It was a beautiful fall day, cool and sparkling. We went to Far Rockaway beach and walked along the shore eastward till we came to an uninhabited section of low sand dunes declining to a broad stretch of smooth yellow beach, up which kept coming the great rollers of the sea.

We sat down upon the sand, huddled in blankets, for the air was fresh, and read aloud, taking turns, the whole of *The Fire-Bringer*. Will's ashes were at Harriet's side. When the reading was over, it was half past four. Then at Harriet's wish we lit a fire, and a few minutes before five o'clock, just as the sun dropped to the level of the water, I opened the urn, which Harriet had given into my hands (as she touched with flame the scarf that held it), and I scattered the ashes over the waves. Then we all knelt and Harriet recited the Ninety-first psalm. The great rollers washed to our feet and, after a few returns, they had sucked the fragments of white bone, the last mortal elements of Will, out into the sea.

And so 'here gather they' still. But now She *has come* — Mnemosyne,

> 'Remembrancer, and bringer out of death.'

XXIX. 'FROM SHUTTING MISTS... LAUGHTER AND RALLYING'

Harriet was a creature of the elements and drew to herself her fellow creatures — the sudden lightning, the rain-releasing cloud-cap and glancing leaves in the sun-burst, the clear starshine, and the noon-warm, multitudinous wing-song of wild nature's self-revealment. Wise in her prodigal insight, she shared with Will a native humor of wisdom which, like Shelley's * 'sincerest laughter' akin to saddest thought, is as brightly elemental and profound as nature's glitter of leaves after dark cloud-rack.

For Harriet, therefore, there were to be no sombre trailings of widowhood over her remembrance of Will — a remembrance which was always quite simply his familiar

presence throughout all the teeming devotions and en-
larging friendships of her after-life. The old symbol of
'handing on the torch' conveys an image strenuously on-
rushing, but Harriet held the torch of her poet delicately
and straightly poised, as a quiet candle to be lit ever newly
in the heart of a friend, and hers was a beautiful diversity
of personal friendships. So, the home-circle of her spacious
'Grove' became a 'House of a Hundred Lights' * illuminated by its first familiar presence in the hearts of other
poets, famed and unfamed; for there the welcoming touch
of her hand was a talisman that conjoined all in her own
and Will's 'poem of life':

> Of wounds and sore defeat
> I made my battle-stay;
> Winged sandals for my feet
> I wove of my delay...
> From the shutting mists of death
> And the failure of the breath...
> O hearken, where the echoes bring...
> Laughter and rallying.

XXX. HEARTH-FIRE 'IN THE COMFORTING SHADOWS OF "THE GROVE"'

At her fireside, seated beside her on the ample chain-
swung couch, many a transcontinental tramp on the trail
to Arcady or Avon has blessed his 'delay' there and, weaving his feet with those winged sandals of Will's song, suddenly he has discovered that he had found his destination.
Such a tramp, in his mid-years, was Nicholas Vachel
Lindsay * who wrote to her there, on a Christmas eve, in
1922:

My dear Cordelia... I know nothing about thee but thy
great kindness of heart, that with thee as with John Ruskin

'every dawn of morning is as the beginning of life.' If I said one word of thee, it would be that thou art Shakespearean, though whether thy soul is Portia, Miranda, Cordelia, Viola, Cleopatra — who can tell? Thy literary sense is the Shakespearean, the events of thy life are Plutarchan and Shakespearean, and likewise thy conversation... Most fraternally — Vachel.

In long earlier days, another Parnassan tramp at her fireside was William Butler Yeats, of whom on his first visit to America in January, 1904, Will wrote to Harriet, who had reported her welcome of Yeats at 'the Grove':

The only thing to care about is that, standing face to face with this young Irishman, you — miraculous reader of hearts and knower of souls — accept him as our brother. My brother he shall be, so long as I have strength to claim him.

'Miraculous reader of hearts' Harriet was, on many planes of human relationship. 'Sister, wife, mother, child' Will describes her to herself in one of his letters.... For her ever-resourceful practicality he confesses his own homage of a 'delighted grin' at her 'absurd effectiveness.' Of her consoling kindness he writes her concerning their boon comrade (Schevill), 'Ferd will smooth his feathers in the comforting shadows of the Grove.'

Will himself first introduced me to Harriet about 1905, at 2970 Groveland Avenue, where after leaving the University he had always his Chicago headquarters along with a few other 'perennials' among her friends.

On my first evening there, we had sat up very late in a fragrant atmosphere of poetry, laughter and midnight regalement, Harriet and Will and I outlasting the others in a trio, till our candles lit us to a landing of the great staircase where we parted — I to enter a spacious bedchamber, undress and blow out my candle.

Shortly after, as I lay in the great four-posted bed, listening up toward the ceiling's glimmery zenith, the faintest of ghostly sounds filtered down, like a lost echo that wandered off into silence, only to return again recurrently and die away into the least of sliding, scuffing, scraping, tinkling murmurs. To my straining senses the semi-darkness grew darker. Like Old Scrooge in Dickens's 'Carol,' listening for the ghost of Marley, I awaited the spectral embodiment of that echo. But still overhead the scuffing tinkle drew nearer, grew faint and far — but never corporeal. The next thing I heard was the breakfast-rap on my door.

At the breakfast table, where I sat down rather night-worn, Harriet was at her presiding place, fresher than the daffodils beside her. She smiled across them at Will, who whimsically returned the smile as she greeted me:

'Hope you slept well!... *Hear* anything — did you?'

My stare was a blank entreaty. Both their smiles met in a burst of laughter — and the sequel was soon out.

My 'Marley's ghost' — was Harriet's 'Home Delicacies Association' then in its first swaddling clothes, hidden away in her ample attic, before that infant industry — born of her genius for gingerbread — had stretched its child-giant limbs and gone forth to become the colossus of Marshall Field's dining emporium and the Pullman Car Service. But Harriet's night-guests must not be disturbed in their slumbers, so *tiptoe* was the watchword overhead for her chefs and their delicate assistants over whom Harriet herself often presided till after sunrise, descending to breakfast to resume her midnight *conversazioni*.

CONCLUSION

Painters and musicians shared with poets that home
where Will Moody's mystically brooding pictures hung on
the walls, with his portrait by Anderson and the land-
scapes of McComas. Ridgely Torrence has characterized
the rare initiative and growth of these interests.[1]

To express Harriet Moody's degree of interest in promot-
ing artists with small incomes, as well as in lame ducks with
no incomes at all, fairly substantial resources are obviously
necessary. A young high school teacher in Chicago, she felt
a strong desire to do more for her invalid mother than her
salary permitted. Having a knack for cooking, she made
some irresistible gingerbread, sold it and received orders for
more. Out of this episode developed the 'Home Delicacies
Association' * a catering enterprise which throve mightily
for many years not through petty economy but sheer excellence of its products.

Few guessed how much she did, year after year, for
Chicago's promising young writers. She believed in Glenway
Westcott before he had written a novel. She detached Hart
Crane, at the age of sixteen, from uncongenial environment
and encouraged him to produce poetry. She helped the
sculptor, Alfeo Faggi, among many others, to find his public.
She promoted many such careers as those of the young com-
posers, Henry Cowell and Harold Triggs.

Individual as this home of hers was, she was independent
of it and of all material scenes and conditions. When she
traveled to New York or Europe, or to California, she took
her own atmosphere with her, and, within an hour of arriving anywhere, her characteristic *salon*, nobody could explain
how, was in full operation.

After her husband's death, in 1910, she retained the
apartment at 107 Waverly Place, New York, which Moody
had never relinquished, and where he had written portions
of his poems and plays. Her unfulfilled wish was to make
this spot a permanent home for poets and a center of poetic
[1] In *The New Republic*, March 9, 1932.

[402]

life. As a matter of fact, it was occupied for years by a succession of poet-friends and was intermittently, during her presence there, the scene of the vivid life that she had the gift of instantly summoning.

In that succession of friends,* my wife and I and our children spent a sparsely impecunious winter (1914–15) at Harriet's Waverley Place apartment, rent-free by her bountiful thoughts of us. And whenever I put forth on far lecture-tours westward, always at Chicago I found welcome in her Groveland Avenue home.

XXXI. HARRIET'S POET–PILGRIMS FROM ALL CLIMES

There throughout the years till her death in 1932, the distinctive red-brick house, set airily apart, was gradually surrounded and dingened by an inseeping murky tide of residential non-descripts. Meanwhile, gaily oblivious of her altered environment, Harriet dispatched her carriage, and later her limousine, with Anton of the smiling moustachios (Marquis of Carabas coachman and chauffeur of 'the Grove' for twenty-seven years), with the perennial barking red setter blithely haunched at his elbow, to welcome her pilgrims at the railroad station. Alone, or paired, or in groups, tarrying by her hearth for days, or weeks, or months, they descended from far climes in freshets of poets, artists and authors, among whom these are some forty * (rostered alphabetically):

Jules Bois, Witter Bynner, Mary and Padraic Colum, Hart Crane, James Daly, Edward Davison, Robert Frost, Zona Gale, Wilfrid Gibson, Stephen Graham, Marjorie Kennedy-Fraser,* Alice Corbin and William Henderson, DuBose Heyward, Vachel Lindsay, Amy Lowell, Percy MacKaye, Edgar Lee Masters, Edwin Markham, John Mase-

CONCLUSION

field, Daniel Gregory Mason, Theodore Maynard, Edna St.
Vincent Millay, Harriet Monroe, Robert Nichols, Yone
Noguchi, Josephine Preston Peabody, O. E. Rölvaag, Carl
Sandburg, Alfredo San Malo, Leonora Speyer, James Ste-
phens, Frank Swinnerton, Rabindranath Tagore (with son,
daughter-in-law and secretary), Eunice Tietjens, Ridgely
Torrence, Willem Van Hoogstraten, William Butler Yeats,
Francis Brett Young.*

Some of them are among the following who dedicated to
Harriet volumes of their own writings: Padraic Colum,
Dr. Eugene Carson, Dr. Martin H. Fischer, Theodore
Maynard, James Stephens, Rabindranath Tagore,* Ridgely
Torrence. And of countless greetings from such pilgrim
friends, these seven are excerpted from letters to Harriet
herself.

James Stephens: I expect to return to the states and I
hope, to Chicago, and to see you. It would be worth going
all them watery miles just for that.

Wilfrid Gibson: I never imagined there was such kindness
in life.

Robert Frost: Come to Franconia and adopt the rest of the
family as you adopted me in Chicago. We can't feed you,
because we haven't learned to feed ourselves in the right
caterer's sense of the word, but we can surround you, the
six of us as I calculate, with one continuous smile of welcome.

Edwin Markham: I wish I was sitting at your hearth again,
listening to your remarkable readings from the pen of the
great soul who was called from you. Those readings are
among my joyous memories.

Yone Noguchi: How often I wish I could fly to your hospitable house and sip tea with you! Of course your house is
more than hospitable, because you are a great personality,
with artistic sympathy — so rare in the world.

Frank Swinnerton: I really don't know how to thank you

for all your kindness to me. I am convinced I should have collapsed if I had not come to your home in Chicago.

Rabindranath Tagore: I do not know if we shall ever meet again — but we *have met* — and that meeting can never be over — and the distances will make it all the deeper and truer by leaving out all trivialities that tend to overcrowd it.... I am sending you, with the greeting of my love and good wishes, a translation of my poem, as the gift of one who has carried home across the seas the memory of your friendship as one of the best boons that your country has given him.

All these friends and many others came not sought-after but seeking, as Torrence discerningly states further in his article before quoted:

It would be a serious mistake to class Harriet Moody as a deliberate collector of celebrities. The truth is that her own personality demanded its suitable food, her mind its material for exchange, her heart the vessels for its overflow. And she had an amazing flair for perceiving and singling out, among multitudes of human beings, those who interested her or who needed her friendship — which among all her givings was the gift she offered most lavishly. Informality of dress, manner, speech all that was inconsequential. But no guest could produce his second-or-third-best intellectual furnishings without detection and challenge. This woman would do all for you that one human being could do for another, but she would not accept your evasions and insincerities.

How deeply Harriet fathomed the spiritual needs of all 'who needed her friendship,' whether publicly known or unknown, and gave them alike her sustenance both spiritual and actual, is evident in this passage of a letter written soon after her death by the young poet, James Daly, who (in 1927) had spent some months at 'the Grove' under her welcoming hospitality:

She was a great friend in every poignant sense of greatness and of 'friend'... the greatest woman I have ever known. A soul so dynamic — so 'rammed with life' as Ben Jonson said of Shakespeare — how empty that soul's going can make this earth seem! Terrifying darkness where before there was an unfailing radiance; and, in her case, a radiance that had fire in it — never a cold, austere radiance. I think of those lines in comment on Goethe's last words:

'No, not more light: more warmth! For we die of cold and not of darkness. It is not the night that freezes, but the frost.'

With thoughts of both Will and herself, E. A. Robinson wrote to her, from Peterborough, N.H., September 29, 1921:

Dear Harriet... There is a shine in all directions that indicates the return of W. V. M. from his temporary submersion under mediocrity and flim-flam; and I'll be mighty glad when his light really shines again with nothing in the way. It will then have extinguished a host of sputtering and unsavory tallow dips.... The world is undoubtedly better for your being in it.... Yours always, E. A. R.

XXXII. THE HOME THAT 'COULD NOT CLOSE ITS DOORS'

Perhaps most lavish among all Harriet's expressions of friendship was her hospitality to Rabindranath Tagore. Of this Sir William Rothenstein wrote her:

I was delighted to see your generous friendship so beautifully acknowledged in Rabindranath's dedication of *Chitra* to you. No one could have been more large-hearted and unselfish than you yourself towards those Indian exiles whom you found near your door. I shall always think of your hospitality, so unbounded and spontaneous, as one of the gracious things of life.

THE HOME WITH OPEN DOORS

After Will's death, Harriet had been 'seriously occupied' abroad and in America with solicitous cares.* Of her return to her Chicago home, in January, 1913, the following account * in her own words reveals how her home became the questing-place of all those who came, like Tagore, 'conferring, after a long separation, about ... a common early home.'

I had been away from home for almost two years, seriously occupied, and I had just come home to rest, when, fairly in the hour of my arrival, I received a note from the editor of an important magazine * saying that she had invited a most distinguished poet (Tagore) to give an address here: that the hostess who had offered to entertain him had been forced to recall her invitation, and that the distracted editor had turned to me for help. But I was adamant. I had freed myself, as I thought, by my long absence, from all sense of duty or obligation, and I declined to undertake this responsibility.

That night I went to bed without regret; but in the early morning I was better advised. It came to me that my home, which had been the home of a poet, could not close its doors to a brother poet. I called my secretary, and asked her to go and say to my friend, the editor, that I would receive the poet. In the meantime I got and read his book of verse, most carefully.

A light powdery snow began to fall just as I was watching for him, and as he arrived, it fell on his picturesque black velvet cap and on his flowing white beard, giving a romantic aspect to his appearance. He was attended by his son with his son's young wife, and by his secretary. These all settled themselves in unobtrusive places in the living room, while the poet came and sat beside me, before going to his room.

I had just come from an ocean journey. The poet's voice was like the lapping of the waves, quiet, rich, sustained. I was soothed and heartened as I listened to him. He was one who talked straight on, without waiting for a reply. This did not seem in the least wearisome. Like all significant conversations, it seemed as if he were talking from the depths of my own being. It was as if we were conferring, after a long separation, about the fundamental doctrines of a common early home, under the teaching and influence of the same father and mother. There was never a moment when he was strange to me, although he commanded my quiet reverence.

Of the second visit by the Hindu poet to 'the Grove' a friend of Harriet, her secretary and intimately a member of her household for many years, has written me this further information concerning an oriental banquet (already grown fabulous in Chicago history) provided offhand by Harriet to scores of Tagore's Hindu compatriots.

In regard to the great Hindu luncheon (or dinner) I should say it came about quite informally. When Mr. Tagore was at 2970, all the Hindus in Chicago and surrounding towns came to see him. There were a great number of them. Some one suggested they should prepare a dinner of Hindu foods. This they did at 2970. Several Hindu young men prepared dishes they liked especially and knew how to make. I remember Mr. Tagore's daughter-in-law prepared a dish of curried chicken. She was much interested in cooking, and learned from Harriet how to make many American dishes, so that she could teach them to girls in the Tagore school in India.

During many years, both in Chicago and London, Harriet continued her rare hospitality to Tagore, before and after he received the Nobel Prize. In May, 1929, Harriet designed and tendered a special luncheon, at *Le Petit Gourmet* (which she owned and directed) in honor of the aged poet's young friend, Sudhindranath Datta,* of Calcutta, and a group of young Chicago poets, among whom was Kathleen Campbell who writes of the occasion in recollection.

I remember the party the way one remembers dreams — without continuity. Rain — firelight between those tree-high candle-sticks at the *Gourmet* — daffodils — the great silver platter passing — grapes, peaches, pears, sculptured from ice-cream... I remember thinking what an extraordinary power Harriet had, to be not there at all, and yet so represented by the faultless service, the lavishness, the bounty, the gaiety of the party, its uncommonness... I want Harriet to be set down in a book, some part of her anyway, and not just left to legend.

XXXIII. MONADNOCK: ANNIVERSARY: 'FAGGOTS OF REMEMBRANCE'

But Harriet herself is the very substance of legend, the primal Homeric stuff of fable: the same that once bourgeoned Penelope and Helen from the busy local looms and 'home delicacies' of the Achaeans to live on as spirit prototypes of their departed time.

To transplant even 'some part of her' from legend to 'set down in a book,' expecting that slip to stay put there, is like setting a sprout of wild honeysuckle in a clay pot by an open south casement and expecting it to refrain from trailing its intransigent blooms and fragrances beyond the narrow lattice of its house of retention. This book is such an earthy retainer and 'slipped' between its shards are two living stems: wild honeysuckle of Harriet and Hymettus-flower of Will — not pressed like wan mementoes but twined as in leaves of the old ballad, upflowering, out-tendriling, forth-reaching toward their own kind.

Of their own kind is the young poet-recorder who recalls,

above, Harriet's party for the friend of Tagore. And like-wise 'as one remembers in dreams... rain... firelight... daffodils... and *Harriet — not there at all*, yet always re-presented by the faultless service... its uncommonness,' so in our remembrance of these letters of Will to her, we feel always 'the lavishness, the bounty, the gaiety' of her essential presence.

How, then, can I record in a book her 'once-on-a-time' actuality — which essentially never *was*? Surely, not at all! For this is a true record, with a true conclusion. And so, like Vachel Lindsay, I avow truly of Harriet that 'the events of her life were Plutarchan and likewise her con-versation,' and therefore as in her life-time for her 'every dawn of morning was as the beginning of life,' so in her after-time she remains, like the morning, ever legendary — as Penelope watchful of her returning Odysseus, or as Helen launching her 'thousand ships' toward battles far off and strange.

Strangely far off was the last word I ever received from Harriet in its interchange of our remembrance of Will two years before her own death.* She was still in their familiar 'Grove' and I in my home in Cornish, lately re-turned there from Peterborough, New Hampshire, where I had spent part of that summer of 1930 at the MacDowell Colony, working in a studio among the woods close by the studio of E. A. Robinson,* with whom I used often to pass our nooning lunch-hour, or walk back to our quarters, evenings, after work.

One such evening toward autumn, having sat awhile by the wood fire in his studio, we looked off from the porch toward his fond vista of Monadnock serene in the sunset, where our thoughts went past the glowing peak westward to Harriet, as we talked of Will, our days and nights with him in earlier contrasted times when 'our little group' were all young together. And I reminded him of an anniversary soon to come.

That night, one of those thoughts took form in a sonnet* which soon afterward I sent to Harriet for October seventeenth, the twentieth anniversary of Will's passing, when I telegraphed to her for E. A. and myself, and her swift reply came back in greeting: 'Yes, dear friends. You and I remembered.'

IN MEMORIAM: W. V. M.
17 October, 1930

Sitting beside old embers of slow fire,
We fed them faggots of remembrance, till
The quickened flames of friendship glowed to fill
Our narrowed hearth with light from a far pyre,
And there — while that strange light became a choir
Of thought — 'E. A.,' I wondered, 'how would Will
Confront, today, if he were with us still,
The loud confounders of Apollo's lyre?'

This much we know: He who of old could feel
The Gloucester Moors heave like a staggered ship
That, shuddering, rights herself to beauty's keel,
Would hold, as then, his poet-helmsman's grip
Serene, where Chaos foams the howling bars,
And chart his haven by the Morning Stars.

PERCY MACKAYE
CORNISH, N.H.
1935

NOTES

ACKNOWLEDGMENTS
NOTES FOR INTRODUCTION AND CONCLUSION

Biographical Data
Bibliography
Index

ACKNOWLEDGMENTS

Note. — On Feb. 22, 1932, Harriet Moody died suddenly at her home in Chicago. Some time before her death, she entrusted the original scripts of these letters to her secretary, a close friend and a member of her household during many years. After Harriet's death, her secretary (who prefers to remain anonymous) prepared them carefully in typed form for publication, omitting some passages and a few whole letters and supplying certain unsigned statements of information (parenthetical in the text), together with occasional footnotes to the text, as here published: a task to which she has given her painstaking zeal and unstinted devotion; and by her authorization the letters are here presented to the public. Concerning some omitted letters she states: 'Letters written from time to time by W. V. M. to Harriet, in which he urges that they "take the step," have not been included.'

At her request and that of a small group of intimate friends of Will and Harriet Moody, including kindred of W. V. M., the present editor has gladly contributed for this volume his portion toward the perpetuation and historical interpretation of these letters by writing the Introduction and Conclusion with their Notes, appending some correlated data of Biography and Bibliography. Incidental to this task a few passages of the letters omitted from the text as here printed have been quoted in these commentaries with specific references made to their dates in the Notes. Of the 340 letters from W. V. M. to Harriet here published, twenty have been heretofore printed, as follows: In *The Play-Book* of March, 1915 (edited by Thomas H. Dickinson, for the Wisconsin Society, Madison, Wis.) — four letters: April 8, 13, 23, 1904, and March 23, 1907. In *William Vaughn Moody: A Study*, by David D. Henry (Bruce Humphries, Inc., Boston, 1934) — sixteen letters (exclusive of the four therein reprinted from *The Play-Book*), viz.: Aug. 19 (postmarked 30th), 29, 1901; May 6, 10, 17, 20, 26, 27, 1902; June 5, 10, 12, 16, 1902; June 2, 5, 9, 1906; May 1, 1907.

For numerous helpful courtesies the editor extends his sincere acknowledgments to the Friend of this Book to whom it is dedicated; to Charlotte E. Moody and Julia Moody Schmalz; to Harriet Moody's secretary; and to the following other mutual friends of Harriet and W. V. M.: Ridgely Torrence, Ferdinand Schevill, Robert Morss Lovett, Daniel Gregory Mason, Lionel Marks, Hamlin Garland, Norman Hapgood, Edgar Lee Masters, Walter Hampden, Marion Morse MacKaye: to the last his especial indebtedness for her suggestion of the title 'Letters to Harriet' and for innumerable insights and labors throughout the course of his undertaking.

NOTES FOR INTRODUCTION AND CONCLUSION

The Roman numeral which precedes each of these notes refers to the corresponding Roman numeral which heads each Section of the text throughout the Introduction and Conclusion. Each passage thus referred to is marked with an asterisk (*) and may readily be found in the text by consulting the number of the Section in which it occurs. In each case, the word or phrase *in italics* corresponds to the word or phrase which is marked in the text with an asterisk (*).

INTRODUCTION NOTES

II. *Mrs. B* ——. The earliest letter of W. V. M. to Harriet, May 20, 1901, commences, 'Dear Mrs. Brainard,' and ends, 'Believe me, dear Mrs. Brainard, Always faithfully yours, Wm. Vaughn Moody.' See Biographical Data (2), under 'Harriet Converse Tilden.' Nearly all of the other letters have no formal salutation at the beginning or ending and are signed simply 'W ——,' the envelopes being addressed to 2970 Groveland Avenue, Chicago, Ill.

II. *Breaking her ankle.* In recording this event which occasioned the writing of these letters, it is needful to understand that Harriet's accident was no ordinary, simple breaking of the ankle. In the darkness, going with Will to the lake shore, both arms joyously raised in pointing to the stars, she stepped off an embankment. The plunging fall was so sudden and severe that the shattered leg-bone was forced through the leather of her shoe. Informed that her foot must be amputated, she refused. For a year the injury caused her to be bedridden, and afterwards required occasional surgical treatment during many years.

III. *This one passage.* Written at Keswick, England; July 22, 1909.

III. *His earliest letter to her.* Chicago; May 20, 1901.

III. *And again.* Paris; July 23, 1902.

III. *Two passages.* Athens, June 3, 1902; and Cornish, N.H., July 6, 1906.

III. *This note to her.* Sept. 18, 1904.

III. *This passage.* March 27, 1905.

III. *The little portrait.* This may refer to the portrait of Harriet, signed 'L. C. Earle, '83,' owned (in 1935) by her niece, Alice Harriet Tilden, which is reproduced in this volume. Cf. W. V. M.'s letter to

Harriet, Dec. 27, 1901; also Nov. 21, 1903, describing a 'delightful picture' of her. W. V. M. himself painted a portrait head of Harriet.

III. *On horse-back.* April 4, 1904, three years after her accident, Will wrote to her from Grand Canyon, Arizona: 'My longing to have you here increased three-fold the moment I felt a horse's sinewy back between my legs. We must ride! And we must do it in this country where one's liberty is conterminous with the horizon, and the horizon is farther away than anywhere else in the world.'

V. *Robert Morss Lovett.* Moody was especially fortunate in securing Prof. Lovett to collaborate with him in their volume, *A History of English Literature* (Scribners, 1902), a delightful work which has held its high place ever since then. For Moody probably could never have written it alone. Commenting upon it, in a letter to Harriet (Dec. 10, 1915), E. A. Robinson wrote:

'I couldn't have written *The Fire-Bringer*, but I can understand how Will could have done it. But I shall never understand how the deuce he wrote that History of English Literature. I should have worked six months over the first chapter and then thrown it away.'

'How the deuce' Moody did it is explained by his having found in Lovett a collaborator exceptionally well-mated in personal friendship and proficient scholarship.

V. *Prof. Mason's slender collection.* E. A. Robinson wrote to Harriet (from Cornwall on Hudson, Nov. 6, 1913) concerning Mason's volume: 'Will's letters are mighty pleasant reading, but it is a great pity there are not more of them.' Fourteen still unpublished letters from E. A. Robinson to Harriet (1911–30) contain valuable allusions to Moody.

V. *Yet unpublished volumes.* Supplied with copious bibliographical data, the volumes still in manuscript are entitled as follows: 'Moody the Mystic, and Other Papers'; 'Early Years of William Vaughn Moody'; 'Later Years of William Vaughn Moody.'

VI. *Colorado Springs.* Prof. Schevill writes (to P. M-K., July 15, 1935): 'Harriet suffered her compound fracture of the ankle on May 16, 1901. W. V. M., Bessie O'Neill, Alice Corbin and myself were present. Will watched over Harriet's recovery till early August when he went west to have his Rocky Mt. trip with Hamlin Garland. Harriet by that time was considerably improved. By late August she was well enough to be moved and had taken a house for September on Mackinac Island, which was doubtless a strong reason for Will's returning. He had hardly returned when the removal to Mackinac proceeded, probably on or near September 1.'

VI. *Letter from Greece.* June 9, 1902. From Athens, W. V. M. wrote

Introduction Notes

to Harriet: 'I have been wrestling all day with the mighty lines of the *Agamemnon.*' These recurred to him four years later, when he and P. M-K. (after attending Josephine Peabody's wedding in Cambridge, June 21, 1906) attended the Harvard Stadium production, in Greek, of Aeschylus' *Agamemnon*, from which the remembered poignant cry of *O tò, tò-tò tò — Apollōn, Apollōn!* reverberates in his letter of Sept. 12, 1906.

VI. *Prof. Schevill.* He comments further: 'In the winter of 1902, Harriet took a cottage near Cape Henry, Virginia. Alice Corbin and Bessie O'Neill went with her, and Will and they stayed on together till the coming Spring. From Cape Henry, Will went (via New York) straight to Greece, where he steeped himself in the atmosphere which he required to bring his Promethean poem to its goal.' — Cf. note after letter of Feb. 11, 1902, and two sequent letters.

VI. *Ancestry.* According to the family records collected by W. V. M.'s sister, Mrs. Julia Moody Schmalz, his middle name, *Vaughn* (originally *Von*, as used by certain of his forbears) had its origin in his maternal Pennsylvania Dutch lineage.

VI. *Harvard paths.* 'In Cambridge, Will Moody lived at 45 Mt. Auburn St. in his Freshman year, at Stoughton 28 during the next two years, and after his return from Europe, at Hilton 23 (in 1893–94) and at Gray's 43 (in 1894–95).' — Statement of Robert Morss Lovett to P. M-K., in a letter, June 16, 1935. During his first three college years (1893–96) P. M-K. roomed at 35 Divinity Hall (not then limited to Divinity students) and during his senior year (1896–97) at Weld, next to Gray's, in the Yard.

VI. *Commencement Part address.* 1897. On the same platform there, President Eliot was then conferring an honorary degree upon Augustus Saint-Gaudens, who — years later, in Cornish (where MacKaye took Moody to meet him at his studio, in February, 1906) — gaily hailed P. M-K. as his '97 Classmate,' in virtue of their mutual sheep-skins. In 1909, P. M-K. was instrumental in arranging the Henry Miller performance of Moody's *Faith Healer* given by Henry Miller at Sanders Theatre, Jan. 24, 1910. Cf. note under XXV.

VII. *Josephine Preston Peabody.* Born in New York City, May 30, 1874, she died in Cambridge, Mass., Dec. 4, 1922.

VII. *Conjoining of our names.* The names are again associated in friendship in the Dedications by E. A. Robinson of three of his own books: — 1923, *Roman Bartholow*, dedicated to Percy MacKaye. — 1929 *Cavender's House*, to the memory of William Vaughn Moody. — 1931, *Matthias at the Door*, to Ridgely Torrence.

VIII. *Like a hard-luck miner.* Cf. W. V. M.'s letter to Harriet, Nov. 8, 1904.

VIII. *Almost as well.* Cf. W. V. M.'s letter to Harriet; Jan. 10, 1904.

VIII. *Harriet's large nature.* Of Will and Harriet, Prof. Schevill wrote P. M-K. concerning this volume: 'I believe you are erecting a monument *aere perennius* to the two greatest souls I have known or shall ever know.'

VIII. *President of the United States.* Theodore Roosevelt's review of E. A. Robinson's *Captain Craig* appeared in 'The Outlook' in August, 1905.

VIII. *Borrowed.* Concerning another incident of borrowing from W. V. M. and E. A. R. by the same overcoat borrower, cf. third note under XVII.

IX. *Moody's accident in Greece,* 1902. Ridgely Torrence recalls (1935) that during his European trip with Moody, in 1907, while they were climbing together Mt. Posilippo, near Naples, Moody — feeling the old pain in his leg again — described to him in detail his fall on Mt. Parnassus, in 1902. Moody said that he had climbed within a few feet of the very summit of the peak and was reaching upward, clutching the rock with both hands, his eyes fixed on the top just beyond, when he suddenly slipped and fell about fifteen feet into a crevice, where his fall was broken by a sharp projection which struck into his thigh on the very spot operated upon three years later by Dr. Bull, in New York, leaving there a wound described by Moody to Harriet (in Mercutio's gay words for his own death-wound) as 'not so deep as a well nor so wide as a church door, but 'twill serve.'

IX. *Our college days.* Though Moody (at Harvard) and P. M-K. (at Leipzig, where he wrote an early play, *Beowulf*, 1899) had made special studies in medieval philology, these studies did not enter into their mutual associations and discussions.

IX. *For several years.* Robinson's plays, *Van Zorn* and *The Porcupine*, respectively first published in 1914 and 1915, were written in 1906 and 1907; but as late as 1911–12 he was at work upon a third play. On Dec. 26, 1911, he wrote to little Arvia MacKaye, at Cornish, N.H.: — 'Tell your father that E. A. has gone crazy again and is writing another bad play.' (Cf. note at top of page 431.)

X. *Olive Tilford Dargan.* In addition to her dramatic works, Olive Dargan — hon. Litt.D., Univ. of N. Carolina, 1924 — is the author of five volumes of poems (1914–22), and of *Highland Annals*, 1925.

X. *Acclaim of Stedman.* 'Compact of noble diction and imaginative fire,' wrote Stedman of Olive Dargan's work in 1904. In 1916, she won the prize of the Southern Society of New York, and in 1924, the Belmont-Ward Fugitive prize. Under her pseudonym, Fielding Burke, she won, in 1932, the Gorky Award, by her novel, *Call Home the Heart*. In 1935 appeared her novel, *A Stone Came Rolling*.

X. *Published in 'The Critic.'* One of these poems by Lindsay was *The Queen of the Bubbles* (now in Lindsay's Collected Poems), accepted by Torrence in November, 1903, and published shortly afterward in *The Critic*, together with Lindsay's drawing for the poem.

X. *Two years after the death of Moody.* Harriet Monroe, editor of 'Poetry' wrote (from Chicago, Dec. 1912), two months after the founding of that journal: 'My dear Mr. MacKaye: I am so glad you approve of our venture, and so grateful for your help. Also I am glad you liked my review of Moody. Your poem to him, *The Fire-Bringer*, is a fine tribute.'

X. *But for the Great War.* On August 1, 1914, the great War opened its planetary drama. On that same day, in Berlin, Max Reinhardt gave the opening performance of an American play, *The Scarecrow*, by P. M-K., which was closed down at once by the cataclysm. Twelve days earlier, July 19, 1914, from W. V. M's old apartment at 107 Waverly Place, New York, Lindsay wrote: 'Percy MacKaye — Dear Friend... Thank you for your letter to Winthrop Ames... I want to keep your interest... My best love and reverence to Poet Arvia.' Lindsay and P. M-K., planned together a chanted ballet-poem for staging which they hoped to secure the Little Theatre of Winthrop Ames, previously director of the New Theatre; but increasing war dementia submerged all such plans.

X. *Gordon Craig's Art.* Cf. *The Sibyl.* Poem, by P. M-K., 'To Edward Gordon Craig upon the publication of his volume, "On the Art of the Theatre."' pp. 14–17, *Uriel and Other Poems*, Houghton Mifflin; 1912. Also, *Three Dance Motives*, Poems for dances of Isadora Duncan, 1910; I. *Lethe*; II. *Dionysus*; III. *The Chase*; in *Collected Poems* (Macmillan, 1916), under 'New Poems,' pp. 117–121.

X. *First book.* In this chart, those books are classified as *first* which first brought their poet authors into marked recognition. For that reason the chart does not tabulate references to these earliest dates of first published books by the following poets: *1895, A Legend of Hollis Hall*, long poem by Percy MacKaye; *1896, The Torrent and the Night Before*, and *1897, The Children of the Night*, by E. A. Robinson (both printed at his own expense, the first without publisher, the second by an obscure publisher of Boston); *1898, The Wayfarers*, verses by Josephine

Peabody; *1898, A Book of Verses*, by E. L. Masters; *1900, A House of a Hundred Lights*, aphoristic poems, by Ridgely Torrence.

X. *These horizon vistas.* The vistas should certainly include the admirable work initiated by Anna Hempstead Branch at Christodora House (Thompson Square, New York City) where, under her sympathetic, creative leadership, as poet-friend of poets, *The Wings*, by Josephine Peabody, was given its first New York performance; the early plays of Stuart Walker were first produced, as well as dramatic rituals by Anna Branch herself; and the significant career of *The Poets' Guild* was first launched. These, however, were chiefly after-developments not associated with Moody and his group during the first decade.

X. *Works of Edgar Lee Masters.* Besides *Maximilian*, published, 1902, Masters wrote at this period the following plays (still unpublished, 1935): — *Althea*, 1906; *The Trifler* (considered for production by Mrs. Fiske), 1907; *Eileen*, and *The Locket*, 1910; *The Leaves of the Tree*, 1911.

X. *Against our conquest of the Philippines.* With these poems by Masters, as profoundly felt protests against America's growing imperialism, may also be grouped Moody's poems, *Ode in Time of Hesitation*, 1899, *Gloucester Moors*, 1900, *On a Soldier Fallen in the Philippines*, 1900; and MacKaye's poems, *The Spirit of Aguinaldo*, 1898, *To Spain in Defeat, To Dewey in Victory, Columbus' Remains at Cadiz, The Ten at Ilo-ilo, Aguinaldo's Illusions, To William Watson, To Senator Hoar*, 1899. (Cf. 'Annals of an Era,' p. 78.)

X. *The New Theatre.* The formal opening (with 'Antony and Cleopatra') in New York, at Central Park West and 62nd Street, on Dec. 15, 1908, was preceded by a Dedicatory Service on the completion of the building, some weeks earlier. The Choral Ode by P. M-K. was sung by the Metropolitan Opera House Chorus, on both occasions.

X. *Conried.* Before the opening of the New Theatre, Heinrich Conried was succeeded by Winthrop Ames as director.

XII. *One of its earliest versions (The Great Divide).* Ridgely Torrence recounts that on New Year's Day, 1906, on returning from an outing in Cos Cob, Conn., with W. V. M. to his room in New York, Moody thrust into his hand a newspaper clipping, exclaiming excitedly: 'Read that!' Torrence read it — a true melodramatic episode of the far west. 'Well?' he queried. 'Well, indeed! Don't you see *it's a play?*' During the next three weeks, Torrence states, Moody completed at white heat a first draft of the play, which he had been working on, its first act based on the episode, and called it *A Sabine Woman.* Cf.

W. V. M.'s letters to Harriet, Dec. 3, 6, 27, 1905, and Jan. 2, 1906.

XII. *Just before his co-starship.* Excerpt from Philadelphia Ledger. July 30, 1905: 'Sothern's plans for *Fenris the Wolf* are delayed by his partnership with Marlowe, but costumes are being made by Karl of London, and Manuel Klein is writing the music.'

XII. *Published chronicles.* Robert Morss Lovett, in his Introduction to Moody's *Selected Poems* (Houghton Mifflin, 1931), and Hamlin Garland, in his *Companions on the Trail*, pp. 87–94 (Macmillan, 1931), have written interesting accounts of the Chicago première of *A Sabine Woman*, at which both Lovett and Garland were present in the audience. But neither account explains its inner cause of conflict nor its after-sequel.

XIV. *On the road.* Cf. second note under XVI, 'A salvaging bonanza.'

XV. *Voices overseas.* In 'The London Morning Leader,' Jan. 24, 1910, reviewing P. M-K.'s first collected *Poems*, William Archer wrote: 'Among America's younger writers, Mr. MacKaye has perhaps only one rival, his friend, William Vaughn Moody, to whom his book is dedicated.'

XVI. *Before I knew Moody and our group.* Jan. 24, 1901, Moody wrote from Chicago University to Robinson: 'I like to hark back and mouse dreamily over... those walks we had from Riverdale to Yonkers, especially the last one.'

At that time when Moody and Robinson were taking long walks together along the Hudson, still all unknown to me, I may have passed them on such another long walk which I took with Pegram Dargan (the gifted poet-husband of Olive), while Dargan was eloquently declaiming the Elizabethan dramatists, wholly skeptical of my eulogies of Sothern as champion of a new dramatic revival of poets. (P. M-K.)

XVI. *A salvaging bonanza.* Eleven years after the play's first production, Harriet dictated (from 2970 Groveland Ave., Chicago, March 6, 1917) the following letter to Alice Corbin Henderson:

'When I was in New York in January, I saw the revival of *The Great Divide*. Mr. Miller has put it on in New York with himself in the lead and Miss Gladys Hansen opposite. I went the first night and sat in a box. The Torrences and Mrs. Crow and Molly Colum were with me. We got in early and the theatre had a dreary dusty look.

'I sat there with my heart in my mouth, thinking of the first first-night and half inclined to believe that the audience of the present hour would not accept *The Great Divide*, turning over in my thought that *The Faith Healer* was more in the mood of an audience today.

'By slow degrees the house filled. Percy MacKaye came in with Vachel Lindsay, and their pleasant faces shone reassuringly in the distance. Mr. Miller, though rather haggard, was in great form for playing, and Miss Hansen gave a much more understanding and sympathetic interpretation of Ruth than any one else has ever done. The house responded with the utmost enthusiasm from point to point, and at the close one realized that it was a real first night rather than a reproduction of the play. All the newspaper comments were as long and as sympathetic as if the play had never been seen in New York before, and I understand it is still running on there, with great success.'

(Earlier she had written (Feb. 17), to another friend:)

'It was greatly cheering to me to see how wonderfully well it is staged. The first night many of Mr. Moody's friends were present, and it seemed almost as if he were there himself, the atmosphere was so buoyant. I felt that I was living over the experience of its first production in 1906.'

XVII. *Differences.* Cf. Moody's letter to Harriet, Jan. 25, 1907. Also page 145, 'Annals of an Era,' 1932.

XVII. *Veteran in full dress.* On Oct. 18, 1907, Stedman had written to Cornish, N.H. the following: 'My dear Robin MacKaye... Your father has invited me to attend the first performance of his new play, and he and Mr. Moody and I are going to sit side by side in full dress! We all think it will be a grand occasion... Affectionately your birthmate, Edmund Clarence Stedman.' Cf. last note under XXIII.

XVII. *Festively toasting.* Concerning that New York première of *Sappho and Phaon* Ridgely Torrence has recalled the following: —
'I know that Will Moody, E. A. and I were enjoying it, greatly interested, and all seemed going finely (in spite of some accidents) till after the second act when Manager Fiske came out before the curtain. His face looked like a wax mask and took the life out of the audience. — That very afternoon, by the way, ——, who had decamped with Will Moody's only overcoat two years before (and Will had worn a mackintosh all winter because of it) turned up at his studio, begging to borrow a dollar. Will asked him, "Where's my overcoat?" — "Pawned." "Where's the pawn-ticket?" "Lost." "Well, here's a dollar. Get out, and don't ever let me set eyes on you again." After the play was over, while we stood in the swarming lobby, who should sail up but —— in great spirits: "Hello, fellows! Wasn't it superb? The American Drama is now in full flower!" Then he beckoned E. A. aside and borrowed another dollar from *him*. So he had seen the show with Will's dollar, and went home with E. A.'s in his pocket. — Our party adjourned to the

Arena restaurant, a super-garden with a big ornamental basin and fountain, where we festively toasted the author, all but Norman Hapgood, who warningly advised him to go right back stage and call a rehearsal of the awful actors.' — Cf. letter from W. V. M. to E. A. Robinson, March 31, 1905, under Section VIII of Introduction.

XVIII. *Acted professionally. Sappho and Phaon* has never been staged as it was written. Its modern *Prologue* and its Herculaneum *Induction* and *Entre-scenes* were omitted by Harrison Grey Fiske and only the central Greek tragedy produced by him. Some years later, a revival of that portion by University students was admirably produced by Prof. Samuel Eliot, Jr., at Smith College, Dec. 2, 3, 1926. Cf. *Scheme of Metrical Motifs in 'Sappho and Phaon,'* with A Letter from P. M-K. to Harrison Grey Fiske, June 7, 1907, in 'Annals of an Era,' edited by E. O. Grover, 1932; pages 460–472.

XVIII. *Disillusionizing facts.* During four days Moody wrote the following: — (*Oct. 17*, 1907) 'Before I knew it I was pouring out my heart to him (Frohman) on what our little group dreamed of trying to do... I swore the daylight black and blue cracking up *The Porcupine.*' (*Oct. 18*) 'Frohman sent back Robinson's play, "not available for stage."' (*Oct. 22*) 'We are all in the dumps... we men in buckram... The cynical critics are slaughtering with all the cosmopolitan refinements of torture.'

XVIII. *Mrs. C. P. Davidge*, then a widow, was the daughter of Henry C. Potter, Episcopal Bishop of New York, and the sister of Mrs. William Hyde (wife of the artist), who neighbored her, summers, at Cornish, N.H. Kindly, generous and brilliant, Mrs. Davidge was an intellectually instigating friend of Moody, and during some years the hospitable benefactress of E. A. Robinson at her winter home in New York, and later on Staten Island, after her marriage to the artist, Henry Taylor.

XVIII. *Island of Mackinac.* From Mackinac Island, Michigan, Sept. 29, 1908, W. V. M. wrote to P. M-K.: 'Congratulations! The *Sun* review of *Mater* was especially first rate... It is a wonderful place here, for beauty and fine traditions — Indian and French stories of the old fur-trading days... I have been deucedly slow in picking up. My doctor forbids city life at present.'

XVIII. *Henri and Julia.* Henrietta Moody (Fawcett) and Julia Moody (Schmalz) sisters of W. V. M. His nephew and namesake, William Vaughn Moody Fawcett, is the son of Henrietta.

XIX. *Social functions.* e.g. The dinner of American Dramatists. The down-town settlement dinner, at which W. V. M. and P. M-K. both first met Edwin Markham of the 'beautiful leonine head.' The

Andrew Carnegie dinner of the Authors Club. The Players Club dinner, in Moody's honor of which P. M-K. still has the printed menu, with its caption, from Shakespeare's *Tempest*, I, 2; 'How, now — moody?' Concerning the last, W. V. M. wrote to his sister, Charlotte, from The Players Club, Nov. 11, 1906: —

'Mr. Miller gave me a dinner at the Players Club last week which was very interesting. The main personage was John Drew, who was amusing and delightful in a quiet way. The dinner began at midnight and when I left at quarter to six in the morning, there was still a knot of old inveterates and enthusiasts of the theatre laying down the law to each other over their wine and walnuts.'

W. V. M. was elected to the Players, Jan. 14, 1907. His proposer was Adolphe E. Borie and his seconder Gutzon Borglum. After the death of W. V. M., an appreciation of his work and personality was written by P. M-K. in *The Players Year Book*, for 1911.

W. V. M. was proposed for the National Institute of Arts and Letters by Edmund Clarence Stedman, was sponsored also by Richard Watson Gilder and Robert Underwood Johnson, and was elected February 28, 1905. (Cf. his letter to Harriet, Jan. 25, 1907.) He was elected to the Academy, Nov. 7, 1908, the second occupant of chair No. 7, succeeding Edward MacDowell. Moody was one of the sponsors of E. A. Robinson, Ridgely Torrence and Percy MacKaye, who were all elected together to the Institute, February 20, 1908. Moody was taken ill with typhoid fever, March 22, 1908, and so did not attend the dinner of the National Institute, at the University Club, New York, in April, 1908, with his poet associates, Robinson, Torrence and MacKaye. By late June he was sufficiently recovered to receive at Yale University the honorary degree Doctor of Letters, June 24, 1908.

XIX. *Guffanti's*. In this stanza of *Uriel*, Guffanti (the 'laird'), Moody, Torrence, Robinson are in turn referred to:

> Thy Parmazan, immortal laird of ease,
> Can never mold, thy caviare is blest,
> While still our glowing Uriel greets the rest
> Around thy royal board of memories,
> Where sit, the salt of these,
> He of the laughter of *a Hundred Lights*,
> Blithe Eldorado of high poesies,
> And he — of enigmatic, gentle knights
> The kindly keen — who sings of *Calverly's*.

From *Uriel and Other Poems*, by P. M-K.; Houghton Mifflin, 1912.

XX. *Shirley Center, Mass.* (Reference to footnote, under XX.) See W. V. M.'s letter to Harriet, postmarked, June 14, 1906. On his trip then from Cornish, N.H., to attend with Harriet the *Agamemnon* performance at the Harvard stadium, Moody went with Percy Mac-Kaye to visit MacKaye's boyhood home at Shirley Center, Mass., where still their two names are recorded together written in pencil in a corner on the board-wall of the little woodland studio (where *The Scarecrow* was written, four summers earlier). On that trip, Moody read aloud some of his poems to MacKaye's mother and to neighbors there, Frank Lawton and his daughter, Shirley Lawton. The latter still recalls his 'magnificent reading' and her own 'ten-year-old girl's impression of the new poet's corduroy trousers and their resemblance in shade to his hair and close-cropped beard.'

At Shirley Center, also, Miss Marrette Longley recorded in a volume of Moody's *Poems*, which he presented to her and her sister, Mary: — 'William Vaughn Moody, with Percy MacKaye called Friday, June 15, 1906. We were together in upper East Room — a perfect June day — a delightful call. Mr. Moody took away with him a beautiful branch of our mountain laurel from Paradise Woods. From our house they went to call on the Lawtons in their Pasture House.'

XX. *The Saint-Gaudens Masque.* Written by Louis Evan Shipman with Prologue by P. M-K. Cf. 'Annals of an Era,' pp. 166, 181, 283, 343, 389.

XX. *Miss Barrymore.* Six weeks later, this passage from the diary of Marion MacKaye (Mrs. P. M-K.), Aug. 18, 1906, gives another Cornish glimpse of W. V. M.: — 'Ethel Barrymore asked us over to play tennis. At the court we found Will Moody, Richard Harding Davis and his wife, and Harry Fuller playing doubles, while Mr. and Mrs. Herbert Adams and Howard Hart and Ethel herself were looking on.'

XX. *A one-act play. Nereida,* later published as *The Cat-Boat,* in the volume by P. M-K. *Yankee Fantasies* (1912). At Cornish, Moody was scheduled to act *the Skipper,* Ethel Barrymore the boy, *Nico,* and Hazel MacKaye (who acted *Anactoria* in 'Sappho and Phaon') the part of *Nereida.*

XXI. *The Three Angels.* Published in full (8 stanzas) in his *Poems and Poetic Dramas,* Vol. I, pp. 144–146; Houghton Mifflin; 1912.

CONCLUSION NOTES

XXIII. *Three diaries.* The regions and dates of Harriet's three diaries are as follows: (1) England: May 25 — July 29, 1909. (2) Maryland (environs of Baltimore): Nov. 10 — Nov. 25, 1909. (3) California (Riverside, Santa Barbara, Hollywood): Dec. 8, 1909 — May 19, 1910.

The itemized places and dates of her first diary are as follows: May 25, 1909, London (Guildford); May 26, British Museum; May 27, South Kensington Museum; June 12, Guernsey — 'Roman foundations, churches of the Conquest, towns of the Commonwealth, relics of French occupation'; June 17, Sark; June 23, Bonchurch, Isle of Wight; June 26, Winchester; June 29, Harriet to London, leaving Will at Winchester; Will goes to Salisbury; June 30, Stonehenge; July 1, London; July 8, Isle of Jersey; July 12, Guernsey, Le Gouffre (Harriet in London, returning to Will at Le Gouffre, Sat. July 17); July 19, London; July 22, Windermere, Ambleside, Keswick, Derwenwater Lake; July 24, Keswick, Boseenthwaite; July 25, Ambleside; July 28, Bowness (Harriet to London, Will to Dartmoor); July 29, London.

XXIII. *Bessie.* Elizabeth O'Neill, whose lively and enlivening personality was almost inseparably a portion of 'the Grove' group of Harriet's Chicago household, including her secretary and Katherine Lyle.

XXIII. *No word from Will.* The next day, July 14, W. V. M. telegraphed from Guernsey: — 'To Mrs. W. V. Moody, Inns of Court, Holborn, London: Doing well. Address Gouffre Hotel. Will.'

On Friday, July 16, Harriet wrote in her diary: 'When I arrived at the Inns of Court, I found a telegram from Will — for which I had been telephoning all day — saying that he was not doing well and would come up to London Monday. I decided to spend Saturday and Sunday with him, telegraphed for a stateroom and got to Southampton to find they had no reservation for me, so I sat up on deck all night,' etc.

On July 16, Will wrote to Harriet: 'Guernsey — Friday aft. — Dearest, I have just telegraphed that I should come up to London Monday unless you suggested some other place. I have not been doing very well today or yesterday — nothing at all alarming or worse than usual, but too much general discomfort and "misery" (I mean it nigger-fashion) to want to remain here, or anywhere away from your blessed comfort. I have tried exerting myself, and it simply won't go. I must keep still, that is all there is to it. Shall leave here by the Monday boat

(I can't very well get off tomorrow) and shall come up to London unless you telegraph me to the contrary. My love — W ——.'

XXIII. *Last letters he ever wrote.* After his return to America and the operation for his failing eyesight, W. V. M. wrote no more letters. Of any letters which he may have written to Harriet in London, while he was elsewhere, during the summer of 1909, there have survived only one letter (from Guernsey, July 16, quoted in full above) and one picture postcard, post-marked, 'Glasgow, 9, Aug. 18, 09, 1.15 P.M.' addressed to 'Mrs. W. V. Moody, 43 Carlton Mansions, Portsdown Road, Maiden Vale, London,' reading as follows: 'Please be sure to call at the bank for my mail. Leave forwarding address. W ——.' (On back of card is a photo of cattle, standing in lake-water, surrounded by mountains, labeled: 'Loch Arklet, Evening.' On the card is printed: 'Loch Arklet is reached by a road from Aberfoyle, about half a mile from Stronaclachar, "the Stonemason's point." Glen Arklet which lies between Stronaclachar and Inversnaid is a pleasant valley.')

XXIII. *The Canterbury Pilgrims.* The large-scale outdoor production of P. M-K.'s Chaucerian play known as 'The Gloucester Pageant,' produced in honor of President Taft at Gloucester, Mass., August 3, 1909, with 1500 citizens, directed by Eric Pape and P. M-K., with music by Walter Damrosch and Charles A. Safford, conductor of the Chorus, at Stage Fort Park, with participation of the U.S. Navy.

XXIII. '*Those adorable children.*' The children were Robin, Arvia and Christy (called by W. V. M. 'the newest one'), who grew up to be poets and artists. (Robin) Robert Keith MacKaye (Harvard, A.B., 1923): author, *Yale University Prize Poem*, 1927; *Honey Holler*, play in 3 acts, Brentano's, 1930; etc. — Arvia MacKaye (Radcliffe), poet, sculptor, illustrator; author, poems in *Harper's*, *Poetry*, anthologies, etc. — Christy MacKaye (Smith; Rollins, A.B., 1932); author, *Wind in the Grass*, a book of poems, Introduction by E. A. Robinson; Harpers, 1932; etc.

XXIV. *Farm.* Soon after Will's death, Harriet bought a large hill-farm at Cummington, Mass., with a small building once owned and used by William Cullen Bryant, whose birthplace adjoins the farm. There, as a memorial to Will, she planned a place of work and refuge for poets, but did not consummate the plan.

XXIV. *Johns Hopkins hospital.* W. V. M. was a patient there from Oct. 6–17, Oct. 28 — Nov. 10, Nov. 25–29, 1909.

In 1909, operations on the brain were far more dangerous than today. In the case of Moody, after two minor operations, the surgeons at Johns Hopkins stated that there were not more than five chances out of a hundred of his surviving a third operation, and even if he should survive, they could not guarantee beforehand either curative results or certainty that the diagnosis of tumor was correct. Under these circumstances, Harriet's decision (made in conference and in unanimous agreement with Will's sister, Charlotte, and his friend, P. M-K.) to permit no further operation but to seek improvement, if possible, through restorative surroundings in California, was in her judgment the only right and feasible decision and accordingly she proceeded to act upon it immediately.

XXIV. *The Scarecrow*. At that production of *The Scarecrow*, by the Harvard Dramatic Club, Cambridge, Brattle Hall, Dec. 7, 1909, in the cast were Robert Benchley (*Bugby*), Samuel Eliot, Jr. (*A Harvard 'Don'*), Timothy Spelman (*Dickon*). Kenneth Macgowan was *Stage-Manager*; Chalmers Clifton, *Composer* of the Music and *Director* of the Pierian Orchestra, in which Robert Edmond Jones played *First Fiddle*. On the Executive Committee were John Silas Reed ('Jack' Reed) and Edward Eyre Hunt. The poster was drawn by Gluyas Williams. These, as students, were then at the dawn of their varied, notable after-careers just as Moody's life-work was at its sundown. One of them, John Reed, died in Russia, October 17, 1920, exactly ten years after Moody's death.

XXV. *Santa Barbara Beach*. This poem by Ridgely Torrence is published in his volume, *Hesperides* (Macmillan, 1925). Another poem about Moody, by E. A. Robinson, is *Broadway Lights*, published in Robinson's *Collected Poems* (Macmillan, 1927).

XXV. *His new play*. This refers almost certainly to his new (last) version of *The Faith-Healer*. Harriet's diary makes no allusion by name to *The Death of Eve*, which she would hardly refer to as a 'play.'

XXV. *Telegram*. 'Jan. 14, 1910. New York. To William Vaughn Moody, Care Potter Hotel, Santa Barbara, Cal. — Producing *Faith Healer* next Wednesday, Savoy Theatre, Rehearsals prove changes to be immense improvement. Have also accepted invitation to play the piece at Harvard, Monday week; good advertisement for play here. Hope you are feeling better. Friendliest greetings to Mrs. Moody and yourself. Henry Miller.' — This telegram was answered as follows: 'Santa Barbara To Henry Miller, 338 Fifth Ave. New York — Hugely delighted by splendid news. Only sorry I can't be there. William Vaughn Moody.'

XXV. *Telegraphic message*. 'Jan. 19, 1910. New York. To William Vaughn Moody, Care Potter Hotel, Santa Barbara, Cal. — A glorious play, gloriously acted, and the audience rose to it gloriously. God bless you. Rann Kennedy, Wynne Matthison, Percy MacKaye.'

From the Players Club, New York, Jan. 23, 1910, Garland wrote: 'Dear Moody: I saw *The Faith Healer* yesterday (with Chas. Francis Browne) and liked it immensely. It is a big original work and should succeed. It is an acting play all the way through and is deeply interesting. Miller is not the man for the part. His personality is too well known and limits the imagination of the hearer. Some new and fervid and poetic personality should be your medium. I am urging him to take the play to Chicago, with a man perhaps like a Walter Hampden in the part, though *he* is not the man needed. — With all good wishes, as ever yours — Hamlin Garland.'

XXV. *Soon in Cambridge.* The Cambridge performance of *The Faith Healer* at Sanders Theatre, took place three days later. Telegram: 'Jan. 24, 1910. Santa Barbara. — Large audience applauding play again and again. Genuine success. Our thanks and united congratulations. F. N. Robinson (for Harvard English Department), Henry Miller.'

In reply to this telegram, W. V. M. wired to Miller: — 'Have had no New York newspaper reports yet, but rejoice in the thought that you are interpreting Faith Healer so splendidly. Thanks for telegram.' Cf. note under VI.

XXV. *From Henry Miller.* Telegram: 'Jan. 29, 1910. New York. To William Vaughn Moody, Hotel Potter, Santa Barbara, Cal. — Newspaper criticism sent Monday. Regret lack of public appreciation, but believe play will live. Glad to hear good reports of your improvement in health. Kind regards to Mrs. Moody and yourself. Henry Miller.'

XXV. *Programme.* Sanders Theatre. Cambridge. January 24, 1910, at 8 o'clock. — Harvard University (seal) Department of English. Henry Miller, in THE FAITH HEALER, a Play in Three Acts, by William Vaughn Moody. — *The Cast:* —

Ulrich Michaelis.......................................Henry Miller
Matthew Beeler.......................................Harold Russell
Mary Beeler, his wife...........................Mabel Bert
Martha Beeler, his sister ....Lillian Dix
Annie Beeler, his daughter....................Gladys Hulette
Rhoda Williams, Mrs. Beeler's niece.............Jessie Bonstelle
Dr. George Littlefield ....Theodore Friebus
Rev. John Culpepper...........................Edward See
Uncle Abe, an old Negro........................Robert McWade
Lazarus, an Indian boy ....James Hagan

The action of the play takes place in the living room of Matthew Beeler's farmhouse near a small town in south-western Missouri.

XXV. *A friend in Cambridge.* Prof. Edward K. Rand of Harvard College. His letter (dated 'Lake View Ave., Cambridge, Mass., Jan. 24, 1910') was as follows:

'Dear Will: We have just come from the *Faith Healer* (at Sanders Theatre) and are still in the heights... I trembled a minute before the final moment. What was to give him his faith again... the knowledge that she had been base? That would make him a villain as black as Theseus. You didn't let the doubt last too long. You showed that his first vision of love was as base as her past had been, and you purified them in that instant with passion both human and divine. The rare moment of creation — one stroke and your world was built.

'Miller, I am afraid, though delightfully simple for the most part, walks clumsily on the higher levels. When he feels poetry coming — especially in description — he blows out sentences by the yard, with a painfully melodramatic effect. If he would speak naturally then, as he generally does, and give the phrases time to visualize themselves, much would be gained. But in general, it was well acted. The audience was enthusiastic — for Cambridge, vociferous. Get well fast, Will, and know that you are always in my thoughts. With affectionate greetings from us both to you and Mrs. Moody, I am Yours ever, E. K. R.'

XXV. *Mr. Mason's letter.* From his old friend, Daniel Gregory Mason. During their college days together at Harvard, Mason composed an admirable music setting for Moody's song, *My love is gone into the east*; and, later, for his song, *Of wounds and sore defeat.* In 1935, he has under way the writing of his personal reminiscences of W. V. M.

XXVI. *Groveland Avenue.* The name of this avenue in Chicago called 'Groveland' during Moody's life-time, was afterwards changed to *Ellis* Avenue.

XXVI. *A play.* For Margaret Anglin. *Tomorrow,* by P. M-K. (Stokes; N.Y.; 1912), first produced not by Miss Anglin, but by Frank Reicher, at the Little Theatre, Philadelphia, Oct. 31, 1913.

XXVI. *Bartlett.* T. H. Bartlett, father of Paul Bartlett, the sculptor. Ten years earlier, Moody had written to Robert Morss Lovett from Chocorua, N.H., August 18, 1900: — 'I am staying with a Mr. Bartlett, ex-sculptor, art-critic, and in spite of himself a magnificent old goat and man of God.' (Cf. Some Letters of *William Vaughn Moody*, edited by Daniel Gregory Mason; Houghton Mifflin; 1913, p. 129) — To Mason Moody wrote of Bartlett: 'The old boy stars the passing hours with immortal phrases.'

XXVI. *Manuscript of the novel.* — Excerpt from diary-journal of Marion MacKaye, 1927: — 'On December 7, E. A. Robinson dined with Percy at the Players. E. A. told him that in writing his novel out of his play, *The Porcupine*, he used up an inch and a half of hard lead pencil. First he cut typewriting paper in two, the long way; then he wrote down each half — 900 words to a page — completing the novel in 75,000 words.' (Cf. third note under IX, on page 418.)

XXVII. *The proposed plan.* The plan proposed by P. M-K. in 1910, to Prof. G. P. Baker, for a *Harvard Theatre in Cambridge*, involved eight definite objects in view, as set forth in P. M-K.'s letter to G. P. B., Oct. 18, 1910, together with a William Vaughn Moody Memorial Committee of the following personnel: George Pierce Baker, Treasurer; Percy MacKaye, Chairman; Mrs. William Perry Northrup (57 E. 58 St., New York), Secretary; John W. Alexander; Winthrop Ames; Hamlin Garland; Mrs. Ben Ali Haggin; Norman Hapgood; Mrs. Edward MacDowell; Josephine Peabody Marks; Daniel Gregory Mason; Mrs. William Vaughn Moody; H. T. Parker; Edwin Arlington Robinson; Ridgely Torrence.

The plan came to no fruition at the time, owing to non-co-operation of the Harvard authorities toward the raising of funds for the purpose; but the initiative thereby set on foot was instrumental in furthering the idea of a great endowed University Theatre which eventuated, sixteen years later, in the erection and launching of the Yale University Theatre, 1926. Strangely, Harvard likewise allowed Yale first to recognize and honor the Harvard poets, Moody and Robinson, by conferring upon them the honorary degree, *Litt.D.*, Moody, 1908; Robinson, 1922.

XXVII. *Twenty-fifth anniversary.* At the least, his anniversary should attain some memorial tablet to Moody at his college room in the Harvard Yard, 28 Stoughton, and another memorial to him at the house of his birth, at Spencer, Indiana — comparable to that organized by the fine initiative of Laura E. Richards at Gardiner, Maine, for the memorial there to Moody's friend, Robinson.

XXVII. *The Fire-Bringer.* By that title a poem by P. M-K., written with thoughts of Moody's last rites in October, 1910, and sent to Harriet at that time, is published in MacKaye's volume, *Uriel and Other Poems* (Houghton Mifflin, 1912) and in his *Collected Poems* (Macmillan, 1916). Cf. fifth note under X. Other poems about Moody by MacKaye are *Uriel* (written 1911), and two Sonnets, one on *The Great Divide* (1906) and one on W. V. M.'s recovery from severe illness (1908). All are published in his *Collected Poems*.

XXVIII. *Long Island's shore.* Walt Whitman himself wrote of that same sea-beach: — 'Down on the long, bare, unfrequented shore, which I had all to myself, I loved, after bathing, to race up and down the hard sand, and declaim Homer or Shakspere to the surf and sea-gulls by the hour.' — Cf. 'Complete Prose Works,' by Walt Whitman. David McKay, publisher, Philadelphia, 1892; page 14.

XXIX. *Like Shelley's.* The last sea-rites of W. V. M. on the Long Island shore bring to mind those of Shelley on the Italian seacoast off which he was drowned, nearly a century earlier. Both were imbued with the majestic spirit of Prometheus — unbound.

XXIX. *The House of a Hundred Lights* is the title of Ridgely Torrence's first slender volume of jewel-faceted poems, 1900.

XXX. *Vachel Lindsay.* Another letter from Lindsay to Harriet is the following, written from Spokane, Washington, March 31, 1925 — this excerpt being the first paragraph of a long letter wherein he proposed to take to the road for good: —

'My dear Harriet Cordelia: You are the finest of all Good Samaritans. You are more than that. Hundreds have turned to you in trouble that was the trouble called aspiration and you have helped them up. Your house is the Castle of Peace and Help, and also it is the Palace of Wisdom. I have met more wise people there than anywhere else on earth. And you have no competitors. There is no second, no third, no imitation Harriet Cordelia. There is only one. Yours faithfully, Vachel.'

XXX. *Home Delicacies Association.* Out of Harriet's addiction for 'homing' both 'delicacies' and the delicate art of poets, there sprang her published *Cook Book*, which might have been her literary masterpiece but for her publisher's uncomprehending veto. For her artist mind (like the chef's in Rostand's *Cyrano*) conceived a perfect reconciliation between Poetry and Pies for which she invited the collaboration of living poets in contributing their pages of homage to both, and several noted poets gladly responded with their manuscripts. But the publisher rejected the Poets by his edict: Pies only! Among the rejected manuscripts was one by Edwin Arlington Robinson.

XXX. *Succession of friends.* In that succession was also Vachel Lindsay, who occupied W. V. M.'s old apartment at 107 Waverley Place, during the summer of 1914. Cf. third note under X.

XXXI. *Some forty.* In this list are included three or four poets who had their homes in Chicago and visited 'the Grove' as neighbors.

XXXI. *Marjorie Kennedy-Fraser.* She wrote to Harriet from Edinburgh, Scotland, Feb. 10, 1918: 'The Preface of my new *Hebridean Songs* (Vol. II) was all written, you know, in your library bedroom upstairs in the month of June, 1916. How inexpressibly kind you were to us! I wonder who has the supreme good luck to be under your sheltering wing at present.'

XXXI. *Francis Brett Young.* From Anacapri, Italy, May 14, 1927, Francis Brett Young wrote to Harriet, in Chicago: — 'Love makes many curious interchanges that are not material. In your husband's plays and poems I can read reflections of your mind and glimpses of the play of light that must have passed between you. Stamped with spiritual integrity and truth, the first thing about all his work is its present vitality. I wish I could feel that many living poets were as acutely alive as Moody is today. Yours always affectionately, Francis.'

XXXI. *Rabindranath Tagore.* From Shantiniketan, Bolpur, India, March 19, 1914, to Harriet in Chicago, Tagore wrote: 'My dear Friend, In memory of the delightful evening we had, reading *Chitra* by your fireside, I have dedicated that little lyrical drama of mine to you, hoping that this dedication will remind you how deeply I value your friendship.... It was to add to the list of the already numerous transgressions you had allowed your poet in the generous exercise of your forbearance. Your affectionate friend, Rabindranath Tagore.'

XXXII. *Solicitous cares.* Immediately after the last rites of W. V. M. (on Oct. 28, 1910), Harriet sailed for Europe with her brother, Will Tilden, who was very ill. When they came back (her secretary states) 'she took him and his wife to Santa Barbara for the winter, then in June (?), 1911, she brought them to Chicago, and from there to Lake Geneva, Wis., for the hot months. In the fall of 1911, the Will Tildens were at 2970 Groveland Ave., till his death in December. In 1912, Harriet went to England three times, the last time at the end of November. She did not stay long. In January, 1913, Tagore made his first visit to Chicago, and stayed at 2970, by her invitation.'

XXXII. *The following account.* It was dictated by Harriet to her secretary.

XXXII. *Magazine.* The magazine, *Poetry*, edited by Harriet Monroe.

XXXII. *Sudhindranath Datta.* Telegram: 'Los Angeles, Calif., April 20, 1929. To Mrs. Moody, 2970 Ellis Ave., Chicago, Ill. — Leaving now. Goodbye. Have advised my friends, Sudhindranath Datta and Boyd Tucker to see you when they are in Chicago. They accompanied me from India. They will go soon. — Rabindranath Tagore.'

XXXIII. *Before her own death.* Harriet died at 'the Grove' on Washington's birthday, 1932. The next day, Dr. Martin H. Fischer, Professor of bio-chemistry in the University of Cincinnati (formerly one of Harriet's pupils in Chicago), wrote to her secretary:

'Thank you for your note which verifies the sad news of the morning paper. Her distress was great on Sunday and I feared — though not so quickly — the inevitable. Her death takes out of my world of the living the greatest and grandest experience of my life.'

XXXIII. *E. A. Robinson.* Born at Head Tide, Maine, Dec. 22, 1869, Robinson died in New York City, April 6, 1935.

XXXIII. *Sonnet.* By P. M-K. 'William Vaughn Moody. In Memoriam. 20 Years after: 1910–1930. To Edwin Arlington Robinson.' First published in the *Boston Evening Transcript*, Sat., Oct. 18, 1930. Also in *Harvard Graduates' Magazine*, December, 1930; and in *Anthology of the MacDowell Club Poets*, New York; December, 1930.

BIOGRAPHICAL DATA

I. William Vaughn Moody

Note. For comprehensive biographical data and comment see the Introduction (92 pages), by Robert Morss Lovett, to *Selected Poems of William Vaughn Moody* (Houghton Mifflin, 1931). Also, *William Vaughn Moody; A Study.* By David D. Henry, Ph.D., State Dept. of Public Instruction, Lansing, Mich. (276 pages with Index. Boston. Bruce Humphries, 1934).

Born. Spencer, Indiana, July 8, 1869, son of Francis Burdette Moody and Henrietta Emily Stoy.

Education. At Spencer, he attended grammar and high school; studied drawing and painting at the local art academy; in music he played the guitar. At Louisville, Kentucky, he attended the Pritchett Institute of Design. In 1884, his mother died, after which he taught a district school near New Albany, Ind. Then for two years, he prepared for college at Riverview Academy, a military school at Poughkeepsie, N.Y., headmaster Harlan Page Amen, afterwards headmaster of Phillips Exeter Academy, who taught him the Classics. 1889–1892, he completed in three years the 4-year course at Harvard College, being an editor of *The Harvard Monthly* there. 1892–1893, travelled abroad (tutoring a pupil) in Black Forest, Switzerland, Italy, England, Greece. Graduated Harvard, A.B., 1893, delivering Class Day poem. 1893–1895, studied medieval philology in Harvard Graduate School, assisting Prof. Lewis E. Gates, in an English course. 1895–1901, was Prof. of English Literature, for short terms at Chicago University.

In July, 1900, he delivered his *Anniversary Ode* at Cambridge, on 125th anniversary of Washington taking command of American army. 1902, published his *A History of English Literature*, with Lovett (Scribner's). In June, 1908, received hon. Litt. D. degree from Yale University. Nov. 7, 1908, was elected a member of the American Academy of Arts and Letters. His published books, with their dates, are listed in the front of the present volume, which deals with his life from May, 1901, till his death at Colorado Springs, Col., Oct. 17, 1910.

II. Harriet Converse Tilden (Moody)

Born. Parkman, Ohio (village of about 200 inhabitants, with no railroad), March 18, year date unknown.

NOTES

Ancestry. Directly descended from Thomas Jefferson, Pres. U.S.A.; also, through Converse (originally de Coniers) family, from French Huguenot settlers in America in 17th Century and during Colonial Wars in Vermont, where Col. Israel Converse was the great grandfather of Harriet's grandfather. The Tilden family came from Kent, England, where Daniel Tilden was made a baronet.

Parentage. Her father was William Mason Tilden. Her mother — Harriet Converse (a first cousin of Mark Hanna's mother) — taught Harriet in her babyhood to read and later to cook and housekeep. When she was about eleven, the family moved to Chicago, where her father became an operator on the Board of Trade and at the Stock Yards.

Education. Sent to Union Springs, N.Y., to board at the Howland School for young girls, Harriet was an excellent student there, especially in German, besides taking part in dramatic entertainments and playing pranks on her teachers. Years afterward, in 1931, an old schoolmate wrote to her: 'Your ardent spirit is unchanged, and your happy expression of it warms the heart and makes me feel young again.' Upon finishing at the Howland School, she went to Europe with another girl and a chaperone — a joyous experience which greatly expanded her views of life. (She did not go abroad again until her marriage with Moody.)

At Cornell University, she completed the four-year course in two years and a half, meanwhile enjoying the natural beauty of the place on long walks and boat rides with fellow students and young professors. There she lived in the home of Hiram Corson, Professor of English Literature, whose teaching deepened her studies of poetry, especially of Chaucer, Shakespeare and Browning, in which her knowledge was minute and her appreciation large and imaginative. Later, elected by both Alumni and Alumnae, she served two terms (1912–1922) as a Trustee of Cornell University, the only woman on the board. After graduating from Cornell, she studied medicine briefly in Philadelphia but, finding it uncongenial, returned to her father's house in Chicago.

A friend of her father was Dr. Daniel Brainard, an eminent Chicago surgeon of great wealth, whose son, Edwin, was a lawyer, very brilliant but dissipated. Harriet and Edwin Brainard were married, and during a number of years she kept his house and entertained his guests. Finally on the death of her father, Harriet secured a divorce and devoted herself to providing her mother with a comfortable living.

At first, on passing examinations, she taught English literature for a time in several of the high schools of Chicago, inspiring her pupils[1] to write stories, plays and verses (all the French forms), several books of which were published.

Of her first meeting with Moody, one tradition relates that W. V. M. was invited by Alice Corbin (then a member of Harriet's household) to one of Harriet's informal Sunday afternoon receptions and met her there. Another tradition gives 'the Little Room,' a small club, as their first meeting place; not long after which, W. V. M. came on a Sunday morning to the door of Harriet's house and left for her a copy of his *Masque of Judgment*, then just published (1900).

In the spring of 1901, Harriet rented a house on the North Shore of Lake Michigan, at Lakeside, where she began to give week-end house-parties of her friends.[2] At these parties it was the custom to gather wood and build a great bonfire on the Lake Shore, and watch the coming of dawn. There, one night in May, while Harriet was going down the bank to the shore, she stepped off a culvert and broke her ankle. It was a very dangerous, complicated fracture. This happened on May 16, 1901. On May 7, 1909, she was married to William Vaughn Moody.

Concerning her immediate family, Harriet resembled her father in temperament and looks. During the lifetime of her aunt, Amelia Converse, who lived in her father's fine old Colonial house in Parkman, Harriet took great pleasure in going back there to visit. She had one cousin, Henry D. Lyman, who founded the American Surety Co., of New York, and two brothers, Will and Fred Tilden. Her niece, Alice Harriet Tilden, graduated from the University of California at Los Angeles, in 1935.

Her business, The Home Delicacies Association, of which she was personal executive, having begun about 1899 in the kitchen of her mother's house at 13th St. and Wabash Ave., was moved to the English basement of a house on Indiana Ave.; then to the top-floor of 2970

[1] Among her pupils were Franklin P. Adams ('F.P.A.,' Columnist), Charles W. Collins (dramatic critic, Chicago Tribune), Alice Corbin (poet), Martin H. Fischer (Prof. of Bio-Chemistry, U. of Cincinnati), Edith Foster Flint (Prof. of English Lit., U. of Chicago), Milton Sills (stage and screen star).

[2] Among her guest-friends there were Samuel Harper, F. J. Miller, R. D. Salisbury, Ferdinand Schevill, Alex. Smith (all professors at the Univ. of Chicago), Dr. Llewellyn Barker, Alice Corbin, Nott Flint, Edith Foster, Katherine Jones, Evelyn Matz, Harriet Monroe, William Vaughn Moody, Elizabeth O'Neill, Beatrice Butler, William Morton Payne, Ralph Fletcher Seymore, Mr. and Mrs. Lorado Taft.

Groveland Ave.; then, in 1913, to the old Bournique dance hall on 23rd St., Chicago. It had also a branch in London, England.

Harriet was the author of *Mrs. William Vaughn Moody's Cook Book*; Scribner's, New York, 1931. She was a member of the Fortnightly, Woman's, College and Arts Clubs of Chicago.

She died, suddenly of bronchial asthma, at 2970 Ellis (formerly Groveland) Avenue, Chicago, on the night of Monday, Feb. 22, 1932. Her funeral service was held privately on Friday, Feb. 26.

On her death, Harriet Monroe wrote of her in *Poetry* (April, 1932): 'Lavish to the last, no defeat was registered in her active life of happy and generous adventure, and the memory of her friendship will enrich many lives.'

BIBLIOGRAPHY

(1) Concerning William Vaughn Moody

Note. The major works of W. V. M., under nine titles, are listed chronologically on the first printed page of this book.

The only volume by a single author which is entirely devoted to the life and works of W. V. M. is *William Vaughn Moody: A Study*, by David D. Henry (Boston; Bruce Humphries, 1934; 276 pages). It contains a very comprehensive list of published writings *by* Moody and a voluminous bibliography of publications *concerning* him and his works. The bibliographical material concerning W. V. M. contained in the following Lists is in large measure (though not wholly) additional to that contained in Mr. Henry's volume.

List A comprises titles of standard *Books*, portions of which deal with W. V. M. and his works. List B comprises material (Periodical *Articles*, *Pamphlets* and *Books* by W. V. M. containing editorial Commentaries on him and his works) deposited in the Chicago University library by Harriet Moody's secretary, who has compiled the list. List C comprises Periodical and Newspaper *Articles* reviewing works by P. M-K., either jointly with works by W. V. M., or inclusively with works by a group of poets or dramatists. List D comprises publications, in verse and prose concerning W. V. M., written by P. M-K. Lists C and D comprise material having special reference to the group-activities, shared by W. V. M., set forth in the Introduction. List B is arranged according to authors; the other lists, according to dates of publication.

LIST A

The American Stage of Today. Walter Prichard Eaton. Small Maynard; 1908.

The American Dramatist. Montrose J. Moses. Little Brown; 1915, 1925.

The Case of American Drama. Thomas H. Dickinson. Houghton Mifflin; 1915.

Chief Contemporary Dramatists. Thomas H. Dickinson. Houghton Mifflin; 1915.

Playwrights of the New American Theatre. Thomas H. Dickinson. Pp. 134–144. Macmillan; 1925.

The Story of the Theatre. Glenn Hughes. 1928.

A History of American Drama, Vol. II.   Arthur Hobson Quinn.   Pp. 1–17.   Harpers; 1928.

Companions on the Trail.   Hamlin Garland.   Pp. 87–94, 439, 449.   Macmillan; 1931.

LIST B

Baker, George P., *Harvard Graduates' Magazine*; December, 1910.

Bicknell, Percy F., 'A Poet in Epistolary Mood.' (A Review of *Some Letters*); *Dial*, 55:300–301; October 16, 1913.

Grabo, C. H., 'Poetry of William Vaughn Moody'; *Chautauquan*, 50: 274–283; April, 1907.

Hagedorn, Hermann, *Independent*; 74– Part I: pp. 314–316; Feb. 6, 1913.

Hutchison, Percy, 'The Poetry of William Vaughn Moody.' (A Review of *Selected Poems*, edited by R. M. Lovett); *New York Times Book Review*, 36:2; April 12, 1931.

K., Q., 'After the Play.' (A Review of the revival of *The Great Divide*); *New Republic*, 10:137; March 3, 1917.

Lessing, O. E., 'Brücken uber den Atlantik, beitrage zum Amerikanischen und Deutschen Geistesleben'; Berlin, Deutsche Verlags-Anstalt, Stuttgart; 1927; pp. 117–129.

Lewis, Edwin Herbert, 'William Vaughn Moody.' A Club Paper, read before the Chicago Literary Club, November 4, 1912; printed for members by The Lakeside Press, R. R. Donnelley & Sons Co.; March, 1913.

Lovett, Robert Morss, 'Memories of William Vaughn Moody'; *Atlantic Monthly*, 147:385–393; March, 1931.

Lovett, Robert Morss, Introduction to *Selected Poems of William Vaughn Moody*; Houghton Mifflin; 1931.

MacKaye, Percy, 'Uriel,' Elegy on the Death of William Vaughn Moody; *Uriel and Other Poems*, 30 stanzas, pp. 1–13; Houghton Mifflin; 1912.

MacKaye, Percy, 9 other publications, itemized under List D.

Manly, John M., 'The William Vaughn Moody Lectures'; *University Record* (University of Chicago) New Series, 3:139–141; April, 1917.

Manly, John M., Introduction to *Poems and Poetic Dramas* and *Prose Plays*, by William Vaughn Moody; Houghton Mifflin; 1912.

Mason, Daniel Gregory, Introduction to *Some Letters of William Vaughn Moody*; Houghton Mifflin; 1913.

'William Vaughn Moody,' *Christian Science Monitor;* August 2, 1920.

'W. V. Moody,' *Life*, 49:837; June 20, 1907.   (A Caricature.)

BIBLIOGRAPHY

'William Vaughn Moody: a Study,' I, 'The Lyrist and Lyric Drama-tist,' by Nash O. Barr; II, 'The Playwright,' by Charles H. Caffin, *Drama*, No. 2:206–211; May, 1911.

'Mr. Moody's Verse,' *The Independent*, 53:1557–1558; July 4, 1901.

'A New American Dramatist,' *Literary Digest*, 33:551–552; October 20, 1906.

Munson, Gorham B., 'The Limbo of American Literature'; *Broom*, pp. 259–260; June, 1922.

Payne, William Morton, 'The Poetry of Mr. Moody'; *Dial*, 30:365–369; June 1, 1901.

Payne, William Morton, 'Two Poetic Dramas'; *Dial*, 36:319–323; May 16, 1904.

Payne, William Morton, 'William Vaughn Moody'; *Dial*, 53:484–486; December 16, 1912.

Rose, G. B., A Review of *The Masque of Judgment; The Sewanee Review*, Part II, 9:332–336; July, 1901.

Schevill, Ferdinand, 'A Remembered April. Recollecting a Spring with a University Poet.' (Inset — *Road-Hymn for the Start*.) *The Circle* (University of Chicago), 2:5–6; June, 1924.

Shorey, Paul, 'The Poetry of William Vaughn Moody.' A Lecture delivered under the auspices of the William Vaughn Moody Founda-tion (University of Chicago), February 3, 1927. Reprinted for pri-vate circulation from *The University Record*, 13:172–200; July, 1927.

Sinclair, May, 'Three American Poets of Today.' *Atlantic Monthly*, 98:325–330; September, 1906. The Same: *Fortnightly Review*, 86: 422–429; September 1, 1906.

Soule, George, 'A Great Pilgrim-Pagan'; *The Little Review*, 1:2–9; December, 1914.

LIST C

'Moody's "Fire-Bringer" and MacKaye's "Fenris."' A Review. *New York Evening Post;* May 9, 1905.

'Recent Harvard Graduates as Men of Letters.' J. M. Groton. *Harvard Graduates' Magazine;* April, 1907.

'A Fresh Generation of American Poet Playwrights: MacKaye, Moody, Young, Aldrich.' *New York Evening Post;* May 11, 1907.

'A Group of Harvard Dramatists.' By George Pierce Baker. *Harvard Graduates' Magazine;* June, 1909.

'The Harvard Dramatists: Moody, MacKaye, Sheldon.' With their

Portraits and Photograph of the Coburn Players, in 'The Canterbury Pilgrims.' *Literary Digest;* June 26, 1909.

'MacKaye's Poems and their Dedication.' By William Archer. *London Morning Leader;* Jan. 29, 1910.

'National Poets: MacKaye and Moody.' *Philadelphia Telegram;* Feb. 7, 1910.

'Poems of MacKaye Dedicated to Three Poet-Friends: Moody, Robinson, Torrence.' By Edwin Markham. *Chicago Examiner;* Feb. 12, 1910.

'Our New Generation of Dramatists.' By Walter Prichard Eaton. *American Magazine;* Nov., 1910.

'In Praise of Vaughn Moody.' Portions of MacKaye's Commemorative Poem. *Boston Evening Transcript;* Oct. 4, 1911.

'The Author of "*The Great Divide*": MacKaye's Stately "In Memoriam" to Moody.' *Indianapolis Star;* Oct. 9, 1911.

'One Poet-Dramatist's Tribute to Another: MacKaye's Elegy on Moody.' Richard Burton. *The Bellman;* Minneapolis; Oct. 14, 1911.

'"Uriel" and "The Fire-Bringer."' ('That winged lyric "The Fire-Bringer" runs like a Victory before William Vaughn Moody's fame. Both poems commemorate the close affection between these poet friends.') *Milwaukee Free Press;* Nov. 25, 1912.

'The Quiet Evening of American Poetry. MacKaye's Elegy on Moody.' By A. W. W. *The Harvard Monthly;* December, 1912.

'The Passing of a Great Singer. The Only Lasting Elegy of the Present Generation of Poets.' *San Francisco Call;* Feb. 17, 1913.

'William Vaughn Moody Finds His Fitting Elegy.' *Book News Monthly;* April, 1913.

'Our American Poets: Moody and MacKaye.' *Review of Reviews;* May 19, 1913.

'Our First Decade Revolutionary Poets: Moody, MacKaye, Robinson, Eastman.' Syndicate Article; *Fort Wayne (Ind.) Gazette;* July 20, 1930.

LIST D
10 Items by P. M-K.

'To William Vaughn Moody.' Sonnet, on the première of 'The Great Divide,' Oct., 1906. *Harvard Monthly;* Feb., 1907.

'To W. V. M. on Recovery from Severe Illness.' Sonnet, summer of 1908. In *Collected Poems;* Macmillan; 1916.

'To the Fire-Bringer.' Poem, on the Last Rites of W. V. M., Oct., 1910.

In *Uriel and Other Poems;* Houghton Mifflin; 1912. Also, in *Collected Poems;* 1916.

'A Harvard Theatre, as a William Vaughn Moody Memorial.' Proposal, Oct., 1910, by P. M-K. to G. P. Baker. Pp. 146–147, *Annals of an Era;* E. O. Grover, edit.; 1932.

'William Vaughn Moody: An Appreciation.' P. 73, *The Players Year Book,* 1911; Players Club, New York; 1911.

'In Memory of William Vaughn Moody.' (Later entitled, 'Uriel') Stanzaic Poem, 8 pages. *North American Review;* Oct., 1911.

'Uriel.' (The Same, with slight emendations.) Elegy on W. V. M. In *Uriel, and Other Poems;* Houghton Mifflin; 1912. 'Also, in *Collected Poems;* 1916.

'Moody and James MacKaye's "Economy of Happiness."' P. 473, *Epoch,* Vol. II, Boni & Liveright; 1927.

'William Vaughn Moody: In Memoriam: 20 Years After.' Sonnet, to E. A. Robinson. *Boston Evening Transcript;* Oct. 18, 1930. Also, *Harvard Graduates' Magazine;* Dec., 1930. Also, *Anthology of the MacDowell Club Poets;* A. Browne; Dec., 1930.

'Will and Harriet Moody.' Being the Introduction and Conclusion, with Notes, for the present volume; 1935.

(2) Concerning Harriet Converse Moody

Note. The only published volume *by* H. C. M. is *Mrs. William Vaughn Moody's Cook Book.* Scribner's; 1931. The following titles are of newspaper Articles *concerning* her.

'Poetry and Pies.' Anne Hard. With half-page portrait of Mrs. Moody. *New York Herald Tribune;* Sunday, June 22, 1930. Pp. 8, 9 and 10.

'Famous Persons Long Have Made House A Mecca. Paintings keep Old Memories Alive.' Bertha Fenberg. With 2 photos of Harriet Moody, in youth and middle age, and photo of interior of her Chicago home. *Chicago News;* July 9, 1931.

'Poet's Widow Dies.' Obituary, with portrait head of Mrs. William Vaughn Moody. *Chicago Daily Tribune;* Thurs., Feb. 25, 1932.

'Harriet Converse Moody.' A Brief Tribute on her Death. Harriet Monroe. P. 53. *Poetry,* A Magazine of Verse; April, 1932.

'A Genuine Friend to Poets.' Carilyn Stevens. 2-column article. *Christian Science Monitor;* March 9, 1932.

'Harriet Converse Moody.' Ridgely Torrence. Signed editorial. *The New Republic;* March 9, 1932. P. 99.

INDEX

A

Abelarde and Heloise: 31, 41, 172
Academy of Music: 341
Acoma: 295
Acropolis: 104, 107, 112
Acts of the Apostles: 391
Adams, Franklin P.: 437
Adams, Mr. and Mrs. Herbert: 425
Adams, Maude: 171
Admirable Crichton: 168, 169
Adonais: 396
Aegean Isles: 105, 107, 108
Aegina: 104, 107
Aeschylus: *Agamemnon:* 120, 121, 267, 271, 273, 284, 286, 417, 425. *Prometheus Bound:* 118
A Garland to Sylvia: 32
Aguinaldo: 420
Aiken, Louis: 196, 198, 207, 219, 221, 222, 247
Albany, N.Y.: 295, 296, 297
Albuquerque, N.M.: 294, 295, 374
Aldrich, Thomas Bailey: 214, 441
Alexander, John W.: 431
Alhambra: 330
Alice ('little Alice'): See Corbin, Alice
Allen, Viola: 218
Amalfi: 89
Ambleside: 426
Amen, Harlan Page: 435
America: 211, 370, 427
American Academy of Arts and Letters: 235, 424, 435
American Dramatists, Society of: 48, 49, 316, 321, 423
American School of Classical Studies, Athens: 104, 105, 112, 123, 134
Ames, Winthrop: 31, 419, 420, 431
Amsterdam, N.Y.: 297
Andritzena: 126
Anglin, Margaret: 41, 42, 45, 46, 254, 255, 256, 260, 261, 262, 263, 264, 271,

276, 277, 290, 291, 296, 298, 302, 315, 316, 339, 341, 353, 354, 355, 392, 430
Anna Karenina: 156
Annisquam: 340
Anniversary of Moody's death: 3, 395, 410, 411, 431
An Ode in Time of Hesitation: 27, 35, 394, 420
Anton: 403
Aphrodite: 124
Apollo: 113, 126, 161, 228, 411
Apollōn: 292, 297, 417
A Prairie Ride: 13
Arachova: 114
Arcadia: 126, 127, 128
Archduke of Austria: 149
Archeology: 112
Archer, William: 421, 442
Arizona: 190, 191, 222, 374, 416
Arts Club, National: 184, 312
Arvia: See MacKaye, Arvia
A Sabine Woman: See *The Great Divide.* Also under Moody, William Vaughn
Ascutney, Mt.: 65, 251, 292
Ashwell, Lena: 315
Athens: 103, 104, 108, 109, 116, 117, 118, 119, 135
Atlantic City: 298, 299
Atlantic Monthly: 441
Attica: 110, 121, 123
Austen, Jane: 46, 279
Austin, Mary: 36
Australia: 272
Authors Club: 424

B

Baker, George Pierce: 20, 21, 395, 431, 440, 441
Baltimore: 251, 386, 387, 426
Barker, Llewellyn: 437
Barnard, George Grey: 56, 63, 64

INDEX

Dunbar, Olivia (Mrs. Ridgely Torrence): 64, 421
Duncan, Isadora: 34, 63, 64, 369, 419

E

Earle, L. C.: 415
Eastman, Max: 442
Eaton, Walter Prichard: 439, 442
Echegaray: 331
Ehrichs, Alma: 18
Ehrichs, Walter: 18, 77
Eldorado: 31, 37, 172
Eleusis: 104, 108, 110, 117
Eliot, Charles W.: 417
Eliot, Samuel Jr.: 423, 428
Elis: 127
Eumenides: 112
Euripides: 135, 141, 292. *Bacchantes*: 139. *Medea*: 214, 271
Eve poem and play, the: See *Death of Eve, The*
Everyman: 188, 339, 353, 354

F

Faggi, Alfeo: 402
Faith Healer, The: See Moody, William Vaughn
Faulkner, Barry: 51, 277
Faversham, William: 227, 228, 351
Fawcett, Henrietta Moody: 63, 235, 423
Fawcett, William Vaughn Moody: 423
Fenris, the Wolf: 32, 39, 41, 230, 242, 421
Ferd: See Schevill, Ferdinand
Fez: 326, 329
Field, Lew: 316. *The Great Decide*: 316
Fire-Bringer, The: See Moody, William Vaughn
Fischer, Martin H.: 404, 433, 437
Fiske, Harrison Grey: 23, 55, 422, 423
Fiske, John: 117
Fiske, Minnie Maddern: 172, 188, 420
Fitch, Clyde: 188, 378
Flagstaff, Ariz.: 200
Flint, Edith Foster: 279, 437
Flint, Nott: 437
Florence: 149, 333

Flowers, names of: 157
Forbes-Robertson: 226, 366
Fortnightly Club: 250, 438
Fountain, The: See Moody, William Vaughn
Franconia: 404
Franzén, Augustus: 25
Frazee, Minnie (niece of W. V. M.): 225
Freund (German translator): 368
Frohman, Charles: 23, 28, 48, 53, 188, 310, 343, 344, 372, 393, 423
Frohman, Daniel: 308, 315
Frost, Robert: 33, 34, 35, 403, 404
Fuller, Harry (Henry B.), artist: 269, 425

G

Galdos: 331
Gale, Zona: 403
Gardiner, Me.: 431
Garland, Hamlin: 17, 76, 78, 79, 80, 414, 416, 421, 429, 431, 440
Gates, Lewis E.: 19, 435
Genoa: 152
German Players: 241, 244
German Plays: By Hauptmann: *Lo's vom Manne*: 177. *Die Waber*: 232
By Sudermann: *Der Sturmgeselle Sokrates*: 180. *Johnannisfeuer*: 214
German Theatre: 171
Gibraltar: 100, 326, 329, 330, 331
Gibson, Wilfrid: 403, 404
Gilbert, Mrs. Anne Hartley (Mrs. G. H.), in *Granny*: 209
Gilder, Jeannette: 250
Gilder, Richard Watson: 28, 224, 234, 241, 284, 285, 350, 424
Glasgow: 427
Gloucester, Mass.: 340, 385, 427
Gloucester Moors: 40, 411
Glück: 369
Goethe: 406
'Good Friday' Procession: 332
Gorky, Maxim: 180
Gouffre: 426
Grabo, C. H.: 440
Graham, Stephen: 403
Gramercy Park: 312, 356

INDEX

INDEX

[457]